Sexism and Youth

Diane Gersoni-Stavn

R. R. Bowker Company

New York & London, 1974
A Xerox Education Company

XEROX

Published by R. R. Bowker Co. (A Xerox Education Company)
1180 Avenue of the Americas, New York, N.Y. 10036
Copyright © 1974 by Diane Gersoni-Stavn
Printed and bound in the United States of America

Library of Congress Cataloging in Publication Data

Gersoni-Stavn, Diane, comp.
    Sexism and youth.

    1.   Sex instruction—Addresses, essays, lectures.
2.   Sex role—Addresses, essays, lectures.   I.   Title.
[DNLM: 1.   Adolescence.   2.   Sex behavior—In
adolescence.   HQ35 G38s   1973]
HQ56.G46   301.41   73-21651
ISBN 0-8352-0710-2

Sexism
and Youth

For my parents
James and Edna Gersoni, with love

Contents

PART 3 Books: Propaganda and the Sins of Omission

Contents

Foreword

Men, have you ever owned a pink toothbrush? Or is pink a color so irrevocably associated with females that you would feel "emasculated" using a pink toothbrush even if it had boar's bristles?

Women, do you wait at the phone for a man's call because "nice girls" aren't supposed to be the aggressors? Then what happens to that passive feminine conditioning when you have to sell yourself at a job interview, ask for a raise, supervise male subordinates, disagree with a man's decision?

Mothers, can you honestly say that you didn't care whether your firstborn child was a girl or a boy? If you admit that, like most people, you were hoping for a boy, do you wonder why?

Fathers, when you're driving the kids to school do you point out the construction site to your son and the lilac trees to your daughter?

Parents, can you ask your 9-year-old daughter and your 8-year-old son to exchange bedrooms without feeling that you'd first have to overhaul the decor in each room: change the wallpaper, curtains, color scheme, toys or books? Would it mean moving your little boy into a room full of ruffles, nurse romances, dolls, and tea sets? Would your daughter suddenly find herself surrounded by unfamiliar football banners on the walls; trucks, war stories, and chemistry sets on the shelves? If children of the same general age cannot move into another room without moving into an entirely alien kind of childhood, someone's being cheated. Are you stunting your children by sex-typing their environments?

Teachers, do you find yourself complimenting the girls in class for what they wear, and the boys for what they make or say or do? If a girl defends herself physically, do you tell her to "act like a lady"? At the same time, are you somewhat tolerant of male combativeness because "boys will be boys"? Have you noticed that most of the women in history texts are queens, witches or wives of famous men? Can you name a dozen scientists, lawyers, reformers, inventors or artists who are women? If you don't know them how can you teach about them?

Guidance counselors, if a boy and girl are honor students in all their high school science courses, do you encourage both of them to prepare for careers in medicine? Or do you tell the boy to be a doctor and the girl to be a science teacher, because "she'll get married and she can always go back to teaching after her children are grown."

These are just a few of the catalytic questions being raised in conferences and consciousness-raising workshops on the subject of nonsexist child rearing and education.

Whether it's a high school rap session in Marblehead, Massachusetts, a feminist conference in San Francisco, a teacher's convention in Milwaukee, or a group of parents in New York City, the people involved seem to respond in the same remarkable way. "I never realized . . ." they murmur. "It's a pattern in my life and I never questioned it before." "I thought I was out of that sex-role trap, but I've been passing it along to my kids in a hundred little ways."

After a great deal of discussion, personal testimony, private epiphanies and public sharing of frustration and rage, the ultimate questions are asked: What can we do about sexism? How can we disprove the myths? Where do we find out more? How can we change our lives, our homes, classrooms, libraries, television fare, toys, games, even our language? How can we make growing up a free, vital, open-ended experience for America's children, no matter what their sex or race?

Feminists who write or lecture around the country have had to answer these queries by referring people to mimeographed doctoral theses or obscure underground journals. We've depended upon the network of women's groups for lists of papers and studies on sex-role socialization, for bibliographies on nonsexist children's books, for news of court cases that have opened sex-segregated schools and courses to attendance by the opposite sex, for information about newly developed nonsexist curriculum materials, for news from education task forces that are working to eliminate sex bias from local school systems, and for pragmatic advice on the challenge of raising free children in a sexist society.

All of us have shared underlined pamphlets and annotated books. We've photocopied dog-eared magazine articles, passing them from person to person, watching them proliferate across the country like chain letters of liberation.

But that was before we had the book you now hold in your hands. By gathering so many of our precious source materials between the cov-

ers of this volume, Diane Gersoni-Stavn has given coherence to the iso-
lated papers and permanence to the project reports. She has assembled
a workbook for humanism, a textbook for a new educational commitment
and a blueprint for revolution.

It is nothing short of revolution that feminists are both making and
recording—and in a profound sense, the publication of *Sexism and Youth*
tells us that feminism has come of age.

Whereas the single-issue suffrage movement bowed gracefully into
oblivion when women won the vote, our generation of "radicals" is evolv-
ing a new kind of feminism whose issues reach deep into every aspect of
adult life.

We are scrutinizing institutionalized "normality." We are challenging the conventional view of marriage, family structure, work, the economic system, abortion, sexuality and the politics of love, housework and
white, male, middle-class power. We are redesigning ourselves from the
inside out—seeking our individual authenticity whether we start by giving
up our phony orgasms or our phony eyelashes.

But in orchestrating a heroic symphony of change for ourselves, we
cannot neglect those who are still practising their scales, note by note.
Unless our revolution extends beyond ourselves to the children who are
coming along behind us, our triumphs will remain a one-generation phenomenon. Then history will remember us only in passing—along with the
suffragists who chained themselves to the gates of public consciousness
for the sake of one victory in one era. We must do more than fight our
sophisticated adult issues. We must not just reinvent ourselves, but also
reach out to reinvent childhood.

To be sure, every woman who achieves and communicates self-
esteem becomes a role model for the aspiring little girls in her life. And
every man who learns to express emotion, to value child rearing as much
as profit-making and to act with compassion as well as reason, makes it
easier for the little boys in his life to become comfortable with vulnerability and human feelings.

Still, it is not enough for us to change ourselves and then to serve
as models. We must also be agents for change. This is where Ms. Gersoni-
Stavn's anthology represents a new maturity for feminism.

Reading this book will help us to extrapolate from our personal
experience those ways in which the entire educational spectrum can be
brightened and humanized for the enhancement of both male and female
development in the growing years. The selections chosen by Ms. Gersoni-
Stavn contain more than theoretical or philosophical insights; each also
suggests constructive recommendations for activism.

We may begin by learning to use the English language without ex-

cluding 51 percent of the population; or by attacking the inequities in a
school district's appropriations for girls' athletic programs; or by planning
a social studies unit on "Woman as Nigger"; or by desexing the sentences
on spelling tests; or monitoring the male-predominated audiovisual
materials; or refusing to teach sex education with a bias *against* "promiscuous" girls and *for* "red-blooded, lusty boys"; or suggesting role-
reversal skits in Family Living class; or checking the number of picture
books that show Mommy in an apron all day; or tossing every *macho* toy
in the junk heap.

Somewhere in these pages there is a plan of action for anyone who
wants to improve the quality of life and the diversity of options for boys
and girls alike. It's a difficult but glorious undertaking.

You can start by breaking the boy-girl color barrier. Buy your son
a pink toothbrush and then read on.

LETTY COTTIN POGREBIN

PREFACE

The women's liberation movement has inspired numerous anthologies. Most contain only historical writings or present an across-the-boards view of various issues: sexism in interpersonal relationships, different professions, the media, etc.

Sexism in youth-directed materials and environments receives an especially brief nod in these books. Yet the vast number of articles published on the subject attests to its importance and the widespread interest in it. Rigid attitudes about sex roles are formed during childhood and adolescence. Before they can be challenged and dispelled, we must understand the primary ways in which they are inculcated.

This anthology provides in one convenient source major analytical essays, personal reminiscences and reflections, community studies, government reports, and resource lists. These deal variously with sexism in socialization, education and the schools, children's literature, films, toys and games. The stereotyping of males as well as females is considered. Some of the articles have not previously been published; most were drawn from a wide range of scholarly and trade journals, women's movement publications, and governmental and private agencies.

The focus of the book is initial and early programming, so materials used by college students are not covered. And coverage is limited to sex-role stereotyping in America. It is important to recognize, however, that the subject is being seriously investigated in many countries, e.g., Germany and Canada, and on an international scale by UNESCO.

A collection of this kind must necessarily be representative rather than fully comprehensive. But most of the important ground-breaking articles in the field have been included. Stringently weeded out at the start were derivative analyses, second-hand summaries, and popularized reports.

Such a collection also contains some inevitable repetition of philosophy and findings. But the articles—by people of both sexes and various ages, backgrounds, and professions—zero in on different types of schools, books, etc.

The selections in this book accurately describe youth-directed materials and environments as they are today. Hopefully, these articles will soon have historic interest only, as parents, teachers, writers, publishers, librarians and others work to make absolutist, inflexible sex-role stereotyping a thing of the past.

I would like to thank all of the copyright holders who graciously consented to the publication of their articles. Thanks go as well to Lillian Gerhardt, with whom I've had numerous fruitful discussions on children's literature, and to Robert Hans Stavn, for sound advice. And the most heartfelt thanks of all for constant encouragement and wise counsel go to Patricia Glass Schuman, my editor and comrade in this venture.

DIANE GERSONI-STAVN
Greensboro, North Carolina
September 1973

INTRODUCTION

The Women's Liberation Movement

The women's liberation movement is a social movement, working for social change. As such, it assumes that many of the behavioral propensities of men and women are due to cultural conditioning.

Nevertheless, it would be foolish to underestimate the effects of biological and psychological differences between men and women. It may well be that the sex hormones do program the fetal brain for masculine or feminine behavior later in life. We know that the male hormone, testosterone, is directly correlated with aggressiveness. Women's libido is significantly affected by the amount of testosterone in their bodies. Male homosexuals have less testosterone than heterosexual males; female homosexuals have more testosterone than heterosexual females. Researchers don't know, however, if the testosterone supply is basic in an individual's makeup or if it is influenced by homosexual behavior. One much-publicized report tells how pregnant women, accidentally given a synthetic hormone with masculinizing effects on the fetus, gave birth to daughters who exhibited "masculine" behavior even though they were raised as "traditional" girls (they were athletic, aggressive, preferred boys' clothes and toys, etc.).

On the other hand, studies of people erroneously raised as the wrong biological sex due to imprecise external genitalia have led many researchers to conclude that gender roles are almost entirely cultural. And, studies of siblings have shown that children with other-sex siblings tend to display more traits of that sex than children with same-sex siblings.

It is true that in most species the male is dominant. However, this fact is of questionable relevance to the human situation where brains have long figured more importantly than physical strength. And feminists can counter with ease claims that men are inherently superior to women. The natural tendency for a human embryo is to be female. The female fetus is more active than the male and more sensitive to new stimuli. Girls have a higher pain threshold than boys, walk earlier, and tend to recover from shock faster. Women take stress better than men and tend to live longer. And then, Freud to the contrary, there's the theory of uterine envy: i.e., that men have engaged in frantic world-building to compensate for their lack of innate physical creativity.

Men often assert that women's physiology must necessarily limit their professional aspirations. They point to the sometimes severe premenstrual, post partum, and menopausal depressions women experience when their hormonal levels are lowest. One study done at the University of London did indeed indicate that a significant number of female admissions to mental hospitals (46 percent) occurred in the week or so preceding and during menstruation. This period also saw 53 percent of all attempted female suicides. However, men exhibit similar depressed symptoms when their testosterone levels decrease during the late forties and early fifties—the age when men aspire to the presidency and other important positions. The "male menopause" and melancholia are only now being seriously investigated. And as for suicide—more than twice as many males as females killed themselves in the United States in 1970.

One anthropologist, Marvin Harris, postulates a cultural theory of female subservience. He suggests that if anatomy were destiny, the bias would be against males since women can do just about everything men can do, and give birth to and nurture new members of the species besides. Harris asserts that ". . . the realization that sexual roles are cultural is not sufficient reason to conclude that they are arbitrary and undetermined . . . Subordination of females happens to occur with remarkable persistence in a great variety of cultures. When a human relationship occurs with great frequency across space and time, we must suppose that there are determinate reasons for it. Culture itself is a form of 'destiny' . . . the institutionalized privilege of being able to exploit women is the reward that modern militaristic societies give to males who serve as cannon fodder."

Most anthropologists agree that in almost all cultures girl and boy babies are treated differently from birth; that barren women have been considered inferior in most societies; that jobs cross-culturally are divided according to age and sex; and that some sex-role identification is necessary. But many—e.g., Laura Bohannon—feel that as a result of the pill and technology, genuinely new conditions exist in today's world with regard to women's roles. And Bohannon asserts that only in industrial society has the father not had a child-rearing role, this due to the physical removal of place of work from residence. (One thinks of the distinction drawn between "maternal *deprivation*" and "paternal *absence*.")

It may never be possible to separate out the precise effects of physiology and cultural conditioning on human beings. Not only do they individually influence people but they interact with each other and with each person's unique essence to affect human behavior. To accord with the reality of this complex interplay of factors, and to accord with an increasingly complex external world, feminists ask simply for options in life styles. Traditional, people-directed women's work—caring for home and family—should be recognized as worthwhile and valuable. Housework is no more boring or useless than much work done outside the home. The homemaker/mother should not be demeaned either by the condescending approval of traditional males or the scornful dismissal of radical feminists. So often even husbands and children who have demanded a full-time wife and mother deride her in later years for not having "grown" and done more with her life.

At the same time, women interested in traditional male activities must be free to pursue them. Traditional women must recognize that work confined to the home does not have the importance in world terms of much work done outside the home. Society can certainly use the skills of all of its citizens. And, even menial/boring jobs outside give the doers a breath of fresh air, the chance to indulge in shop talk and on-the-job camaraderie.

In any event, we must strip our minds of stereotyped assumptions as far as possible. Full-time homemakers may bring more imaginativeness, resourcefulness, and positive skills to their jobs than professional workers. Professional women may make better wives and mothers than full-time homemakers. Successful professional women (and men) may still derive their greatest satisfaction from their families. Not all strong, aggressive men are chauvinists. Not all dainty, carefully made-up women are traditionalists. Many women and men will continue to want partners who exhibit traditional traits. Many will not, however, and so the point for everybody is options.

Women who work outside the home now do so mostly for economic reasons. Almost two-thirds of them are single, divorced, widowed, separated, or have husbands earning less than $7000 a year. Since one out of three marriages ends in divorce, many women are catapulted into work situations lacking requisite skills and psychological preparedness to work. High school counselors must make girls aware of this, along with the following figures taken from latest reports and pamphlets issued by the

Women's Bureau, Employment Standards Administration, U.S. Department of Labor. In March 1972, one out of ten women workers was head of a family. In 1971, nearly three out of ten families headed by women had incomes below $3000. For black families headed by women, the 1971 figure was four out of ten. About one out of nine families is headed by a woman; almost two out of five poor families are headed by women. About three out of ten black families are headed by women; almost three out of five poor black families are headed by women. In 1972, 4.4 million working mothers had 5 million children under six years of age. Yet there are only some 905,000 licensed day care slots available for these children. Of workers not covered by the Fair Labor Standards Act, 40 percent are women; 57 percent of black women workers and 22 percent of white women workers are not covered by the Act.

In any event, 43 percent of all women today are in the labor force, compared to 23 percent in 1920. Nine out of ten girls will work outside the home at some point in their lives. The average woman worker today is married and 39 years old, compared to 1920 when she was single and 28. Though women presently constitute about two-fifths of all workers, they have accounted for three-fifths of the increase in the civilian labor force in the last decade.

In years to come more women, influenced by "span plan" thinking, will train for careers and work for reasons of personal fulfillment. And men may have to readjust some priorities to accept this. The life expectancy for a baby girl today is 74 compared to 55 in 1920. There are 80 girls graduating from high school today for every 100 girls 17 years old in the population; in 1920 there were 20. Alan Pifer, President of the Carnegie Corporation of New York, pointed out in 1971 that women comprise 75–90 percent of the qualified students who don't go on to college, even though a greater proportion of women than men complete high school. There are 18 women graduating from college today for every 100 women 21 years old in the population; in 1920 there were two. About half of today's women marry by age 21 and have their last child at 30. After this child has entered school, the mother may have 30–35 years of life ahead of her. Popular magazines are warning her about time weighing heavily on her hands, the empty nest syndrome, etc.

Stereotyped thinking still holds that women make unreliable employees. Yet there is not significantly more absenteeism among women than among men. In 1971, men 17 years of age and over lost an average of 4.9 days, compared to 5.5 days for women. Women lost an average of 3.8 workdays due to acute illness, while men lost 3.2 days for this. However, men more often than women were absent because of such chronic conditions as arthritis, heart trouble, rheumatism, and orthopedic impairment. Studies indicate that women's illnesses usually keep them away from work for shorter periods of time than do men's illnesses, that women's absences cause no more financial loss than men's, and also, that men change occupation more often than women.

In considering turnover, it is important to realize that the figures for men and women are much closer with higher status jobs than with lower status jobs. The Department of Labor cites a recent study in asserting that: "The overall turnover rates were much less favorable for women than for men 'mainly because women are disproportionately represented at the lowest level, where turnover is highest for both sexes.'" The greatest average of sick days also occurs among people making the lowest salaries.

Economic discrimination against women workers is rampant. Women with full-time, year-round jobs earn on the average only $3 for every $5 earned by similarly employed men—a bigger gap than existed 16 years ago. In 1971, women's median earnings were $5593; men's, $9399. White men earn the most money, followed by minority men, then white women, then minority women. Ninety-seven percent of private household workers are women; 76 percent of clerical workers; 61 percent of retail sales workers; 57 percent of service workers; 40 percent of professional workers; 30 percent of operatives. Only 17 percent of managers, 15 percent of nonretail sales workers, and 3 percent of craftsmen are women. Yet the average woman worker is as well educated as the average man worker. A 1972 United States Office of Education report, "A Look at Women in Education," found that programs sponsored by the Manpower Development and Training Act and the Vocational Education Act channeled women workers into low-paying jobs. The report also found that the Office of Education funded sex-biased career tests and put out sex-biased workbooks and public information materials.

Nevertheless, largely thanks to concerted feminist efforts, changes are occurring. A few companies are sponsoring day-care centers for their employees; others are considering reducing the 40-hour week to 35. It is being urged that part-time jobs be upgraded in status, and more of them made available to mothers. Most importantly, women are slowly being admitted into fields hitherto denied them by rule or custom. They are working as senatorial pages, diesel truck drivers, apprentice shipfitters, aircraft and auto mechanics, electricians, sheet metal workers, shoe repair(wo)men, cheese and watch makers, embalmers, cabinetmakers, ministers and rabbis, foresters, sports reporters, plumbers, furniture movers, longshore(wo)men, door(wo)men, mail(wo)men, patrol(wo)men, FBI agents. More women are entering law and medical school, becoming engineers and politicians. Professions in which women have traditionally numbered heavily—teaching and librarianship, for example—are being attacked for their pyramid structure which sees women workers at the bottom and male administrators at the top. And such traditional, formerly suspect "women's work" as midwifing is enjoying a new vogue. Academic women—e.g., members of the Modern Language Association and the National Council of Teachers of English—are forming their own groups and caucuses and issuing reports and guidelines on sexism. Some churches and Y's are establishing forward-looking programs for girls. Women are popping up on news shows as reporters as well as weatherwomen; women athletes are appearing in television ads. Previously unacclaimed women of achievement are now being nationally acknowledged—e.g., Jeannette Rankin, first member of the National Organization for Women's Susan B. Anthony Hall of Fame. Rap and consciousness-raising groups are as common in suburbia as on college campuses, and the drop-out wife is the latest object of media attention. Women are objecting to rigid abortion laws and forced pregnancy leaves, demanding easier access to credit cards, and learning self-defense. Rape victims are coming out of their own peculiarly horrifying closets and establishing crisis centers and hot lines. Democratic and Republican women are working together for women's issues in the Women's Political Caucus. Black women have formed their own feminist organization to deal with their particular problems. Women are initiating their own publishing and film ventures—The Feminist Press, Lollipop Power, New Seed Press, Media Plus, Inc., New Day Films, etc. They are holding their own art shows, film and even pornography festivals. High school free presses, and counter-culture presses and film companies (Times Change Press, Newsreel, etc.) are doing titles on sex roles as well as on political themes. Radical women are decrying the status of the groupie as sex object. More women are engaging in more rugged sports, including crew racing, soccer, football, and basketball. A few universities have established academic/athletic scholarships for women. The military is being pressured to give women the same job options and benefits that military men get. In many cases, these represent token rather than substantive changes. But they are changes, and feminist pressure is increasing, not slacking off.

Women's Liberation and Other Movements

Many of the concerns of the women's movement cohere with those of other movements, e.g., ecology. For example, writers like Letty Cottin Pogrebin, Ellen Peck, Betty Rollin, and Angela Barron McBride are presenting what they believe to be realistic reassessments of formerly sentimentalized or scorned motherhood. In 1972, Ellen Peck founded the

National Organization for Non-Parents. Some women, e.g., busy professionals, are choosing to have just one child and perhaps to give it company by adopting other children or by living in a blood or chosen extended family (Margaret Mead is one such example). These actions have
some common cause with measures urged by some social ecologists—e.g.,
baby rationing, parent licensing, the taxation of big families, and the
removal of preferential tax deductions for families with children. Many
people, however, will rightly continue to feel that a life without children
can be very empty.

A major spinoff from the women's movement is the new attention
being paid to the problems of men, children, and the elderly. Men are
starting to request paternity leaves and the right to be respected if they
work as nursery school teachers, secretaries, stewards, or house husbands.
The strain of always being strong and emotionless is being analyzed in
terms of the extra stress it places on men—stress which may reveal itself
in a greater incidence of ulcers and heart attacks, and in a shorter life
span. Researcher Lawrence Podell tends to underestimate women's problems but he aptly comments about men: "Who can be *that* sure he
is achieving to his potential, gaining the most important goals, or being
as happy as he might? Women are immersed in the kinship network,
and men are enmeshed in the bureaucratic nexus . . . both dream of
being one's own boss."

The new spotlight on children examines not only the effect of sex-
role stereotyping on them but their sexuality, the battered child syndrome, and their rights under the law (for example, girl delinquents are
often faced with more stringent penalties and given less chance for independent action than boys, while boys in school are often disciplined more
severely than girls for the same offenses).

In one cross-cultural study, Ruth Hartley found that among four
different groups of children (Caucasians and American Japanese in
Honolulu; Europeans and Maoris in New Zealand), female children were
seen as being more desired by parents than male children because female
children were more helpful around the house, nicer, and more obedient.
Hartley says about the male: "Is it to be wondered at that he later fiercely
asserts and desperately defends a superiority to which his claims must be
constantly validated? . . . These data suggest that the more egalitarian
and less sex-separated culture offers the boy, as well as the girl, a superior
opportunity to feel consistently wanted and worthwhile." Other studies
show, however, that American schoolboys learn early to value men's
work and status in life above women's.

As initial phases of the women's movement sought to do away with
the sexual double standard, so do such writers as Simone de Beauvoir and
Susan Sontag now call our attention to the sexuality of old people—es-

pecially older women. Dirty old men are laughed at and perhaps secretly envied; dirty old women are unmentioned or held in disgust.

There are many similarities in the way women, the young, and the old are viewed and treated. All are accused of being childlike; all have trouble getting employment and credit ratings; all are dependent on the generosity of others; all are in some ways second-class citizens.

The Problems and Promise of Women's Liberation

Alice Rossi and others have pointed out that though women are in a majority numerically, they hold strength in no one geographic area and so can't form a powerful voting bloc. And while the struggles of minorities for equality may increase family solidarity, women's struggles increase tension within the family unit.

Human beings are often amazingly naive and short-sighted. They tend to plunge into successive social movements venerating the different ideologies, expecting utopia, and forgetting that living means compromise. Women currently attracted to the women's movement should be aware of the problems commitment may bring. Many women, mentally persuaded that they should have independence and careers, will be unable to accept this emotionally. Independence and careers will often come only at the price of family tension. Sometimes they will cause the breakup of the family unit—a unit tremendously important to most people, since it can provide intimacy, trust, and a bulwark against loneliness. Most women, like most men, will have indifferent jobs, not exciting careers; those embarking on supposedly exciting careers may find that the reality won't equal the expectation. Women will find that it is extremely difficult to interrupt a career with child-rearing and then take the career up again. And they will find that no one adequately warned them how taxing it would be to try to have a family and a career simultaneously.

Other issues have been raised by the movement. Does feminist action encourage unisex? What will be feminism's long-range effects on both sexes? Day-care centers are undeniably a necessity for working mothers, but how will we guarantee their quality? Will they provide children with necessary warmth and affection?

These problems and questions certainly don't invalidate the women's movement. They merely require that women discipline themselves to assess themselves and their situations realistically, and to anticipate the consequences of their actions. It is in fact a testimonial to the movement that despite problems and unresolved questions—many of them congruent with increased options—interest and belief in it grow steadily on the grass roots level. Radical women publicize the issues and are vital in keeping the middle from becoming complacent. (Of course, the first people to call attention to social issues are always considered radical. And programs or behavior considered radical in one era may be commonplace in another.) The middle has the most appeal for most women, however, and ensures that at least needed reforms will occur by making society happy to settle for its programs in place of radical change.

Feminist foremothers, the original suffragists, were a small group of pioneers going against the mainstream of their time. They faced all the dangers and knew all the excitement of pioneers. There are many more women in the ranks in today's movement—"average" women who are working not so much for specific, dramatic goals but for self-satisfying, self-respecting, self-chosen life styles. Because of their efforts, their daughters may be able to be homemakers without apology and/or career women without explanation.

As women gain these options, they should keep in mind the words of Shirley Chisholm: "The softness, warmth, and gentleness that are often used to stereotype us are positive human values . . . The strength that marked Christ, Gandhi, and Martin Luther King was a strength born not of violence but of gentleness, understanding and genuine human compassion."

Sexism and Youth

The articles in this book document the way in which child-directed environments and materials serve to arbitrarily limit children's world views and behavioral options. Studies by Lynne B. Iglitzin and Judith Fiedler show that by the fifth grade, children have already typed jobs in the home and outside by sex. As children's options are limited, so are the options of the adults they become. Relatively few articles have been published analyzing the effects of sexist materials on boys. Yet boys are obviously conditioned by them, and several of the authors explain how.

Part I, "Socialization/Indoctrination," contains general observations on language—a major, initial socializing agent—and on the false assumptions inherent in sex-stereotyped child rearing. To be truly liberated, women must not just drift passively; as far as possible they must take an active role in shaping their lives. They will never be able to do this if they are socialized from the beginning to be dependent and passive.

Part II, "Dear Old Sexist School Days," considers the general atmosphere of schools; the particular sexist practices of administrators, teachers, and counselors; the ways in which different kinds of schools, e.g., vocational, discriminate against girls; the potential of feminist studies courses; and various solutions to the problem of sexism in elementary and secondary education. In a study done in the 1960's, James Gallagher found that high-achieving girls and boys did similarly on written tests, but that boys were far more expressive in the classroom. Why must intelligent girls feel inhibited about displaying their intelligence?

Sexism in colleges and the ways in which college students manifest previous sex-role conditioning are beyond the scope of this book. Nevertheless, readers should be aware of Matina Horner's studies of superior college students which show that "A girl who maintains the qualities of independence and active striving which are necessary for intellectual mastery defies the conventions of sex-appropriate behavior and must pay a price in anxiety . . . negative attitudes expressed toward and about successful women have remained high, and perhaps even increased and intensified, among male and female subjects." Horner's studies led her to formulate her much-quoted theory that women are motivated to avoid success. Sociologist Marcia Millman describes how only men share in the theoretical American value system where identity is based on achieved and not on ascribed traits. Women's identity is still determined by ascribed traits (sex, appearance, marriage and husband's identity). Florence Howe has analyzed the discrepancies between women's higher education and the social goals set for them. Colleges orient girls towards careers but social pressure gears them towards marriage and motherhood which college does nothing to prepare them for.

In response to all this, women's colleges are no longer rushing to become coeducational (just as integration is no longer a primary goal of many blacks). Smith, Wellesley, Mount Holyoke, and Wheaton, among others, have determined to remain single-sex schools to keep the option of the woman's school alive and to resist male domination of education in America. Alan Pifer, President of the Carnegie Corporation of New York, has detailed some changes demanded by female professors: the revision of nepotism rules; authorized maternity leaves, with guaranteed job reservation and postponement of tenure decision; tenure-granting to part-time personnel; the appointment of women to decision-making committees; and concerted attempts to recruit, hire, and promote women. Clearly, the educational system at all levels is being reevaluated for its treatment of and influence on girls and women.

Part III of *Sexism and Youth* is entitled "Books: Propaganda and the Sins of Omission." This is by far the most extensive section because most of the studies done on sexism in children's materials have concentrated on readers and other books. The various authors consider the stereotyped images of girls and women in picturebooks and basal readers; folk and fairy tales; middle-grade and high school novels; novels about minorities; social studies, language arts and science textbooks; and children's encyclopedias. There are also articles evaluating books which purport to present females in non-stereotyped ways, and an article reflecting on feminist criticism as a discipline.

Numerous workshops are being held in communities and universities across the country to analyze the problem of sexism in children's books. The first textbook complaint under Title IX of the Education Amendments Act of 1972 was filed with the Department of Health, Education and Welfare in May, 1973 by the Committee To Study Sex Discrimination in the Kalamazoo Public Schools. And juvenile book publishers are stating their intention to bring out more novels and biographies about girls and women. Similarly, adult book publishers are increasing their production of books about women. Biographies are being issued of such relatively unknown women as Jane Digby and Mary Ellen Peacock. Authors are being reevaluated in the light of feminist awareness. Sylvia Plath, Doris Lessing, and other women writers are gaining a broader following and getting more exposure in college literature courses. Personal testimony is being put forth by women as a valid, authoritative form of expression; they no longer accept the notion that only those books written from the male viewpoint and in a "masculine" style deserve to be called great. Nor do they buy the idea that male-centered stories and plays are drama while female-centered stories and plays are soap opera. College women and others have established feminist literary magazines, and even a feminist book club. And prestigious publications—e.g., *The New York Times*—are taking care to include book and play reviews written from a feminist viewpoint.

Part IV of *Sexism and Youth* deals with "Media Mix and the Games Children Play." The authors show how comic books, sports, games, toys, television programs, and audiovisual materials socialize children. One study of comic books not included here found that male figures appear on the average of 194.5 times compared to 70.1 times for female figures. Where females do appear—e.g., in teen romances—they are pining for the men of their dreams to notice them (the men invariably do). As for toys, Robert Liebert and other researchers have conducted studies indicating that ". . . children will alter their choices of toys to conform with the indicated preferences of their own sex . . . stated preferences of the opposite sex had no effect whatsoever."

Television is an especially powerful socializing agent, since modern children spend many thousands of hours in front of their sets. Cartoons take up much of their viewing—cartoons which *TV Guide*'s Edith Efron, after intensive scrutiny, termed sexist: "Vacuous brunette sorority-girl cartoons. Sexy blondes with curves and no brains. Wives are ugly, whining nags in curlers." And, though not specifically aimed at children (beyond the weekend morning toy ads), television commercials are of course seen and absorbed by children. In these ads, women are still presented primarily as incompetents and sex objects. Even some of the ads attempting to remedy this visualization are offensive—e.g., the ones where young women put down the lifestyles of their mothers, or where attractive men praise "older" women who aren't a day over 30.

Like children's TV shows and films, adult TV series and movies (which children of course see) are being scrutinized and panned for sexism. Very few women in TV series are professional women, and the many housewives featured are bland stereotypes. Feminist critics are decrying the lack of female-identity-crisis movies to parallel all those about men. They are also protesting the fact that older women in movies, with the exception of comediennes, are usually bitchy, neurotic, weird, murderous, or dull.

Conclusion

Sexism and Youth can touch only in passing on the most important aspect of socialization—how children are reared in the home. Each home offers a unique setting, and there is no way to run controlled studies of home environments. Sexual stereotyping is so widespread and pervasive that even enlightened parents may be unwittingly guilty of it. Even if children attend a modern school which allows them full play intellectually, the experience is nullified if they return home to stereotyped toys, games, and expectations.

We must raise our children as humanists. This obviously entails the elimination of sex-role stereotyping. Further, it means that we must teach athletic kids not to look down on more studious ones; studious ones not to disparage athletes and athletic ability; artistic kids not to view their classmates as philistines; politicos not to disdain uncommitted kids as trivial; "hip" kids not to scorn everybody else as pathetically "straight." Above all, it means teaching children that none of these talents and outlooks precludes the others; that they can all be present in one person.

Hopefully, *Sexism and Youth* will be a consciousness-raising experience for readers which will encourage them to apply the same techniques of evaluation and criticism in their homes that the authors of the articles have applied to schools, books and the media. And, to be sure, it will hopefully make readers examine more carefully the tools they use as teachers, librarians, etc. Only individual desire and ability, not presumed or behavioral norms or outside pressures, should determine what girls and boys become and do. The word is options.

PART 1

Socialization/Indoctrination

WHY I WON'T CELEBRATE BROTHERHOOD WEEK

Every American hears a lot about brotherhood and doing unto your neighbor as you would have him do unto you. Strains of John Denver's singing "I wish every man could be free" are familiar to all of us as is the advisability of practicing brotherly love and listening to the views of the man on the street.

But I wonder if enough thought has been given to the probable effect of referring to all people in masculine terms—"brother," "man," "he," "him," and every job title ending in "man" (fireman, policeman, congressman, chairman, journeyman, salesman, tradesman, etc., *ad nauseum*). Even the word "humanity" contains the word "man"!

The general use of "he" and "him" and "man" rather than "people" might make syntax flow more smoothly, but what does it do to feminine egos and self-concepts? There must be some reason why American women, given political and social advantages unavailable to many sisters in other lands, have not attained more power.

Perhaps one reason lies with the negative self-image caused by repeatedly hearing people referred to in masculine terms. Everyone from animals pictured in books to the Holy Ghost in the popular song, "American Pie" seems to be a "he."

Maybe Freud wasn't so far off when he recognized penis envy. Young girls learn early and thoroughly that boys are the ones who count. The sexist English language makes that message abundantly clear.

Do young girls picture a fifty-fifty mixture of men and women when they hear society referred to in masculine terms more often than not? Or do they somehow feel, understandably, left out? They are! Do they feel, atypical, peculiar, and, worse, abnormal? (After all, the proverbial man

Note: By Anne McEvoy Schmid. Reprinted with permission from The Emma Willard Task Force on Education, *Sexism in Education*, 3rd ed., copyright © 1972 (Box 14229, University Station, Minneapolis, Minnesota 55414).

on the street is always used to signify the norm.) Does "he" really mean both sexes to them? Does "man" really mean both men and women? Or does red mean red, green mean green, tree mean tree, her mean her, and he mean he? Consider the following and be your own judge:

Many years ago, my sister Janie came home from kindergarten with an exciting story to tell mother. However, as mother was entertaining some friends and busily engaged in conversation, Janie was not getting the attention she desired. One of mother's friends, noting the child's frustration, said, "Sometimes you have to hit that woman with a brick to get her attention." Thereupon, my sister marched out to the garden, got a brick, and was just about to strike when all noticed what was happening.

The other day at school, I was talking to a teacher aide who has two boys, eight and ten. They had just been watching the Olympic games on television, and she mentioned that she had pointed out a certain country's 100-man team. Her boys looked and saw some women on the team and questioned this. They told their mother they had thought she said it was a 100-man team. So what were *women* doing on it?

The point is, children interpret words literally. When they read "cow," they picture a cow; when they hear "house," they picture a house; when they are told that someone needs to be hit with a brick, they oblige, and they can't understand what women are doing on a 100-man team. When they see and hear and read "him," "he," "his," "man," "mankind," "brotherhood," "chairman," "postman," and all the others, they picture men or boys—not girls or women. The continued exposure, indeed the barrage of male-gender words, drives home the fact that this is indeed a man's world.

We all know that language is *reflective* of change, but this does not mean that language cannot or should not be progressive itself.

If little girls read and hear "one" or "them" rather than "he" or "him," if they are exposed to chairperson, congressperson, clergyperson, tradesperson, salesperson, and the like, perhaps they will stop picturing men or boys in these positions.

Of course these words sound awkward and even ridiculous to us now, but so did many new words when we first heard them.

It does not take a student of the subject to recognize that there is nothing static about the English language. What is grammatically "correct" has changed throughout history, as has what sounds "acceptable" or "normal."

It is probable that the above changes would cause the English language to be less smooth and flowing. Perhaps it does sound less forceful and dramatic to say "People do not live by bread alone" or "People's reach should exceed their grasp, or what's a heaven for?"

In my opinion initial awkwardness and (perhaps) some losses in force and drama are a small price to pay for the elimination of sexism from the English language.

In the last analysis, we must ask ourselves, What is more important—syntax or souls?

Not so much like drops of water, though water, it is true, can wear holes in the hardest granite; rather, drops of liquid sealing-wax, drops that adhere, incrust, incorporate themselves with what they fall on, till finally the rock is all one scarlet blob.

"Till at last the child's mind *is* these suggestions, and the sum of the suggestions *is* the child's mind. And not the child's mind only. The adult's mind too—all his life long. The mind that judges and desires and decides—made up these suggestions. But all these suggestions are *our* suggestions!" The Director almost shouted in his triumph.

All Are Harmed

The point, of course, is that the high caste Alphas are programmed just as thoroughly, and in a manner just as destructive of their personalities, as are the low caste Gammas. Thus, analyses of the system of slavery in the American South have pointed to the adverse influence of that institution on the attitudes and character of Southern *whites*. Specifically, slavery produced the attitude that physical labor is demeaning, and produced also a perversion of the slave-owner's own humanity. Lincoln expressed this in the observation, "As I would not be a slave, so would I not be a slave-holder."

There is a close parallel, it seems to me, with respect to man's inhumanity to woman. Returning to the dictionary as an authoritative source of meaning and attitudes, we find that "male" also connotes *aggressiveness, brutality,* and *force,* with specific reference to the use of guns (n.b., boys are given guns to play with; only girls or a sissy would play with dolls). And to avoid being considered feminine, or effeminate, no "real man" would say or do anything that might mark him with female characteristics of *tenderness, sensitiveness,* or *gentleness.*

Thus, a recent news report quoted aircraft-based bomber pilots off Viet Nam as saying that they take a strong sense of "masculine pride" in the daily task of raining tons of bombs on the countryside and people of that small country. Similarly, analyses of the Pentagon Papers have noted, on the part of the all-male participants, a demonstrable concern about counseling restraint and thereby betraying "weakness." At the same time, it has been noted, no one suffered loss of face or status for having urged increased aggression—no matter how wrong such counsel subsequently proved to be. Indeed, nowhere in the Pentagon Papers does any male permit doubts to be raised as to his manhood by questioning, in precise terms, any escalation of killing, maiming, and devastation. Rather, there are only occasional and indirect references to such essential human concerns by comments pointing to possible adverse public reaction through demonstrations. In short, few men would publicly express "masculine pride" in refusing to fight in an immoral war, or in putting a child to bed, or in washing out a diaper—or, indeed, in so many of the other human activities that count in life.

The point is that our children, both boys and girls, all have the right to a healthy personhood. Just as our daughters as well as our sons should have *strength, courage,* and *independence,* so should our sons as well as our daughters have *sensitiveness, tenderness,* and *gentleness.* Thus, in seeking to end the sexist programming of children, the psychological liberation of women is a valid and increasingly recognized goal. But the fundamental civil liberties issue is the equal right of every individual, male as well as female, to become a completely human being—the most basic of all libertarian concerns.

fields. The articles were collated into two equal sets of booklets, and the names of the authors were changed so that the identical article was attributed to a male author (e.g., John T. McKay) in one set of booklets and to a female author (e.g., Joan T. McKay) in the other set. Each student was asked to read the articles in her booklet and to rate them for value, competence, persuasiveness, writing style, and so forth.

As he had anticipated, Goldberg found that the identical article received significantly lower ratings when it was attributed to a female author than when it was attributed to a male author. He had predicted this result for articles from professional fields generally considered the province of men, like law and city planning, but to his surprise, these coeds also downgraded articles from the fields of dietetics and elementary school education when they were attributed to female authors. In other words, these students rated the male authors as better at everything, agreeing with Aristotle that "we should regard the female nature as afflicted with a natural defectiveness." We repeated this experiment informally in our own classrooms and discovered that male students show the same implicit prejudice against female authors that Goldberg's female students showed. Such is the nature of a nonconscious ideology!

It is significant that examples like these can be drawn from the college world, for today's students have challenged the established ways of looking at almost every other issue, and they have been quick to reject those practices of our society which conflict explicitly with their major values. But as the above examples suggest, they will find it far more difficult to shed the more subtle aspects of a sex-role ideology which—as we shall now attempt to demonstrate—conflicts just as surely with their existential values as any of the other societal practices to which they have so effectively raised objection. And as we shall see, there is no better way to appreciate the power of a society's nonconscious ideology than to examine it within the framework of values held by that society's avant-garde.

Individuality and Self-Fulfillment

The dominant values of today's students concern personal growth, on the one hand, and interpersonal relationships on the other. The first of these emphasizes individuality and self-fulfillment; the second stresses openness, honesty, and equality in all human relationships.

The values of individuality and self-fulfillment imply that each human being, male or female, is to be encouraged to "do his own thing." Men and women are no longer to be stereotyped by society's definitions. If sensitivity, emotionality, and warmth are desirable human characteristics, then they are desirable for men as well as for women. (John Wayne is no longer an idol of the young, but their pop-art satire.) If independence, assertiveness, and serious intellectual commitment are desirable human characteristics, then they are desirable for women as well as for men. The major prescription of this college generation is that each individual should be encouraged to discover and fulfill his own unique potential and identity, unfettered by society's presumptions.

But society's presumptions enter the scene much earlier than most people suspect, for parents begin to raise their children in accord with the popular stereotypes from the very first. Boys are encouraged to be aggressive, competitive, and independent, whereas girls are rewarded for being passive and dependent (Barry, Bacon, and Child, 1957; Sears, Maccoby, and Levin, 1957). In one study, six-month-old infant girls were already being touched and spoken to more by their mothers while they were playing than were infant boys. When they were 13 months old, these same girls were more reluctant than the boys to leave their mothers; they returned more quickly and more frequently to them; and they remained closer to them throughout the entire play period. When a physical barrier was placed between mother and child, the girls tended to cry and motion for help; the boys made more active attempts to get around the barrier (Goldberg and Lewis, 1969). No one knows to what extent these sex differences at the age of 13 months can be attributed to the mothers' behavior at the age of six months, but it is hard to believe that the two are unconnected.

As children grow older, more explicit sex-role training is introduced. Boys are encouraged to take more of an interest in mathematics and science. Boys, not girls, are given chemistry sets and microscopes for Christmas. Moreover, all children quickly learn that mommy is proud to be a moron when it comes to mathematics and science, whereas daddy knows all about these things. When a young boy returns from school all excited about biology, he is almost certain to be encouraged to think of becoming a physician. A girl with similar enthusiasm is told that she might want to consider nurse's training later so she can have "an interesting job to fall back upon in case—God forbid—she ever needs to support herself." A very different kind of encouragement. And any girl who doggedly persists in her enthusiasm for science is likely to find her parents as horrified by the prospect of a permanent love affair with physics as they would be by the prospect of an interracial marriage.

These socialization practices quickly take their toll. By nursery school age, for example, boys are already asking more questions about how and why things work (Smith, 1933). In first and second grade, when asked to suggest ways of improving various toys, boys do better on the fire truck and girls do better on the nurse's kit, but by the third grade, boys do better regardless of the toy presented (Torrance, 1962). By the ninth grade, 25 percent of the boys, but only 3 percent of the girls, are considering careers in science or engineering (Flanagan, unpublished; cited by Kagan, 1964). When they apply for college, boys and girls are about equal on verbal aptitude tests, but boys score significantly higher on mathematical aptitude tests—about 60 points higher on the College Board examinations, for example (Brown, 1965, p. 162). Moreover, girls improve their mathematical performance if problems are reworded so that they deal with cooking and gardening, even though the abstract reasoning required for their solutions remains the same (Milton, 1958). Clearly, not just ability, but motivation too, has been affected.

But these effects in mathematics and science are only part of the story. A girl's long training in passivity and dependence appears to exact an even higher toll from her overall motivation to achieve, to search for new and independent ways of doing things, and to welcome the challenge of new and unsolved problems. In one study, for example, elementary school girls were more likely to try solving a puzzle by imitating an adult, whereas the boys were more likely to search for a novel solution not provided by the adult (McDavid, 1959). In another puzzle-solving study, young girls asked for help and approval from adults more frequently than the boys; and, when given the opportunity to return to the puzzles a second time, the girls were more likely to rework those they had already solved, whereas the boys were more likely to try puzzles they had been unable to solve previously (Crandall and Rabson, 1960). A girl's sigh of relief is almost audible when she marries and retires from the outside world of novel and unsolved problems. This, of course, is the most conspicuous outcome of all: the majority of American women become full-time homemakers. Such are the consequences of a nonconscious ideology.

But why does this process violate the values of individuality and self-fulfillment? It is *not* because some people may regard the role of homemaker as inferior to other roles. That is not the point. Rather, the point is that our society is managing to consign a large segment of its population to the role of homemaker solely on the basis of sex just as inexorably as it has in the past consigned the individual with a black skin to the role of janitor or domestic. It is not the quality of the role itself which is at issue here, but the fact that in spite of their unique identities, the majority of America's women end up in the *same* role.

Even so, however, several arguments are typically advanced to counter the claim that America's homogenization of its women subverts individuality and self-fulfillment. The three most common arguments invoke, respectively, (1) free will, (b) biology, and (3) complementarity.

1. The free-will argument proposes that a 21-year-old woman is perfectly free to choose some other role if she cares to do so; no one is standing in her way. But this argument conveniently overlooks the fact that the society which has spent 20 years carefully marking the woman's ballot for her has nothing to lose in that twenty-first year by pretending to let her cast it for the alternative of her choice. Society has controlled not her alternatives, but her motivation to choose any but one of those alternatives. The so-called freedom to choose is illusory and cannot be invoked to justify the society which controls the motivation to choose.

2. The biological argument suggests that there may really be inborn differences between men and women in, say, independence or mathematical ability. Or that there may be biological factors beyond the fact that women can become pregnant and nurse children which uniquely dictate that they, but not men, should stay home all day and shun serious outside commitment. Maybe female hormones really are responsible somehow. One difficulty with this argument, of course, is that female hormones would have to be different in the Soviet Union, where one-third of the engineers and 75 percent of the physicians are women. In America, women constitute less than 1 percent of the engineers and only 7 percent of the physicians (Dodge, 1966). Female physiology *is* different, and it may account for some of the psychological differences between the sexes, but America's sex-role ideology still seems primarily responsible for the fact that so few women emerge from childhood with the motivation to seek out any role beyond the one that our society dictates.

But even if there really were biological differences between the sexes along these lines, the biological argument would still be irrelevant. The reason can best be illustrated with an analogy.

Suppose that every black American boy were to be socialized to become a jazz musician on the assumption that he has a "natural" talent in that direction, or suppose that his parents should subtly discourage him from other pursuits because it is considered "inappropriate" for black men to become physicians or physicists. Most liberal Americans, we submit, would disapprove. But suppose that it *could* be demonstrated that black Americans, *on the average*, did possess an inborn better sense of rhythm than white Americans. Would *that* justify ignoring the unique characteristics of a *particular* black youngster from the very beginning and specifically socializing him to become a musician? We don't think so. Similarly, as long as a woman's socialization does not nurture her uniqueness, but treats her only as a member of a group on the basis of some assumed *average* characteristic, she will not be prepared to realize her own potential in the way that the values of individuality and self-fulfillment imply she should.

The irony of the biological argument is that it does not take biological differences seriously enough. That is, it fails to recognize the range of biological differences between individuals within the same sex. Thus, recent research has revealed that biological factors help determine many personality traits. Dominance and submissiveness, for example, have been found to have large inheritable components; in other words, biological factors *do* have the potential for partially determining how dominant or submissive an individual, male or female, will turn out to be. But the effects of this biological potential could be detected only in males (Gottesman, 1963). This implies that only the males in our culture are raised with sufficient flexibility, with sufficient latitude given to their biological differences, for their "natural" or biologically determined potential to shine through. Females, on the other hand, are subjected to a socialization which so ignores their unique attributes that even the effects of biology seem to be swamped. In sum, the biological argument for continuing America's homogenization of its women gets hoist with its own petard.

3. Many people recognize that most women do end up as full-time homemakers because of their socialization and that these women do exemplify the failure of our society to raise girls as unique individuals. But, they point out, the role of the homemaker is not inferior to the role of the professional man: it is complementary but equal.

This argument is usually bolstered by pointing to the joys and importance of taking care of small children. Indeed, mothers *and* fathers find child-rearing rewarding, and it is certainly important. But this argument becomes insufficient when one considers that the average American woman now lives to age 74 and has her *last* child at about age 26; thus, by the time the woman is 33 or so, her children all have more important things to do with their daytime hours than to spend them entertaining an adult woman who has nothing to do during the second half of her life span. As for the other "joys" of homemaking, many writers (e.g., Friedan, 1963) have persuasively argued that the role of the homemaker has been glamorized far beyond its intrinsic worth. This charge becomes plausible when one considers that the average American homemaker spends the equivalent of a man's working day, 7.1 hours, in preparing meals, cleaning house, laundering, mending, shopping, and doing other household tasks. In other words, 43 percent of her waking time is spent in activity that would command an hourly wage on the open market well below the federally-set minimum for menial industrial work.

The point is not how little she would earn if she did these things in someone else's home, but that this use of time is virtually the same for homemakers with college degrees and for those with less than a grade school education, for women married to professional men, and for women married to blue-collar workers. Talent, education, ability, interests, motivations: all are irrelevant. In our society, being female uniquely qualifies an individual for domestic work.

It is true, of course, that the American homemaker has, on the average, 5.1 hours of leisure time per day, and it is here, we are told, that each woman can express her unique identity. Thus, politically interested women can join the League of Women Voters; women with humane interests can become part-time Gray Ladies; women who love music can raise money for the symphony. Protestant women play Canasta; Jewish women play Mah-Jongg; brighter women of all denominations and faculty wives play bridge; and so forth.

But politically interested *men* serve in legislatures; *men* with humane interests become physicians or clinical psychologists; *men* who love music play in the symphony; and so forth. In other words, why should a woman's unique identity determine only the periphery of her life rather than its central core?

Again, the important point is not that the role of homemaker is necessarily inferior, but that the woman's unique identity has been rendered irrelevant. Consider the following "predictability test." When a boy is born, it is difficult to predict what he will be doing 25 years later. We cannot say whether he will be an artist, a doctor, or a college professor because he will be permitted to develop and to fulfill his own unique potential, particularly if he is white and middle-class. But if the newborn child is a girl, we can usually predict with confidence how she will be spending her time 25 years later. Her individuality doesn't have to be considered; it is irrelevant.

The socialization of the American male has closed off certain options for him too. Men are discouraged from developing certain desirable traits such as tenderness and sensitivity just as surely as women are discouraged from being assertive and, alas, "too bright." Young boys are encouraged to be incompetent at cooking and child care just as surely as young girls are urged to be incompetent at mathematics and science.

Indeed, one of the errors of the early feminist movement in this country was that it assumed that men had all the goodies and that women could attain self-fufillment merely by being like men. But that is hardly the utopia implied by the values of individuality and self-fulfillment. Rather, these values would require society to raise its children so flexibly and with sufficient respect for the integrity of individual uniqueness that some men might emerge with the motivation, the ability, and the oppor-

tunity to stay home and raise children without bearing the stigma of being peculiar. If homemaking is as glamorous as the women's magazines
and television commercials portray it, then men, too, should have that
option. Even if homemaking isn't all that glamorous, it would probably
still be more fulfilling for some men than the jobs in which they now find
themselves.

   And if biological differences really do exist between men and women
in "nurturance," in their inborn motivations to care for children, then
this will show up automatically in the final distribution of men and
women across the various roles: relatively fewer men will choose to stay
at home. The values of individuality and self-fulfillment do not imply
that there must be equality of outcome and equal numbers of men and
women in each role, but that there should be the widest possible variation in outcome consistent with the range of individual differences among
people, regardless of sex. At the very least, these values imply that
society should raise its males so that they could freely engage in activities
that might pay less than those being pursued by their wives without
feeling that they were "living off their wives." One rarely hears it said of
a woman that she is "living off her husband."

   Thus, it is true that a man's options are limited by our society's sex-
role ideology, but as the "predictability test" reveals, it is still the woman
in our society whose identity is rendered irrelevant by America's socialization practices. In 1954, the United States Supreme Court declared that a
fraud and hoax lay behind the slogan "separate but equal." It is unlikely
that any court will ever do the same for the more subtle motto that successfully keeps the woman in her place: "complementary but equal."

Interpersonal Equality

> Wives, submit yourselves unto your own husbands, as unto
> the Lord. For the husband is the head of the wife, even as Christ
> is the head of the church; and he is the savior of the body. There-
> fore, as the church is subject unto Christ, so let the wives be to their
> own husbands in everything. (Eph. 5)

As this passage reveals, the ideological rationalization that men and
women hold complementary but equal positions is a recent invention of
our modern "liberal" society, part of the equalitarian veneer which helps
to keep today's version of the ideology nonconscious. Certainly those
Americans who value open, honest, and equalitarian relationships generally are quick to reject this traditional view of the male–female relationship; and, an increasing number of young people even plan to enter
"utopian" marriages very much like the following hypothetical example:

Both my wife and I earned Ph.D. degrees in our respective disciplines. I turned down a superior academic post in Oregon and accepted a slightly less desirable position in New York where my wife could obtain a part-time teaching job and do research at one of the several other colleges in the area. Although I would have preferred to live in a suburb, we purchased a home near my wife's college so that she could have an office at home where she would be when the children returned from school. Because my wife earns a good salary, she can easily afford to pay a maid to do her major household chores. My wife and I share all other tasks around the house equally. For example, she cooks the meals, but I do the laundry for her and help her with many of her other household tasks.

Without questioning the basic happiness of such a marriage or its appropriateness for many couples, we can legitimately ask if such a marriage is, in fact, an instance of interpersonal equality. Have all the hidden assumptions about the woman's "natural" role really been eliminated? Has the traditional ideology really been exorcised? There is a very simple test. If the marriage is truly equalitarian, then its description should retain the same flavor and tone even if the roles of the husband and wife were to be reversed:

Both my husband and I earned Ph.D. degrees in our respective disciplines. I turned down a superior academic post in Oregon and accepted a slightly less desirable position in New York where my husband could obtain a part-time teaching job and do research at one of the several other colleges in the area. Although I would have preferred to live in a suburb, we purchased a home near my husband's college so that he could have an office at home where he would be when the children returned from school. Because my husband earns a good salary, he can easily afford to pay a maid to do his major household chores. My husband and I share all other tasks around the house equally. For example, he cooks the meals, but I do the laundry for him and help him with many of his other household tasks.

It seems unlikely that many men or women in our society would mistake the marriage *just* described as either equalitarian or desirable, and thus it becomes apparent that the ideology about the woman's "natural" role nonconsciously permeates the entire fabric of such "utopian" marriages. It is true that the wife gains some measure of equality when her career can influence the final place of residence, but why is it the unquestioned assumption that the husband's career solely determines the initial set of alternatives that are to be considered? Why is it the wife who automatically seeks the part-time position? Why is it *her* maid instead of *their* maid? Why *her* laundry? Why *her* household tasks? And so forth throughout the entire relationship.

The important point here is not that such marriages are bad or that their basic assumptions of inequality produce unhappy, frustrated women. Quite the contrary. It is the very happiness of the wives in such marriages that reveals society's smashing success in socializing its women. It is a measure of the distance our society must yet traverse toward the goals of self-fulfillment and interpersonal equality that such marriages are widely characterized as utopian and fully equalitarian. It is a mark of how well the woman has been kept in her place that the husband in such a marriage is often idolized by women, including his wife, for "permitting" her to squeeze a career into the interstices of their marriage as long as his own career is not unduly inconvenienced. Thus is the white man blessed for exercising his power benignly while his "natural" right to that power forever remains unquestioned.

Such is the subtlety of a nonconscious ideology!

A truly equalitarian marriage would permit both partners to pursue careers or outside commitments which carry equal weight when all important decisions are to be made. It is here, of course, that the "problem" of children arises. People often assume that the woman who seeks a role beyond home and family would not care to have children. They assume that if she wants a career or serious outside commitment, then children must be unimportant to her. But of course no one makes this assumption about her husband. No one assumes that a father's interest in his career necessarily precludes a deep and abiding affection for his children or a vital interest in their development. Once again America applies a double standard of judgment. Suppose that a father of small children suddenly lost his wife. No matter how much he loved his children, no one would expect him to sacrifice his career in order to stay home with them on a full-time basis—*even if he had an independent source of income.* No one would charge him with selfishness or lack of parental feeling if he sought professional care for his children during the day. An equalitarian marriage simply abolishes this double standard and extends the same freedom to the mother, while also providing the framework for the father to enter more fully into the pleasures and responsibilities of child rearing. In fact, it is the equalitarian marriage which has the most potential for giving children the love and concern of two parents rather than one.

But few women are prepared to make use of this freedom. Even those women who have managed to finesse society's attempt to rob them of their career motivations are likely to find themselves blocked by society's trump card: the feeling that the raising of the children is their unique responsibility and—in time of crisis—ultimately theirs alone. Such is the emotional power of a nonconscious ideology.

In addition to providing this potential for equalized child care, a truly equalitarian marriage embraces a more general division of labor which satisfies what might be called "the roommate test." That is, the labor is divided just as it is when two men or two women room together in college or set up a bachelor apartment together. Errands and domestic chores are assigned by preference, agreement, flipping a coin, given to hired help, or—as is sometimes the case—left undone.

It is significant that todays' young people, many of whom live this way prior to marriage, find this kind of arrangement within marriage so foreign to their thinking. Consider an analogy. Suppose that a white male college student decided to room or set up a bachelor apartment with a black male friend. Surely the typical white student would not blithely assume that his black roommate was to handle all the domestic chores. Nor would his conscience allow him to do so even in the unlikely event that his roommate would say: "No, that's okay, I like doing housework. I'd be happy to do it." We suspect that the typical white student would still not be comfortable if he took advantage of this offer, if he took advantage of the fact that his roommate had been socialized to be "happy" with such an arrangement. But change this hypothetical black roommate to a female marriage partner, and somehow the student's conscience goes to sleep. At most it is quickly tranquilized by the thought that "she is the happiest when she is ironing for her loved one." Such is the power of a nonconscious ideology.

Of course, it may well be that she *is* happiest when she is ironing for her loved one.

Such, indeed, is the power of a nonconscious ideology!

Bibliography

BARRY, H., III, BACON, M. K., and CHILD, I. L. "A Cross-Cultural Survey of Some Sex Differences in Socialization." *Journal of Abnormal and Social Psychology* 55 (1957): 327–332.

BROWN, R. *Social Psychology.* New York: Free Press, 1965.

CRANDALL, V. J., and RABSON, A. "Children's Repetition Choices in an Intellectual Achievement Situation Following Success and Failure." *Journal of Genetic Psychology* 97 (1960): 161–168.

DODGE, J. D. *Women in the Soviet Economy.* Baltimore: The Johns Hopkins Press, 1966.

FLANAGAN, J. C. "Project Talent." Unpublished manuscript.

FRIEDAN, B. *The Feminine Mystique.* New York: Norton, 1963.

GOLDBERG, P. "Are Women Prejudiced Against Women?" *Transaction* 5 (April 1968): 28–30.

GOLDBERG, S. and LEWIS, M. "Play Behavior in the Year-Old Infant: Early Sex Differences." *Child Development* 40 (1969): 21–31.

GOTTESMAN, I. I. "Heritability of Personality: A Demonstration." *Psychological Monographs* 77 (1963): Whole no. 572.

KAGAN, J. "Acquisition and Significance of Sex Typing and Sex Role Identity." In *Review of Child Development Research, vol. 1,* ed. by M. L. Hoffman and L. W. Hoffman. New York: Russell Sage Foundation, 1964. Pp. 137–167.

McDAVID, J. W. "Imitative Behavior in Preschool Children." *Psychological Monographs* 73 (1959): whole no. 486.

MILTON, G. A. "Five Studies of the Relation between Sex Role Identification and Achievement in Problem Solving." Technical Report No. 3, Department of Industrial Administration, Department of Psychology, Yale University, December, 1958.

SEARS, R. R., MACCOBY, E. E., and LEVIN, H. *Patterns of Child Rearing.* Evanston, Ill.: Row, Peterson, 1957.

SMITH, M. E. "The Influence of Age, Sex, and Situation on the Frequency of Form and Functions of Questions Asked by Preschool Children." *Child Development* 3, (1933): 201–213.

TORRANCE, E. P. *Guiding Creative Talent.* Englewood Cliffs, N.J.: Prentice-Hall, 1962.

THE SOCIAL CONSTRUCTION OF THE SECOND SEX

> The passivity that is the essential characteristic of the "feminine" woman is a trait that develops in her from the earliest years. But it is wrong to assert a biological datum is concerned; it is in fact a destiny imposed upon her by her teachers and by society.
>
> Simone de Beauvoir

During the last thirty years social science has paid scant attention to women, confining its explorations of humanity to the male. Research has generally reinforced the sex stereotypes of popular mythology that women are essentially nurturant/expressive/passive and men instrumental/active/aggressive. Social scientists have tended to justify these stereotypes rather than analyze their origins, their value, or their effect.

In part this is due to the general conservatism and reluctance to question the status quo which has characterized the social sciences during this era of the feminine mystique. In part it is attributable to the "pervasive permeation of psychoanalytic thinking throughout American society." [1] The result has been a social science which is more a mechanism of social control than of social inquiry. Rather than trying to analyze why, it has only described what. Rather than exploring how men and women came to be the way they are, it has taken their condition as an irremediable given and sought to justify it on the basis of "biological" differences.

Nonetheless, the assumption that psychology recapitulates physiology has begun to crack. Masters and Johnson shattered the myth of woman's natural sexual passivity—on which her psychological passivity was claimed to rest. Research is just beginning into the other areas. Even without this new research new interpretations of the old data are being explored. What these new interpretations say is that women are the way they are because they've been trained to be that way. As the Bems put it: "We overlook the fact that the society that has spent twenty years carefully marking the woman's ballot for her has nothing to lose in that twenty-first year by pretending to let her cast it for the alternative of her choice. Society has controlled not her alternatives, but her motivation to choose any but the one of those alternatives." [2]

This motivation is controlled through the socialization process. Women are raised to want to fill the social roles in which society needs them. They are trained to model themselves after the accepted image and to meet as individuals the expectations that are held for women as a group. Therefore, to understand how most women are socialized we must first understand how they see themselves and are seen by others. Several studies have been done on this. Quoting from one of them, McClelland stated that "the female image is characterized as small, weak, soft and light. In the United States it is also dull, peaceful, relaxed, cold, rounded, passive and slow." [3] A more thorough study which asked men and women to choose out of a long list of adjectives those which most closely applied to themselves showed that women strongly felt themselves to be uncertain, anxious, nervous, hasty, careless, fearful, dull, childish, helpless, sorry, timid, clumsy, stupid, silly, and domestic. On a more positive side, women felt that they were understanding, tender, sympathetic, pure, generous, affectionate, loving, moral, kind, grateful, and patient. [4]

This is not a very favorable self-image but it does correspond fairly well with the social myths about what women are like. The image has some nice qualities, but they are not the ones normally required for that kind of achievement to which society gives its highest social rewards. Now one can justifiably question both the idea of achievement and the qualities necessary for it, but this is not the place to do so. Rather, because the current standards are the ones which women have been told they do not meet, the purpose here will be to look at the socialization process as a mechanism to keep them from doing so. We will also need to analyze some of the social expectations about women and about what they define as a successful *woman* (not a successful person) because they are inextricably bound up with the socialization process. All people are socialized to meet the social expectations held for them, and it is only when this process fails to do so (as is currently happening on several fronts) that it is at all questioned.

Let us further examine the effects on women of minority group status. Here, an interesting parallel emerges, but it is one fraught with much heresy. When we look at the *results* of female socialization we find a strong similarity between what our society labels, even extols, as the typical "feminine" character structure and that of oppressed peoples in this country and elsewhere.

In his classic study on *The Nature of Prejudice,* Allport devotes a chapter to "Traits Due to Victimization." Included are such personality characteristics as sensitivity, submission, fantasies of power, desire for protection, indirectness, ingratiation, petty revenge and sabotage, sympathy, extremes of both self and group hatred and self and group glorification, display of flashy status symbols, compassion for the underprivileged, identification with the dominant group's norms, and passivity.[5] Allport was primarily concerned with Jews and Negroes, but compare his characterization with the very thorough review of the literature on sex differences among young children made by Terman and Tyler. For girls, they listed such traits as sensitivity, conformity to social pressures, response to environment, case of social control, ingratiation, sympathy, low levels of aspiration, compassion for the underprivileged, and anxiety. They found that girls compared to boys were more nervous, unstable, neurotic, socially dependent, submissive, had less self-confidence, lower opinions of themselves and of girls in general, and were more timid, emotional, ministrative, fearful, and passive.[6]

Girls' perceptions of themselves were also distorted. Although girls make consistently better school grades than boys until late high school, their opinion of themselves grows progressively worse with age and their opinion of boys and boys' abilities grows better. Boys, however, have an increasingly better opinion of themselves and worse opinion of girls as they grow older.[7]

These distortions become so gross that, according to Goldberg, by the time girls reach college they have become prejudiced against women. He gave college girls sets of booklets containing six identical professional articles in traditional male, female, and neutral fields. The articles were identical, but the names of the authors were not. For example, an article in one set would bear the name John T. McKay and in another set the same article would be authored by Joan T. McKay. Each booklet contained three articles by "women" and three by "men." Questions at the end of each article asked the students to rate the articles on value, persuasiveness and profundity and the authors on writing style and competence. The male authors fared better in every field, even such "feminine" areas as Art History and Dietetics. Goldberg concluded that "Women are prejudiced against female professionals and, regardless of the actual accomplishments of these professionals, will firmly refuse to recognize them as the equals of their male colleagues."[8]

This combination of group self-hate and distortion of perceptions to justify that group self-hate are precisely the traits typical of a "minority group character structure."[9] It has been noted time and time again. The Clarks' finding of this pattern in Negro children in segregated schools contributed to the 1954 Supreme Court decision that outlawed such schools.

These traits, as well as the others typical of the "feminine" stereotype, have been found in the the Indians under British rule,[10] in the Algerians under the French,[11] and in black Americans.[12] There seems to be a correlation between being "feminine" and experiencing status deprivation.

This pattern repeats itself even within cultures. In giving TATs to women in Japanese villages, De Vos discovered that those from fishing villages where the status position of women was higher than in farming communities were more assertive, not as guilt-ridden and were more willing to ignore the traditional pattern of arranged marriages in favor of love marriages.[13]

In Terman's famous 50-year study of the gifted, a comparison in adulthood of those men who conspicuously failed to fulfill their early promise with those who did fulfill it showed that the successful had more self-confidence, fewer background disabilities, and were less nervous and emotionally unstable. But, they concluded "the disadvantages associated with lower social and home status appeared to present the outstanding handicap." [14]

The fact that women do have lower social status than men in our society and that both sexes tend to value men and male characteristics, values, and activities more highly than those of women has been noted by many authorities.[15] What has not been done is to make the connection between this status and its accompanying personality.

The failure to extensively analyze the effects and the causes of lower social status is surprising in light of the many efforts that have been made to uncover distinct psychological differences between men and women to account for the tremendous disparity in their social production and creativity. The Goldberg study implies that even if women did achieve on a par with men it would not be perceived or accepted as such and that a woman's work must be of a much higher quality than that of a man to be given the same recognition. But these circumstances alone, or the fact that it is the male definition of achievement which is applied, are not sufficient to account for the lack of social production. So research has turned to male/female differences.

Most of this research, in the Freudian tradition, has focused on finding the psychological and developmental differences supposedly inherent in feminine nature and function. Despite all these efforts, the general findings of psychological testing indicate that: (1) Individual differences are greater than sex differences; i.e. sex is just one of the many characteristics which define a human being. (2) Most differences in ability in any field do not appear until elementary school age or later. "Sex differences become more apparent with increasing education even if it is coeducation." [16]

An examination of the literature of intellectual differences between the sexes discloses some interesting patterns. First, the statistics themselves show some regularity. Most conclusions of what is typical of one sex or the other are founded upon the performances of two thirds of the subjects. For example, two thirds of all boys do better on the math section of the College Board Exam than the verbal, and two thirds of the girls do better on the verbal than the math. Bales' studies show a similar distribution when he concludes that in small groups men are the task-oriented leaders and women are the social-emotional leaders.[17] Not all tests show this two-thirds differential, but it is the mean about which most results of the ability test cluster. Sex is an easily visible, differentiable and testable criterion on which to draw conclusions; but it doesn't explain the one third that doesn't fit. The only characteristic virtually all women seem to have in common, besides their anatomy, is their lower social status.

Second, girls get off to a very good start. They begin speaking, reading, and counting sooner. They articulate more clearly and put words into sentences earlier. They have fewer reading and stuttering problems. Girls are even better in math in the early school years. Consistent sex differences in favor of boys do not appear until high-school age.[18] Here another pattern begins to develop.

During high school, girls' performance in school and on ability tests begins to drop, sometimes drastically. Although well over half of all high-school graduates are girls, significantly less than half of all college students are girls. Presumably, this should mean that a higher percentage of the better female students go on to higher education, but their performance *vis-à-vis* boys' continues to decline.

Girls start off better than boys and end up worse. This change in their performance occurs at a very significant point in time. It occurs when their status changes, or to be more precise, when girls become aware of what their adult status is supposed to be. It is during adolescence that peer-group pressures to be "feminine" or "masculine" increase and the conceptions of what is "feminine" and "masculine" become more narrow.[19] It is also at this time that there is a personal drive for conformity.[20]

One of the norms of our culture to which a girl learns to conform is that only men excel. This was evident in Lipinski's study of "Sex-Role Conflict and Achievement Motivation in College Women," which showed that thematic pictures depicting males as central characters elicited significantly more achievement imagery than female pictures.[21] One need only recall Asch's experiments to see how peer-group pressures, armed only with our rigid ideas about "femininity" and "masculinity" could lead to a decline in girls' performance. Asch found that some 33 percent of his subjects would go contrary to the evidence of their own senses about something as tangible as the comparative length of two lines when their judgments were at variance with those made by the other group members.[22] All but a handful of the other 67 percent experienced tremendous trauma in trying to stick to their correct perceptions.

When we move to something as intangible as sex-role behavior and to social sanctions far greater than the displeasure of a group of unknown experimental stooges, we can get an idea of how stifling social expectations can be. It is not surprising, in light of our cultural norm that a girl should not appear too smart or surpass boys in anything, that those pressures to conform, so prevalent in adolescence, should prompt girls to believe that the development of their minds will have only negative results. The lowered self-esteem and the denigration of their own sex noted by Smith [23] and Goldberg [24] are a logical consequence. These pressures even affect the supposedly unchangeable IQ scores. Corresponding with the drive for social acceptance, girls' IQs drop below those of boys during high school, rise slightly if they go to college, and go into a steady and consistent decline when and if they become full-time housewives.[25]

These are not the only consequences. Negative self-conceptions have negative effects in a manner that can only be called a self-fulfilling prophecy. They stifle motivation and channel energies into those areas that are likely to get some positive social rewards. Then those subject to these pressures are condemned for not having strived for the highest social rewards society has to offer.

A good example of this double bind is what psychologists call the "need for achievement." Achievement motivation in male college sophomores has been studied extensively. In women it has barely been looked at; women didn't fit the model social scientists set up to explain achievement in men. Girls do not seem to demonstrate the same consistent correlation between achievement and scores on achievement tests that boys do. For example, Stivers found that "non-motivated for college" girls scored higher on achievement motivation exams than "well-motivated for college" girls.[26] There has been little inquiry as to why this is so. The general policy followed by the researchers was that if girls didn't fit, leave them out. Nonetheless some theories have been put forward.

Pierce postulated that part of the confusion resulted from using the same criteria of achievement for girls that were used for boys—achievement in school. Therefore, he did a study of marriage vs. career orientation in high-school girls which did show a small but consistent correlation between high achievement motivation scores and marriage orientation.[27] In 1961 he did another study which showed a very strong correlation between high achievement scores and actual achievement of marriage within a year of high-school graduation. Those who went on to college and/or did not get married had low achievement scores.[28]

Although he unfortunately did not describe the class origins and other relevant characteristics of his study it does seem clear that the real situation is not that women do not have achievement motivation but that this motivation is directed differently from that of men. In fact, the achievement orientation of both sexes goes precisely where it is socially directed—educational achievement for boys and marriage achievement for girls. Pierce suggested that "achievement motivation in girls attaches itself not to academic performance, but rather to more immediate adult status goals. This would be a logical assumption in that academic success is much less important to achievement status as a woman than it is for a man." [29]

He goes on to say that "girls see that to achieve in life as adult females they need to achieve in non-academic ways, that is, attaining the social graces, achieving beauty in person and dress, finding a desirable social status, marrying the right man. This is the successful adult woman. . . . Their achievement motivations are directed toward realizing personal goals through their relationship with men. . . . Girls who are following the normal course of development are most likely to seek adult status through marriage at an early age." [30]

Achievement for women is adult status through marriage, not success in the usual use of the word. One might postulate that both kinds of success might be possible, particularly for the highly achievement-oriented woman. But in fact the two are more often perceived as contradictory; success in one is seen to preclude success in the other.

Horner just completed a study at the University of Michigan from which she postulated a psychological barrier to achievement in women. She administered a TAT word item to undergraduates that said "After first term finals Anne finds herself at the top of her medical school class." A similar one for a male control group used a masculine name. The results were scored for imagery of fear of success and Horner found that 65% of the women and only 10% of the men demonstrated a definite "motive to avoid success." She explained the results by hypothesizing that the prospect of success, or situations in which success or failure is a relevant dimension, are perceived as having, and in fact do have, negative consequences for women. Success in the normal sense is threatening to women. Further research confirmed that fear of social rejection and role conflict did generate a "motive to avoid success." [31]

Ability differences correlate strongly with interest differences [32] and women have a definite interest in avoiding success. This is reinforced by

typical of girls, Bronfenbrenner maintains, and involves the risk of "over-socialization."

He doesn't discuss the possible negative effects such oversocialization has on girls, but he does express his concern about what would happen to the "qualities of independence, initiative, and self-sufficiency" of boys if such training were applied to them. "While an affectional context is important for the socialization of boys, it must evidently be accompanied by and be compatible with a strong component of parental discipline. Otherwise, the boy finds himself in the same situation as the girl, who, having received greater affection, is more sensitive to its withdrawal, with the result that a little discipline goes a long way and strong authority is constricting rather than constructive." [49]

That these variations in socialization result in variations in personality is corroborated by Schachter's studies of first and later-born children. Like girls, first children tend to be better socialized but also more anxious and dependent, whereas second children, like boys, are more aggressive and self-confident. [50]

Bronfenbrenner concludes that the crucial variable is the differential treatment by the father and "in fact, it is the father who is especially likely to treat children of the two sexes differently." His extremes of affection, and of authority, are both deleterious. Not only do his high degrees of nurturance and protectiveness toward girls result in "over-socialization," but "the presence of strong paternal power is particularly debilitating. In short, boys thrive in a patriarchal context, girls in a matriarchal one." [51]

His observations receive indirect support from Douvan who noted that "part-time jobs of mothers have a beneficial effect on adolescent children, particularly daughters. This reflects the fact that adolescents may receive too much mothering." [52]

The importance of mothers, as well as mothering, was pointed out by Kagan and Moss. In looking at the kinds of role models that mothers provide for developing daughters, they discovered that it is those women who are looked upon as unfeminine whose daughters tend to achieve intellectually. These mothers are "aggressive and competitive women who were critical of their daughters and presented themselves to their daughters as intellectually competitive and aggressive role models. It is reasonable to assume that the girls identified with these intellectually aggressive women who valued mastery behavior." [53]

There seems to be some evidence that the sexes have been differentially socialized with different training practices, for different goals, and with different results. If McClelland is right in all the relationships he finds between child-rearing practices (in particular independence and mastery training), achievement-motivation scores of individuals tested, actual achievement of individuals, and indeed, the economic growth of whole societies,[54] there is no longer much question as to why the historical achievement of women has been so low. In fact, with the dependency training they receive so early in life, the wonder is that they have achieved so much.

But this is not the whole story. Maccoby, in her discussion of the relationship of independence training to analytic abilities, notes that the girl who does not succumb to overprotection and develop the appropriate personality and behavior for her sex has a major price to pay: a price in anxiety. Or, as other observers have noted: "The universe of appropriate behavior for males and females is delineated early in development and it is difficult for the child to cross these culturally given frontiers without considerable conflict and tension." [55]

Some anxiety is beneficial to creative thinking, but high or sustained levels of it are damaging, "for it narrows the range of solution efforts, interferes with breaking set, and prevents scanning of the whole range of elements open to perception." [56] This anxiety is particularly manifest in college women,[57] and of course they are the ones who experience the most conflict between their current—intellectual—activities, and expectations about behavior in their future—unintellectual—careers.

Maccoby feels that "it is this anxiety which helps to account for the lack of productivity among those women who do make intellectual careers." The combination of social pressures, role-expectations and parental training together tell "something of a horror story. It would appear that even when a woman is suitably endowed intellectually and develops the right temperament and habits of thought to make use of her endowment, she must be fleet of foot indeed to scale the hurdles society has erected for her and to remain a whole and happy person while continuing to follow her intellectual bent." [58]

The reasons for this horror story must by now be clearly evident. Traditionally, women have been defined as passive creatures, sexually, physically, and mentally. Their roles have been limited to the passive, dependent, auxiliary ones, and they have been trained from birth to fit these roles. However, those qualities by which one succeeds in this society are active ones. Achievement orientation, intellectuality, and analytic ability all require a certain amount of aggression.

As long as women were convinced that these qualities were beyond them, that they were inferior in their exercise and much happier if they stayed in their place, they remained quiescent under the paternalistic system of Western civilization. Paternalism was a pre-industrial scheme of life, and its yoke was partially broken by the industrial revolution.[59]

only to men or women, there is a great deal of overlap for most jobs. Virtually every task, even in the most primitive societies, can be performed by either men or women. Equally important, what is defined as a man's task in one society may well be classified as a woman's job in another.[74] Nonetheless, the sexual division of labor is much more narrow than dictated by physical limitations, and what any one culture defines as a woman's job will seldom be performed by a man and vice versa. It seems that what originated as a division of labor based upon the necessities of survival has spilled over into many other areas and lasted long past the time of its social value. Where male strength and mobility has been crucial to social survival, male dominance and the aura of male superiority has been the strongest. The latter has been incorporated into the value structure and attained an existence of its own.

Thus, male superiority has not ceased with an end to the need for male strength. As Goode pointed out, there is one consistent element in the assignment of jobs to the sexes, even in modern societies: "Whatever the strictly male tasks are, they are defined as *more honorific* (emphasis his). . . . Moreover, the tasks of control, management, decision, appeals to the gods—in short the higher level jobs that typically do *not* require strength, speed or traveling far from home—are male jobs." [75]

He goes on to comment that "this element suggests that the sexual division of labor within family and society comes perilously close to the racial or caste restrictions in some modern countries. That is, the low-ranking race, caste, or sex is defined as not being *able* to do certain types of prestigious work, but it is also considered a violation of propriety if they do it. Obviously, if women really cannot do various kinds of male tasks, no moral or ethical prohibition would be necessary to keep them from it." [76]

Sex roles originated in economic necessities but the value attached to any one role has become a factor of sex alone. Even cross-culturally, these roles, and the attitudes associated with them, are ingrained by common socialization practices. Barry, Bacon, and Child discovered that "pressure toward nurturance, obedience and responsibility is most often stronger for girls, whereas pressure toward achievement and self-reliance is most often stronger for boys." [77] These are the same socialization practices traditionally found in Western society. As the Barry, Bacon, and Child study showed, these socializations serve to prepare children for roles as adults that require women to stay near the home and men to go out and achieve. The greater emphasis a society places on physical strength, the greater the sex-role differentiation and the sex differences in socialization.

These sex-role differences may have served a natural function at one time, but it is doubtful that they still do so. The characteristics we observe in women and men today are a result of socialization practices that were developed for survival of a primitive society. The value structure of male superiority is a reflection of the primitive orientations and values. But social and economic conditions have changed drastically since these values were developed. Technology has reduced to almost nothing the importance of muscular strength. In fact, the warlike attitude which goes along with an idealization of physical strength and dominance is proving to be positively destructive. The value of large families has also become a negative one. Now we are concerned with the population explosion and prefer that our society produce children of quality rather than quantity. The result of all these changes is that the traditional sex-roles and the traditional family structures have become dysfunctional.

To some extent, patterns of child-rearing have also changed. Bronfenbrenner reports that at least middle-class parents are raising both boys and girls much the same. He noted that over a 50-year period middle-class parents have been developing a "more acceptant, equalitarian relationship with their children." [78] With an increase in the family's social position, the patterns of parental treatment of children begin to converge. [79] He likewise noted that a similar phenomenon is beginning to develop in lower-class parents and that equality of treatment is slowly working its way down the social ladder.

These changes in patterns of child-rearing correlate with changes in relationships within the family. Both are moving toward a less hierarchical and more egalitarian pattern of living.

As Blood has pointed out, "today we may be on the verge of a new phase in American family history, when the companionship family is beginning to manifest itself. One distinguishing characteristic of this family is the dual employment of husband and wife. . . . Employment emancipates women from domination by their husbands and, secondarily, raises their daughters from inferiority to their brothers. . . . The classic differences between masculinity and femininity are disappearing as both sexes in the adult generation take on the same roles in the labor market. . . . The roles of men and women are converging for both adults and children. As a result the family will be far less segregated internally, far less stratified into different age generations and different sexes. The old asymmetry of male-dominated, female-serviced family life is being replaced by a new symmetry." [80]

All these data indicate that several trends are converging at about the same time. Our value structure has changed from an authoritarian one to a more democratic one, though our social structure has not yet caught up. Social attitudes begin in the family; only a democratic family can raise children to be citizens in a democratic society. The social and economic organization of society which kept women in the home has likewise changed. The home is no longer the center of society. The primary male and female functions have left it and there is no longer any major reason for maintaining the large sex-role differentiations which it supported. The value placed on physical strength which reinforced the dominance of men, and the male superiority attitudes that this generated, have also become dysfunctional. It is the mind, not the body, which must now prevail, and woman's mind is the equal of man's. The "pill" has liberated women from the uncertainty of childbearing, and with it the necessity of being attached to a man for economic support. But our attitudes toward women, and toward the family, have not changed concomitantly with the other developments. There is a distinct "cultural lag." Definitions of the family, conceptions of women and ideas about social function are left over from an era when they were necessary for social survival. They have persisted into an era in which they are no longer viable. The result can only be called severe role dysfunctionality for women.

The necessary relief for this dysfunctionality must come through changes in the social and economic organization of society and in social attitudes which will permit women to play a full and equal part in the social order. With this must come changes in the family, so that men and women are not only equal, but can raise their children in a democratic atmosphere. These changes will not come easily, nor will they come through the simple evolution of social trends. Trends do not move all in the same direction or at the same rate. To the extent that changes are dysfunctional with each other they create problems. These problems must be solved not by complacency but by conscious human direction. Only in this way can we have a real say in the shape of our future and the shape of our lives.

References

1. Rossi, A. "Equality between the Sexes: An Immodest Proposal." In Robert J. Lifton (ed.), *The Woman in America*. Boston: Beacon Press, 1965. Pp. 102–103.
2. Bem, S. and Bem, D. "We're All Nonconscious Sexists." *Psychology Today* (1970):4(6), 26.
3. McClelland, D. "Wanted: A New Self-image for Women." In Robert J. Lifton (ed.), *The Woman in America*. Boston: Beacon Press, 1965. P. 173.
4. Bennett, E. M. and Cohen, L. R. "Men and Women: Personality Patterns and Contrasts." *Genetic Psychology Monographs* (1959):59, 101–155.
5. Allport, G. *The Nature of Prejudice*. Reading, Mass.: Addison-Wesley, 1954. Pp. 142–161.

6. TERMAN, L. M. and TYLER, L. "Psychological Sex Differences." In Leonard Carmichael (ed.), *Manual of Child Psychology.* New York: Wiley & Sons, 1954. Pp. 1080–1100.
7. SMITH, S. "Age and Sex Differences in Children's Opinion concerning Sex Differences." *Journal of Genetic Psychology* (1939):54, 17–25.
8. GOLDBERG, P. "Are Women Prejudiced against Women?" *Transaction,* April 1969, 28.
9. CLARK, K. and CLARK, M. "Racial Identification and Preference in Negro Children." In T. M. Newcomb and E. L. Hartley (eds.), *Readings in Social Psychology.* New York: Holt, Rinehart & Winston, 1947.
10. FISHER, L. *Gandhi.* New York: Signet Key, 1954.
11. FANON, F. *The Wretched of the Earth.* New York: Grove Press, 1963.
12. MYRDAL, G. *An American Dilemma.* New York: Harper, 1944.
13. DE VOS, G. "The Relation of Guilt toward Parents to Achievement and Arranged Marriage among the Japanese." *Psychiatry* (1960):23, 287–301.
14. MILES, C. C. "Gifted Children." In Carmichael, *op. cit.,* p. 1045.
15. See: BROWN, R. *Social Psychology.* New York: The Free Press, p. 162; Reuben Hill and Howard Becker (eds.), *Family, Marriage and Parenthood.* Boston: D. C. Heath, 1955, p. 790; Goldberg, *op. cit.,* p. 28; Myrdal, *op. cit.,* Appendix V; and Goode, W. J., *The Family.* Englewood Cliffs, New Jersey: Prentice-Hall, 1965. P. 70.
16. TYLER, L. "Sex Differences," under "Individual Differences" in the *International Encyclopedia of the Social Sciences,* Vol. 7, 1968, New York: The Macmillan Co. Pp. 207–213.
17. BALES, R. F. "Task roles and social roles in problem-solving groups." In T. M. Newcomb, E. Maccoby, and E. L. Hartley (eds.), *Readings in Social Psychology* (3rd ed.). New York: Holt, Rinehart & Winston, 1958.
18. MACCOBY, E. "Sex Differences in Intellectual Functioning." In E. Maccoby (ed.), *The Development of Sex Differences.* Stanford: Stanford University Press, 1966. Pp. 26 ff.
19. NEIMAN, L. J. "The Influence of Peer Groups upon Attitudes toward the Feminine Role." *Social Problems* (1954):2, 104–111.
20. MILNER, E. "Effects of Sex-role and Social Status on the Early Adolescent Personality." *Genetic Psychological Monographs:* 40, 231–325.
21. LIPINSKI, B. *Sex-role Conflict and Achievement Motivation in College Women.* Unpublished doctoral dissertation, University of Cincinnati, 1965.
22. ASCH, S. E. "Studies of Independence and Conformity. A Minority of One against a Unanimous Majority." *Psychological Monographs* (1956):70, No. 9.
23. SMITH, *op. cit.*
24. GOLDBERG, *op. cit.*
25. BRADWAY, K. P. and THOMPSON, C. W. "Intelligence at Adulthood: A Twenty-five Year Followup." *Journal of Educational Psychology* (1962):53, 1–14.
26. STIVERS, E. N. *Motivation for College of High School Boys and Girls.* Unpublished doctoral dissertation, University of Chicago, 1959.
27. PIERCE, J. V. and BOWMAN, P. H. "The Educational Motivation Patterns of Superior Students Who Do and Do Not Achieve in High School. U.S. Office of Education Project #208. *Co-operative Research Monograph No. 2,* U.S. Printing Office, Washington (1960):33–66.

28. PIERCE, J. V. "Sex Differences in Achievement Motivation of Able High School Students." *Co-operative Research Project No. 1097*, University of Chicago (December 1961).
29. *Ibid.*, p. 23.
30. *Ibid.*, p. 42.
31. HORNER, M. "Femininity and Successful Achievement: A Basic Inconsistency." In Bardwick, et al., *Feminine Personality and Conflict.* Belmont: Brooks/Cole, 1970. See also pp. 97–122 in this text.
32. TERMAN & TYLER, *op. cit.*, p. 1104.
33. MACCOBY, 1966, *op. cit.*, p. 26.
34. *Ibid.*, p. 27.
35. MACCOBY, E. "Woman's Intellect." In Farber & Wilson (eds.), *The Potential of Women.* New York: McGraw-Hill, 1963. P. 30.
36. *Ibid.*, p. 31. See also: Sherman, J. A. "Problems of Sex Differences in Space Perception and Aspects of Intellectual Functioning." *Psychological Review* (July 1967):74, No. 4, 290–299; and Vernon, P. E. "Ability Factors and Environmental Influences." *American Psychologist* (Sept. 1965):20, No. 9, 723–733.
37. BRONFENBRENNER, U. "Some Familial Antecedents of Responsibility and Leadership in Adolescents." In Luigi Petrullo and Bernard M. Bass (eds.), *Leadership and Interpersonal Behavior.* New York: Holt, Rinehart, & Winston, 1961. P. 260.
38. LEVY, D. M. *Maternal Overprotection.* New York: Columbia University Press, 1943.
39. MACCOBY, 1963, *op. cit.*, p. 31.
40. WITKIN, H. A., DYK, R. B., PATERSON, H. E., GOODENOUGH, D. R., and KARP, S. A. *Psychological Differentiation.* New York: John Wiley and Sons, 1962.
41. CLAPP, J. *Sex Differences in Mathematical Reasoning Ability.* Unpublished paper, 1968.
42. SONTAG, I. W., BAKER, C. T., and NELSON, V. A. "Mental Growth and Personality Development: A Longitudinal Study." *Monographs of the Society for Research in Child Development* (1953):23, No. 68.
43. MACCOBY, 1963. *op. cit.*, p. 33.
44. KAGAN, J. and Moss, H. A. *Birth to Maturity: A Study in Psychological Development.* New York and London: John Wiley and Sons, 1962. P. 275.
45. *Ibid.*, p. 225.
46. WINTERBOTTOM, M. "The Relation of Need for Achievement to Learning Experiences in Independence and Mastery." In Harold Proshansky and Bernard Seidenberg (eds.), *Basic Studies in Social Psychology.* New York: Holt, Rinehart & Winston, 1965. Pp. 294–307.
47. SEARS, R. R., MACCOBY, E., and LEVIN, H. *Patterns of Child Rearing.* Evanston, Ill.: Row, Peterson, 1957.
48. BRONFENBRENNER, *op. cit.*, p. 260.
49. *Ibid.*
50. SCHACHTER, S. *The Psychology of Affiliation.* Stanford: Stanford University Press, 1959.
51. BRONFENBRENNER, *op. cit.*, p. 267.
52. DOUVAN, E. "Employment and the Adolescent." In F. Ivan Nye and Lois W. Hoffman (eds.), *The Employed Mother in America.* Chicago: Rand McNally, 1963.

53. KAGAN and Moss, *op. cit.*, p. 222.
54. McCLELLAND, D. C. *The Achieving Society.* Princeton: Van Nostrand, 1961.
55. KAGAN and Moss, *op. cit.*, p. 270.
56. MACCOBY, 1963, *op. cit.*, p. 37.
57. SINICK, D. "Two Anxiety Scales Correlated and Examined for Sex Differences." *Journal of Clinical Psychology* (1956):12, 394–395.
58. MACCOBY, 1963, *op. cit.*, p. 37.
59. MYRDAL, *op. cit.*, p. 1077.
60. MONTAGU, A. "Anti-feminism and Race Prejudice." *Psychiatry* (1946):9, 69–71.
61. KENISTON, E. and KENISTON, K. "An American Anachronism: The Image of Women and Work." *American Scholar* (Summer 1964):33, No. 3, 355–375.
62. ROSSI, *op. cit.*
63. ADORNO, T. W., et al., *The Authoritarian Personality.* New York: Harper, 1950.
64. STEPHENS, W. N. *The Family in Cross-cultural Perspective.* New York: Holt, Rinehart & Winston, 1963.
65. D'ANDRADE, R. "Sex Differences and Cultural Institutions." In Maccoby (ed.), 1966, *op. cit.*, p. 189.
66. BLOOD, R. O., and WOLFE, D. M. *Husbands and Wives.* Glencoe: The Free Press, 1960.
67. BLOOD, R. O. "Long-range Causes and Consequences of the Employment of Married Women." *Journal of Marriage and the Family* (1965):27, No. 1, 46.
68. GOODE, *op. cit.*, p. 76.
69. HILL and BECKER, *op. cit.*, p. 790.
70. HALLENBECK, P. N. "An Analysis of Power Dynamics in Marriage." *Journal of Marriage and the Family* (May 1966):28, No. 2, 203.
71. BLOOD, *op. cit.*, p. 47.
72. BARRY, H., BACON, M. K., and CHILD, I. L. "A Cross-cultural Survey of Some Sex Differences in Socialization." *Journal of Abnormal and Social Psychology* (1957):55, 330.
73. SPIRO, M. E. *Kibbutz: Venture in Utopia.* Cambridge: Harvard University Press, 1956.
74. D'ANDRADE, *op. cit.*, p. 191.
75. GOODE, *op. cit.*, p. 70.
76. *Ibid.*
77. BARRY, BACON, and CHILD, *op. cit.*, p. 328.
78. BRONFENBRENNER, U. "Socialization and Social Class through Time and Space." In Maccoby, Newcomb and Hartley, *op. cit.*
79. BRONFENBRENNER, U. "The Effects of Social and Cultural Change on Personality." *Journal of Social Issues* (1969):17, No. 1, 6–18.
80. BLOOD, *op. cit.*, p. 47.

MEN: BEING A BOY

As boys go, I wasn't much. I mean, I tried to be a boy and spent many childhood hours pummeling my hardly formed ego with failure at cowboys and Indians, baseball, football, lying, and sneaking out of the house. When our neighborhood gang raided a neighbor's pear tree, I was the only one who got sick from the purloined fruit. I also failed at setting fire to our garage, an art at which any five-year-old boy should be adept. I was, however, the neighborhood champion at getting beat up. "That Julius can take it, man," the boys used to say, almost in admiration, after I emerged from another battle, tears brimming in my eyes but refusing to fall.

My efforts at being a boy earned me a pair of scarred knees that are a record of a childhood spent falling from bicycles, trees, the tops of fences, and porch steps; of tripping as I ran (generally from a fight), walked, or simply tried to remain upright on windy days.

I tried to believe my parents when they told me I was a boy, but I could find no objective proof for such an assertion. Each morning during the summer, as I cuddled up in the quiet of a corner with a book, my mother would push me out the back door and into the yard. And throughout the day as my blood was let as if I were a patient of seventeenth-century medicine, I thought of the girls sitting in the shade of porches, playing with their dolls, toy refrigerators, and stoves.

There was the life, I thought! No constant pressure to prove oneself. No necessity always to be competing. While I humiliated myself on football and baseball fields, the girls stood on the sidelines laughing at me, because they didn't have to do anything except be girls. The rising of each sun brought me to the starting line of yet another day's Olympic decathlon, with no hope of ever winning even a bronze medal.

Note: By Julius Lester. Reprinted with permission from *Ms.*, July 1973, 11:1, 112–113.

Through no fault of my own I reached adolescence. While the pressure to prove myself on the athletic field lessened, the overall situation got worse—because now I had to prove myself with girls. Just how I was supposed to go about doing this was beyond me, especially because, at the age of 14, I was four foot nine and weighed 78 pounds. (I think there may have been one 10-year-old girl in the neighborhood smaller than I.) Nonetheless, duty called, and with my ninth-grade gym-class jockstrap flapping between my legs, off I went.

To get a girl friend, though, a boy had to have some asset beyond the fact that he was alive. I wasn't handsome like Bill McCord, who had girls after him like a cop-killer has policemen. I wasn't ugly like Romeo Jones, but at least the girls noticed him: "That ol' ugly boy better stay 'way from me!" I was just there, like a vase your grandmother gives you at Christmas that you don't like or dislike, can't get rid of, and don't know what to do with. More than ever I wished I were a girl. Boys were the ones who had to take the initiative and all the responsibility. (I hate responsibility so much that if my heart didn't beat of itself, I would now be a dim memory.)

It was the boy who had to ask the girl for a date, a frightening enough prospect until it occurred to me that she might say no! That meant risking my ego, which was about as substantial as a toilet-paper raincoat in the African rainy season. But I had to thrust that ego forward to be judged, accepted, or rejected by some girl. It wasn't fair! Who was she to sit back like a queen with the power to create joy by her consent or destruction by her denial? It wasn't fair—but that's the way it was.

But if (God forbid!) she should say "Yes," then my problem would begin in earnest, because I was the one who said where we would go (and waited in terror for her approval of my choice). I was the one who picked her up at her house where I was inspected by her parents as if I were a possible carrier of syphilis (which I didn't think one could get from masturbating, but then again, Jesus was born of a virgin, so what did I know?). Once we were on our way, it was I who had to pay the bus fare, the price of the movie tickets, and whatever she decided to stuff her stomach with afterward. (And the smallest girls are all stomach.) Finally, the girl was taken home where once again I was inspected (the father looking covertly at my fly and the mother examining the girl's hair). The evening was over and the girl had done nothing except honor me with her presence. All the work had been mine.

Imagining this procedure over and over was more than enough: I was a sophomore in college before I had my first date.

I wasn't a total failure in high school, though, for occasionally I would go to a party, determined to salvage my self-esteem. The parties usually took place in somebody's darkened basement. There was generally a surreptitious wine bottle or two being passed furtively among the boys, and a record player with an insatiable appetite for Johnny Mathis records. Boys gathered on one side of the room and girls on the other. There were always a few boys and girls who'd come to the party for the sole purpose of grinding away their sexual frustrations to Johnny Mathis's falsetto, and they would begin dancing to their own music before the record player was plugged in. It took a little longer for others to get started, but no one matched my talent for standing by the punch bowl. For hours, I would try to make my legs do what they had been doing without effort since I was nine months old, but for some reason they would show all the symptoms of paralysis on those evenings.

After several hours of wondering whether I was going to die ("Julius Lester, a 16-year-old, died at a party last night, a half-eaten Ritz cracker in one hand and a potato chip dipped in pimiento-cheese spread in the other. Cause of death: failure to be a boy"), I would push my way to the other side of the room where the girls sat like a hanging jury. I would pass by the girl I wanted to dance with. If I was going to be refused, let it be by someone I didn't particularly like. Unfortunately, there weren't many in that category. I had more crushes than I had pimples.

Finally, through what surely could only have been the direct intervention of the Almighty, I would find myself on the dance floor with a girl. And none of my prior agony could compare to the thought of actually dancing. But there I was and I had to dance with her. Social custom decreed that I was supposed to lead, because I was the boy. Why? I'd wonder. Let her lead. Girls were better dancers anyway. It didn't matter. She stood there waiting for me to take charge. She wouldn't have been worse off if she'd waited for me to turn white.

But, reciting "Invictus" to myself, I placed my arms around her, being careful to keep my armpits closed because, somehow, I had managed to overwhelm a half jar of deodorant and a good-size bottle of cologne. With sweaty armpits, "Invictus," and legs afflicted again with polio, I took her in my arms, careful not to hold her so far away that she would think I didn't like her, but equally careful not to hold her so close that she could feel the catastrophe which had befallen me the instant I touched her hand. My penis, totally disobeying the lecture I'd given it before we left home, was as rigid as Governor Wallace's jaw would be if I asked for his daughter's hand in marriage.

God, how I envied girls at that moment. Wherever *it* was on them, it didn't dangle between their legs like an elephant's trunk. No wonder boys talked about nothing but sex. That thing was always there. Every time we went to the john, there *it* was, twitching around like a fat little worm on a fishing hook. When we took baths, it floated in the water like a lazy fish and God forbid we should touch it! It sprang to life like lightning leaping from a cloud. I wished I could cut it off, or at least keep it tucked between my legs, as if it were a tail that had been mistakenly attached to the wrong end. But I was helpless. It was there, with a life and mind of its own, having no other function than to embarrass me.

Fortunately, the girls I danced with were discreet and pretended that they felt nothing unusual rubbing against them as we danced. But I was always convinced that the next day they were all calling up all their friends to exclaim: "Guess what, girl? Julius Lester got one! I ain't lyin'!"

Now, of course, I know that it was as difficult being a girl as it was a boy, if not more so. While I stood paralyzed at one end of a dance floor trying to find the courage to ask a girl for a dance, most of the girls waited in terror at the other, afraid that no one, not even I, would ask them. And while I resented having to ask a girl for a date, wasn't it also horrible to be the one who waited for the phone to ring? And how many of those girls who laughed at me making a fool of myself on the baseball diamond would have gladly given up their places on the sidelines for mine on the field?

No, it wasn't easy for any of us, girls and boys, as we forced our beautiful, free-flowing child-selves into those narrow, constricting cubicles labeled *female* and *male*. I tried, but I wasn't good at being a boy. Now, I'm glad, knowing that a man is nothing but the figment of a penis's imagination, and any man should want to be something more than that.

PART 2

Dear Old Sexist School Days

THE SCHOOL'S ROLE IN THE SEX-ROLE STEREOTYPING OF GIRLS: A FEMINIST REVIEW OF THE LITERATURE

The renewed feminist critique of traditional sex roles requires that we examine where and how these roles are learned. This article will review research studies, informal reports, and speculative writings that bear on the school's role in elaborating and reinforcing damaging sex roles.

Developmental psychologists have tended to assume a "separate but equal" approach in their studies of sex roles. That is, implicit in most discussions of sex roles is the assumption that "girls learn their girl role" and "boys learn their boy role" in a relatively benign social context. There is little concern with the *content* of sex roles or the consequences of "appropriately" feminine and masculine characteristics for the psychological health, self-actualization, and achievement of women and men; the political and cultural realities of male-dominated society are ignored or minimized, and certainly left unchallenged. Most developmental studies, then, accept traditional sex roles as "given" and merely attempt to discover at what age "sex-role appropriate" learning occurs. However, even within the context of "descriptive neutrality" (read "traditional sexism") certain findings are relevant to the present discussion.

1. Children learn the content ascribed to sex roles at an early age. The male/female distinction is clear to children beginning at about age two and is one of the earliest concepts they learn.[1] By the preschool years, children not only know which sex they are but know the behavior patterns, play preferences, and psychological characteristics expected of them.[2]

2. As children grow older their awareness of "appropriate" sex-role

Note: By Betty Levy. Reprinted with permission from the author and *Feminist Studies*, Summer 1972, 1:1, 5–23.

behavior increases and becomes more restricted and stereotyped.[3] However, boys are more aware of the female role than girls are of the male role, which suggests the presence of sex-role avoidance in boys.[4]

3. Both girls and boys increasingly value and prefer the male role. Fifteen of the 20 studies of sex-role acceptance reviewed by Oetzel[5] showed greater sex-role acceptance by males, supporting Brown's[6] suggestion that the wide latitude given to girls in expressing preference for masculine activities is due to the higher status awarded masculine activities. Girls are allowed to be tomboys; boys are censured if they are sissies. These studies also confirm Smith's[7] classic study of 100 boys and girls ages eight to 15 who "voted" whether girls or boys possessed the greater degree of each of 19 desirable and 14 undesirable traits. He reported that with increasing chronological age both boys and girls develop a better opinion of boys and a progressively poorer opinion of girls. Kohlberg's review of early sex stereotypes indicated that both girls and boys learn to attribute more power and prestige to the male role: "At early ages (three–four) the father is not awarded more prestige than the mother, but by ages five–six he is. . . . Girls between the ages of five and eight do not show an increase in preference for same-sex objects and activities, whereas boys do."[8] What these studies do not tell us is *how* children learn to ascribe different values to male and female roles, and, ultimately, to view the female role as inferior.

4. Studies of adults reveal that both females and males think it preferable to be male and to have male children. A 1946 survey by *Fortune* magazine found that while 91 percent of the men would want to be males if they could be born again, 25 percent of the women would prefer to be male.[9] According to a 1955 Gallup poll, between five and 12 times as many women as men recall having wished they were of the opposite sex. Similarly, a mass of evidence demonstrates that American parents tend to prefer boys. More mothers of girls have postpartum depression than do mothers of boys; pregnant women dream twice as often about male babies; mothers who have only daughters are happier about a new pregnancy than are mothers of sons; if the first child is a boy the interval before a second child is conceived is longer than if the first child is a girl; and the likelihood of having a third child is greater if the first two children are both girls than if they are both boys.[10]

5. The sex-role training of girls involves less tolerance for aggressive behavior and greater permission and even encouragement of dependency.[11] Competency, independence, objectivity, logical thinking, self-assertiveness, and self-confidence all are stereotypically attributed to and reinforced in males, while emotional expressiveness, sensitivity to others, as well as incompetence, dependency, subjectivity, poor logic, submissive-

ness, and lack of self-confidence are stereotypically attributed to and reinforced in females.[12]

The remainder of this paper will discuss how schools function to reinforce these attitudes and behavior and thus perpetuate existing inequalities between the sexes.

Educational researchers and critics of the schools recently have demonstrated the contradiction between what schools *say* they do and what they *actually* do. The ostensible purpose of schools is to educate. Liberal reformers who accept this purpose at face value bemoan the fact that schools are "failing," i.e., not educating. Silberman[13] indicts the "mindlessness" of school personnel for the "grim, joyless, and oppressive" classrooms. More sophisticated analysts move beyond the stated purpose of schools to examine their actual and multiple functions. In an important essay, Reimer writes:

> Schools in all nations, of all kinds, at all levels, combine four distinct social functions: custodial care, social-role selection, indoctrination, and education as usually defined in terms of the development of skills and knowledge. . . . It is the conflict among these functions which makes schools inefficient. It is the combination of these functions which tends to make the school a total institution . . . and which makes it such an effective instrument of social control.[14]

Reimer describes the institutional values of conformity, dependence on others for learning, and hierarchy or social stratification. The revolutionary Brazilian educator Freire asserts that there is no "neutral" education: education is either for "domination" or for "freedom."[15] Most schools, he contends, effectively "domesticate" and "pacify" the masses, since they transfer "prepossessed and pre-digested reality," divorced from both its origins and its uses. Illich[16] has focused on the "hidden curriculum" of the school, the structure of the school as opposed to what happens in schools. Friedenberg has noted: "In school . . . it is indeed true that the medium is the message . . . what is taught isn't as important as learning how you have to act in society, how other people will treat you, how they will respond to you, what the limits of respect that will be accorded to you really are."[17] Wasserman[18] contrasts the educational mythologies with the realities of education for oppression. She maintains that the current crisis in schools is created by the increasing incompatibility between the stated educational function and the unstated socialization, job selection, and indoctrination functions.

Looking more closely at how this incompatibility is revealed in schools, Jackson[19] describes the conflict between the demands of institutional conformity—i.e., between learning to be passive and to acquiesce to the network of rules, regulations, and routines, and meeting the demands of intellectual scholarship. Holt [20] describes how the classroom discourages thinking and intellectual risk-taking. The reason why students "fail" at learning is because they "succeed" in mastering coping strategies to meet the institution's demands. Students trained in "answer-grabbing" and "teacher-pleasing" do not become critical thinkers. Silberman [21] empirically confirmed Holt's classroom observations and found a correlation between fifth-graders' desire for teacher approval and their rejection of intellectual challenges. Other studies indicate that not only do children respond to institutional reward structures, but they often are more aware of institutional demands than they are of the requirements of learning itself. White,[22] for example, found that elementary school pupils have no "cognitive map of content" to help them perceive connections between subjects, but rather they have a "map of school experience"—that is, work and evaluation demands of the teachers. In a comparative study of elementary schools in four urban neighborhoods, Leacock [23] found that children consistently reflected a stronger emphasis on "good behavior" than on "good work" when they were interviewed about what they thought their teachers wanted.

All students must learn to adapt to these oppressive demands of schools. Beyond this common socialization, however, are experiential differences by class, race, and sex. Rather than providing "equality of opportunity" for all students, schools in fact perpetuate existing inequalities in our society. Grannis [24] in a ground-breaking article, offers three models he believes typify American schools and describes the effects these different structures have on children's behavior and social role training. In the "factory model" school, working-class children are taught in highly authoritarian, routinized, and rigid, hierarchically organized patterns that emphasize assignments, recitation, and rote learning. These children are socialized to accept monotonous factory and white collar jobs. In the "corporate model" school, suburban middle-class children are taught in nongraded, team-teaching, highly "rationalized" instructional situations preparing them for the coldly task-oriented team and committee aspects of corporate life. The third model, the "family school," similar to the British infant school model in its concern for the whole life of the child, is said to typify only nursery schools. None of these models has been demonstrated to be "better" for raising students' achievement, but both the "factory" and the "corporate" models effectively perpetuate class differences by initiating pupils into a conception of work fitting their "proper place" in society.

Within schools, the two major mechanisms for perpetuating social distinctions are "tracking" and "teacher's expectations." In a thorough critique of urban schools, Rothstein [25] describes tracking, or the formal mechanisms by which certain types of students (particularly women, minority-group, and working-class students) are channeled into educational tracks, leading to dead-end and low-paying jobs. Rosenthal and Jacobson [26] introduced the concept of "teacher's expectations," of the interpersonal self-fulfilling prophecies that operate in the classroom and affect students' performance. Post-Pygmalion studies support the existence of this phenomenon and reveal the way teachers "expect" and then obtain differential performance from lower-class and minority-group students.[27]

In summary, schools promote an ideology of equality, but in reality they perpetuate inequality; schools profess that "learning" is their major purpose, but "teach" institutional conformity and nonthinking.

Most of the above remarks concerning the functions of schools are by now familiar and well worn. What the critics have failed to examine, however, is how the traditional demands of the schools function to perpetuate traditional sex roles. Elementary schools reinforce girls' training for obedience, social and emotional dependence, and docility. That girls on the whole like school better than boys [28] and perform better in most respects [29] may be due in part to the consistency of the sex role demands of home and school. At the secondary school level, passive learning continues to be rewarded or no intellectual demands are made on girls; and it is expected that girls' education is chiefly a preparation for marriage and child-rearing. The prevalence of "role conflict" and decreased intellectual performance among many bright high school and college women is the result.[30]

The early socialization of girls toward obedience and approval seeking predisposes them to accept more readily the school's demands of conformity to rules and "doing what you are told." Observations by Crandall et al.[31] of children during free play suggest that girls' more than boys' achievement in elementary school, but not in preschool, was more affected by their need for parent and teacher approval. Stein [32] tested Crandall's findings in a controlled reinforcement situation and found that while girls did not perform better if praised, they were more affected than boys by disapproval. Tulkin et al.[33] found that fifth- and sixth-grade "high-need-for-approval" girls were the most popular, whereas "high-need-for-approval" boys were the least popular. Furthermore, girls' awareness that they are less valued than boys also may contribute to their conforming, dependent behavior. Kohlberg [34] states that girls reach the "good-girl" stage of moral development earlier than boys, and stay there longer. He suggests that this is because girls are forced to distinguish between the "prestige of goodness" and the "prestige of power" in sex-role learning.

Perhaps this means that girls learn that if they *have* to be a girl, they had better be a *"good"* one, since they have little else going for them.

> [The girl] internalizes a definition of maturity which is the early acceptance of quietness, obedience, and poise. Because these are character traits instilled in her from the time she is one, and because they correspond to the demands of the school system, she often does better in school. Which is why she's called more mature.[35]

The schools' emphasis on neatness, order, punctuality, and performance of often meaningless and monotonous tasks is an important part of the "domesticating" function of schools, particularly in the case of girls. Hartley has presented evidence that developmentally the traditional housekeeping aspect of the female sex role is the most thoroughly learned. Noting girls' imitation of domestic activities as well as their unhindered access to tools (both real and play) of the domestic trade at home and at school, he concludes: "The definition of this aspect of the female sex role seems to proceed without interruption and with continuous reinforcements, almost from the cradle on."[36] More recently, Poloma and Garland[37] presented evidence supporting a "toleration of domestication" hypothesis for married professional women; that is, even in dual-career marriages the woman has been so thoroughly trained in her domestic function that she puts her family role before her professional role, will often discontinue work because of family demands, and often does not perceive these choices forced upon her as discriminatory.

We need to know how the "domestication" of girls is strengthened in school. Do, in fact, teachers reward girls' docility and conforming behavior more than boys'? How do teachers respond to girls' needs-for-approval relative to boys'? What characterizes "mature" versus "immature" girls in the eyes of the teacher? How do teachers react to "inappropriately socialized" girls? What are the subtle ways in which girls are channeled into "feminine" interests and activities?

There is a triple aspect to sexist accounts of the effects of elementary schools on sex roles. First, there is more concern for what happens to boys than for what happens to girls. Second, female teachers are blamed for "feminizing" boys. Third, these biased studies rest on assumptions of inappropriately traditional sex-role stereotypes. Lest the charge of "sexism" appear too strong, the following representative quotation is offered:

> Countless teachers, the overwhelming majority of whom are women, expect boy pupils to behave, react, and learn like girls. Even though frequently unaware of it, many of these women value neatness and cleanliness above individual initiative. They prefer

conformity, mental passivity, and gentle obedience—at which girls
excel—to the aggressive drive and originality of many boys.[38]

Sexton has decried the schools' "feminizing" influence on boys. She
writes: ". . . the school is too much a woman's world, governed by wom-
en's rules and standards. . . . The subject matter seems all too frilly and
feminized. . . . Though the boy must learn to be his own authority, the
school insists that he obey its authority. . . . This is not good preparation for real manhood." [39] By implication, the schools' "feminization" or
"domestication" training *is* good preparation for "real womanhood." The
fact that girls are being doubly trained—at home and at school—to be
docile and conforming is not of concern. What is of concern is that boys
might be treated badly in school, that is, "like girls." The fact that the
school as an institution demands conformity and obedience for both sexes
is not discussed. The fact that most schools are oppressive places for most
children is not noted. Rather, female teachers are labeled the enemy in
the destruction of male minds.

Evidence supporting ·the "inappropriate treatment of boys" hypothesis comes mainly from two sources. First are studies that claim that
children perceive the elementary school as a "feminine" environment.
Kagan [40] and Kellogg [41] showed that primary school girls and boys tend
to label school objects as "feminine." This sex-typing was not a clear-cut
trend, however, as boys labeled fewer objects "feminine" than did girls,
and certain objects more frequently were associated with males than
females.

Second, much evidence has been marshaled to demonstrate female
teachers' discrimination against boys. A much-quoted study by Meyer and
Thompson [42] found that sixth-grade boys received more disapproval or
blame contacts from their teachers than did girls. Jackson and Lahaderne [43] found that boys received eight to ten times more prohibitory
messages (order-keeping and misbehavior-punishing messages) than girls.
Yet, in three of the four classrooms observed, boys received more than
their share of all types of interactions with the teacher. The researchers
concluded that the teachers used instructional and managerial interactions
with boys as "devious strategies for social control." In their review of the
literature, Sears and Feldman [44] suggest that while boys, in general,
receive more teacher disapproval in the lower grades than do girls, girls
receive more approval for conformity, and interact less with their teachers. Thus, rather than being discriminated against, boys appear to be more
intense or salient stimuli for teachers, and they receive more attention
from them while girls either are ignored or rewarded for conformity and
obedience.

Other recent studies support this hypothesis of boys' saliency in the eyes of the teacher. In contrast to earlier claims of female teachers' bias against boys during reading instruction, Davis and Slobodian [45] found that female first-grade teachers did *not* discriminate against boys or favor girls during reading periods. Good's and Brophy's recent findings [46] support the same conclusion. Moreover, Felsenthal [47] found that female first-grade teachers interacted more with boys in both positive and negative ways and tended to call on volunteering boys more than volunteering girls during reading instruction. Preliminary findings from the Columbia Classroom Environments Project [48] indicate that in second-grade classrooms, boys more than girls are "off-task" in daily activities, are more "controlled" by their teachers, but also receive more teaching time, more skill work, and more individual tutorial attention. Add to this Torrance's earlier finding [49] that teachers say they reward the creative behavior of boys three times as often as they do the creative behavior of girls and the "message" to girls becomes clear—be quiet, be good, be conforming; originality, self-assertion, and "center stage" activities are reserved for boys.

One study which indicated that nursery school teachers reward both girls and boys for traditionally "female" play activities was reported by Fagot and Patterson.[50] The so-called "feminine" behaviors included painting, art work, playing with dolls and the doll house, playing in the kitchen, and listening to stories; while so-called "masculine" behaviors included playing with building blocks and transportation toys, climbing, and riding tricycles. Observing three-year-olds in two nursery classes intermittently for a year, they found that teachers reinforced girls 363 times for sex-typed behaviors, and 353 of these were for "feminine" behaviors. They reinforced boys less for sex-typed behavior (232 times) but 199 of these were for "feminine" behaviors. However the boys' peer reinforcement apparently overcame the teachers' so-called "feminizing" influence since the boys did not become more "feminine" in their behavior preferences over the year. The researchers do not comment on the 3:2 ratio of sex-typed reinforcements given to girls or mention what effect the girls' peer group had on what apparently is a more intense sex-typing of female children.

Many studies have demonstrated that teachers discipline boys more harshly than girls,[51] and that the majority of teachers' "behavior problems" are boys.[52] Westbrook [53] confirmed earlier studies that indicated that teachers are more disapproving of extroverted behavior (impertinence, disobedience, interrupting, etc.) than of introverted behavior (fearfulness, shyness, sensitiveness). Yet, clinicians view introverted or withdrawal tendencies as being more serious.[54] Ullman [55] studied differences between girls and boys in school adjustment and observed that boys tended to act out while girls turned their conflicts on to themselves. He concluded that although teachers rate girls as being better adjusted, they do so uncritical of the standard of adjustment and unaware of the way in which girls are making their so-called "adjustment." Interpretations of school adjustment research usually are along the lines of Sexton's concerns that boys are being "emasculated" by their female teachers,[56] rather than that girls, by being allowed and encouraged to turn their anger against themselves, perhaps are being less noticeably but more seriously damaged. Furthermore, a boy harshly yelled at from across the room may temporarily feel put down, but also may learn to defend and assert himself.

Bardwick[57] speculates that a boy learns in school that he can get attention and respect for nonconforming behavior, both from his teacher and his peers. Thus, teacher criticism, a seemingly negative response, may actually lead boys toward greater independence, autonomy, and activity. Spaulding found[58] that, compared to boys, a disproportionate number of teachers' negative remarks to girls concerned incorrect answers, a pattern that could only reinforce girls' sense of inferiority. If teacher criticism of girls is less harsh than criticism of boys, as Spaulding indicates, it may be even more difficult for girls to learn to fight back. The girl who is reassuringly (patronizingly?) told that everything will be all right, while the teacher supportingly (controllingly?) has her/his arm around her, is less likely to develop self-assertive behaviors that carry the risk of disapproval.

Other evidence indicates that even by the preschool years, boys tend to make more realistic achievement assessments than do girls.[59] Perhaps the criticism boys receive tends to be more task-oriented, helping them better to evaluate their skills. Girls may be receiving more general and more personal criticism. This latter type of criticism discourages what Minuchin[60] calls "self-differentiation . . . or . . . increasingly refined perceptions of one's patterns of strengths and deficits," and may lead to an oversensitivity to criticism and to doing tasks in order to gain social approval rather than to meet one's own standards.

One solution often proposed for the "feminization" of males is to place more adult male teachers in the primary grades. The evidence in support of this position is scanty. First, research on imitation learning and sex-identification has not shown a clear-cut trend for same-sex models to promote sex-typed behaviors. In fact, many researchers conclude[61] that the father, rather than the mother, is the major socializer of "sex-appropriate" behavior for both boys and girls. It is not at all clear whether the sex of the teacher/model has an influence distinct from cultural sex-role definitions and the institutional demands of the school which probably are shared and communicated equally by both male and female teachers. Comparing children in male-taught and female-taught kindergartens, Brody and Laosa found no evidence that the sex of the teacher was associated with girls' and boys' scores on sex-role measures, toy, game and occupation-choice measures, sex-typing of school objects, or achievement strivings. They conclude:

> The fears of Sexton and others about boys being "feminized" seem clearly unfounded. There is no need to believe that female teachers cannot handle boys adequately simply because they are female, nor any reason to expect that the presence of a male teacher will have any dramatic effect on children of either sex.[62]

One way in which traditional sex roles *are* reinforced is through the authority structure of the school itself. Eighty-five percent of all elementary school teachers are women; 78 percent of all elementary school principals are men.[63] School children do not need to be taught the differential status of men and women—they learn it simply by attending school. It would be interesting to determine empirically what effect, if any, elementary schools that employ women and men on an equal basis in all positions, have on children's ideas of sex roles.

Another mechanism of sex-role reinforcement is segregated classes and activities. A number of primary grade schools have been "experimenting" with sex-segregated classes. The teachers write glowingly of programs "specifically tailored to the needs of each sex." The all-boy classes emphasize large muscle physical activity, team games, building, repairing, and other tasks "ordinarily performed by fathers," arts and crafts with wood, rock, clay, and other "male" materials. The all-girl classes include activities such as "dressing up like mother and playing house," and playing with crayons, paper, and pasting materials. Although they noted that "in the mixed group which stressed masculinity, the girls seemed to enjoy the program as much as the boys," these informal reports did not discuss the varied needs of children or concern themselves with the rigid role definitions they impose on girls and boys by restricting their activities.[64]

Within unsegregated classes certain activities such as cooking and sewing are encouraged primarily for girls, and other activities such as woodwork and mechanical work are encouraged primarily for boys. Physical education and playground activities frequently are sex-segregated. Even in "free schools" where there is no conscious attempt to sex-type, the policy of allowing children to "follow their own interests" usually results in condoning the pervasive sex-typed activities the children have learned outside the school. Effective "open classrooms," while basically noninterventionist, still require children to master basic skills. But intervening to require nonsex-typed choices and activities and more "sex-role free" flexibility has not yet become one of "open classroom" concerns.

As children move through elementary school, certain subjects such as English come to be regarded as "girls' subjects" while math and science are perceived as "boys' subjects." Stein and Smithells [65] found that school children's sex-typing of these activities progressively became more rigid. The mechanisms by which this sex-typing occurs were not investigated in their study, but clearly they are of concern and should be studied.

There are a number of descriptive studies of sex-typing in elementary school reading materials. A 1946 study of third-grade readers found striking differences in the treatment of the sexes. Females were portrayed as "sociable and kind, but helpless, inactive, and uncreative" while males were portrayed as "the bearers of knowledge and wisdom." [66] More recently, a 1971 study, also of third-grade readers, reported a similar picture. The characteristics of the females in the stories reviewed closely resembled Jenkin's and Vroegh's [67] "most feminine woman imaginable"— appreciative, affectionate, charming, considerate. The range of occupations of the females is even more limited than the real restriction of women in the work force.[68] A thorough study of twelve elementary school reader series and award-winning trade books revealed a heavy preponderance of boys' stories "in which boys are portrayed as smarter than girls, with greater initiative and achievement" and girls often are portrayed as "younger sister ninnies" who have mishaps and need to be helped. Men assume a variety of roles in the stories and, if fathers, play creatively with their children. Women almost exclusively are portrayed as mothers and teachers. Mothers are "forever wearing aprons" and are cast in supportive, passive roles.[69] A recent survey of trade books for young children revealed "the general image of the female ranges from dull to degrading to invisible." [70]

Children's readers are not the only culprits. An analysis of mathematics textbooks in New York City school libraries revealed that even math problems are presented in social contexts which reinforce sex-role stereotypes. In one series, for example, women and girls shop, cook, sew, and get sick; while men and boys build things, drive cars, go camping, and earn money.[71] Sex-typing in elementary social studies books also has been examined,[72] and studies in other subject areas very likely would show that traditional sex-role stereotypes are imbedded in all school materials, songs, games, posters, educational films, and so on—all of which teach girls and boys "what's expected." As yet there are no studies of the effect of sex-typed school materials on the self-concepts, career aspirations, and achievements of girls.

The teachers' separation of boys and girls for seating, lining up, hanging up coats, and so on also calls attention to sex distinctions and sex roles (e.g., "Girls line up first."); the choice of class helpers also teaches sex roles ("Boys, move the chairs"; "Girls water the plants."). The protocols of a microanalysis of a single urban classroom were filled with such comments. At one point the teacher requested a boy for a thumbtacking job because "it's difficult for girls to climb up." [73] And after calling on three boys in a row who were unable to answer a question, the teacher asked, "Do I have to call on a girl?" [74] Such behaviors daily elaborate and reinforce traditional sex roles, yet no classroom observations studies have focused specifically on interactions of this type.

Studies of "expectancy effects" concerning how teachers' expectations of sex-role behaviors operate in the classroom have not been conducted. Specific areas that call for examination include differential expectations about the interests and competencies of girls and boys, differences in disciplining them, and types of activities of girls and boys strongly rewarded or punished. Furthermore, we need to know how teachers differentially perceive and stereotype the same behaviors of girls and boys. Are there differences between girls and boys in behaviors represented by labels such as "withdrawn," "aggressive," and so on? How then do teachers *react* to these differences?

Although there have been many studies of elementary school children's sex-role conceptions and preferences, there is little data on whether or not they differentially perceive the same behaviors in girls and boys. How rigidly do children require compliance to traditional sex-role standards? How do children perceive the school demands on them for "sex-appropriate" behaviors? What is the association of level of cognitive development to stereotyping?

A few studies indicate that sex roles are not immutable but can be changed with a change in the school environment. Minuchin [75] compared 100 middle-class fourth-graders in a "traditional" school and a "modern" school. She found that in the modern school, which had more flexible attitudes about sex roles, girls showed less concern for approval than in the traditional school. Modern school girls also were found to be equally competent to boys in problem solving, whereas in the traditional school the boys were better problem solvers. Since sex differences in "need-for-approval" and problem-solving skills are not measurably great before elementary school, it is not clear to what extent these differences can be attributed to differences between schools. Joffee [76] reported a participant-observation study of a nursery school in which the general attitude toward sex roles was a deemphasis on sex-typed behavior and an accepting, relaxed attitude toward "violations" of traditional sex roles. There were no indications of sex or sex role in the activities or structure of the school—even bathrooms were shared. All the children knew their correct gender identity, but "there did not exist among the children any patterned recognition of appropriate sex roles; the children as a group did not perceive certain activities or modes of behavior as being the exclusive property of one sex." The only instances in which sex differences were invoked by the children were as reciprocal "last ditch attempts at behavior control"—that is, yelling "boys only" or "girls only" to maintain control of an activity, area, or toy.

Other exploratory studies are revealing. Chasen [77] found that after two months of a short daily reading program designed to raise career aspirations, preschool girls indicated more range of response to the question, "What do you want to be when you grow up?" Selcer [78] found fewer sex-role stereotypes among children from women's liberation and nonmainstream families than among children from Orthodox Jewish families on three measures—toy preference, sex-role stereotype questionnaire, and the question: "What are the differences between girls and boys?" The free-play behaviors of these children also indicated rigid sex-typed play in the Orthodox Jewish nursery school and relatively nonsex-typed play in the women's liberation nurseries. As more day care centers are created for young children and as feminists press for changes in primary education, more programs designed to expand role flexibility for girls and boys will be created. But the research validation of such programs barely has begun. We need to know much more about the effects of broad social changes in sex roles on the sex-role definitions, expectations, and behaviors of girls and boys.

The same male-dominated authority structure, sex-segregated courses and programs, and conventional sex typing in textbooks, and the sex-role stereotyping of the teachers of elementary schools also are found at the secondary school level. Counselors guide female students into "feminine" occupations and tend to assume the girls desire marriage more than in fact they do.[79] A thorough documentation of the sex bias against women in New York City vocational and technical high schools and the misrepresentation of women in high school textbooks was reported by the New York City Chapter of the National Organization of Women.[80] There are more boys' than girls' high schools in New York City. There are more restricted programs and more restricted course offerings within programs for girls in both girls' and coeducational high schools. Two of the four specialized academic high schools only recently began to admit girls and that innovation occurred only after a court battle. As 14-year-old Alice de Rivera, who filed the court suit and won the right to attend Stuyvesant High School, said:

> Aside from being discouraged to study for a career, women are discouraged from preparing for jobs involving anything but secretarial

work, beauty care, nursing, cooking, and the fashion industries.
. . . This means that if a girl is seeking entrance to a vocational
school she is pressured to feel that certain jobs are masculine and
others feminine. She is forced to conform to the Board of Education's image of her sex.[81]

And that image is far from liberated. Nationally, more than half of the
females in public vocational-education programs are being trained in
home economics and about one third in office practices.[82] Thus by
completion of high school the tracking of female students is all but
complete and inescapable.

The institutional sexism of high schools is supplemented and
reinforced by the attitudes and behaviors of the teachers. A recent
exploratory study by Aderen et al.[83] surveyed the sex-role attitudes and
classroom behaviors of twenty secondary school teachers in and around
New York City. A short form of the Broverman Sex-Role Stereotype
Questionnaire—an 82-item bipolar list of traits (e.g., not at all aggressive—
very aggressive)—was used to assess teachers' sex-role ideals, but the
instructions were changed from the usual form, which asks the respondent
to identify sex-role stereotypes to, "What do you think an adolescent male
or female *should* be like?" The teachers were asked to rate each trait on
a scale of 0–70 according to how they thought an adolescent male and
an adolescent female should exhibit that trait.

Results indicated that most of the teachers differentiated ideal
behaviors by sex. Only 3 of the 19 respondents said all characteristics
should be the same for both sexes. For the 16 other teachers, 9 of the 82
items were highly stereotypic (72 percent or more agreement), 21 items
were moderately stereotypic (50–74 percent agreement), but no items
were equalitarian (i.e., marked "same" for both males and females). The
nine items that were highly stereotypic were the more general characteristics mentioned on the questionnaire. Seventy-five percent or more of
the respondents wanted adolescent males to be more masculine, dominant,
independent, and assertive, and to be less emotional, ready to cry, and
concerned about their appearance. They wanted females to be more
feminine, submissive, dependent, unassertive, emotional, ready to cry,
and concerned about their appearance. Except for "concern for appearance," the items that were desired for males were those generally
considered more socially desirable characteristics.[84]

Classroom observations of these same teachers indicated that many
of them acted out their sex-role stereotypes in the classroom. For example,
a music teacher taught the boys how to tune their instruments, but tuned
the girls' instruments for them. In an English class reviewing for exams,
the teacher typically first called on a boy for the answer and then called

on a girl for an illustration. When the class became noisy the teacher yelled at the girls for chattering. Although stereotyped in their ideals for adolescent male and female behavior, a few teachers did not treat boys and girls differently or give evidence of sex stereotyping in the classroom. Apparently, these teachers' attitude of "liberal professionalism" (i.e., treat everyone equally) in the classroom prevented our observation of their sex-role stereotypes in practice. These stereotypes are so pervasive and often so subtle (they are, in fact, a "nonconscious ideology") [85] that more sophisticated techniques of observation in and out of the classroom are required to measure students' perceptions of their teachers' attitudes and the effects of these attitudes on the students.

An additional instrument was administered to this same sample of secondary school teachers. Teachers received brief individual statements about four students, and were instructed to describe how they thought the student would act and how they as teachers would discourage or encourage that student. For each statement, boys' and girls' names were alternated. Results indicated stereotyped responses for each statement. Teachers indicated they would treat a "withdrawn" boy more firmly than a "withdrawn" girl. A "withdrawn" girl would gently be encouraged to participate, whereas a "withdrawn" boy would firmly be made to "crack his shell" and become more assertive. Responding to a statement for a hypothetical "model student," teachers who were asked to describe a female "model student" tended to claim that she couldn't truly be intelligent but was probably "compensating" for something. No such comments appeared in the descriptions of the male "model student." If a student was presented as a "warm person who wants to help people," this characteristic in a girl often was seen as incompatible with academic ability and as implying specific vocational goals (teaching, nursing, social work). A "warm-and-helpful" boy was perceived either as a potential behavior problem because of his interest in others' business, or as potentially helpful academically to others. In other words, warmth and helpfulness—traditionally "feminine" characteristics—were perceived as having social-emotional consequences when displayed by girls and as having positive academic consequences when displayed by boys. Teachers responding to a "competent student interested in math and science" indicated they would encourage the student, if a boy, to build on that interest and encourage it in other areas; but if the student were a girl they expressed concern that she develop competencies in areas besides mathematics and science to avoid becoming "lopsided." Despite the claims of our respondents that they "treated all students fairly and equally," the differential evaluation according to sex-role stereotypes was evident. That these responses appeared in such a small sample simply underscores their all-pervasiveness.

A recent study by Gaites [86] explores perceptions of ideal male and ideal female students. Teachers were given short descriptions of male or female students and were asked to imagine what these students' future lives would be like. Results indicated a greater and wider range of expectations for male students; teachers rarely expected females to be involved in anything other than marriage and child rearing.

There are, then, a few studies documenting sex-role stereotypes in the "expectations" teachers have for their male and female students. Intervention studies designed to change these expectations have yet to be attempted.

Concluding Remarks

The first phase of the renewed feminist wave of criticism, analysis, and polemic seems to have peaked and the difficult application of feminist analysis to the traditionally male-biased social sciences barely has begun. Studies of "sex-role socialization" typically have accepted the *content* of sex roles as given and have attempted to clarify the variables affecting the learning *process* along sex-role lines. This objectification and reification of sex roles has prevented our understanding of how sex-role learning is taught and elaborated in patriarchal society. That "appropriate" sex-role learning for girls, while functional to the maintenance of male-dominated society, is detrimental to girls' psychological development has often been acknowledged. But this fact has been overlooked in the overriding concern that schools might be "emasculating our boys." There is not even a word in our language to represent the "castration" or "emasculation" of females. We need serious research into how traditional sex-role stereotypes affect girls' learning and development and how schools continue to perpetuate and elaborate these stereotypes. Most importantly, new educational environments must be designed to eliminate restrictive sex-role learning so that girls and boys can be free to explore their full human potential.

References

1. JEROME KAGAN, "Check One: ☐ Male ☐ Female," *Psychology Today* 3, No. 2 (July 1969): 39–41.
2. DANIEL G. BROWN, "Sex Role Development in a Changing Culture," *Psychological Bulletin* 55 (1958): 232–242; William Ward, "Process of

Sex-Role Development," *Developmental Psychology* 1, No. 2 (1969): 163–168.

3. ALETHA H. STEIN and JANCIS SMITHELLS, "Age and Sex Difference in Children's Sex-Role Standards about Achievement," *Developmental Psychology* 1, No. 3 (May 1969): 252–259.

4. RUTH HARTLEY and FRANCES HARDESTY, "Children's Perceptions of Sex-Role in Childhood," *Journal of Genetic Psychology* 105, No. 1 (1964): 43–51; W. W. Hartup and S. G. Moore, "Avoidance of Inappropriate Sex-Typing by Young Children," *Journal of Consulting Psychology* 27 (1963): 467–473.

5. ROBERTA OETZEL, "Annotated Bibliography," in *The Development of Sex Differences*, ed. by Eleanor Maccoby (Stanford: Stanford University Press, 1966), pp. 223–322.

6. BROWN, "Sex Role Development."

7. S. SMITH, "Age and Sex Differences in Children's Opinions Concerning Sex Differences," *Journal of Genetic Psychology* 54 (1939): 17–25.

8. LAWRENCE KOHLBERG, "A Cognitive-Developmental Analysis of Children's Sex-Role Concepts and Attitudes," in *The Development of Sex Differences*, ed. by Eleanor Maccoby, pp. 105–106.

9. E. ROPER, "Women in America, The *Fortune* Survey," part one. *Fortune Magazine*, August 1946.

10. EDWARD H. POHLMAN, *The Psychology of Birth Planning* (Cambridge, Mass.: Shenkman, 1969).

11. JEROME KAGAN and H. A. Moss, *Birth to Maturity: A Study in Psychological Development* (New York: John Wiley and Sons, 1962).

12. INGE K. BROVERMAN et al., "Sex-Role Stereotypes: A Current Appraisal," *Journal of Social Issues* 28, No. 2 (1972): 59–78; A. C. Sherriffs and R. F. Jarrett, "Sex Differences in Attitudes About Sex Differences," *Journal of Personality* 35 (1953): 161–168; A. C. Sherriffs and J. P. McKee, "Qualitative Aspects of Beliefs About Men and Women," *Journal of Personality* 25 (June 1957): 451–464.

13. CHARLES SILBERMAN, *Crisis in the Classroom* (New York: Vintage, 1970).

14. EVERETT REIMER, *An Essay on Alternatives in Education* (Cuernavaca, Mexico: CIDOC Cuaderno No. 1005, 1970).

15. PAULO FREIRE, "Cultural Action for Freedom," *Harvard Educational Review* (Monograph Series No. 1. Cambridge, Mass., 1970), pp. 1, 6.

16. IVAN ILLICH, "After Deschooling, What?" *Social Policy* (September/October, 1971): 5–13.

17. EDGAR FRIEDENBERG, "What Do the Schools Do?" *This Magazine Is about Schools* 3, No. 1 (Winter, 1969): 33.

18. MIRIAM WASSERMAN, "School Mythology and the Education of Oppression," *This Magazine Is about Schools* 5, No. 3 (Summer, 1971): 23–36.

19. PHILIP W. JACKSON, "The Student's World," *The Elementary School Journal* 66 (1966): 343–357.

20. JOHN HOLT, *How Children Fail* (New York: Delta, 1964).

21. MELVIN L. SILBERMAN, "Classroom Rewards and Intellectual Courage," in *The Experience of Schooling*, ed. by M. L. Silberman (New York: Holt, Rinehart, and Winston, 1971).

22. MARY ALICE WHITE, "The View from the Pupil's Desk," *The Urban Review* 2 (1968): 5–7.

23. ELEANOR LEACOCK, *Teaching and Learning in City Schools* (New York: Basic Books, 1969).
24. JOSEPH C. GRANNIS, "The School as a Model of Society," in *Learning of Political Behavior*, ed. by N. Adler and C. Harrington (New York: Scott-Foresman, 1970), pp. 135–147.
25. RICHARD ROTHSTEIN, "Down the Up Staircase: Tracking in Schools," *This Magazine Is about Schools* 5, No. 3 (Summer, 1971): 103–139.
26. ROBERT ROSENTHAL and LENORE JACOBSON, *Pygmalion in the Classroom* (New York: Holt, Rinehart, and Winston, 1968).
27. RAY C. RIST, "Student Social Class and Teacher Expectations: The Self-Fulfilling Prophecy in Ghetto Education," *Harvard Educational Review* 40, No. 3 (August, 1970): 411–451; P. C. Rubovits and M. L. Maehr, "Toward an Explanation of the Rosenthal-Jacobson Findings" (Paper presented at the American Educational Research Association, New York, February, 1971).
28. PHILIP W. JACKSON, *Life in Classrooms* (New York: Holt, Rinehart, and Winston, 1968).
29. ELEANOR MACCOBY, "Sex Differences in Intellectual Functioning," in *The Development of Sex Differences*, ed. by Eleanor Maccoby, pp. 24–39.
30. JAMES J. GALLAGHER, "Sex Differences in Expressive Thought of Gifted Children in the Classroom," *Personnel and Guidance Journal* 45, No. 3 (November, 1966): 248–253; Matina Horner, "Fail: Bright Woman," *Psychology Today* 3 (November, 1969): 36–38; M. C. Shaw and J. T. McCuen, "The Onset of Academic Underachievement in Bright Children," *Journal of Educational Psychology* 51 (1960): 103–108.
31. V. CRANDALL and A. RABSON, "Children's Repetitive Choices in an Intellectual Achievement Situation Following Success and Failure," *Journal of Genetic Psychology* 97 (1960): 161–168; V. Crandall et al., "Parents' Attitudes and Behaviors and Grade School Children's Academic Achievements," *Journal of Genetic Psychology* 104 (1964): 53–66.
32. ALETHA H. STEIN, "The Influence of Social Reinforcement on the Achievement Behavior of Fourth Grade Boys and Girls," *Child Development* 40, No. 3 (1969): 727–736.
33. STEVEN R. TULKIN, JOHN P. MULLER and LANE K. CONN, "Need for Approval and Popularity: Sex Differences in Elementary School Students," *Journal of Consulting and Clinical Psychology* 33, No. 1 (1969): 35–39.
34. LAWRENCE KOHLBERG, "A Cognitive-Developmental Analysis. . . ."
35. SARAH SPINKS, "Sugar 'n Spice," *This Magazine Is about Schools* 3, No. 3 (Summer, 1969): 65.
36. RUTH HARTLEY, "A Developmental View of Female Sex-Role Definition and Identification," *Merrill-Palmer Quarterly* 10, No. 1 (1964): 7.
37. MARGARET M. POLOMA and NEAL T. GARLAND, "The Married Professional Woman: A Study in the Toleration of Domestication," *Journal of Marriage and the Family* (August, 1971): 531–540.
38. JACK H. POLLACK, "Are Teachers Fair to Boys?" *Today's Health* 46, No. 4 (1968): 21.
39. PATRICIA SEXTON, "Schools Are Emasculating Our Boys," *Saturday Review*, June 19, 1965, p. 57.
40. JEROME KAGAN, "The Child's Sex Role Classification of School Objects," *Child Development* 35 (1964): 1051–1056.

41. R. A. KELLOGG, "A Direct Approach to Sex-Role Identification of School-Related Objects, *Psychological Reports* 24 (June, 1969): 839–841.
42. W. J. MEYER and G. C. THOMPSON, "Sex Differences in the Distribution of Teacher Approval and Disapproval Among Sixth Grade Children," *Journal of Educational Psychology* 47 (1956): 385–396.
43. PHILIP W. JACKSON and HENRIETTE M. LAHADERNE, "Inequalities of Teacher-Pupil Contacts," *Psychology in the Schools* 4 (1967): 204–208.
44. PAULINE SEARS and D. FELDMAN, "Teacher Interactions with Boys and Girls," The *National Elementary Principal* 46, No. 2 (November, 1966): 31.
45. O. L. DAVIS and J. SLOBODIAN, "Teacher Behavior Toward Boys and Girls During First Grade Reading Instruction," *American Educational Research Journal* 4, No. 3 (May, 1967): 261–269.
46. T. L. GOOD and J. E. BROPHY, "Questioned Equality for Grade One Boys and Girls," *Reading Teacher* 25 (December, 1971): 249–252.
47. H. FELSENTHAL, "Sex Differences in Teacher-Pupil Interaction during First Grade Reading Instruction" (Paper presented at the Annual Meeting of the American Educational Research Association, Minneapolis, Minn., March, 1970).
48. J. C. GRANNIS, S. W. KAMINSKY, and W. W. FURMAN, "Teachers' and Pupils' Roles in Variously Structured Classroom Settings and Subsettings: A Report from the Columbia Classroom Environments Projects" (Paper presented at the Annual Meeting of the American Educational Research Association, Chicago, Ill., April 6, 1972).
49. E. P. TORRANCE, *Rewarding Creative Behavior: Experiment in Classroom Creativity* (Englewood Cliffs, N.J.: Prentice-Hall, 1965).
50. BEVERLY FAGOT and GERALD R. PATTERSON, "An in vivo Analysis of Reinforcing Contingencies for Sex-Role Behaviors in the Preschool Child," *Developmental Psychology* 1, No. 55 (1969): 563–568.
51. R. L. SPAULDING, "Achievement, Creativity, and Self-Concept Correlates of Teacher-Pupil Transactions in Elementary Schools." Cooperative Research Project No. 1352. Washington, D.C.: U.S. Department of Health, Education, and Welfare, Office of Education, 1963.
52. FRANCES BENTZEN, "Sex Ratios in Learning and Behavior Disorders," *The National Elementary Principal* 46, No. 2 (November, 1966): 13–17.
53. A. WESTBROOK, "Teachers' Recognition of Problem Behavior and Referrals of Children to Pupil Personnel Services," *Journal of Educational Research* 63, No. 9 (May–June, 1970): 391–394.
54. G. A. W. STAUFFER, JR., "The Attitude of Secondary School Teachers Toward Certain Behavior Problems of Children," *School Review* 64 (1956): 358–362.
55. C. A. ULLMAN, "Identification of Maladjusted School Children" (Public Health Monograph No. 7, 1952. Washington, D.C.: U.S. Department of Health, Education, and Welfare).
56. PATRICIA SEXTON, "Schools Are Emasculating Our Boys."
57. JUDITH M. BARDWICK, *Psychology of Women: A Study of Bio-Cultural Conflicts* (New York: Harper and Row, 1971).
58. R. L. SPAULDING, "Achievement, Creativity, and Self-Concept Correlates of Teacher-Pupil Transactions in Elementary Schools" (Cooperative Research

Project No. 1352, Washington, D.C.: U.S. Department of Health, Education, and Welfare. Office of Education, 1963).

59. V. J. CRANDALL, U. NATKOUSKY, and A. PRESTON, "Motivational and Ability Determinants of Young Children's Intellectual Achievement Behaviors," *Child Development* 33 (1962): 643–661.

60. PATRICIA P. MINUCHIN, "The Schooling of Tomorrow's Women," *School Review* 80, No. 2 (February, 1972): 204–205.

61. For example, see Miriam M. Johnson, "Sex-Role Learning in the Nuclear Family," *Child Development* 34(1963): 319–333.

62. JERE E. BRODY and LUIS M. LAOSA, "The Effect of a Male Teacher on the Sex-Typing of Kindergarten Children," mimeographed (The University of Texas at Austin, 1971), p. 47.

63. KAREN BRANAN, "What Can I do About . . . Sex Discrimination?" *Scholastic Teacher* (Elementary School Teachers' Edition, November, 1971), p. 20.

64. "Boys Are Different," *Instructor* (December, 1970), pp. 50–54.

65. STEIN and SMITHELLS, "Age and Sex Differences in Children's Sex-Role Standards About Achievement."

66. IRVIN L. CHILD, ELMER H. POTTER, and ESTELLE M. LEVINE, "Children's Textbooks and Personality Development," *Psychological Monographs* 40, No. 3 (1946).

67. NOEL JENKIN and KAREN VROEGH, "Contemporary Concepts of Masculinity and Femininity," *Psychological Reports* 25 (1969): 679–697.

68. JANICE POTTKER, "Female Sex Role Stereotypes in Elementary School Readers" (Master's Thesis, University of Maryland, 1971).

69. *Dick and Jane as Victims: Sex Stereotyping in Children's Readers* (Princeton: Women on Words and Images. A Task Force of Central New Jersey NOW, 1972).

70. ELIZABETH FISHER, "Children's Books: The Second Sex, Junior Division," *The New York Times Book Review* (May 24, 1970), p. 6.

71. "Sex Bias in the Public Schools" (New York City Chapter of NOW, 1971), p. 19.

72. JAMIE KELEM FRISOF, "Textbooks and Channelling," *Women: A Journal of Liberation* 1, No. 1 (Fall, 1969): 26–28.

73. LOUIS M. SMITH and WILLIAM GEOFFREY, *The Complexities of an Urban Classroom: An Analysis toward a General Theory of Teaching* (New York: Holt, Rinehart, and Winston, 1968), p. 53.

74. Ibid., p. 45.

75. PATRICIA P. MINUCHIN, "Sex Differences in Children," *The National Elementary Principal* 46, No. 2 (November, 1966): 45–48.

76. CAROLE JOFFEE, "Sex Role Socialization and the Nursery School: As the Twig is Bent," *Journal of Marriage and the Family* 33, No. 3 (August, 1971): 467–475.

77. BARBARA CHASEN, "Sex Role Stereotypes: Self-Image of Pre-Kindergarten Boys and Girls in Regard to Doll Preference, Work Preference, and Sex Role Stereotype Questions" (Unpublished paper, New York University, May, 1971).

78. BOBBI SELCER, "How Liberated Are Liberated Children?" *The Radical Therapist* 2, No. 5 (February, 1971): 14–15.

79. ROBERT RIORDAN, "Feminine Sex Role Concepts Among High School Counselor and Students" (Ph.D. Dissertation, *Bibliography Abstract*, 1965).
80. New York City NOW, "Sex Bias."
81. ALICE DE RIVERA, "On De-segregating Stuyvesant High," in *Sisterhood Is Powerful*, ed. by Robin Morgan (New York: Vintage, 1970), p. 366.
82. *American Teacher*, November, 1971.
83. ALEX ADEREN et al., "A Survey of Secondary School Teachers' Sex Role Stereotypes and Sex-Typed Classroom Behaviors" (Unpublished paper, Teachers College, Columbia University, January, 1972).
84. INGE K. BROVERMAN et al., "Sex Role Stereotypes: A Current Appraisal," *Journal of Social Issues* 28, No. 2 (1972): 59–78.
85. SANDRA L. BEM and DARYL J. BEM, "Case Study of a Nonconscious Ideology: Training the Woman to Know Her Place" (Pittsburgh, Pa.: KNOW, Inc., 1970), p. 7.
86. A. J. H. GAITES, "Teachers' Perceptions of Ideal Male and Female Students: Male Chauvinism in the Schools" (Paper presented at the American Educational Research Association, Chicago, Illinois, April, 1972).

THE SCHOOLING OF TOMORROW'S WOMEN

In this paper, the "liberated woman" is defined to be one who can make personally meaningful choices about the pattern of her life. The "liberating society" is one that accepts and supports such efforts. It follows that an optimal education provides an environment and a set of experiences that equip a woman to make and implement such choices.

The issues involved in the education and development of women are, for the most part, a special case of more general issues. The definition and goal for liberated women express a viewpoint about the goals of human development in general—a viewpoint that highlights choice, effectiveness, individuality, and fulfillment as psychological goals for any individual. The concern with social forces that facilitate or block individual choices is relevant for other subgroups as well: for Blacks, or Jews, or Chicanos, or the poor. The search for an optimal liberating education for women is part of the more general search for optimal forms and qualities of schooling. Any discussion of women, the society that surrounds us, or the characteristics of an education that might best serve our development is a special case of the ongoing discussions about human development, about current society as a context for such development, and about the specific socializing experiences—child rearing, education, etc.—that shape any human being in some directions rather than others.

Legal and social reform in this country will not automatically ensure the liberation of women. If a female Utopia were implemented tomorrow at a societal level, would all women be able to use their opportunities in an optimal way? The answer must be "no" unless there were concurrent concern for the growth experiences that shape the capacity to respond to opportunities that exist in the environment.

What kind of education might facilitate the development of a

Note: By Patricia Minuchin. Copyright © 1972 by The University of Chicago Press. Reprinted with permission from *School Review,* February 1972, 80:2, 199–208.

woman capable of meaningful choices and the active implementation of a personal life style and pattern? I will use the elementary school level as my frame of reference—the years when basic attitudes, perceptions, and skills are first developed and consolidated in a setting beyond the family —but the points are generic and apply to more advanced education as well.

Four goals or educational tasks seem pertinent for a school that would be relevant to the development of a liberated young female: (1) minimization of stereotypes; (2) provision of broad exposure to experiences, ideas, and models; (3) education in skills for choice, problem solving, and evaluation; and (4) enhancement of self-differentiation and self-knowledge.

The Minimization of Stereotypes

Any school is a small society. It offers most children their first paradigm of a larger society beyond the family and subtly teaches something about the parameters of possible development. It offers models of adult roles and possible life styles. It teaches attitudes and expectations for girls and for boys through the organization and content of its curricula and through the tone and nature of its teacher–child relationships. To the extent that the school is rigid and narrowly sex typed in these aspects, it probably hampers the growing girl unnecessarily in the exploration and understanding of her own possibilities.

Sex-linked conceptions of what is appropriate and to be expected are fairly common in this culture: the conception that girls are not good at math and science; that they are not manually skillful or interested in or apt to respond to training in such skills; that they are less logical and analytic in the use of their minds than males; that they tend to be docile, obedient, and dependent, are not as aggressive or high-spirited as boys, are more verbal and less athletic, tidier and more interested in clothes; that they will be centered around home and family in their adult roles; that careers are not apt to be serious or long term, and are apt to follow along certain traditional lines.

Such conceptions are not without foundation. On an average and to this point in time, sex differences in many of these areas are observable, and certainly they have been documented recurrently by systematic research.[1] Traditional developmental theory, perhaps for this reason, has accepted such differences as a given and as a value, defining socialization in this area as the shaping of the child toward "appropriate sex-typed responses" and assessing the success of such socialization through direct measurement of sex typing in the child's behavior patterns—the closer the match the better.[2]

My viewpoint is different. It does not deny a probable and necessary core of sex-role identification in the growing child or the fact that many children come into school exemplifying attitudes, interests, and personality styles that are consistent with conventional sex-linked expectations. The school needs to accept and provide for these differences. But the school shapes as well as reflects behavior, and it can lean either toward rigid maintenance of the status quo or toward openness to change. What this viewpoint stresses is the development of a school atmosphere that expects and values variety, that acknowledges changing patterns and encourages exploration, and that minimizes the probability of a "self-fulfilling prophecy" with regard to sex-linked behavior, whereby the growing girl comes increasingly to exemplify the attitudes, roles, and adjustments that are predicted for her.[3]

Exposure to Experiences, Ideas, and Models

By almost any definition of education, one of the primary functions of the school is to introduce the child to the culture—its accumulated knowledge, its ways of thinking, its skills, and ways of functioning. The more effective, broad, and involving this exposure is, presumably, the more the growing girl can begin to select her interests, sense her affinities, and try different pathways.

Any school supplies some of this "grist" through the range of subject matter to which the child is exposed over the years. The issue is how to make this exposure meaningful and useful, rather than superficial, so that knowledge is integrated and available to the child as she grows and changes. Relevant, here, are those educational approaches and programs which have stressed multifaceted experiences; the study of human adaptation in many eras and settings; the selection of curricula that hold potential excitement and relevance for children at different developmental stages; the exposure to many adults in different roles; the availability of multiple media as pathways for the consolidation of learning; and a continuing problem-centered interaction among the children, the natural environment, and the human community in which they are embedded. If second-graders are studying the city around them, they are apt to discuss and hypothesize about its functions—its necessities, supply lines, institutions, essential work roles—then move out into the community to observe the bridge under construction, watch the vegetables arriving at market, talk with people working in the local stores; read and write around the same theme and experiences; consolidate what they have seen and discussed, not only through verbal means, but by painting, block building, the creation and enactment of an original play.

What is important to the girl's development as an independent, knowledgeable person, cognizant of her choices and of the elements and tools of her culture, is an education that involves her with multiple fields, ideas, media, and people, and that puts her at the center of her own learning process.

Skills for Choice, Problem Solving, and Evaluation

From some points of view, optimal schooling must provide an education in the processes and tools of thinking: problem solving, decision making, "learning how to learn." If one sees the forging of a life pattern as a continuous process of perception, reasoning, choice, and evaluation, then the learning and exercise of such skills during the school years become essential and relevant for the more personal issues that will arise for women in the course of their development.

Many streams of educational philosophy and practice have converged in recent years to challenge the nature of traditional, subject-dominated, rote learning and to argue for the development of more vital, open-ended, and searching processes of thought. Such a perspective is exemplified by "open classrooms"; by the inquiry- and discovery-oriented curricular revisions of Suchman and of Bruner[4]; by programs directed at productive thinking[5]; and by the branch of education that stemmed from Dewey and has persisted and evolved in the intervening years.[6] Such approaches stress the central and active role of the student and the element of choice in learning activities. They teach techniques of researching a problem or idea. They highlight a process that goes from uncertainty to relative resolution, from hunch to verification, and that usually involves obstacles, the confrontation with conflicting authorities, and the development of plausible alternatives. They call, usually, for problem-centered interaction with other people, both teaching adults and the highly important peer group, who offer discussion, argument, and experiences of their own.

In the school context, the subject matter is basically intellectual: What will happen to various metals under high heat? What makes man human and how does his functioning compare with other animals? Why did the pioneers move westward, who made their laws, how did they educate their children? How can the dollar be worth something different today than it was yesterday, and what have the Japanese, English, and Germans to do with it? But it seems likely that there is considerable paralearning about the processes of thought and resolution, and that such experiences build the intellectual armamentarium necessary to think about and direct one's own life: to tolerate confusion and uncertainty; to develop alternative solutions; to experiment, make decisions, and evaluate their outcome. Such processes are certainly relevant to the selections and complex amalgamations any woman must make in relation to marriage, children, home, and work.

Self-Differentiation and Self-Knowledge

Whatever the skills and knowledge that can be brought to bear, it is clear that the development of a personally meaningful life pattern rests centrally on a differentiated understanding of oneself. Does the school have a role in enhancing self-knowledge?

Educators would differ, theoretically, in their conception of how central such a function or responsibility need be; and, in practice, schools vary widely in the attention they give to such a goal. Of course, any child learns a good deal about herself in the course of schooling, whether the school recognizes it or not. By the time she has come through the elementary school years, any girl has developed some image of how successful she is, how she is evaluated comparatively, what she's "good at," how she strikes adults and classmates, even in the most traditional and impersonal of school atmospheres. Optimal education experience in this respect, however, probably requires more—both more *supportive* experiences that build confidence in oneself and more *differentiated* experiences that build increasingly refined perceptions of one's own reactions.

Schools which have regarded individuality and self-knowledge as central educational goals have usually considered the teacher–child relationship, in the early years especially, a major vehicle for such development. They have stressed, not only the warm and supportive aspects that come instantly to mind, but the role of the teacher as a person who comes to know the child so well that reactions to the child's efforts and behavior can be unique and differentiated—recognizing individual strides, developing personalized standards, helping with moods and effect, suggesting new materials and leads, capitalizing on interests, working with individual patterns of strength and deficit. Such a teacher does not always say, "That's lovely" to a painting; she may well say, "That's the first time I've seen you use that fine bright orange"—reflecting her clear knowledge of this child's unique efforts and products as well as her appreciation and support.

Such approaches have also seen the child as learning most about herself if the program has some of the features described in the two previous points. The more active and varied the role of the learner, the more media available for expressing knowledge and feeling, the more opportunities for work-oriented interactions with peers and adults, the better the child comes to know her own capacities, modes of learning, interests, and impact on people.

An optimal education for liberating young women requires not only that she come to know her adequacy in formal comparative terms, as exemplified by traditional evaluative procedures, but that she come to know and value herself as a unique person, with her own pattern of interests, skills, feelings, and relationships.

What difference would such an education make? Would schooling of this nature really move young women toward liberation?

A difficult question to answer. Few of us seriously doubt that people are shaped by their environment and experiences. School experiences, which occupy, like the family, so much of the child's life space for so many years, must certainly affect attitudes, perceptions, and decisions. But such convictions are hard to verify when variables are complex and interrelated, and it is difficult to map systematically the specific connections between aspects of the school environment and the particular nature of female development.

In a comparative study of schoolchildren, my colleagues and I gathered some material which suggests that different kinds of schooling have differential impact on, among other things, sex-role development.[7] The children in the study were nine-year-old, fourth-grade, middle-class urban children—48 girls and 57 boys. They were attending four different schools, selected for study because they represented different points along what we called a "modern-traditional continuum" of educational philosophy and practice. The most "modern" school exemplified many of the ideas discussed earlier: individual rather than stereotyped conceptions of people and possibilities; an emphasis on processes of inquiry and problem solving; varied materials and multiple media; active roles for each child and for the peer group in learning; supportive and individualized teacher–child relationships. The most "traditional" school, by definition, was more conventional in its expectations for children. It was organized around subject matter, achievement levels, and traditional materials for learning, and it was more formal in its conception of the teacher's role as an authority figure and as the director and evaluator of learning.

We tested the children over a wide range of functioning (cognitive development, interpersonal perceptions, aspects of self-image), including their attitudes toward male and female roles, images of future roles and development, and the extent of sex typing in their fantasies and play. We found a core of sex-typed responses in these nine-year-olds, as a total group: preferences, projections—fantasy themes that would be predicted on the basis of culturally familiar sex-typed expectations. But we found, as other researchers have, that girls were less sex typed than boys and, in addition, that girls from "modern" backgrounds departed most from the conventional expectations and patterns. These girls were most apt to see their present lives and their future roles in exploratory terms. They saw their future lives in terms of continuity with their individual interests rather than in terms of exclusive interest in wife and mother roles or conventional expectations of secretary and nurse careers. Their fantasies and projective play were less sex typed than those of most of the girls; they involved a wider variety of themes, were less centered on home and family, were more apt to deal openly with conflict, and were less dependent in tone.

It is important to point out that such reactions characterized girls whose families often held "modern" attitudes as well and whose mothers sometimes exemplified complex role amalgamations; such reactions were most notable in girls whose homes and schools were congruent in their orientation. In our research, such a finding constituted a "confounding" or entanglement, making it difficult to separate clearly the relative effects of school and home. At the same time, it points to an obvious reality: the school is a socializing force, but it interacts with other major forces in its impact on development. When we survey the roster of influential forces, there is little danger that the family or the probable impact of models and attitudes in the larger culture will be overlooked. There is more danger that the school will be overlooked as a significant force in shaping development. It was clear that the girls from the most modern school of our study were affected not only by attitudes and models in their homes but by the nature of their education as well—by the value placed on intellectual attitudes of challenge and search in any area, by their exposure to both women and men in varied and changing work roles, by the school's acceptance of personal feeling and style and its high respect for them as individuals.

We are in the early stages of understanding the impact of educational experience on the course of personal development, but it seems evident that the nature of schooling, from the earliest years on, shapes the capacities and strengths of the growing female. If we are to understand such forces, we shall probably have to look at schools in all their complexity, as small societies and total educational environments, rather than at specific pieces of curriculum for teaching one point or another. And if we are to implement on any sizable scale a kind of educational experience that equips young women to choose, fight for, and carry out personally meaningful life patterns, we may need to make dramatic changes in the prevailing organization of many schools: the values they represent, the relationships they foster, and the form and content of the learning experiences they offer.

References

1. ELEANOR E. MACCOBY, ed., *The Development of Sex Differences* (Stanford, Calif.: Stanford University Press, 1966).
2. JEROME KAGAN, "Acquisition and Significance of Sex Typing and Sex Role Identity," in *Review of Child Development Research*, ed. by M. L. Hoffman and L. W. Hoffman (New York: Russell Sage Foundation, 1964).
3. E. LEACOCK, *Teaching and Learning in City Schools* (New York: Basic Books, 1969); and R. Rosenthal and L. Jacobson, *Pygmalion in the Classroom: Teacher Expectation and Pupils' Intellectual Development* (New York: Holt, Rinehart & Winston, 1968). These authors offer illustrations of self-fulfilling prophecies regarding other subgroups in the educational system.
4. R. SUCHMAN, "Inquiry Training: Building Skills for Autonomous Discovery," *Merrill Palmer Quarterly* 7 (July 1961): 147–169; J. S. Bruner, *The Process of Education* (Cambridge, Mass.: Harvard University Press, 1960); and Bruner, *Man: A Course of Study* (Cambridge, Mass.: Education Development Center, 1967).
5. M. V. COVINGTON, R. S. CRUTCHFIELD, and L. B. DAVIES, *The Productive Thinking Program* (Berkeley, Calif.: Brazelton Printing Co., 1966).
6. B. BIBER and P. MINUCHIN, "The Role of the School in the Socialization of Competence," in *Achievement in American Society*, ed. by B. Rosen, H. Crockett, and C. Nunn (Cambridge, Mass.: Schenkman Publishers, 1969); B. Biber, E. Shapiro, and D. Wickens, *Promoting Cognitive Growth from a Developmental-Interaction Point of View* (Washington, D.C.: National Association for the Education of Young Children, 1971).
7. P. MINUCHIN, B. BIBER, E. SHAPIRO, and H. ZIMILES, *The Psychological Impact of School Experience* (New York: Basic Books, 1969); P. Minuchin, "Sex-Role Concepts and Sex Typing in Childhood as a Function of School and Home Environments," *Child Development* 36 (1965): 1033–1048.

DIARY 1972 OF A MAD 12-YEAR-OLD

Monday

My whole class went to see "The Hellstrom Chronicle." Everyone was crowded into one line, and there was a lot of screaming and pushing going on. I felt somebody pushing me in the back. My gut reaction was to punch whoever did it right back, so I did. It was John C., and I hit him right in the stomach. The teacher pulled me out of line and said he was appalled by my unladylike actions.

Wednesday

I had another student council meeting today. I arrived late, unfortunately, because the principal of the school was at this particular meeting. After about ten minutes I was called on to speak, and I brought up the subject of playground areas. The main question was why the fifth- to seventh-grade boys had a large area and the girls had a very small area—an enclosed street. I said I thought there might be some arrangement where boys and girls share areas. Well, the principal didn't like any kind of complicated arrangements to share playgrounds. "After all," he said, "girls don't like to play games. They like to sit around and talk. . . ."

After lunch I went to the German delicatessen to buy some gum. I was getting out my money when the owner got very impatient and treated me as if I was an invalid. He started showing me how to count my money and called me "girlie." I grabbed my money back and told him I knew how to count it, thank you, and not to call me girlie. I told him I was planning to buy my gum somewhere else.

Note: By Suzy Kitman. Reprinted with permission from *Ms.*, September 1972, 1:3, 62–63; 123.

Saturday

Went to see a girl friend today, and she acts as though her brother were God the Messiah. He has endless privileges. Their parents act as though he can do no wrong, and no present is too much to reward him with. He has special desserts, a telephone, television, and a big room. Now, the girl isn't exactly out in the cold. She's terribly spoiled also. But anyone who comes into that house could sense the glowing vibrations the parents have for her brother. My friend seems insecure, always follows a crowd, and is deathly afraid of her parents.

Monday

Well, I've been stamped as the girl who wants to be a boy, go out for the football team, and join the Army, none of which happens to be true. The main problem is that the boys seem to think of Women's Liberation the way it was treated in a skit I saw on a Bob Hope TV special: a man running around with an apron on saying some stupid thing about how his wife is never home because of football practice.

When you bring up household chores like dusting, washing dishes, and waxing floors, boys have thought up some great answers. This is one of my favorites—"Well, since it's been that woman's work is cleaning for so many years, I guess it must be heredity already." What? I almost flew out of my seat when I heard that one. I just recently heard an even worse one, an explanation of why men get better jobs. Because "girls are smarter in grammar school, but in high school boys are smarter, and that's why men get better-paying jobs and why they are more fit to hold them!" It was a girl who said that. She had learned it from her father.

Thursday

There's a new rage with the boys to call girls "broads" and other less desirable names. I must admit I was flabbergasted. My only response was to call this boy a "goon," a word that I'd heard in some old gangster movie.

Another thing. I personally hate it when girls go around giggling and asking boys to teach them how to tie their shoelaces. (A difficult task, as we all know.)

Monday

Last night, my brother called me into his room. I was all the way downstairs, but I went up anyway and there he stood, holding two piles of dirty laundry. He said he wanted me to wash and dry his clothes by eight o'clock the next morning. (My mother was away.) Assuming I would be bent over and ready, he put them in my arms, but they dropped right through because I flatly refused to do his dirty work. . . .

Saturday

One of the kids who's always teasing me about my opinions asked me what I wanted to do after college. He said, "I suppose you want to be in the Army or be a truck driver?" and everyone, including some of my girl friends, laughed. It wasn't really funny. I didn't like it, but it made me start thinking about what I really *do* want to be. I guess I do want to get married, but it has to be someone who agrees with the way I think. Someone who will not just "go along" with me, and who is willing to share the chores. I only want to have two children, because there are too many people who have more kids than they can support, and I think that's really bad. Children are a big responsibility. I hope that my husband and I would have the kinds of jobs where we could each take turns with the children—maybe working four days a week, different hours, or something like that. I don't want to have to do all the cooking and cleaning, but I think that we could work it out evenly so that we share the work.

I'd really like to work in a job where I could travel and have an expense account. Maybe I'll be a marine biologist, or an oceanographer.

Thursday

When I went into my Social Studies class today, I noticed that we had a student teacher. He looked decent so I decided to start talking with him. He came over to my desk, and I brought up women and how we get treated and asked him what he thought about it. He got very edgy and kept saying I had to look at it from his point of view. "How would you like it if men started invading *your* jobs?" he asked. We talked until the period ended and not once did he let me finish a sentence. He said I should forget about the cause, mainly because I'm too young to know anything about it anyway.

Sunday

Last night, I was baby-sitting with Mary J., the eight-year-old who always gives me a hard time. This time, she closed me into the pantry when I was getting her bedtime cereal. I got the door open okay, but I was mad. I really gave it to her. Then she got really sulky and sat down at the table and put her feet up right under my nose. Before I realized it, I was thinking, "What kind of terrible tomboy is this?" I slipped that time. But, hopefully, it won't happen again.

Tuesday

I really got disgusted today with M., the girl who sits next to me in English. Every single day she comes in all starry-eyed about her boyfriend. The only thing she ever thinks about is him or the next party! I finally asked her if there wasn't anything else she was interested in, and she just looked at me and then said, "Well, *you* wouldn't understand"—as if she felt sorry for me. It makes me sick the way all of the girls act about their boyfriends. Every day one of them is sobbing her heart out because she and her boyfriend have broken up—as if it were the worst thing in life. Then a week later she's going with someone else! It's as if they all swap partners every month—I wonder what will happen when they've all gone steady with each other about six times!

I don't understand why they want to tie themselves down to one boy right now. Why can't girls just be good friends with a lot of boys, instead of plastering themselves to one? Everything they do is to please the boys—the way they dress, the way they talk, even the activities they join. It's supposed to be the most important thing in life—to get a boy and wear his ID so the whole world knows that you're going steady. I don't see why girls have to sit around getting all upset if a boy doesn't call or ask them out? Why can't they call *him?* Why is it such a big deal anyway if you don't have a boyfriend?

Wednesday

Today there was a meeting for anyone who wanted to work on the set of a play we're doing. I went because I wanted to learn how to do carpentry and stuff with building. They told me that only boys could do the actual building of the set, and that girls had to paint scenery if they wanted to work on it.

Tuesday

A guidance counselor came from the high school today to talk to us about the high school. He began to talk about the classes we would be taking—two in particular. Home economics for girls and shop for boys. Well, I had heard a lot of things about home economics from older friends, and I really didn't want to take it. I asked him if *I* could take shop, and was there ever an uproar of laughter! He said many girls did want to take shop, but all the teachers felt it was wise for women to know how to sew.

Friday

During math today my teacher told the class about a new activity—playing baseball every Monday and Friday afternoon. There are eight teams: girls against girls, boys against boys. Of course, we don't get mixed teams. The teachers were afraid the girls won't be able to stand up to the boys' strength and great athletic ability. My teacher commented, "About five years ago I knew a girl who was fantastic in sports—maybe history will repeat itself!" It cracked the boys up, but none of the girls laughed at it!

DOES DIFFERENT EQUAL LESS?:
A HIGH SCHOOL WOMAN SPEAKS OUT

Being a high school woman means getting a course in synchronized swimming when you signed up for water polo.

Being a high school woman means putting on a short skirt and makeup when you go with a request to an unsuspecting principal.

Being a high school woman means you are required by law to drop out of school if you are pregnant or if you are married. Almost always it means being pressured to have a boyfriend. And almost as often it means being denied access to birth control information.

Being a high school woman means having one whole gym class devoted to a woman from a downtown department store so she can tell you how to buy a bra that fits.

Being a high school woman means being furious and having teachers, counselors, school psychologists, your parents, and your friends say "I don't see why you are so upset."

Being a high school woman means having a guidance counselor hand you the pink vocations journal with pictures of women working as secretaries, dental hygienists, librarians, elementary school teachers, lab technicians, key punch operators, and factory workers. There's not one picture of a woman operating heavy machinery or of her being in a leadership position. Who wouldn't rather stay home and have kids? Too bad we don't have that choice. Women make up 40 percent of the labor force—only 11 percent of us won't need a job.

Being a high school woman means going to the employment service section of the guidance office and being told by the counselor that the employer wanted her to recommend a boy for the job.

Note: By Constance Williams. Reprinted with permission from *School Library Journal,* January 1973, 19:5, 36–38. Copyright © 1973 by the Xerox Corporation.

Being a high school woman means worrying about student guidance files, which students are not allowed to see. Unaware of these files' content, students have no way of challenging their validity. Women are especially vulnerable to these files since women are directly affected by guidance counselors who track students into appropriate areas and levels of study. (Last year many of us tried to see our secret guidance files. Some of us succeeded, many of us failed, depending on who our parents were and how well our counselor liked us.)

Being a high school woman means noticing that all of the flutists in the orchestra are women, the trombonists men, the conductor a man, and that all of the music has been composed by men.

Being a high school woman means having to overcome the very active part school plays in keeping women from exploring our full capabilities. This means realizing that you've only been taught half the story—and it was *his* story, not ours. We have few models for nonstereotyped life styles. We see very few of our own kind developing their intellectual and creative potential. Without models, women's aspirations are lower than men's. Our expectations are lower than men's. The 1968 report of the President's Commission on the Status of Women reports that only 40 percent of college freshpeople are women. Only one in three of B.A. and M.A. degrees are earned by women in the United States—and only one in ten of the doctorates were earned by women. Among the top 10 percent graduating high school seniors, there are twice as many girls as boys—with no college plans. The commission found that some of the reasons for the loss in motivation on the part of high school women was the stereotyping of women in our culture and the lingering ideas of female inferiority, both of which persist in U.S. history books.

Being a high school woman means trying to recover the history that was taken from us. It means reading about old suffragettes, revolutionaries, writers, inventors, and national leaders. (*Generations of Denial, 75 Short Biographies of Women in History* by Kathryn Taylor is a good pamphlet to start with.)

Being a high school woman means seeing women treated as supplementary materials in textbooks. Used in a variety of ways, our texts in nearly all fields reinforce the stereotyped image of American women and our place in society. They generally leave out most women of importance and minimize the legal, social, and cultural disabilities they face. In an article entitled "Women in U.S. History Text Books" (*Social Education*, March 1971) author Janice Law Trecker examines 12 of the most popular history texts, and concludes that

> . . . based on information included in these commonly used high
> school texts, one might summarize the history and contribution of

American women as follows: "Women arrived in 1619. They held the Seneca Falls Convention in 1848. During the rest of the 19th Century, they participated in reform movements, chiefly temperance, and were exploited in factories. In 1923 they were given the vote. They joined the armed forces for the first time during the Second World War and thereafter have enjoyed the good life in America." Add the names of the women who are invariably mentioned, Harriet Beecher Stowe, Jane Addams, Dorothea Dix, and Frances Perkins, with perhaps Susan B. Anthony, Elizabeth Cady Stanton, with almost as frequently Carrie Nation, and you have the basic text.

Unfortunately, this is an all too accurate description of the history book used in my school, which is titled *Quest for Liberty*. It sums up the plight of American women in history this way:

> The 19th amendment, ratified in 1919, permitted women to vote; the campaign for women's suffrage had been carried on for more than seventy years by such dedicated women as Lucy Stone, Susan B. Anthony, Julia Ward Howe, Elizabeth Cady Stanton, Lucretia Mott, Amelia Bloomer, Carrie Chapman Catt, and Frances Willard. These women had also spoken out for abortion, birth control, temperance, women's rights, and lesser reforms. The work women did during World War I created sympathy for their campaign. In 1920, two million women voted in their first national election."

While the entry "Women" appears in the index of this book, no such entry exists under the heading "Men." They are all listed individually.

Being a high school woman means looking through 3,175 biographies on the West High library shelves to find that approximately 83 are about women.

Being a high school woman means looking for books about feminists in the school library and finding only two. One is about Lucretia Mott and the other about Susan B. Anthony. While you're flipping through the card catalogue trying to find the Carrie Chapman Catt entry—here is a sampling of the books you would find if you were in my high school: Man In Nature, Man Against Storm, Man In Space, Man Probes the Universe, Man and his Physical Universe, Manned Space Flight, Man's Conquest of Space, Man In the Fictional Mode, Man In the Poetic Mode, Man In the Dramatic Mode, and Women in American Life.

Being a high school woman means walking into the library and being greeted by similar looking women on the covers of *Seventeen, Glamour, McCall's, Ladies' Home Journal* and *American Girl*. Sometimes that makes you feel bad about eating that candy bar (none of the models have pimples) and sometimes you just get mad that there is no copy of *Off Our Backs* on the magazine shelf.

How many school libraries have a copy of *Our Bodies, Ourselves,* and the *Birth Control Handbook,* or Wilhelm Reich's *Mass Psychology of Fascism?*

Being a high school woman means needing information on sex, birth control, and abortion and then finding out that all those books are on closed shelves in the school *and* public library. Like it or not, if schools are interested in teaching what students are interested in learning, then a comprehensive course in sexuality should be offered.

Being a high school woman means you form groups just to talk about the things that make us angry. (Why can't we have tampax machines in the bathrooms? I hate it when guys call me chick! How did we end up making armbands for the demonstration while men made all the speeches?) Some women in my high school were angry. We immersed ourselves into books about women. *Sisterhood is Powerful,* edited by Robin Morgan, was taken off our school library shelf because there are articles by lesbians in it. (Last spring, the Madison Board of Education ruled that it was up to individual high school principals as to whether or not he—and they all are men—wants to allow gay people into the building. This means that a student can be expelled for being gay!) Besides Morgan's book, our group discussed Shulamith Firestone's *Dialectic of Sex, The Case for a Feminist Revolution,* sections from Margaret Mead's *Male and Female,* Engels' *The Origins of the Family,* and short excerpts from Freud, Reik, and Erikson just to see what we were up against.

Being a high school woman also means being aware of important women of today, including our grandmothers, mothers, and friends, as well as Bernadette Devlin, Shirley Chisholm, Margaret Mead, Madame Binh, Angela Davis, Martha Mitchell, Golda Meir, and all of the new film-makers, doctors, librarians, poets, lawyers, workers, prostitutes, mental patients, and prisoners and sharing with each other the struggle we all have in common. For a while, we had a women's group out at the Wisconsin girls' reform school. Groups in other parts of the city have formed their own track team and for the first time organized so that their coach receives an equal salary as the boys' track team coach. Students are attempting to do their sociology projects on sexism in the school system by doing research to find out the number of men and women in school-related jobs and then recording the differences in salary and rank level.

Our group presented a radio show for a university class on Sexism in the School System. Women are publishing their own newspapers and establishing their own therapy groups. We are setting up a rape crisis center. There is so much work to be done.

We are reading books by women describing their experiences, including *The Bell Jar* by Sylvia Plath, *The Golden Notebook* by Doris Lessing, *Nightwood* by Djuna Barnes, *Diary of an Ex-prom Queen* by Alix Kates Shulman and the *Diaries* of Anais Nin (Vols. I, II, and III), and *Les Guerillères* by Monique Wittig (she calls it a novel, but it's the best poetry I've ever read). From there many of us were prompted to share our poetry with each other. One of our most enjoyable projects was watching old movies at the State Historical Society, one from every decade from 1920 to Doris Day.

In essence, being a high school woman means needing information—and support. We must have books, films, and records about all kinds of women in all aspects of life. We also need reviews of the images of girls and women in all high school materials—new and old.

Obviously, we need the help of our teachers and counselors, but more importantly, we need the help of the information specialist—the school librarian.

It has been said that society determines the status of women, while the educational system perpetuates it. Will you help us in the long overdue struggle to break this cycle—and acquire the knowledge we need to eliminate sexism in this society?

Bibliography

BARNES, DJUNA. *Nightwood.* New Directions, 1961.

BOSTON WOMEN'S HEALTH COURSE COLLECTIVE. *Our Bodies Ourselves.* New England Free Press, 1971.

CHAPIN, JUNE R., RAYMOND J. McHUGH and RICHARD GROSS. *Quest for Liberty.* Enterprises, 1971.

CHERNIAK, DONNA, and FEINGOLD, ALLAN, eds. *Birth Control Handbook.* McGill Students Society, 1970.

ENGELS, FREDERIC. *The Origins of the Family.* International, 1942.

FIRESTONE, SHULAMITH. *Dialectic of Sex.* Bantam, 1971.

GRIFFIN, S. "Rape: the All American Crime." *Ramparts,* September 1971. Pp. 26–35.

LESSING, DORIS. *The Golden Notebook.* Ballantine, 1962.

MEAD, MARGARET. *Male and Female.* Mentor, 1955.

MORGAN, ROBIN. *Sisterhood is Powerful.* Random, 1970.

NIN, ANAIS. *Diaries of Anais Nin.* Swallow, 1966.

PLATH, SYLVIA. *The Bell Jar.* Harper, 1971.

REICH, WILHELM. *Mass Psychology of Fascism.* Farrar, 1970.

SHULMAN, ALIX KATES. *Diary of an Ex-prom Queen.* Knopf, 1969.

TRECKER, JANICE LAW. *Women in U.S. History Text Books.* Social Education, March 1971.

WITTIG, MONIQUE. *Les Guerillères.* Viking, 1971.

SEGREGATED ACADEMIC AND VOCATIONAL SCHOOLS: SEPARATE BUT NOT EQUAL

Opportunities for girls are further limited by restricted admissions in schools. Academic and vocational high schools in large school districts sometimes exclude one sex entirely or require higher admissions standards for girls than for boys. Simply because of their sex, students may find themselves ineligible for the school offering the best or only courses in their field of interest.

Until recently, New York City excluded girls from two of the city's high quality public academic high schools specializing in science, mathematics, and technology. Two years after a court order opened the first school, the Board of Education was still listing these schools for "boys only" in its official catalogue.[1]

Vocational high schools in big cities are also frequently sex segregated. A 1971 telephone survey by OE's Office of Legislation found, for example, that the District of Columbia had four (two for men, two for women); Baltimore, four (also two for each); and New York City, 18 (13 for males, five for females).

Separate does not mean equal. Boys' vocational high schools tend to offer training for more diverse and better-paying jobs. The segregated schools in New York City prevent girls from taking courses in 17 different vocational fields: architectural drafting, dental labs processing, jewelry making, industrial chemistry, and upholstery as well as areas in heavy industry. Boys are excluded from two.[2]

A comparison of Boston's two trade high schools, one for each sex, is particularly revealing.

Note: From *A Look At Women in Education: Issues and Answers for HEW.* Report of the Commissioner's Task Force on the Impact of Office of Education Programs on Women. Published November 1972 by the U.S. Office of Education, Department of Health, Education, and Welfare.

Boys at Boston Trade High choose from courses in automobile mechanics, basic electronics, cabinetmaking, carpentry, drafting, electrical technology, machine shop, painting, plumbing, printing, sheet metal, and welding. At Trade High School for Girls, on the other hand, students are only offered programs in clothing, foods, beauty culture, and commercial art. The average expected wage for trades taught at Trade High School for Girls is 47 percent less than that for the trades available at Boston Trade High School for Boys.[3]

In addition, nonvocational course offerings at these schools are determined by sex. At Trade High School for Girls, students take typing and merchandising, while boys at Boston Trade learn geometry, trigonometry, and physics. Girls can study biology but not chemistry. Interestingly, the Boston school system makes exceptions for boys who want to be admitted to the girls' trade school (seven were enrolled in 1970), but no exceptions have ever been made for girls who sought admission to the trade school for boys.[4]

References

1. National Organization for Women (NOW), New York City Chapter, Education Committee, *Report on Sex Bias in the Public Schools* (New York, N.Y., 1971), p. 3.
2. Bureau of Educational and Vocational Guidance in cooperation with the Office of High Schools, *The Public High Schools, New York City, 1971–72* (New York, N.Y.: Board of Education of the City of New York, 1972), pp. 18–23.
3. GAIL BRYAN, *Discrimination on the Basis of Sex in Occupational Education in the Boston Public Schools,* mineographed. (Prepared as part of an investigation by the Boston Commission to Improve the Status of Women, 1972), p. 6, n. 1.
4. *Ibid.,* p. 4.

REPORT ON SEX BIAS IN THE PUBLIC SCHOOLS– EXCERPTS

The following excerpts are public testimony in the case of Bonnie Sanchez and Laura Edelhart against Harold Baron, Principal of Junior High School 217, and Hugh McDougall, District Superintendent of District 28, New York City Board of Education (69 C 1615) given in United States Courthouse, Brooklyn, New York, on January 29, 1971, and March 19, 1971. Prosecution lawyers came from the New York Civil Liberties Union and the Center for Constitutional Rights.

The Court ruled that there is a basis for a class action suit by female students against the New York City Board of Education.

Excerpts of Testimony of Laura Edelhart

After I got home, I started calling the Board of Education. But I never got through to anyone. I must have made a dozen calls at least.

Q: Did anyone at the Board of Education ever tell you anything to do about this matter?

Well, eventually I was told that because the school was decentralizing that I should go back to the school for this problem; that it wouldn't be a matter of the Central Board any more.

Q: And did you do that?

Yes, I did. I called the school. I spoke to Mr. Baron . . . , and he said that we have too many boys in the school to be able to allow the girls to take metalwork and mechanics.

Note: 3rd ed. 1973. Copyright © Education Committee, National Organization for Women, New York City Chapter, 28 East 56th Street, New York, New York 10022. Reprinted with permission.

Q: Mrs. Edelhart, when you were in high school, did you attempt to take a metalworking course?

Mr. Maurer: Objection.

The Court: How long ago was it?

The Witness: About 20 years ago.

The Court: Objection sustained. Unrelated.

Mr. Ennis: Your Honor, I wish to show that it is related, in this sense: I wish to show that the only named plaintiff in this case was the named plaintiff because she had the support of her mother. She had the support of her mother because her mother was also denied permission to take a metalwork class when she was in high school, and it is because of that continuing problem—

The Court: I am not persuaded. The objection is sustained.

Q: Mrs. Edelhart, do you think that having taken the course it was valuable for your daughter?

Mr. Mauer: Objection.

Yes, I do.

The Court: What is the relevancy of that?

Mr. Ennis: Well, Your Honor, I wish to establish that, having taken that course, Bonnie Sanchez was a more self-reliant and capable individual than she was before.

The Court: Let us assume that is so. What has that got to do with the policy?

Mr. Ennis: It has to do with whether or not that policy is damaging the lives of female students in high school. We intend to show that it is; that the Board of Education policy is depriving female students of the opportunity to become self-reliant people—

The Court: Do you expect to offer any statistics on it, or do you expect to rely on the testimony?

Mr. Ennis: We will offer statistics, Your Honor.

Excerpts of Testimony of Gigi Gordon, JHS 217
(Van Wyck), Ninth Grade

Q: Can you tell me what shops are available at your school?

They have sewing and cooking available to the ninth grades. That is only for girls. And for the boys, they have metal and printing, and I think they also have ceramics.

Q: What shop are you taking now?

We just changed shops and I was assigned to sewing.

Q: Which shop did you want to take?

I wanted to take printing.

Q: Did you make any attempt to take printing?

Yes, I did. I went to several people, one of them was Mr. Wydlock, and he told me he would check into the matter and he would try to get me into the boys' shop. Then I saw him again and he said he thought they were all filled up. And then I saw him a third time and he said there was no room in the boys' shop for any more girls.

Q: Do you know whether there are any more girls in there now?

No, there aren't any girls.

Q: Did he say it was a boys' shop specifically?

Yes.

Q: How many shops are there for boys?

Two or three; it depends upon what periods. There are two in one period and three in another.

Q: How many for girls?

Two.

Q: Do you know what the percentage of boys and what the percentage of girls was?

I don't know the percentages, but it is about evenly distributed.

Q: Are there any other classes or subjects for credit that only have boys?

Yes. There is an AVI Squad, which is a squad with audiovisual aids, and it is for boys. And the boys are supposed to set up equipment to show films, and projectors, and things like that. I tried to get into that and the teacher said it would be okay to get into it. We had to fight for that, but we got into it. And the teacher said that he would show us how to work the things. And he showed us how to work them. And then we never got called to be on the squad. We never got called to set up any such equipment.

Q: Did you ask to—

Yes. We went to the teacher. We asked him why we weren't called. He said, "Well, there are plenty of other boys who can do the job and they have been on the squad longer than you."

Q: You mentioned Mr. Wydlock before. Can you tell me who he is?

He is the Dean of Boys. He is also in charge of the shops for girls and boys, but mostly the boys.

Q: And what did he tell you yesterday?

He said that the shops were all filled up with boys and that he didn't think I could get in because of the boys, because there was no room for any more girls in the shop.

Q: Now you are scheduled to take sewing; right?

Yes.

Q: When is that course given?

Mondays and Wednesdays, the third and fourth periods.

Q: And when is the printing course given?

The same time.

Q: Do you know of any other girls who tried to get into the print course?

Yes. Helen Kartis.

Q: Did you speak to the principal about your discussions with Mr. Wydlock?

No, because the principal is not available to discuss matters with students.

Q: Did you try?

I have tried before on different issues than this and the principal doesn't speak to the students unless it is a matter of extreme urgency; and even then he is usually at suspension hearings.

Q: Did you try this time?

No. But I did speak to the assistant principal, Mr. Niler.

Q: What did he say?

He said that I should ask the shop teachers if they wanted girls in their classes.

Excerpts of Testimony of Julie Nives, JHS 217 (Van Wyck), Ninth Grade

Q: Could you tell me how the gym classes are set up in your school?

Yes, there is a boys' gym and a girls' gym. We have it once a week for two periods.

Q: What do you learn in the girls' gym?

At the beginning, the first marking period, we did volley ball, and after that, after the marking period was over, we continued doing that. So me and some friends complained because we were supposed to have a new curriculum each marking period. And they said, "O.K., we will try to do something," and they did. Finally they got us records which had exercises on them, but the exercises were not working out very well because they were only to slim your waistline and help you walk down the street, well, things like that. So after a while it wasn't really working out well. So then we complained again, you know, we should have something a little more, you know, better, because nobody was getting prepared—you have to wear gym suits—and so they had not done anything about it and we refused to get dressed. That day we went down, we were looking around for some guy—our assistant principal—to complain to, and he wasn't there. And the Dean sent us back into gym, and since then we have not been doing anything.

Q: Can you tell me what the boys do in gym?

The boys do exercises. They play basketball. They can go out when it is warm, which the girls are not allowed to do. They play handball. Baseball. They have certain teams after school for just baseball, basketball, track teams, which the girls do not have.

Q: Have you asked to do any of the sports which the boys do?

We asked for basketball. They said there wasn't enough equipment. The boys prefer to have it first. Then we will have what is left over. We haven't really gotten anywhere.

Q: Gigi mentioned the AVI program before. Did you also try to get into that?

Yes, I was with her. And my teacher, who is also our science teacher, he tried—We complained to him a few times that he has not been calling us down to use the projectors. And he said that he would try to but there were too many boys that were taken care of first. And one day he did call me down and then he said, "Oh, forget it. I have somebody else to do the job."

Excerpts of Testimony of Catherine Reinheimer, JHS 104, Eighth Grade

Q: Why did you decide to testify?

Because last year and this year my friends and I have tried to get into ceramics. We are not allowed to take it. The only thing girls can take is sewing and cooking.

Q: What are the boys' shops?

Wood, metal, printing, and ceramics.

Q: How do you students get into these shops? Can they choose them or are they assigned to those classes?

No, they are assigned.

Q: Are any girls assigned to either printing, metal, wood, or ceramics?

No, just cooking and sewing.

Q: Are any boys assigned to sewing and cooking?

No.

Q: Have you tried to get into any of the boys' shops?

Yes, ceramics.

Q: How did you try to get into those?

I asked our assistant principal, Miss Piccarelli. We asked her if we could change from sewing or cooking to ceramics, and she said, "No. Those are boys' shops; you can't get into them."

Q: Did you ask anybody else?

Yes. After she said we couldn't, when we had group guidance, where we can tell the things we have problems with to our group guidance teacher we told her we can't get into ceramics. She said to bring it up at the student body conference. So our representative of our grade brought it up at the conference and she didn't have any luck with it.

Q: So right now you can't take any of those classes, wood, metal, printing, or ceramics?

No.

Q: When Miss Piccarelli told you that you couldn't come into the shop class, the ceramics class, did you try to speak with the principal of the school?

No, because Miss Piccarelli was closer to the children than Mr. Frank was—like, he did very, very important things—well, Miss Piccarelli told us today she is in charge of the Department of Shops—

Q: Would you recognize that the principal is in charge of the school?

Yes.

The Court: Do you deny that a counselor has authority to advise the children as to what the policy is concerning the exclusion of a particular course? . . . don't impose the obligation on the child to go to a higher authority before she understands she is excluded.

Excerpts of Testimony of Marcy Silverman, Jamaica High, Eleventh Grade

Q: Are there any classes or activities or programs within the classes that are open to male students and not to female students?

Well, within my physics class last year, our teacher asked if there was anybody interested in being a lab assistant, in the physics lab, and when I raised my hand, he told all the girls to put their hands down because he was only interested in working with boys.

Q: Did you make any further attempts to become a lab assistant?

Yes. I spoke to Mr. Chailiff. He is the head of the student organization, and I told him what my physics teacher had said and he said he would see, you know, what might be done; but I never heard about it again.

Q: Are there any other activities in the school that women are not members of, and have you attempted to be in any other activities?

Yes. There is an Honor Guard, which are students who, instead of participating in gym for the term, are monitors in the hall, and I asked my gym teacher if I could be on the Honor Guard Squad. She said it was only open to boys. I then went to the head of the Honor Guard, a Mr. Baron, who said that he thought girls were much too nasty to be Honor Guards. He thought they would be too mean in working on the job, and I left it at that.

Q: Is the Honor Guard a credit activity?

Yes. If you're a member of the Honor Guard, you get credit for the term's work of physical education.

The Court: How do you get appointed to it? How does a boy get appointed to it?

They just come into the boys' gym and say "Who wants to be on it?" And those who want to be on it are on it, but they never came in and said that to our girls in gym class.

Q: Are there other classes that you take that the boys and the girls are separated or the boys and the girls have different curricula?

Yes. The hygiene classes are—there's boys' hygiene and girls' hygiene and I know in some of the boys' hygiene classes they—I'm not quite sure if it's specifically in the curriculum but there has been discussion of birth control in the boys' hygiene classes, and when we attempted to, you know, discuss it in our girls' classes, they told us that we couldn't do it, we couldn't talk about things like that, and girls have tried to bring in booklets to distribute in the class, so as—you know, if we couldn't have a discussion, maybe we could distribute some material, and they told us to get it out of the school.

Q: To your knowledge, are there any other programs that are open to the boys and not to the girls?

Well, along with—in the hygiene program last week there was a—at a student council meeting, at which I was home room representative, a teacher spoke as a narcotics advisor in the school. There is a new program in the school, and he said he would be distributing material to the boys' hygiene classes on drug abuse and they would be starting a new program together. But he mentioned nothing about the girls' classes.

Q: You are taking gym now, is that correct?

Yes, I am.

Q: Do you have the same activities in your gym classes that the boys do?

No, we don't. Right now we're doing folk dancing and we asked—there were about 20 girls in the class that I knew who would like—who would have liked to go out and run track as the boys do. They play ball out in the recreational fields, and I asked one of the gym teachers if we could get a group of girls who would like to go out and run track or play ball in the fields. Since there are about six or seven gym teachers and since they divide the boys' classes up with teachers taking certain groups out, if we could do this in our class. First she said I should get the names of 50 girls who would want to do it. I proceeded to ask around and I had about 30 girls in the first day who wanted to do it, and then the next day in gym she said to forget about it because she had spoken to Mrs. Klein, the head of the girls' Health Education Department. She said that just couldn't be done.

Q: Are the girls able to go out at all or is it just a question of running track?

The girls are only allowed to go out in the very, very early part of the term, at the beginning of September, and then again in June, which comes to a total of about three weeks. When the boys go out—they go out all the time, except, you know, when the weather just doesn't permit.

Q: Do the boys and girls have the same equipment in their gym classes?

The only equipment in my years of gym in Jamaica High School, the only equipment I've ever seen is basketball and a volley ball. And the boys have ropes. They have pegboards that they use for climbing. I don't know. I've never been in the boys' gym. I've only heard from friends, but I know the equipment that we use and it's not the same. . . . All I've ever seen is a basketball and a volley ball and a record player.

Q: What other programs in gym do you have? You play baseball?

We don't. We spend a lot of time—I think there are a few weeks that we are supposed to be playing baseball, but every time we keep learning over and over again, which leaves about two or three days left to actual game playing.

Q: You play volley ball?

Yes, we play volley ball also.

Q: And when you go outside, what sort of classes do you have?

We play this game. I don't know. It's called Ogre Take, where you just throw the ball and you run around.

Q: And you're running around a lot?

There is no equipment, though, and when I asked if we could play soccer, since I saw other—the boys' gym classes playing it and since I've played soccer on my own time, I was told that the boys use the fields and, you know, because of that we're not allowed to use them. Because they get priority. The teacher told me that.

Excerpts of Testimony of Leslie Lubin, Jamaica High, Eleventh Grade

In the fall of my junior year I tried to get on the Honor Guard Squad.

Q: What happened at that time?

I had talked to a few of the boys' gym teachers because they were the head of the Honor Guard and they told me that I could not be an Honor Guard because I was a girl.

The Court: What teachers did you talk to?

I had spoken to Mr. Malin and Mr. Baron about it.

Q: Is the Honor Guard the same Honor Guard that Marcy Silverman testified to earlier this morning?

Yes, it is.

Q: Is that an alternate to gym, a credit course alternate to gym?

Yes.

Q: Did you ever try again to be on the Honor Guard?

I had continued speaking to Mr. Malin about it and I managed to sway him to believe that he needed a girl on his squad.

Q: Why was that?

Because I had told him that it was not right to have boys guarding the girls' bathrooms. You needed a girl to go in there because otherwise a boy would have to interrupt a teacher's classroom to have a female teacher go into the bathroom to, you know, control what was going on in there.

Q: So at that point did he agree to let you be on the Honor Guard?

Yes.

Q: And how long did you serve on the Honor Guard?

For about four months.

Q: What happened at the end of that four-month period?

I was walking around the halls with my Honor Guard button on and it seems that Mr. Sugar, who is the principal, and Mr. Baron, who is the head of the boys' gym department, had seen me with the button on and they told Mr. Malin, who at the time was head of my squad, that he would have to fire me.

Q: Did Mr. Malin tell you that?

Yes.

Q: Did he fire you for that reason?

Yes.

Q: So that you're not now on the Honor Guard any longer?

No.

Excerpt of Testimony of Pamela Charney, Bronx High School of Science, Twelfth Grade

Q: Approximately how many girls are there in your school?

There are 3,600 students, and it's—well, they say there is—no one ever tells you anything about admissions being different, but if you look at the old yearbooks, it's approximately two thirds male and one third female.

Excerpts of Testimony of Susan Horowitz, Bronx High School of Science, Eleventh Grade

Q: Have you ever attempted to participate in the Stage Squad program at Bronx Science?

Yes. I originally wished to join the Stage Squad in the beginning of my sophomore year, and I went—there was an ad in the Daily Bulletin, which is posted every day in the homeroom, which advertises extracurricular openings, and there was an ad for interested boys to join the Stage Squad.

Q: Is that what the ad said interested boys?

Yes, interested boys to join the Stage Squad, please come to such-and-such room. And I wanted to be on the squad so I went, and the advisor of the Stage Squad, Mr. Schlessel. . . . He said that the work only involved moving around heavy chairs and things like that and that I couldn't do that.

Q: Do you receive any sort of credit if you serve on the Stage Squad?

Yes. You get service credit, which is credited toward your credit total, which is used if you want to join Arista.

Q: What is Arista?

It's an honor society. It looks good on your record. It helps you get into college and things like that.

Q: After you were not permitted to join the Stage Squad in your sophomore year, what did you do then?

I sort of forgot about it. I just assumed that I couldn't join, and then after that I was attending the Women's Lib Club, and we were discussing things, like Stage Club and the Prince—

Q: Excuse me. The Women's Lib Club, is this a club in the school?

Yes. It's a school-sanctioned club. And we discussed things that were in the school that were not open to women, such as the Stage Squad and the Prince Squad and the Audio Visual Squad. . . .

EXPELLING PREGNANT STUDENTS

Discrimination is particularly severe for one group of students—those who become pregnant. Every year over 200,000 young women under 18 give birth.[1] Usually these young women are expelled from school at the first sign of pregnancy. Out of 17,000 school districts surveyed in 1970, fewer than one third offered pregnant school-age girls any education at all.[2] School districts that did allow students to study during pregnancy usually kept them at home or segregated them in special classes for various reasons—on moral grounds, for special protection, or for convenience.[3]

None of these reasons justify denying a young woman the right to regular public education with her peers. There is no evidence that pregnant students are morally contagious. Class attendance poses no greater health hazard to pregnant women than performing a job, doing housework, or caring for other children—all things that women commonly do up until childbirth.

Expulsion compounds the already serious problems of teenage pregnancy. Of every 100 pregnant teenagers who leave school, 85 never come back. Rejected, cast out with a child to support and often no salable skills, these teenagers are nine times more likely to commit suicide than their peers.[4]

Eighty-five percent will keep their babies, either to raise an illegitimate child alone or to enter into an early marriage that is three or four times more likely to end in divorce than marriages in any other age groups.[5] Their children are four times more likely to have psychological problems than those with older parents. Among the teenage mothers who remain unmarried, 85 percent go on welfare.[6]

Note: From *A Look At Women in Education: Issues and Answers for HEW*. Report of the Commissioner's Task Force on the Impact of Office of Education Programs on Women. Published November 1972 by the U.S. Office of Education, Department of Health, Education, and Welfare.

References

1. National School Public Relations Association (NSPRA), *Schoolgirl Pregnancy: Old Problem, New Solutions* (Washington, D.C.: NSPRA, 1972), p. 1.
2. *Ibid.*, p. 6.
3. *Ibid.*, pp. 6–11.
4. EDWIN KIESTER, JR., "The Bitter Lessons Too Many Schools Are Teaching Pregnant Teenagers," *Today's Health* (June 1972), p. 54.
5. MARION HOWARD, "Comprehensive Community Programs for the Pregnant Teenager," *Clinical Obstetrics and Gynecology*, vol. 14, no. 2 (June 1971), pp. 473–474.
6. KIESTER, *The Bitter Lessons* . . . , p. 54.

CONSCIOUSNESS-RAISING IN THE CLASSROOM: SOME GAMES, PROJECTS, DISCUSSION-OPENERS, ETC.

1. Have the girls complete either or both "I would (would not) like to be a man because . . ." For the boys, substitute "woman." This should indicate what the students see as the privileges and burdens of each sex, and how they perceive the division of roles.

2. An alternate phrasing of the above—"If I were a boy (girl), I would (like to) . . ." Do the students feel that they can't do or become these things given their actual sex. For instance, if a girl says, "If I were a boy, I would climb trees and play baseball," she should be asked if she does climb trees and play baseball, why not if she doesn't, would she like to, what makes her think she can't.

3. Cut out pictures of people of various facial types and have students each describe one and speculate on what that person may be like. Do they react more favorably to women who fit the traditional concept of "feminine" and men who fit the traditional concept of "masculine?" How wide a range of fantasizing do they do about people of each sex— e.g., in terms of occupations? What aspects of personality and life style do they concentrate on with each sex—e.g., do they speculate on marital status and number of children more frequently with women than with men?

4. Draw a series of stick figures (indistinguishable as to sex) holding objects or doing something (e.g., holding a broom, driving a van, holding a bat). Have the students make up stories about them.

5. Take the students on a discrimination trip, including a mock job interview, a men-only restaurant, a housecleaning, an application for credit at a department store, etc.

Note: Reprinted with permission from The Emma Willard Task Force on Education, *Sexism in Education,* 3rd ed., copyright © 1972 (Box 14229, University Station, Minneapolis, Minnesota 55414).

6. Keep a running list of "ways I have benefited by being a male (or female) today." Or keep two parallel lists, plus and minus.

7. To illustrate how selective generalization works, give some facts about men and have the students generalize from them. For example: FACT: Men have a much higher incidence of heart disease than women. GEN.: Employer to male job applicant: "I'm sorry but we just can't afford to hire a man for this job. You might have a heart attack and die." FACT: The male hormone testosterone is considered by many endocrinologists to be the cause of aggression. GEN.: Men are always fighting and getting violent. They can't be trusted in positions of power.

8. Word association games—Have the students sit in a circle and have each, in turn, say a word or phrase that is used negatively about women (shrill, hysterical, hag, old maid). Then do the same for men (cocky, bastard, henpecked). How many of the male words are actually antiwoman? (For example, bastard and son-of-a-bitch reflect on his mother; henpecked reflects on his wife.)

9. Role-reversal games—Conduct a marriage ceremony in which the mother gives away the groom, they're pronounced woman and husband, and become Mrs. and Mr. Jane Smith. Have students conduct interviews with prominent men, asking them for their favorite home repair techniques, how they combine marriage and career, what size suit they wear, how they manage to stay young and handsome. This should illustrate the absurdity of some of our conventions that keep men's and women's roles strictly defined.

10. "Today is my 80th birthday"—Have students look back at their lives since leaving high school. This should show their aspirations and expectations.

11. Cut out questions from Ann Landers, Dear Abby, and Ellen Peck that relate to female and male behavior and sex roles and relationships between the sexes. Have the students write their own answers.

12. Set up a display of cosmetics, beauty equipment, etc., with labels explaining how each is used. If you can get away with it, have the boys put on makeup and discuss how it affects their self-perception. If the girls are at the makeup wearing age, have them discuss how they feel with and without makeup.

13. Allow each student 10 minutes to make a list of characteristics of women (or men). If they have difficulty, tell them to try thinking of one woman (or man) they know. Then divide them into small groups (three to five) and have them first read their lists, then say which characteristics on the list are true of themselves, then which characteristics they like. Then have the small group, as a team, select ten items from the combined lists that they think are most important. It is essential that they

agree on the meaning of each characteristic. Then have them rank the items from one to ten. Who is the person they have created? The ideal woman (or man)? The typical woman (or man)? Are the characteristics positive or negative? Try several variations: girls working on female characteristics and boys on male, vice versa, both sexes working on the same sex, all-female and all-male small groups, mixed small groups. Have the teams compare their results.

14. Have girls write on "What I like best about being a woman," "What I hate most about being a woman," "What I like most in men," "What I hate most in men."

Reverse for boys.

Compare and discuss the male and female likes and dislikes. Are they complementary, similar, dissimilar, etc?

15. List words and phrases referring to unmarried women. To unmarried men.

16. Have females pretend they are male and plan their future. Reverse for males.

17. Have female students pretend that marriage is *not* an alternative and plan their future.

18. Have students monitor TV ads, TV programs, and comic strip characters for examples of sexism.

19. Have class line up in a straight line and tell them to pick their position on the basis of their importance. (*Do not* try to tell them what to judge importance on.)

What usually happens is that males are at the front of the line and the majority of females in the last half of the line.

20. Have males sit in a circle and the females sit in a circle around them.

Each female picks a male to observe his verbal and nonverbal communication. (They may not say anything while the males are talking.)

Pick one of the four for the males to discuss:

What they like about being male.

What they don't like about being male.

What they like about females.

What they don't like about females.

When the males are finished, each female gives her observations of what the male she was watching said (verbally) and did (nonverbal motions, etc.). The males may not say anything while the females are discussing them.

Reverse everything with the females in the center circle.

When that is finished (males have finished saying what the females said and did), have general discussion of how everyone felt, their reactions, etc.

21. Make up a collage or montage or simply draw what society considers to be the "ideal woman" and the "ideal man." Then students explain their ideal. (Include physical description, emotional characteristics, personality, and mannerisms.)

The same thing can be done using their peers—"popular girl" or "popular boy."

22. Students can analyze nursery rhymes or children's stories which include women alone or both women and men (boys and girls). What is the role played by each person? What do they think this implies or suggests as to the way girls and boys see themselves?

23. Students can watch television "situation" shows concerning or including women. Analyze the role of the woman in that particular segment. Present to class, either by skit or report.

24. Rewrite "Love Is" according to women's liberation.

25. Pick certain comic books and discuss the roles portrayed in them.

"LET BROTHER BAKE THE CAKE"

I, for one, am not ready to take the advice given the heroine in the children's book, "Up a Road Slowly." I'm not ready to "accept the fact that this is a man's world and learn how to play the game gracefully." I've never been graceful, and I have a low tolerance for games with unfair rules. So do third-graders. And that is what this article is about. If the effort of educating our elementary school children toward realization of female equality seems like an uphill battle strewn with rocks and thorns, do what Joe Hill says, and " 'put your wooden shoes on, pard'," and remember that the kids will be with you all the way!

Materials I have used with my eight- and nine-year-olds this school year include library books, textbooks, newspaper and magazine pictures and articles, a flannel-board story I made, and other devices.

Methods vary. I have used storytelling, a skit, discussion, creative writing, and others. One method I have found especially enlightening is criticism of existing materials. For example, most basic readers have many more stories about boys than they do about girls. And, frequently, boys are shown doing more "fun," active things than girls, who are somewhere in the background. Or girls are little sisters being shown how to do something by big, wise brother. Like little Amy, who gets stuck in a closet and is afraid of the dark (girls are frequently afraid in literature) and big brother Stuey "saves the day" by inventing a flashlight and then goes after Mother and the key. We use Scott-Foresman books in St. Paul, and for that reason I give these examples. Scott-Foresman is no worse than the others.

Children enjoy examining the stories and comparing the number featuring boys with the number featuring girls. One fourth-grader in a co-worker's class gave me a list that indicated boys starred in 41 selections,

Note: By Anne McEvoy Schmid. Reprinted with permission from *American Teacher,* November 1972, CE 4–5.

a boy and a girl together in five, and girls were featured in only two! (I must admit to ignorance of what book she evaluated; these figures were shocking even to a skeptic like myself, and I think I might have been guilty of a little "oversell.") One of my nonreaders enjoyed counting the number of pictures of boys and girls in a reader. She found that boys appeared almost three times as often as girls.

Once this spring, while reading a story to my class, I became disgusted with big brother Sam exhorting Betty with "It's your own fault . . . you never stick to anything. You start to collect or make something, but if anything goes wrong, you quit."

Well, after this reinforcement of any latent ideas anyone might have had about feminine flightiness and lack of tenacity, I quit, telling my class why.

One of the youngsters suggested the story be read with sex-role reversals, and he proceeded to read orally in this manner. My sister, an elementary school librarian, frequently employs this device, especially when Mother and Father are conversing. The children to whom she is reading never notice, but Mother definitely comes off sounding more forceful and aggressive than Father! At my sister's suggestion, I tried doing some spur-of-the-moment editing when reading orally, and it does make sense. Carolyn Haywood may write "policeboys," but when I read "Ramona the Pest," policegirls patrol just as frequently as boys. (Maybe a little more often.)

We had a lot of fun the day I read "What Will I Be From A to Z," a soft-cover "career guide for primary pupils" that shows women performing six out of 20 jobs: homemaker, librarian, nurse, office worker, teacher, and violinist. In the discussion that followed, we decided which jobs could be performed by women and discovered that all, with the possible exception of quarterback, could and should be handled by women. This lesson got pretty noisy—I've found that children aroused to excited anger like to shout things like "unfair," and "who says girls can't do that!" About the time the decibels were rising to a dangerous degree, the bell rang, and because it was one of my first lessons on "consciousness-raising," I was wondering how much had sunk in. Believe me, I felt pretty good when I saw a mother later that afternoon and she told me her son had come home and said, "Guess what? We found out today that girls can be judges!"

Another lesson that has been successful involves using a flannel board and teacher-made manila pictures of Sally and Sam, two friends who went to grade school and college together. Both were excellent students, and after graduating with honors in the same field, they went to apply for a job at the same company.

Sally was given a typing test, resulting in a mundane, dead-end job, and a small paycheck. Sam, after passing a battery of tests to determine his executive potential, went on and eventually reached a high-level administrative position. Sam vacations in Bermuda, while Sally drives to her aunt's home in a neighboring state. Sam entertains Sally in his apartment; Sally lives at home with Mother because she can't afford to live alone. The children are informed, after the story is over, that job discrimination is illegal and immoral. They are told also that it still exists and that we must do all we can to fight it. It doesn't hurt kids to learn young that eternal vigilance is the price of freedom.

A lesson I particularly like, and one that should be done every Feb. 15, involves reading the proceedings of the trial of Susan B. Anthony, the feminist who was arrested for voting in the presidential election of 1860. This lesson, although well received by my students, is probably better suited to older youngsters. I do feel, however, that they got the main point. I think everybody understood Anthony's feeling when she told the judge, "I shall never pay a dollar of this unjust penalty," and my students said, "Oh, good!" when I said that she stuck to her promise and never did pay that fine.

One of my favorite projects, and one that showed the class the power of direct action, was our evaluation of Hallmark's "What Girls Can Be" and "What Boys Can Be." While these two books are notorious to most feminists, it is unfortunately true that their bright colors and attractive pictures make them a "must-see" item for children. So I read these books orally.

The girls' book pictured a nurse, stewardess, ballerina, model, movie star, dress designer, nursery-school teacher, singer, secretary, artist, candy-store owner (the sole businesswoman), and ended with a frilly white bride, aproned housewife, and mother.

The boys' book went through fireman, baseball player, busdriver, policeman, cowboy, doctor, sailor, pilot, clown, zoo owner, farmer, TV actor, and the last two pages showed an astronaut and President of the United States. Quite a switch from the ending of the book for girls, isn't it?

We especially reacted to the last few pages. After noting that there is no bridegroom walking down the aisle, and that if that astronaut and President were married, we weren't told about it, my pupils were outraged. I heard cries of "Girls can be President!" "My doctor is a woman!" "Unfair books," and "Lousy writing." Finally, one child suggested we do something about it, and another answered, "Let's write to the author and tell him what we think!"

We did, and several weeks later we received a letter from Hallmark telling us that because of "some criticism" they were discontinuing production of the books and they had stopped shipping them to retail stores.

While there are many specific lessons that can and must be drawn up, and many materials already obtainable that must be compiled and organized into teachable units, there remains much more material to be produced. The "Miss Muffet Fights Back" booklist should be extended, and the Feminist Press can't carry the whole load. We need good books (text and trade), and it isn't going to happen overnight. It isn't going to happen unless we let publishers know that we won't buy sexist materials. (Like the old-time unionist said, you have to hit 'em where their heart is, in their pocketbook!)

Unfortunately, there seems to be a dearth of visual aids. I have yet to see a poster-sized picture of Susan B. Anthony, and while I was able to get a beautiful poster of Sojourner Truth, the well-known abolitionist and feminist, it was only because I happened to be in a small, out-of-the-way bookstore and saw it there. I am also unable to get big pictures of women doctors and dentists, suitable for wall or bulletin-board display along with a reminder to visit your doctor or dentist twice a year or whatever. Pictures of women doing jobs formerly done by men are sorely needed for display in elementary schoolrooms. It is our job to provide suitable role models.

The number of films and filmstrips on feminism is increasing, but there is nothing available for primary-grade students. Why is it that people invariably start at the wrong end of the curriculum? Common sense and research tell us that the best way to change opinions and attitudes is to work with the very young.

Children identify with like-sex characters, just as small girls identify with Mommy and small boys identify with Daddy. Schoolboys encounter plenty of active, intelligent problem-solving male role models. However, girls are all too often forced to identify with fearful Amys or Caddie Woodlawns who learn to give up their tomboyish ways, often the most admirable qualities they have, and to adjust to (just) being a girl. Or they identify with the Presidents' wives who, admirable women though they may be, gained fame mainly through their husbands' accomplishments. There aren't enough Pippi Longstockings, and the Carrie Nations and Elizabeth Blackwells are too often ignored or made to look ridiculous by male historians.

Identification and imitation are psychological processes that explain how people learn. Our girls and boys learn something besides phonics and comprehension skills when they read the available readers, and they learn something besides the Presidents' names and the important battles when they read American-history books. They learn that to be female in America is to be relatively unimportant. They learn that it is important for girls to look pretty, and to depend on the omnipresent, omnipotent male. They learn that they had better learn to like the way they look in an apron and that they might as well give up any ideas they might have once had about doing anything adventurous or dangerous, like being an astronaut or a member of a safari.

Feminism in education is more than material; it is a point of view and an attitude that permeates the entire curriculum and affects nearly every aspect of teacher–pupil behavior. It is giving a spelling test and making sure that the sentence examples you dictate are nonsexist and contain just as many references to girls as to boys. It is giving sentences that might destroy a few stereotypes. If the weekly list contains "dishes," let Father do them. If it contains "cake," let Brother bake it. If it contains "package," let Sister carry it into the house.

When devising worksheets, use nonsexist language. One vocabulary test I made this year had this sentence in it: "Father *hustled* after baby as she crawled toward the stairway." And I don't need to tell an elementary-school teacher what an obvious reversal this is. When I wrote some material for a unit on animal adaptation this winter, I was careful to refer to the animal as "it" rather than "he." It is surprising how frequently animals encountered in books are referred to as "he," unless of course, they are wearing an apron or hair ribbon!

Classroom duties should be carried out in nonsexist ways. Girls shouldn't be given housekeeping tasks more frequently and boys should not automatically be given the privilege of operating equipment or doing the "heavy work." (In third grade, girls are just as capable as boys of lifting and carrying.) And if anyone wants to give girls secretarial duties because their handwriting is "naturally neater," I invite them to try to decipher some of my girls' work!

One favorite practice that I am thinking of eliminating next year is the habit of lining up in sex-determined rows, although I am not sure this is so important.

Feminism must be taught, and caught, in the classroom. It must not be relegated to a two-week unit on women in history and then neglected the rest of the year. Eventually, a teacher will become so attuned to discrimination that his or her ears will perk up when he or she is confronted with any offensive material. The teacher will become adept at editing films, filmstrips, texts, or people, and so will the students. I have heard many reminders this year: "You mean 'she and he' not just 'he,' or 'people' not 'men.'" When I lapse, my students remind me. And this from a class that laughed in September when I made reference to a woman doctor, and said things like, "You mean nurse. Women can't be doctors!"

The other day, a teacher who had a hamster lost behind some pipes in her room was told to have a boy who's good in science go home and ask his father what would be an effective way to lure the animal out. Next time I hear a remark like this, I'll take a lesson from my students and say, "Hey, wait a minute!"

CHANGING THE SCHOOL ENVIRONMENT

When my then nine-year-old daughter announced two years ago that she wanted to raise horses when she grew up and would marry a rich man to finance the project, I realized that all those stories she had been reading about a girl and her horse were getting to her. She was modeling herself and her future on fictional and cultural projections of a woman's role, and the fact that I was a career-oriented Ph.D. candidate was not sufficient by itself to overcome the seduction of those images. I would have to do something to change her total environment and it would have to be done before the crucial years of adolescence when parental influence declines and peer-group influence increases. In order to avoid the psychological damage which would result from my making a decision about her future and attempting to impose it upon her, I decided to try to effect a substitution of more constructive images of women for the old images she was following.

The first step was helping her to see the fictional and relative nature of those images. So I began to watch television with her, discussing with her the one-sided picture of women it presents. We talked about the women we knew who were doing other things in life. I pointed out to her how different she was from some of the silly little girls we saw in situation comedies. I was helping her to develop a critical sense and to see the gap between fiction and her own potential. I could have prevented her from watching television in order to protect her from those stereotypes, but I would also have had to keep her home from school and keep her from reading books to protect her from them. We also began to examine her home and school reading material and to discuss the images of women presented in her books.

Note: By Dorin Schumacher. Reprinted with permission from *Women: a Journal of Liberation,* 1972, 2:4. Copyright © 1972 by *Women: A Journal of Liberation* (3028 Greenmount Avenue, Baltimore, Maryland 21218).

She began to complain about the sports program in her school and about the fact that there were organized activities for the boys but nothing for the girls. All the girls could do was to hang around the swings because the playing field was taken over by the boys' games. It became obvious that we had somehow to change the school environment too, and that this was going to be a much more difficult task. It would have been even more difficult, however, had the school in question been a public school. In our favor was the fact that her school was a university-related laboratory-demonstration school which prides itself on its "dedication to individual growth and development."

It is a small, attractive school which communicates a cheerful and friendly atmosphere. The children look happy and busy. It has about 250 students in kindergarten through ninth grades, most of whom come from white, middle-class, highly educated academic or professional families. Because it is associated with a university School of Education, it is heavily involved in the process of teacher education and influences a great many potential teachers and their future students. Many of its mostly male faculty teach in the university School of Education and many of them are working for graduate degrees there. Students from the School's degree programs do student teaching at the school and hundreds come each year to observe classes in progress. The teachers write their own curricula which they constantly revise.

Imagine my shock then when my first approaches to the school met with male supremacist responses. I asked for a discussion group on the school's role in motivating the girl students to be added to a PTA small discussion group meeting. The assistant principal was not interested and said so: "After all," he said, "this school already stands for individual development. There is no prejudice here. Besides, most parents would not want their daughters to have careers." He referred me to the PTA president, a recently divorced, Freudian-oriented professor of social work. It was predictable that he would take me for drinks to a dimly lit bar and say that he did not think the school should play a role in creating castrating females and that I should be careful about projecting my own neuroses onto my daughter.

When the discussion group finally came off, it was like the theater of the absurd. It was directed by a woman psychologist who stated that the research showed that women had less native intelligence than men; and one of the most active participants was a civil liberties lawyer who got into the group by mistake, but who stayed to argue for the preservation of cultural differences: Italians make better spaghetti, Blacks can run faster than Whites, and women are happy staying home and nurturing. The principal came in long enough to state, "There is no point in educating women; they all have the nesting instinct."

But my husband and I tried to stick to what little real evidence we had. He brought my daughter's school readers to the group and did an analysis of the sex-role stereotypes contained therein. One of them was titled *Deeds of Men,* and the other contained almost no stories about girls except for one in which an active girl was referred to as a tomboy. We also reported on the sports program and were able to say that we had personally observed the fact that no activities were provided for the girls and that we had made complaints to no avail. I cannot emphasize strongly enough how important it is to bring in solid evidence in situations like this, because the discussions can get bogged down in debates about the reliability of children's accounts and the question of parents' rights to make value judgments about what is good for their children.

The discussion was most productive, however, because it put us in contact with several parents who were already very much concerned about the general question of their daughters' full development, but who were not aware of the negative information which we presented. We did not have a great deal of evidence but what we had was reliable and impressive; it showed the other parents that changes should be made. After the discussion, the PTA president kept saying what a shame it was we had had such small participation and so little interest shown in the subject.

We then brought up the subject at a seventh-grade "Mothers' Meeting" (this was my son's class) and it threw the meeting into chaos. (Usually they are a bore.) Half the mothers turned on me and verbally attacked me and my ideas but listened to my husband when he made the same points. Husbands can be excellent allies in these situations, especially if you can get them to attend "Mothers' Meetings." The other half of the mothers were nodding vigorous assent. The teacher checked out his classroom library and found out that it was true that the adventure and discovery stories were about boys and love stories were about girls. But he told me that if I wanted them to be different I would have to write them myself. Some of the other mothers began to question the science-math teacher to find out if he was giving girls as much encouragement as he was giving boys. Naturally he said yes. But more support among parents had been identified.

We were still handicapped by a lack of access to the classroom to gather more and better evidence for the need for change. We needed to make more parents aware of the school's real expectations of its girl students to counteract its appealing propaganda about individual development and freedom. Our only hope at the time was to educate parents so they would bring pressure to bear on the school. And we were very much handicapped by the unavailability of good resource material to recommend to the school. So what followed that year was largely reactive on our part.

The principal of the school sent out an announcement of a PTA event which he dreamed up that consisted of having the "ladies" bring desserts wrapped in gaily decorated boxes to be auctioned off to the highest male bidder who could then, we were told, buy himself a harem. I began to fantasize filling a box with chicken bones or obscene messages, or staging a guerrilla theater action of parents parading around dressed in aprons, banging loudly on pots and pans with wooden spoons. Not surprisingly, no one was interested in fulfilling my fantasies so the demonstration never got off the ground. But the children were talking about it in school and it got back to the principal as an ominous and imminent occurrence.

He was sufficiently worried to invite me in to discuss my concerns. After a couple of hours of discussion during which he complained about a lack of professionalism among female public school teachers and blamed the problems of public education on women, and I spoke about the need to develop career motivation at an earlier age, he invited me to address the faculty and present my ideas to them. But I didn't want the school to get off that easily. I wanted to have a concrete program to present that would last beyond the two or three years that these teachers might teach at the school. I desperately needed resource materials to recommend and did not have the time to search for them.

The next thing that happened was that some of the teachers—the males—in the name of the "Faculty," challenged the fathers to play a basketball game to raise money for the school. I decided to do an action on my own to draw attention to the attitudes of the school administration and faculty, particularly as it was manifested in the sports program. I signed myself up for the father–teacher basketball game. When my team showed up for the practice meeting, I discovered that two of the fathers were professional football players and several of the others had played varsity basketball in college. I had played junior varsity basketball one year in high school: girls' rules of course. I did manage to make a basket during the practice session and no one was more surprised than I. The week of the big game I underwent a series of personal trials which included taking Ph.D. orals, receiving the news that my husband had been denied tenure but was having a site visit from a federal granting agency for a big grant request to fund his new research; and I got what felt like the flu.

But I played in the big game anyway, wiped out as I was. And my daughter was terrific. She came out and encouraged me saying, "Just try mommy; you don't have to get a basket, just try." Several of the mothers and girl students came up and said, "We know what you're trying to do and we think it's great. You've got a lot of guts." And I was wondering what the hell I was doing out there making a fool of myself and dealing with side issues. I never did learn men's basketball rules and I ran around the court feeling as though I was in a Kafka-esque world of confused and jumbled visual impressions where everyone understood what to do but me. But the next day at school my daughter played baseball with the boys for the first time.

At first they would not let her up to bat, but when she insisted she got up to bat and made a hit. And she has been getting better ever since. Last week she caught a pop-fly and put out my departmental chairman's son. And I never suggested directly that she should play organized sports. I showed her most of all that I was not afraid to go out and try something in an all-male environment that I was not sure I could succeed at—something I had never before allowed myself to do. It gave her the courage to try something she wanted very much to do but had been afraid to try. And she saw that just because something is labeled "For Men Only" it does not mean that women have to accept that definition and restriction.

Then the year was over. We still had not been able to get to the central place of organized instruction—the classroom and the classroom materials. But this year, I was invited by a new Black parent of a girl to be the discussion group leader at a PTA meeting on the topic of the school's role in preparing girls for roles in society. And when she invited me to do it, she said, "You know, sexism is just like racism; it's all around us and it's there in very subtle ways."

Our discussion group identified problem areas in school environment, and made recommendations for positive change: how it could be brought about and lists of resource materials to facilitate it. Resource materials were becoming available and we followed the models available in new courses for women in higher education. These recommendations started circulating and seemed to engender the respect that words on paper and bibliographies get in an academic environment. We presented them to the principal and the new PTA president. I let it be known in the course of the discussion that the university to which the school was related was under investigation by HEW for discrimination against women and that I considered the school to fall within the purview of that investigation. I also mentioned that I had been appointed to the council which had been established to advise the Chancellor of the University on these matters. This seemed to give us the muscle we had been looking for. We presented the following recommendations:

I. Sports Program:

That a sports program for girls be instituted.

That an integrated, that is for boys and girls playing together, sports program be instituted also.

That a special effort be made to teach individual competencies which may be used throughout an individual's active life.

That, if necessary to accomplish the above, a female sports teacher be hired. This teacher would not be hired to direct a sports program for girls but as an equal to team-teach both boys and girls. Hopefully, this would be a person who could provide such activities as creative dance for boys as well as girls.

II. Professional Women Speakers:

That a school policy be adopted of having professional women speak to the students about their work. There are many mothers of students in the school who are actively pursuing careers. Women doctors, lawyers, scientists, politicians, even ministers, would provide needed role models for girl students as well as provide an important picture of professional women to boy students.

III. Books:

That a committee be formed to seek out and examine books which provide constructive role models for girls and do not provide sex stereotypes of males or females. This committee will develop a bibliography of such books and will make recommendations for purchase for classroom libraries and for the school libraries. It will also send book lists to parents and request the purchase of recommended books for the school libraries. It will also make a study of books presently available in the school to identify those which present a particularly negative self-image to boy or girl students.

IV. History and Social Studies:

That an effort be begun to include women's achievements and contributions to history and culture in the history and social studies curricula.

V. Teaching of Literature and Talking About Stories:

That in discussions in the classrooms concerning stories and books which do present a one-sided picture of women and men (i.e., male characters actively doing, exploring, inventing, playing a variety of roles; female characters engaged in domestic tasks, human relationships, emotional expression), that the teachers discuss the one-sidedness of these pictures and help the students to explore other possibilities for individuals (intellectual achievement for women, emotional expressivity and involvement in human relationships for men).

VI. Music and the Arts:

While it is recognized that our cultural sex roles do not encourage aesthetic expression and appreciation in males, an effort must be made to continue to encourage girls in these activities. Open discussion about individual male and female contributions to the arts would enable students to feel comfortable with individual interests and capabilities which differ from predominant cultural expectations. Subtler kinds of encouragement of boys may be interpreted by the girls as discouragement. The committee recognizes the complexity of the situation and recommends open discussion whenever possible.

VII. Student Government:

It is hoped by the committee that some ways may be explored to facilitate and encourage the active participation by girls in leadership positions. One approach which the committee recommends is discussions before nominations, elections, etc., of leadership *qualities* which can be developed and learned by males and females alike; examples of women leaders provided; discussions of cultural expectations and how they can influence individuals' expectations of themselves.

The day after our committee meeting which drew up the recommendations, the sports teacher announced the inclusion of girls on intramural sports teams. The principal wrote to me stating a commitment to the education of female students and his intention of purchasing the recommended resource materials and circulating them among the teachers. The Program Director on the Board stated his intention of doing a PTA program on the subject of the education of women. We will be watching closely to ensure that as future teachers come to observe the school classes they will hear teachers and students discussing the accomplishments of women in history, in the professions, in life, and in self-fulfillment.

Next September, my daughter will be in seventh grade. Two years ago the sports teacher told me that girls get passive and unmotivated in junior high and there is "nothing you can do about it." But now there is hope for her and for all of us.

FEMINIST STUDIES: THE SCHOOLS AND SEX-ROLE STEREOTYPING

A teacher at a Boston junior high school has an unusual focus for her ancient history courses. In addition to providing the usual information about the lives of famous men, she also teaches about the lives of women and children. This approach identifies her as one of a small but growing number of teachers who are helping students question society's differential treatment of men and women. All of these teachers share the understanding that both women and men are detrimentally affected by the old assumption that men are superior to women. This understanding is the core of feminism.

By the very nature of the subject, feminist courses are interdisciplinary, problem-oriented, and personal. For example, in a Women in Society course in a suburban high school in Massachusetts, students use various frameworks to discuss the forces and institutions that affect women's lives. Is a woman's identity determined by her biology or her socialization? Are women oppressed? (If so, by whom or what?) Do women have a history and culture of their own?

Students in the course, including a few males, look at their own lives in order to understand the lives of women generally. They also look at the lives of others. Class discussions flow from assignments, such as conducting an in-depth interview of a female relative about her childhood or adolescence; reading fiction and autobiography about growing up (e.g., *Memories of a Catholic Girlhood,* by Mary McCarthy; *A Tree Grows in Brooklyn,* by Betty Smith; "Down with Childhood," in *The Dialectic of Sex,* by Shulamith Firestone; a story by Marge Piercy in *The Bold New Women,* edited by Barbara A. Wasserman); and by studying psychologi-

Note: By Carol Ahlum and Jackie Fralley. Reprinted with permission of the authors and *Today's Education,* December 1972, 61:9, 26.

cal, physiological, and anthropological information about adolescence (e.g., *Our Bodies, Ourselves,* New England Free Press, 791 Tremont St., Boston 02118; *How To Take the Worry Out of Being Close,* by M. and R. Gray, P.O. Box 822, Oakland, CA 94612; and *Sex and Temperament in Three Primitive Societies,* by Margaret Mead).

In the best feminist curriculum, the consideration of race and class is interwoven with the analysis of sex stereotyping. For example, at an urban high school in New Jersey a teacher presenting units on sex-role socialization plans assignments which show these interconnections. In her integrated class, a comparative analysis of the stereotyped images of men and women in the ads of *Life* and *Ebony* magazines led students to question why they held different images of women and men. This teacher runs her classroom like a laboratory. The class might separate into twos to discuss and tape-record feelings about women's liberation and then replay their conversations before the group. Or they might role-play or brainstorm.

The excitement of exploring untraveled ground characterized the History of Women course at a Wyoming high school last spring. The teacher was a man who became involved in a feminist curriculum because of his interest in incorporating current issues into his teaching of history. Using Eleanor Flexner's *Century of Struggle* as the text, he supplemented students' reading with brief primary source excerpts about the anthropological roots of sex-role differences and the status of women in earlier times.

In the spring of 1970, students at a high school on Long Island requested a course about women and asked a teacher (and feminist) and students from SUNY/College at Old Westbury to help them set it up. The Women in Society course, offered that fall, focused on consciousness-raising in which students talked about their own sex-role socialization and that of women and men generally. As the class progressed, students decided to produce a play to present their ideas to fellow students in the American history program. After each presentation of their musical skit, "You've Come a Long Way, Baby," the class conducted small-group workshops about the issues in the play.

Another skit, "Some of My Best Friends are Women," was produced the following semester, the second time the course was taught. Students performed the skit at a statewide conference on the social studies in March 1972. Here, too, they conducted a workshop-type discussion about the play, this time with 100 teachers, curriculum developers, and textbook editors.

Good feminist courses can't be copied; they grow out of the teacher's awareness of student needs and concerns. But a teacher who is interested in developing such a course can learn much by sharing the ideas and materials of those who have already developed this kind of curriculum.

The Clearinghouse on Women's Studies has published a list of high school feminist studies for teachers. The Feminist Press also has free materials available. The mailing address for both organizations is: SUNY/ College at Old Westbury, Old Westbury, N.Y. 11568. Other resource groups, which will send material if you enclose a large self-addressed, stamped, return envelope, include: KNOW Press, P.O. Box 86031, Pittsburgh 15221; and the Women's History Research Center, Inc. (which also asks for a donation) 2325 Oak St., Berkeley, CA 94708.

Resources for courses can be found in everyone's area. So hunt around for local feminist groups and ask them for advice and materials.

REALISTIC COUNSELING FOR HIGH SCHOOL GIRLS

Data distributed by the U.S. Department of Labor indicate that over half of today's high school girls will work full time for up to 30 years, and 90 percent of these girls will be employed for other significant periods of time. At present, women comprise 40 percent of the workforce in this country; 10 percent of the families in the United States are headed by women.

Women are, however, concentrated in jobs that pay poorly. According to census statistics in 1969, the median salary for women was $4,977 compared to $8,227 for men. Further, the unemployment rate for women is much higher than that for men. Forty percent or 1.8 million of the families with incomes below the poverty level were headed by women in 1970 (U.S. Department of Labor, 1970).[1]

Few high school girls seem to be aware of these facts. They are not, therefore, preparing seriously for positions that will enable them to earn a living and, in many cases, to support a family. Here is a problem with which the counselor and teacher need to be concerned as they work with high school girls during the years when important decisions are being made.

Origins of the Problem

Studies find that high school girls consistently have low aspiration levels compared to boys at this level. They are not motivated to achieve, largely because of their poor self-concepts. A statewide survey of California teenagers in 1968 found that in general girls had a negative self-

Note: By Iris M. Tiedt. Copyright © 1972 by the American Personnel and Guidance Association. Reprinted with permission from *The School Counselor,* May 1972, 19:5, 354–356.

image. Forty-two percent of the girls doubted that they could be successful. They saw marriage as having priority over a career and usually did not consider the possibility of both marriage and a career. Only one third planned to continue any kind of college course work. The researchers concluded: [2]

> The teenage survey revealed that today's girls are unaware that, married or not, most of them will be employed for many years, that many will never marry, that many will be widowed for many years, that probably 3 in 10 will be divorced, that more than 1 in 10 will be heads of families, that adequate and reliable child care at modest cost is in very short supply, and that if current childbearing trends continue, 40 potentially productive years of life will lie ahead after their youngest child is in school.

Girls from low socioeconomic backgrounds, furthermore, were even less certain about their potentials. Forty percent of the sample were unsure that they would complete high school. All of them planned, however, "to get married" after graduation, and none of them planned to continue their education after high school. Even more pessimistic is their expectation that they would be on welfare if something happened to their husbands.[3]

Through the socialization process the child learns from birth to differentiate behaviors appropriate to the sex roles. From early childhood little Jimmy knows that he will be an active member of the labor force of our country. When asked what he will be, he answers, "a pilot, a policeman, a farmer. . . ." He does not answer, "a daddy." By contrast, a small girl, playing with her dolls, almost surely will reply, "a mommy." [4]

Ginzberg and others [5] substantiate this attitude toward a career in their study of mature educated women:

> One of the striking differences that we found between our parallel investigations of the career development of men and women was that men followed a relatively simple and straightforward pattern compared with the much more complex career and life patterns characteristic of the majority of our women.

Cultural expectations tell a girl in many ways that she should marry and have a family. She is taught to be feminine—which is usually interpreted to mean passive, submissive, dependent, docile, and narcissistic (ref. note 4). She is conditioned not to be assertive and competitive and to consider herself intellectually inferior to men. To defy these expectations obviously requires an especially strong personality.

Few girls, furthermore, see models of women who are intelligent, attractive, and respected in their careers. Instead they observe well-dressed men in positions of responsibility as they make decisions and assume leadership roles. They see women more typically as housewives dependent on a husband's money and position. They come in contact with women teachers and librarians who have been frequently carica-tured. They know secretaries, beauticians, clerks, waitresses, and house-hold workers who hold the lower-paid jobs in society that require minimal training.

How Can the Counselor Help?

Our aim must be to improve the self-concept of girls as early as pos-sible. In order to be effective, the counselor's efforts should not be passive, but active; in other words, the counselor should not wait for girls to ask for help. They do not know that they need it. As we have pointed out, they are largely unaware of the problems that are involved.

The counselor needs first of all to be informed about the problems of young women, as well as about the problems of the mature woman that the girl will become. To operate best, furthermore, he must be she, for studies show that male counselors tend to provide male-oriented counsel-ing that is not in the best interests of women.[6]

Counseling in this case will involve much more than the one-to-one consultation. The counselor should experiment with varied approaches such as:

1. Developing a file of inexpensive materials for the counseling cen-ter or the school library, including items such as (a) *Mademoiselle*'s col-lege and career articles, (b) information about the National Organiza-tion for Women (NOW), and (c) careers in the Armed Services.

2. Helping girls form discussion groups about mutual problems, alternative futures, etc.

3. Speaking to classes of mixed sexes about the problems of women in our society, encouraging questions and discussion.

4. Inviting speakers to come to school to address large or small groups; for instance, a woman lawyer to provide a career model for girls, a member of NOW to discuss the work of this organization, a panel of women to discuss today's woman.

5. Brainstorming with teachers to discover ways of helping girls through daily contacts, books studied in the curriculum, classes offered, and so on, including the selection of texts that present real women, not stereotypes.

6. Publicizing opportunities available to girls—materials in the li-brary, interesting kinds of jobs, group meetings, speakers.

7. Recommending books for purchase by the library, including books about the feminist movement and equality for women such as *Born Female* by Caroline Bird (McKay), and good biographies such as *Eleanor and Franklin* by Joseph Lash (Norton).

8. Instigating curricular changes that permit girls to enroll in any vocational courses available in school; avoiding segregation by sexes as much as possible, considering, for example, how many courses in physical education can be coeducational.

9. Designing courses specifically to aid girls, particularly those in lower socioeconomic families; designing instruction to provide information that will help girls plan for a career, that will help motivate them to achieve and to consider themselves as individuals of considerable worth.

10. Subscribing to some of the newer publications for women, for example, *The Spokeswoman*—an independent monthly newsletter of women's news ($7 for individuals)—and *NOW Acts*—a monthly publication that covers issues and actions related to the equality movement ($5).

Counselors should also encourage girls themselves to work with any of the activities described. They will learn much and gain confidence as they develop a bibliography of books about women or make contacts by phone or letter to invite a speaker to come to the school. They will also have ideas about how the counselor can best help high school girls.

References

1. U.S. Department of Labor. Bureau of Labor Statistics. Washington, D.C.: U.S. Government Printing Office, December 1970.
2. ROBIN MORGAN (ed.), "High School Women: Three Views," in *Sisterhood Is Powerful* (New York: Random, 1970), p. 5.
3. Advisory Commission on the Status of Women, *California Women* (Sacramento: Author, Documents Section, 1971).
4. BOOCOCK, S. S., "A Funny Thing Happened on the Way to Maturity," *Association of American University Women Journal*, November 1971.
5. GINZBERG, E., et al. *Life Styles of Educated Women* (Columbia University, 1966), pp. 4–5.
6. CHESLER, P., "Men Drive Women Crazy," *Psychology Today*, July 1971.

Bibliography

TIEDT, I. M. Improving self-concepts of young women through English instruction. (Paper presented at California Association of Teachers of English Convention, San Francisco, February 1972.)

LET THEM ASPIRE!: A PLEA AND PROPOSAL FOR EQUALITY OF OPPORTUNITY FOR MALES AND FEMALES IN THE ANN ARBOR PUBLIC SCHOOLS— EXCERPTS

Removing Sexual Stereotypes

We feel, based on a number of interviews, that many educators (as well as the general public) regard girls by and large as somewhat helpless, mechanically inept, slightly frivolous, future homemakers. This can be borne out by the following types of comments made by high-placed people in our schools:

"I'd like to see a high school course in Household Maintenance for girls."

"What do you want to take *that* course for? You just want to be with the boys." (This is a principal talking to a female student.)

"I'm all for a course that teaches girls to wire lamps and things."

"When a girl signs up for Industrial Arts, we call her in to see how serious she is."

That these statements are simply reflections of societal prejudices and not proof of the inferiority of girls can be shown by the fact that women in many other countries function very effectively in roles other than housewife-mother. In Taiwan, women help build buildings; in Russia, women are skilled engineers, bricklayers, doctors, and technicians; in

Note: By the Committee to Eliminate Sexual Discrimination in the Public Schools, rev. ed. January 1973; further addenda April 1973. Reprinted with permission of Marcia Federbush, author.

127

France, women scale mountains with Alpine gear. In fact, during World War II in our own country, women built and flew the airplanes.

There is an increasingly vocal desire on the part of women nowadays —and there soon will be on the part of growing girls—not to be thought of as helpless. A way the schools can help erase this negative stereotyping so prevalent in our society, is to give girls as well as boys experience and encouragement from the earliest grades in the use of building equipment and tools. Girls must build with blocks and construction toys. They must put together models and gain a feeling of competence with tools and machines. Not to give them these privileges assures that they will grow up feeling helpless when confronted with mechanical situations. It also guarantees that women will continue to have more menial jobs than men with considerably lower pay.

Likewise, boys must learn to help themselves—to cook for themselves and to sew their own torn shirts. There may not always be someone else to perform these services for them. If we do not train both girls and boys to feel at home with household as well as mechanical skills, we are guaranteeing that women will continue to be dependent on men for technical help and men will continue to be dependent on women for household services. The emphasis on care of preschool children, now required of girls alone in home economics classes, would certainly be influential in helping boys realize that they, too, must someday share in the care of their children.

We would recommend, then, that at the elementary level girls and boys alike be called on to build, to sew, to cook, to solve mechanical problems, and so on. At the junior high school level, particularly in the seventh grade in which girls have traditionally been required to take a home economics course and boys an industrial arts course, we ask that Ann Arbor return in modified fashion to patterns used here many years ago, in which both boys and girls were required to study home economics and industrial arts. We would urge that the contents of these courses be redesigned to appeal greatly to students of both sexes, because these are areas which can provide a lifetime of enjoyment and usefulness.

Emphasis on Family Cooperation in Future Curriculum Guides

It is clear that there have been no sexual prerequisites for purely academic subjects, and yet high school boys and girls have only to thumb through the pages of electives open to them to know what directions their lives are expected to follow.

The current Curriculum Guide, which is about to be reprinted, describes all courses available to high school students. Of the 21 Home Economics courses offered, ten have a clear or obviously implied sex prerequisite. Others are presumably intended for girls, although the word has been omitted. At least six of the 21 courses lead girls directly toward a path of *homemaking* or *housekeeping*. Throughout the entire school system, there is no other battery of courses so completely tailored to groom a particular group of students for a specific adult career!

Such phrases as "man's role in the kitchen," and "their (girls') place in society," appear in the Home Economics section of the Guide. We ask that at both the high school and the junior high school levels, there be a drastic rethinking of the emphases in the home economics area. Since girls and women tend to do more than their share of the care of children, and since there tends to be a lack in American society of paternal involvement in the upbringing of young children, it is suggested that boys should be encouraged to take courses in child-care (till now required of all junior high school girls). Stress on personal grooming either should be required of both sexes or should be relegated to extracurricular club status, if included at all. When girls are encouraged to concentrate on their appearance, it is most often with the intent of making them marriageable. In addition, television and other media constantly bombard girls with the necessity of personal grooming for the sake of popularity.

More appropriate coeducational courses for today's society might deal with management of home life in families in which all adults are working, or cooperative family living, stressing the sharing of traditional roles.

Bachelor cooking versus cooking for the family

Next semester the high school course currently listed as Foods (Boys) will be labeled Bachelor Cooking (or a name similar to that). It will be open to boys who, we are told, want to learn efficient, quick, and enjoyable cooking techniques, without having to prepare full, family-style meals and to learn rules of etiquette taught in conjunction with girls' courses. Providing this special emphasis for boys assumes that they will not have to do the family cooking, while the emphasis for girls implies that girls will necessarily marry and devote time to complete meal service. We ask that this course be opened to girls whose interests in cooking are more casual than traditional concepts assume.

The course might also be labeled, "Cooking for Apartment Living," or "Cooking for One," or perhaps, "Cooking for Fun," as all cooking should be.

Sex prerequisites

From our interviews with administrators and counselors, we are quite under the impression that Dr. Westerman's directive to eliminate sex prerequisites for enrollment in courses will be difficult to attain, partly because of custom, and partly because of the inability of teachers and administrators (and parents and students) to recognize sexual discrimination when it occurs. For one thing, several of the upper schools seem to be having so many problems to contend with at the present time (such as split-shift arrangements and the maintenance of racial harmony) that they have not yet seriously begun to make provisions for the new policy. For another, some schools are proud of their "for boys only" or "for girls only" courses. Tappan Junior High School, for example, feels that it is doing girls a fine service by providing a course for them in Crafts, and Pioneer High School thinks that a separate course in Bachelor Cooking is what male students need. A third difficulty about which we caution the Administration to be on guard is the assumption on the part of school personnel that providing separate courses with the same name to boys and to girls is providing equal education. (This will be dealt with in the next section.) The fourth difficulty we foresee is that some courses have become so ingrained in the school program, that it will be very hard to adapt them to the new policy.

Will the emphasis on Clothing, Child Care, Personal Grooming, and Foods in junior high school Home Economics be changed somewhat in an attempt to reach boys, or will the sentence, "All girls are required to take one semester of this course in the seventh grade," simply be removed on the assumption that only girls will continue to sign up for it?

We recommend, then, that the Administration require all schools to detail plans for complying with Dr. Westerman's directive, with the aim of *attracting* both boys and girls to currently segregated programs. We ask, too, that high standards of compliance be set before judging the written proposals acceptable.

Clothing

Despite Dr. Westerman's directive to eliminate sex prerequisites for courses, there will apparently continue to be "Clothing" courses specifically for girls next semester (for example, in Scarlett Junior High School). It is argued that boys and girls become modest trying on the clothes they are making in front of each other. Since the schools are not offering clearly parallel courses for boys (making boys' clothes), then they should try to overcome this problem instead of excluding boys.

We feel that sewing programs should be expanded to include

courses in which some boys might definitely be interested, such as upholstery, interior decorating, clothes designing, and tailoring. After all, men do go into these fields, and the high school is the logical place for people to gain the skills they will later need.

We would also ask that the emphasis on "fashion" be minimized in clothing classes. This concept makes young women all too conscious of values which only emphasize vanity and superficial attractiveness. Practicality, usefulness, and awareness of good tailoring in clothing should be stressed instead. Stressing high fashion is also discriminatory against poor children who must make do with what they have.

If home economics classes place a value on having fashion shows as a culminating activity for sewing classes, then this value must apply to boys as well as to girls, and both sexes must be included.

Separate but equal

It is our impression that schools may wish to promote "separate but equal" classes for boys and girls as a way of adjusting to Dr. Westerman's directive, and we ask the Administration *not* to accept this as a means of ensuring educational equality. In racial matters, "separate but equal" facilities have always meant "separate but inferior" for the oppressed group. A great number of comments made by vice-principals, counselors, and teachers assure us that this has the same implications for boys and girls. The following are examples:

> "We *do* have a shop course for girls. They make crafts."
>
> "I want to start a boys' class in sewing so I can teach them how to take a sewing machine apart." (This teacher lets girls "piddle around unscrewing the pedal.")
>
> "I used to teach 'Physics for Girls.' We taught them how to put plugs together and wire toasters."
>
> "We had to separate that class so we could teach the girls the kinds of things they'd be interested in."

Certainly it should be the nature of education to broaden students' horizons and to elicit new interests. We feel that when teachers talk of "girls' interests," it is more frequently the teacher's assumption of what girls' interests should be.

To guarantee that girls make furniture in addition to crafts, learn electricity in addition to plug wiring, learn barbecuing as well as family meal planning, and so on, we insist that industrial arts and home economics courses, just as language courses, *all* be open to both sexes. If trying on clothes in a sewing class proves too embarrassing when both girls and boys are present, then unless there is a *clearly* comparable course for both sexes, provisions will have to be made to overcome this problem rather than to exclude boys.

Protective counseling

We ask that no extra counseling be given to girls signing up for courses traditionally reserved for boys (and likewise, for boys signing up for courses habitually considered female). Girls must not be asked why they want to "take a course like that." It must not be hinted that they are really only interested in being with boys. They must not be questioned as to their seriousness in wanting to take the course any more than boys are. When girls express an interest in industrial arts, counselors must avoid giving them protective warnings about having to tie their hair back and remove their jewelry. Regulations applicable to all members of the class should be given during the opening session or printed in the curriculum guide. At present, it is an act of courage for girls to sign up for these courses, and derisive, protective, and cautionary warnings only serve to frighten them away. Similarly, boys desiring to take any kind of home economics course must in no way be intimidated. Perhaps the most important aim of education should be to encourage boys and girls to have independent interests, which make them feel competent, secure, and happy. No student should be turned away from pursuing a desired course of study!

Unjustifiable excuses for omitting girls

In our various encounters with school-related personnel, we have come across the following justifications (among others) for keeping girls out of certain courses or activities:

"There's no place for a girl to take a shower."

"What about insurance? What if a girl fell off a 16-foot ladder?"

"Where would a girl go to the toilet?"

"But a girl would get her hair caught in the machinery."

"We can't let girls do metal work because they have to wear masks and work with sparks."

"The unions won't let them in, so why should we train girls for jobs they won't be able to get?"

"But boys have to swim nude!"

"If girls were in the class, we'd have to make crafts instead of real woodwork."

"The weights are too heavy for girls to carry."

"Girls aren't interested in that sort of thing."

"Girls wouldn't want to take off their jewelry and tie back their hair for that course."

"The millage didn't pass, so we couldn't let girls take Industrial Arts."

We submit that *none* of these reasons is valid.

If the room is not equipped with a shower, then one of the sexes will have to use the gym shower, wash with soap and water, or remain greasy. If teachers are worried about long hair, then long-haired girls (and boys) should be required to fasten it back in some way. (Teachers have never expressed to us their worry about boys with long hair.)

At any rate, no interested student, regardless of sex, color, weight, or any other physical feature, should be refused admittance into any course in which she (he) is interested. Changes may have to be made in conventional thinking patterns, but these will be necessary if our schools are to be humane to all students and are to bring out the best potential that each young person has to offer.

Biased teachers

We have frequently heard statements such as, "That teacher wouldn't be caught dead having a girl (or a boy) in his (or her) class." We have also heard of teachers demanding such exacting standards for students of one sex or the other in traditionally unisexed classes that the student has dropped out eventually. We insist in all such cases, if the teacher does not respond to administrative pressure to cease such behavior, that it be the teacher, not the student who is displaced from the course.

Practical nursing

Students in the Practical Nursing Program, which comes under Ann Arbor's Occupational Education Department's jurisdiction but caters mainly to high school graduates, complain of being rigidly stereotyped into outmoded sex roles in the expectations placed on them concerning conduct, dress, and answers on examinations. Separate roles for males and females and double standards of morality are said to be emphasized in some classes. "You didn't have to apply here if you didn't want to abide by our standards," is evidently the response given students who wish to assert any degree of individuality of judgment in their appearance. Male students must wear their hair shorter and female students must wear their skirts longer than is accepted practice among actual hospital personnel. Nurses in books are still always referred to as "she," although there is a movement afoot to replace this with "he," as in other subject area texts. Books should be used which refer to nurses as "she or he," or "he or she."

Since this Program comes under the School System's auspices, standards applying to other students with regard to personal comportment, clothing length, and hair style should apply here also. And since the program is covered by Title VII and Title VIII of the Public Health Service Act, care must be taken to ensure that sex discrimination in admission of students and against employees is prohibited. The Program should be reviewed for the overall uniform treatment of students.

Home building

Pioneer High School has recently initiated a home-building course under the sponsorship of local people in the building industry. This course is currently limited to boys. In this program, high school boys learn home-construction techniques and actually build a salable house, an accomplishment which should certainly be available to girls.

The two arguments given to us (as late as March 1971) for the exclusion of girls were:

(1) The unions will not admit women, so why should we train girls for jobs they won't be able to get.

(2) The sponsors will withdraw their money if we let girls take the course.

Until fairly recently, our schools were in no way encouraging Black students to enter apprenticeship programs because the trade unions would not admit Blacks. The same faulty rationale is now being used against girls. In effect the schools are saying, "The unions are behaving illegally and we will be accomplices in this." Schools *must* be forerunners in opening new avenues of pursuit to youngsters, even in untraditional areas. By saying, "We can't train girls because the unions won't let them in," school systems are helping to perpetuate sexual discrimination in the building trades indefinitely: Unions will only accept trained and qualified workers; women cannot receive training in schools (or anywhere else, for that matter); therefore, they will not be allowed to enter the unions. Fortunately, there are civil rights laws forbidding unions to discriminate on account of sex. Fortunately, too, there are civil rights laws forbidding places which train workers, as well as sponsors of such training programs, to discriminate on the basis of sex. Our schools receive some federal funds. In addition, the Vocational Education Department has applied for federal funds to supplement the home-building program. As recipients of federal money, the schools are most assuredly breaking the law in refusing admittance to girls in the home-building program.

In keeping girls out of this vocational program because they will not go into the field professionally, our schools seem to be assuming that all boys taking the course become home builders. They do not! A great goal of education should be to give students competence in a skill which will give them personal satisfaction for the rest of their lives. The schools should in no way refuse to educate those who cannot swear that they will base their entire future professions on a particular course of study. For girls (and boys) who will become architects, and for girls (and boys) who may wish to participate in building or remodeling a structure, as well as for girls (and boys) who may wish to go into the building trades, the home-building course is vital.

The second argument above (that of the course's sponsors' withdrawing their money if girls are admitted) is certainly immoral. The school experience must be for the benefit only of the students. No benefactor, industry, or pressure group should be permitted to dictate which students are to be restricted from qualifying for a course. If this policy is not clearly spelled out, then any group wishing to donate money to the schools for a special course might choose which students are to be ineligible to benefit from it.

We have been in close contact with the Michigan Civil Rights Commission. They have suggested that we bring a suit against the building trades for excluding women, against the sponsoring group for financing a discriminatory course, and against the Ann Arbor Public Schools for refusing to train female students. We have chosen the following course of action:

1. We are negotiating the initial stages of a suit against the building trades through the Civil Rights Commission in Detroit. We have also requested and received a letter from the business manager of one of the construction unions to the effect that the building trades will not discriminate on the basis of sex. Copies of this letter have been sent to appropriate school personnel. Excluding women from union membership is clearly in violation of the Michigan Fair Employment Practices Act.

2. We have asked the chairman of the board of sponsors of the course to request from his committee a ruling that girls will be admitted to the course under the same conditions as boys. The committee voted to accept qualified female students, provided that they receive no special considerations.

3. We are not eager to sue the schools. We insist, however, that they join the two above groups in announcing that the home-building course will be unreservedly available to qualifying girls. For them not to do so is in violation of the Fair Employment Practices Act.

New building design

We are confident that the schools are serious in their desire to eliminate sexual discrimination. If this is true, then this decision must have far-reaching consequences.

Since we have been told repeatedly that it is unfeasible for girls to take certain industrial arts classes because there is no place for them to shower afterwards, it will be necessary for the Board to insist that plans for new buildings include facilities for both boys and girls. Home economics classes, too, must have changing rooms for both sexes, if embarrassment when trying on clothes is a legitimate reason for keeping boys out.

We ask the Board, also, to ensure that future schools *not* be built with one high-ceilinged gym and one low-ceilinged. In order for a great many students of both sexes to be able to participate in sports, it will be necessary to build all gyms, large and small, with high ceilings to accommodate such activities as basketball and volleyball.

Foreword to the Athletics Section

Since this report was written, a number of significant changes have been made which will affect school athletics throughout Michigan. Senate Bill 1106, which would allow girls to play on noncontact teams with boys, passed the Legislature and is now Act Number 138 of the Public Acts of 1972. (This law may be illegal from the beginning in its restricting girls to noncontact sports.) Also, in court action on behalf of two young women tennis players of Ann Arbor, games can no longer be forfeited because girls are on teams. The Federal Judge hearing the case felt, in addition, that it was depriving female students of equal opportunity to forbid them to play in contact sports. The regulations of the MHSAA (Michigan High School Athletic Association) have therefore been changed so that girls may now play on teams with boys, and males may coach female students. The generally overprotective regulations for girls are now called "recommendations" in the Association's new recognition of the possible existence of sexually discriminatory policies (which it will not admit publicly). The recommendations are still there, however (with minor changes), as a warning of how the MHSAA would prefer girls' athletics to operate. The Ann Arbor School Board, in the fall of 1972, voted to join the Association for one year only on condition that it rid itself of practices and policies which make for discrimination based on race and on sex. The Board appointed a committee to help carry this out.

Meanwhile, a new federal law has been passed essentially forbidding sex discrimination in the schools. It is Title IX of the Education Amendments of 1972. It reads, "No person in the U.S. shall on the basis of sex be excluded from participation in, be denied the benefits of, or be subjected to discrimination under any education program receiving Federal financial assistance." The guidelines to Title IX include sex discrimination in athletics in publicly funded schools within the coverage of the law. They require that physical education classes, as other classes, be coeducational, and spell out that "Instruction, training, coaching, facilities, equipment, and opportunities to practice and compete in the same or similar athletic activities must be provided equally to students of both sexes in terms of both quantity and quality." Male and female coaches of the same-named activity must also be paid the same incremental wages. In short, Title IX asks essentially that female and male athletics be funded equally. But this is not the only law which must be considered in making a case for equal opportunity in athletics.

The old Brown Decision of 1954, which attempted to desegregate schools racially, said, "In the field of education, the doctrine of 'separate but equal' has no place."

And now, people are beginning to include "sex" as one of the categories deserving "equal educational opportunity," the phrase derived from the 14th Amendment's Equal Protection of the Laws clause.

The coming (!) Equal Rights Amendment specifies, "Equality of rights under the law shall not be denied or abridged by the United States or by any State on account of sex," and this includes the right of students of both sexes to participate equally in programs offered by a school. Basically, it asks that the same laws apply to all people, without bias.

The Equal Pay Act and the Equal Employment Opportunities Act forbid discrimination in employment and in pay for employees on account of sex. New York passed a law in 1971, and a few other states have followed suit, saying that no person may be excluded from courses of instruction or from athletic teams by reason of sex.

Although school systems have been remiss in following these laws, particularly in regard to athletics, it looks as if the handwriting is on the wall: they now have no option *but* to provide equal opportunity in athletics as well as in other areas. Filing a complaint is as easy as writing a letter to the Office for Civil Rights in Washington.

But how can school systems provide equal and not separate programs when there are actual or societally created average differences in such parameters as height, weight, strength, and speed between the sexes? Many critics rightly assert that the new legislation to establish coed teams will give only the one or two top female athletes in many sports the chance to participate in interscholastic team competition. Even where individual skill counts, as in track or in swimming, the best girl would rarely be able to break the record of the best boy. This would further discriminate against female students. We are left, then, with a tricky philosophical problem of providing a program that will be healthy physically, psychologically, and morally for students of both sexes, will take into account actual differences in ability level between the sexes, will provide equal opportunity for *all* students in the public schools, and will provide a unitary guiding system of values for female and male students. If a practice is considered harmful to one sex, can it really be so good for the other?

A good solution to the problem will have to take into account a number of factors and must satisfy a number of conditions.

1. The solution must be workable in the near future and must not be unattainably complicated.

2. It must not get rid of the best aspects of existing male and female sports, but on the other hand *must* eliminate the most detrimental of each. For example, female athletics usually do not turn away any interested student. Male students certainly deserve this right. And current male athletics tend to place an exaggerated emphasis on aggressive competition which, evidence indicates, may serve to bring out the hostilities rather than the cooperative tendencies of young people. A good program should lessen this syndrome in order to be healthy for both sexes.

3. It must recognize that parents of female children pay as much in school taxes as parents of male children (or more, since girls outnumber boys) and are entitled to equal expenditures on their behalf.

4. The solution must seek to ensure that students of varying athletic ability levels, from the highly skilled to the relatively inept, will be able to find satisfactory athletic activities of choice. All are children of the public, and all deserve equally the benefits of education—the chance to gain interests and skills that will be personally rewarding throughout life.

5. It must allow girls to enjoy the opportunity for full encouragement, training, competition, excitement, publicity, and physical activity which they have been denied for so long. This is particularly crucial at a time when a chief problem in city high schools and junior highs is "tough girls" and "girl gangs."

6. It must be recognized that although interscholastic athletic activities are engaged in voluntarily, they are financed mainly by public

funds and are conducted in the name of the public schools. They must therefore provide equality of opportunity for both sexes.

7. The solution must take into account the fact that students as a group nowadays seem to be less interested in intense competition in many areas of life than they were some years ago. Personal satisfaction, competence, cooperation, and enjoyment seem to be the goals of many young people. On their own and in "lifetime sports" gym classes, they are happily engaging in athletic activities with members of the other sex.

8. The solution must not permit students to be turned away from activities and programs in which they are interested and potentially capable, by virtue of their sex.

9. It must seek first to resolve the inequities in athletics before putting athletic and nonathletic activities on a par and allowing students to choose a certain equivalent expenditure of extracurricular activities (as is done in some California cities).

Need we emphasize that these goals will not easily be attained? But by using some ingenuity, school systems should be able to come up with equitable solutions. Perhaps we should say that they *must* come up with equitable solutions—or else the law will be brought in.

Basically these solutions will have to aim for new kinds of athletic programs based on interest and ability, enthusiasm and enjoyment, or on some sort of physical ratios, rather than on the sex of the participants. Using these criteria, we would end up with various assortments of predominantly male teams, strictly coed teams, and predominantly female teams, all given the opportunity to compete interscholastically and pleasurably with comparable teams. This seems also to be the direction in which many students' thoughts are headed. A workable solution will realistically have to allow for average real (and possibly some assumed) differences between the sexes in such parameters as height, weight, strength, and speed.

In some California towns, two methods are being used to attack the problem in school and in recreational athletics. There are some teams set up solely by age brackets for children, young adults, and older adults, with several categories in each. In some other athletic programs, there are a certain number of spots designated for females and a certain number for males. Basketball teams, for example, may have two spots reserved for young women. There is also a height criterion. Any given team is allowed only a certain total height of all members additively. Therefore, if there is one person more than six feet tall, there must also be one about five feet tall. These programs are said to be working successfully.

The Ann Arbor Recreation Department is now required by city

ordinance to open all of its activities to people of both sexes. If an activity
is offered which caters predominantly to one sex, it must be counter-
balanced by one geared mainly to the other.

The public junior and senior high schools in Michigan and in most
other states have a long tradition of highly competitive, male interscholastic sports, tightly controlled by the male-oriented State High School
Athletic Association. When the high schools in Michigan held their basketball playoffs for about a month in the spring of 1972, it was as though
there were not a female student in the schools of Michigan. In order to
offset this and to provide a philosophically as well as a practically sound
and equitable athletic program for both females and males in Michigan
schools, we would recommend the following solution to the athletic
dilemma. It could serve at least temporarily, until such a time when teams
are completely based on criteria other than sex.

This solution was presented to the Ann Arbor Board of Education in
April 1973 by Marcia Federbush of our Ann Arbor Committee to Eliminate Sex Discrimination in the Public Schools. It is called the *components
approach* and represents what we feel is a more legal and more workable
approach than what other groups are currently advocating. We must
emphasize that in publicly funded education, there is no room for a doctrine of "separate but equal," which almost invariably ends up "separate
and vastly unequal" for the more oppressed group. As needed variations
are made in perfecting the wording of this approach, they will be included in future editions of *Let Them Aspire*.

(1) Before anything else, we must make a firm commitment
to equal opportunity and to adherence to Title IX by specifying
that *no student may be excluded from a team or an athletic activity
because of his or her sex*. We can't legally limit girls to only noncontact sports. New York has a State law which may surprise you. It
reads, "No person shall be disqualified from state public and high
school athletic teams by reason of that person's sex, except pursuant
to regulations promulgated by the commissioner of education." I'm
going to define *team* in such a way as to make this easier to accept,
but we must bear in mind that equal opportunity in publicly funded
education means that each student will be able to benefit from
activities available to other students.

(2) Each team, sport, or category will consist of the male
and the female participants in that sport, in one or a variety of
arrangements, *from essentially sex-separated to completely sex-
integrated*. Teams such as Basketball, Gymnastics, Track, Golf,
Tennis, Skiing, Volleyball, and a number of other activities which
historically have appealed to—and have been considered acceptable

for—both sexes, then, will represent both the males and females in the sport. We will call a single activity category a "Team" whenever possible.

(3) Where sports exist which traditionally attract preponderantly one sex over another, the sports will be grouped into clusters of related activities, such as *Football-Flag Football-Touch Football; Hockey-Field Hockey-Soccer; Baseball-Softball; Wrestling-Judo-Karate;* and so on, so that components catering to males and to females will be represented within a cluster. These multi-sports groupings we will refer to as "Clusters."

(4) Male and female coaches within a Team or a Cluster, in consultation with students, together shall coordinate, supervise, and budget for activities for men and women students equitably, ensuring that a common set of values, policies, and regulations for practice and participation applies to both sexes, and that balanced predominantly sex-separated or strictly coeducational opportunities for both sexes exist within the category. Coaches of both sexes shall be paid the same salary for the same activity. Both male and female coaches shall be qualified insofar as possible to assist with the coaching of students of both sexes within a Team or a Cluster; and women and men coaches shall cooperate in the coaching, training, and accompanying of female and male students engaging in team sports. Coaches in public schools, as other teachers who come in contact with youth, must be able to teach students of both sexes and to deal with them humanely, equitably, wisely, and reliably.

(5) Each Team or Cluster will be composed of "Components," which may be essentially male, essentially female, predominantly male, predominantly female, strictly coeducational, interscholastic, intramural, or limitedly extramural. Attempts will be made, within each team or cluster, to create components which are coeducational and based on factors such as ability, height, interest in participation, and so on. Students may be assigned by sex when this factor is necessary to create components with equal representation of the two sexes. If our schools decide to separate Interscholastic Athletics from Intramural and Limited Extramural Athletics, Teams will also be organized across sexual lines, representing both males and females equitably within the sport, either in strictly coeducational or in predominantly one-sexed components.

(6) Teams which compete interscholastically in sports in which females as well as males regularly participate shall be represented in contests with other schools either by one highly coeducational component or by an essentially male component and an essentially female component together contributing toward the success and the score of the team. Interscholastic competition shall

be arranged in such a way that, whenever possible, male and female athletes represent the team in a day's competition. For example, in the absence of strictly coeducational components, the male varsity basketball component and the female varsity basketball component, or the female gymnastics component and the male gymnastics component will represent the Team as a meet. So that the component of one sex will not be featured more prominently at a meet, the component to play first will be determined either by the toss of a coin or in prearranged fashion.

(7) In cases in which a Cluster component basically of one sex—for which there is no direct counterpart for the other sex—competes in interscholastic athletics, it will be ascertained that a comparable component consisting chiefly of members of the other sex will also have the opportunity to compete interscholastically. This is the case, for example, where women students tend to play field hockey, and male students ice hockey. Within each Cluster, attempts should be made to provide an activity appealing to members of both sexes. If a school wishes to maintain a sport which attracts a great deal of attention for one sex, such as football, then endeavors should be made to build a sport gaining competency and recognition for the other sex.

(8) Where females and males play interscholastically within the same sport, their seasons of play will coincide so that components of both sexes can represent their school together. They will therefore have equal use of facilities and equipment. Intramural, limitedly extramural, or other components of *both sexes* may participate in seasonal sports outside of the regular season.

(9) Participating schools will inform other schools with which they play that their girls' as well as their boys' components, or their coeducational component, will appear at competitions in such activities as basketball, track, swimming, gymnastics, tennis, golf, and volleyball, and that arrangements must be made accordingly for fair competition. Schools will only play with teams and join leagues that will welcome students of both sexes to participate in competition. Attempts will be made to arrange league and interscholastic games within reasonable access to the school's students.

(10) In order to build an equal opportunity, coeducational athletic program, when this concept tends to be relatively foreign to Michigan interscholastic athletics, intramural, limitedly extramural, and new interscholastic programs will attempt to offer coaching and team play opportunities on a coeducational basis using any of a variety of methods of grouping students. An eventual interscholastic athletics program should be an outgrowth of a fine physical education or intramural program.

(11) The athletic program will be led by co-directors, male and female, paid the same salary and receiving the same benefits. The two directors will cooperate in organizing and coordinating the predominantly male, predominantly female, and truly coeducational components into an effective and sound athletic program for all students.

(12) A team, or a component of a team, may be considered a predominantly girls' team or a predominantly boys' team if it contains up to 15 percent of members of the opposite sex. If the number of qualifying students of the opposite sex seeking team membership exceeds 15 percent of the total of qualifying students seeking team membership, the school must establish in that sport an additional coeducational team and/or one composed predominantly of members of the opposite sex.

We ask school systems everywhere to recognize the inevitability and reasonableness of this approach in publicly funded, coeducational educational institutions, and to work toward its implementation so that both sexes receive the full measure of equal opportunity they deserve.

The athletic program

The Michigan High School Athletic Association governs the interscholastic athletic activities of all high schools and junior highs in the state. There are about 223 Representative Council and Committee positions governing all facets of the Association. Of these, *seven* women comprise the Girls Athletics Advisory Committee. *All other office holders regulating high school and junior high school athletics in Michigan are men.* Included among the sports represented by men alone are swimming, basketball, track and field, tennis, golf, and gymnastics, all of which everyone would agree should be open to women. There are also a variety of committees dealing with other phases of the Association's activities, not one of which includes a woman. This indicates without a doubt that no attempt has been made to attain female competence in interscholastic athletics in the schools of Michigan.

Included in the handbook of the Michigan High School Athletic Association are clearly prejudicial rules which pertain exclusively to girls. These have been created by the Girls Athletic Advisory Committee, some of them fairly recently. They severely handicap fine girl athletes interested in competition. Girls cannot benefit from the coaching available to boys (all girls' teams must be coached by women), and they cannot play on teams including boys. They must therefore join outside organizations, such as the Amateur Athletic Union (AAU) and pay fees for coaches, for pool time, for busing, and for entrance to competitions.

We have informed Marilyn Jean Kelly and Annetta Miller, the two women members of the State Board of Education, of these inequities, and they have called for a complete report from the Michigan High School Athletic Association. If the Board of Education does not revise its rulings which affect high school girls throughout the state, a prominent University professor and some of his students are willing to sue on behalf of an outstanding 16-year-old female tennis player in an Ann Arbor high school. Because she has not been able to be coached by her school's tennis coach (a male) and has not been able to play on teams with boys (although she is more capable than the male tennis players), she has had to be coached expensively outside the schools. She has also had to pay for entrance and busing fees to competitive games.

Our point in bringing this to the attention of the Ann Arbor Board of Education is that the Ann Arbor schools by and large follow the restrictions of the MHSAA in regard to girls' athletics. There is an *enormous* disparity between the interscholastic athletic programs for boys and girls in our schools.

We would like to see the Ann Arbor schools strive for an athletic program which would provide every school child with some activity meaningful for him or her personally, without regard to prejudicial state rulings or to antiquated philosophies that prevent girls from functioning effectively.

Coaches

Coaches and assistant coaches are generally members of the regular teaching staff who devote extracurricular time to coaching sports. Although this list includes tennis, golf, track, gymnastics, swimming, and basketball, sports in which girls traditionally compete, none of these coaches is available to girls. (One would think that girls might at least rate the use of the tennis coach, since tennis was first introduced to America by Mary Ewing Outerbridge in 1874.) Since the Michigan High School Athletics Association specifies that women must coach girls and that girls may not be on teams with boys, and since the Ann Arbor schools are not likely to hire a female coach especially for a limited number of girls, it seems that girls may not benefit from the services of these coaches. No girl, no matter how extraordinary, is known ever to have benefitted from the athletic trainer, who receives 30 percent above base pay.

Who coaches girls? The "Girls Athletic Club" in a school includes the two or three women gym teachers in that school. These women, who receive 11 percent above base pay, coach all the girls' sports, with the exception of an occasional extra teacher or college student who helps out.

Assuming that the two Ann Arbor high schools have all of the usual male coaches, the percentages above base or contract salary add up to 304 percent per high school, or 608 percent for the two high schools, an equivalent of six salaries. Assuming that there are two female teachers in each high school who run the entire extracurricular athletic program for girls, each receiving 11 percent above base, then the four of them earn a total of 44 percent of a salary. The Cheerleaders' coach—who helps girls to spur on boys' sports—receives 14 percent above base. (Coaching the cheerleaders is actually a very time-consuming job.) If the coaching salaries for Modern Dance (which may include some boys), Cheerleaders, Aquaneers, and Girls Athletic Club are added, allowing two of these last in each school, girls' athletic coaches in the two high schools receive altogether a total of 88 percent of one salary.

There are a few ways to remedy this situation and to make it more equitable to both sexes:

Since the state rules do not specify that boys must be coached by men, women can be sought to coach as many teams as possible. This would permit girls who desired it to receive specialized coaching along with the boys. They would still be unable to play on coed teams, however. There have actually been at least two cases in which extraordinary women athletes, a tennis player and a golfer, have been denied positions in the Ann Arbor school system, although they would have been superb teachers and coaches, and would certainly have upgraded the programs for girls. (Both had no trouble finding positions in local universities.)

The junior high school coaches are paid on a percentage basis, as are the male coaches in the high schools. The football, basketball, and wrestling coaches are paid a higher percentage than any of the girls' coaches, but the differences are not extraordinary. (Although it appears that junior high school girls and boys have the same access to coaching, it must be pointed out that each of the junior highs provides girls with only a limited number of sports, while most of the activities are available to boys in each school. There is no junior high school girls' gymnastics, for example.) Women coaches for high school girls might also request a percentage above salary for each sport coached. (It is not clear why they have not done this.)

A suggestion which would benefit fine girl athletes would be for the school system to break the rules of the MHSAA and to permit girls who wish to receive specialized coaching in such fields as track, gymnastics, swimming, golf, and tennis, to be coached and to play along with the boys. Two of our four junior high schools already have male coaches for girls' teams, which means that some rules are already being broken. As mentioned previously, the rules are clearly prejudicial and are being reviewed by the State Board of Education. The Ann Arbor Board of Education should certainly join in insisting that the MHSAA make its rules undiscriminatory.

Meanwhile, the incoming president of the Ann Arbor Education Association has promised that the inequities in the pay for male and female coaches and in the variety of coaching offered to boys and to girls will be studied and changed. We are aware that some alterations are now in progress. We ask the Board not to sign a contract with the AAEA until such drastic inequalities are resolved. We also ask the Board to issue a statement that would permit girls to be coached by men and to play on teams with boys when no comparable athletic activity is available to them. If this means that boys will have to wear swim suits (now provided or rented by the schools to girls), then this is just one of the prices that will have to be paid for providing quality, equal educational opportunity for boys and for girls. (Physical education classes during school hours now are coeducational and stress Life Sports.) Paying for elementary school coaching might be studied.

We must ensure that girls who are extraordinary athletes and who wish to pursue sports careers professionally (they pay very well) and avocationally may receive their training and the use of facilities through the schools. These privileges are accorded to boys. Girls should not have to spend great sums to receive their training and competitive experience elsewhere. As mentioned earlier, a law professor and his students are interested in bringing suit to ensure that girls will have access to the best athletic opportunities the schools can offer.

A final alternative would be for the schools to drastically cut the emphasis on the boys' interscholastic program!

Athletic budget

In last year's Annual Financial Report, the expenditures for high school activities are listed. All of the boys' sports for which coaches are provided are itemized. If the disbursements for all of them in the two high schools are totaled, it becomes evident that $68,025 was spent on boys' interscholastic athletics last year, *not including coaching salaries.* (There are items in the budget, such as Six A League and South Central League, which we assume to be boys' activities, but which we have not included in our addition.) If the expenditures for girls' athletic activities are summed, it will be found that the figures for the two schools total $6,296, not including coaching. *Last year, Ann Arbor spent more than 10 times as much money for boys' athletics as for girls'.* At the junior high school level, only Slauson School itemized its Boys Athletics and Girls Athletics, $1,399 for boys versus $190 for girls (plus an incredible $752 for girls' swim suits). Thus the extreme imbalance also extends down to the junior high schools. Women junior high school gym teachers tell us also that great sums are spent on boys' football, which are not itemized in the budget.

School officials concerned with the budget tell us that high school football brings in such large receipts that the sport has paid off the cost of a stadium. They imply that because boys' sports bring in so much money, a greater expenditure is justified. A moment's reflection should reveal that it is the amount *expended* on a pupil which indicates the school's concern, not the amount received. Public schools are not supposed to be profitmaking institutions. If a sport is able to raise money for the schools, so much the better. But the receipt of money must not be used as a rationalization for the huge imbalances in the expenditures between girls and boys. It is not the fault of girls that in our culture nothing they do can draw the audiences attracted to male sports. Our schools, however, might take a look at Iowa. There, girls' basketball is a successful, moneymaking venture, providing far more interest and revenue than boys' basketball. Our schools, however, would have to change their negative attitude toward girls' spectator sports to institute such a program.

We insist that the Ann Arbor Board of Education review the huge disparity between boys' and girls' athletic financing, and either lessen one or heighten the other. Girls must be provided with the serious opportunity to enjoy, to participate in, and to excel at sports, even to aim for Olympic competition if they wish. At present, it seems that an extraordinary amount of money is being spent to benefit a limited number of students.

Extracurricular activities with credit; scholarships

Until very recently, boys were able to receive school credits for participating in football, wrestling, tennis, cross-country, swimming, baseball, basketball, golf, track, gymnastics, and hockey instead of gym. This list coincides with the list for which coaches and funding are provided. There are no girls' activities listed for credit. We are told that this has been changed, but certainly not because it was unfair to girls.

It has also been pointed out to us by a female high school student that boys have another advantage over girls: they may receive athletic scholarships.

Removing junior high school gym teachers

It may be of interest to the Board of Education that last year each junior high school had three male and three female gym teachers. This year, with the necessity of saving money, one physical education teacher was cut from each school, *none of them male.* This means that two women teachers now must do the work that three did last year. (One school has a third part-time teacher.) To quote one highly experienced teacher, "I can't give the girls any more than I'm doing now. I'm too tired." It is obviously the girl students who will suffer from this willingness to cut back on female staff exclusively.

We ask that the Board search for a way to relieve this clear-cut imbalance, possibly by seeking competent university students to coach girls in some of the sports now denied them. We ask, too, that in the future, if a similar situation arises, the Administration take meticulous care not to eliminate teachers serving one sex in greater proportion than teachers serving the other.

Junior high school required gym

In order to encourage girls to learn the excitement, the personal skill, and the formal rules of team and individual sports, it would be preferable for girls to have their required semester of physical education in the seventh grade when they first enter junior high school, rather than in the ninth grade as has now been proposed by the Administration. By the time they are in the ninth grade, it may be too late to alter unfortunate habits and attitudes against athletic activities. The junior high school gym teachers have recommended that girls be given one required semester of daily gym in the seventh grade and one semester during the alternate season of the eighth grade to provide the necessary skills and inspiration from the beginning. At the seventh-grade level, they say, girls' bones and muscles and attitudes are more flexible than at the later time.

We ask the Board to find a means of honoring these teachers' wishes.

Bathing caps

If girls are required to wear bathing caps in these days of "unisex" hair styles, then there is no conceivable reason for boys not to wear them also. Or, on the other hand, if boys are not required to wear caps, then girls must be permitted to go without them as well.

An announcement to swimmers must be made to this effect.

Culminating day

When one thinks of interscholastic sports, one pictures teams from various schools regularly playing those from other schools in the same category, until one team accumulates the greatest number of victories. If a team builds up enthusiasm to win a certain game and then loses, the members feel greatly let down, but then they can always hope to win the next game. This also allows (hopefully) a large number of students to participate in different games. Not so for junior high school girls in Ann Arbor.

At the end of a season's practice in a sport, there is a single culminating day, in which selected eighth- and ninth-grade teams from each school compete with similar teams from other schools. (There are two interscholastic game days in basketball now.) An entire season of a sport culminates in one or two games, in which only a few chosen girls may take part. It is small wonder that the win or loss of that game takes on exaggerated emotional significance (refusal to shake hands, accusations of cheating, etc.) in the lives of some of the girls. When girls ask, "Why can't we compete with other schools the way boys do," the answer tends to be, "We haven't the facilities, the busing, or the staff." There has always been a feeling in our schools that young, teen-aged girls are delicate and need to be protected. It has been felt that they should not be too competitive or play in spectator sports. One look at junior high school girls today should convince an observer that they, as well as boys, need constructive outlets for their competitive tendencies. Ann Arbor has had girl athletes of Olympic caliber who have received no help from our schools. They have not been able to receive coaching (from a male) or play on a coed team or compete with other schools.

We ask the Board of Education to ascertain that junior and senior high school girls will have the same accessibility to a well-rounded interscholastic sports program as boys have. It is somewhat ironic that while we are fighting for the state's athletic rules to permit junior high school girls as well as boys to be able to play in ten games of interscholastic basketball instead of only five, junior high school girls in Ann Arbor may participate in only one or two.

Gentlemen first

We have been told by junior high school gym teachers that at the beginning of the school year, the proposed calendar for the boys' athletic program is sent to the Administration and approved. After this, the schedule for girls' sports is fitted around the boys' program with regard to the scheduling of interscholastic games and the use of pools, gyms, and equipment. Women in physical education have become accustomed to second-rate treatment and have probably not complained about this before. The girls apparently do receive approximately equal usage of the facilities, although the number of female participants is smaller than that of male, but they are granted this usage generally out of season.

We ask that boys and girls equally be provided with encouragement, aspiration, and opportunity to explore the excitement of team and individual sports, particularly at the junior high school level when students, by and large, are just being introduced to the athletic programs of the schools. It is not necessary to throw boys directly into a highly competitive, seasonal schedule, while letting girls practice and play only when it is convenient.

Football

It has been brought to our attention that the junior high school boys' football program seems to be subsidized out of proportion with respect to girls' athletic programs. While women gym teachers in some schools have been begging for years for new mats, new fans, and other equipment, the boys' football teams seem always to receive whatever they request, from busing to expensive new uniforms. We ask the Board to scrutinize the extraordinary discrepancy in funds given to football as opposed to other sports, particularly those for girls. It is unnecessary for the extreme favoritism shown to boys in sports to begin so markedly at the junior high school level.

Male coaches for female (and male) teams

We are told that the state ruling regarding female coaches for girls' teams was created in 1949 for three reasons, most of which are still used by some male physical education directors in our schools.

When asked, for example, why junior high school girls cannot be coached in swimming along with the boys, it is said that: (1) Male coaches would be tempted to take physical liberties with girls. (They seem trustworthy, however, when teaching girls English.) (2) Male coaches would push girls too hard competitively. (3) Women coaches fear that their limited coaching jobs would be usurped by men. (4) In the case of swimming, boys would have to wear swim suits (which might easily be arranged).

It is number 2 to which we wish to direct your attention.

We are told that the reason the girls' athletic program is so vastly different from and less competitive than the boys' is that "we don't want to fall into the same pitfalls that plague the boys' athletic program." This suggests that maybe the boys' athletic program can use some changes to make it more humane. Perhaps male coaches would not only push girls too hard; perhaps they are pushing boys too hard also. It seems feasible that our entire system of athletics which so discriminates against girls must also be discriminating against a vast number of boys who are not star athletes, when we emphasize highly competitive team sports so strongly.

Most of the team coaches and assistant coaches, for whom high supplementary wages are guaranteed (for boys' sports) in the Master Agreement, are not trained physical education teachers. They are generally teachers of other subjects who have skill in the sport they coach.

If the schools need fear that male coaches would push girls too hard or be indiscreet with them, this strongly suggests that the schools ought to formulate a policy with regard to the coaching of coaches of interscholastic sports. They should be instructed not only in psychological aspects of competition, but also in anatomy, physiology, and other areas pertinent to athletic training. They might then be qualified to coach girls reliably. Since the State Board of Education will undoubtedly change its ruling concerning the necessity of having female coaches for girl athletes, the Ann Arbor schools should begin to plan accordingly.

Wednesday use of gyms

The recent Ann Arbor School Boards have probably made an error in deciding to build Scarlett Junior High School and its as yet unfinished duplicate school with one high-ceilinged gym and one low-ceilinged one, although undoubtedly some money was saved. While sports such as gymnastics, dancing, and wrestling can be carried out in a high-ceilinged room, the team sports of basketball and volleyball, which attract a great many participants, cannot be played in a low-ceilinged gym. With several boys' and several girls' teams in a sport, the current four-day-a-week schedule will not permit a full interscholastic and intramural program for both sexes to take place. And since the boys' teams engage in an energetic interscholastic schedule, it is (again) the girls' teams which suffer. No longer is it feasible, either, to have two girls' teams playing on a half court simultaneously, for now Ann Arbor girls play the same full-court rules that boys do. Tappan Junior High School has a recreation building which apparently is totally unusable for volleyball and basketball. With the great increase in the number of students each school now is handling, the most desirable solutions would be to add a gym to each junior high school, or to raise the ceilings of the low-ceilinged gyms. Since we do not expect favorable responses to these suggestions, we will instead suggest that the current restrictions on the use of the school buildings (in order that students may receive religious instruction) on Wednesdays be stopped. So that more team participation on the part of students may take place, those who wish to receive religious training might choose a different day on which to practice in the gym. Schools now have teachers' meetings on Wednesdays. It has been suggested to us by gym teachers that one teacher might attend the meeting while another coaches an athletic activity.

We urge the Board to be sure that extracurricular sports activities will continue even when all the junior high schools are on a split schedule.

Policy regarding athletics

In line with the suggestion . . . that the Board of Education formulate a policy concerning the coaching of coaches, we feel that an overall change of athletic policy should be evaluated, dealing at least with the following points:

1. Methods for achieving a truly equal-opportunity athletic program for female and male students, with a guiding set of athletic values applicable and healthful to all.

2. The possibility of having more intramural or limitedly interscholastic athletic activities, as opposed to rigorously competitive, interscholastic league sports, to allow students of *all* ability levels, not just the star athletes, to participate in a sport of their choosing.

3. Means of encouraging more girls to participate in sports, and allowing more interscholastic competition for girls than at present, including their performance in spectator sports. We feel that policy for boys and for girls should be the same.

4. Ways of approximating equality in the athletic budget for males and females and of ensuring that the programs offer equal expenditure of time, interest, recognition, coaching skill, and use of equipment and facilities (see *Foreword* to this section).

Family Living

We hope that teachers of the Family Living courses at the high schools use better judgment than some of their textbooks in discussing such subjects as deviancy and premarital sex.

> Differences in the meaning of a sexual relationship. In a sexual involvement, the girl has more to lose than the boy, in several different ways. Even if no unanticipated pregnancy occurs, girls tend to be more emotionally committed than boys before they will have sexual relations. Girls tend not to engage in sex activity unless they believe that the boy really loves them and that the relationship is a meaningful one. For a boy, sexual enjoyment may be an end in itself, not especially dependent upon commitment

to a relationship with this particular girl. This difference in their approach to sexual relations can be extremely damaging to a girl's conception of herself when she later realizes that this is the case. She is hurt when sex represents a meaningful love relationship to her but she finds that to him it does not have that implication. This is especially destructive because many girls who have premarital sexual relations have a special need and desire for a rewarding and supportive relationship with someone outside their families. Our studies of thousands of young people who do and do not engage in premarital sex show that girls from unhappy families with serious problems are much more likely to have premarital sexual relations than are girls from happy families. *The secure girl who has received emotional support and nurture at home in her growth toward maturity is better able to take the long view and to think of the potential effect on her own and the boy's future if they should become too deeply involved with each other too early* [italics not used in original]. Thus, unfortunately, the girl who most needs a good permanent relationship is the one most likely to suffer the trauma of the disillusioning conclusion that she has been used or exploited by someone of her own age whom she cared for.

Further, research studies show that the girl who has sexual relations in one love affair tends to follow the same pattern afterwards when she is going with a different boy. Although in each affair a girl may believe that this time it is truly love and that they are equally committed to each other, still her pattern of behavior tends to become promiscuous. She may after a while have the fatalistic feeling that after all she is no longer a virgin so what does it matter.[1]

In the above example, the authors seem to condone promiscuity in boys and not in girls. They discuss girls' need for love and permanence (as opposed to boys' enjoyment of sex as an end in itself), and say that girls who engage in premarital sex are insecure and come, by and large, from troubled homes. They do not consider the possibility that the same may be true of boys—that boys from secure homes may wish to be emotionally involved with their sex partners and may not need to prove themselves sexually as much as boys who have received inadequate family love. Nor is the boy's future the girl's responsibility.

"Further, research studies show that the girl who has sexual relations in one love affair tends to follow the same pattern afterwards when she is going with a different boy." That sentence can certainly be read with the sexes interchanged. In the authors' minds, the disgrace caused by losing one's virginity is the crux of the problem. This is the epitome of the double standard.

The book currently used in Ann Arbor's high school classes handles this issue more equitably, but then states the following with regard to students' stepping out of conventional roles ("deviance"):

> *People who exhibit traits of the opposite sex* are often regarded with some misgivings. Girls who have highly developed masculine skills are generally accepted as tomboys. But after the age of twelve or thirteen, a girl who is a good ball-player or who plays boys' games with boys is often regarded with some doubt. There are other more acceptable athletic skills such as swimming, water skiing, tennis, and golf; but even in these sports, a girl who is regularly more outstanding than boys may be viewed with some skepticism.
>
> Boys who have highly developed feminine skills and interests are regarded with amused tolerance as young children, but if they grow up to talk and act like girls this is generally seen as undesirable.[2]

By failing to add any suggestion of the value of one's own individual differences and areas of competence, the message left with the student is, "You'd better not be interested in different things than most members of your sex. If you do, you're queer (deviant)." The girl student is clearly told not to be more outstanding than boys.

It would be desirable to scrap some of these books currently used to teach Family Living type courses, aside from their promoting double standards of morality and teaching students to aim for the cultural norm. For instance, sex and love, subjects of intense personal interest to adolescents, are handled in a cold, textbook-like approach, with standard questions at the end of each chapter.

We ask that teachers of these courses be chosen with exquisite care to ensure that they are greatly sensitive to the problems of youth, and are not guilty of imposing separate standards on boys and on girls.

We ask, too, that sex education classes, currently in the elementary schools, avoid imparting these double standards, and of emphasizing stereotyped sexual roles.

Sex Education

We should like to call attention to a number of aspects of Ann Arbor's Sex Education program which must be upgraded or modified.

Although the school officials in charge of the Sex Education program insist that there is no formal emphasis in the elementary schools on the expected roles of various family members, in practice many teachers are actually stressing strongly what girls, boys, mommies, and daddies are supposed to do in families. We ask vehemently that in view of the fact that many women are now striving to function according to their abilities outside of the home, and since many families, especially young couples, are working toward total cooperation and encouragement of individual competence in family living, teachers must be instructed by the administration to deemphasize stereotyped roles of family members in every way possible. Stressing role playing leads young children to categorize their parents in roles which they may not even represent in actuality.

At the present time, too, when many people are living in a variety of untraditional settings, such as communal groupings or marriageless partnerships, the Ann Arbor Sex Education program and the state guidelines for sex education are singularly anachronistic, with their total stress on normal, middle-class (usually white) family life with two happy, role-playing parents.

Also, particularly for young children, it is preferable for matters pertaining to reproduction to be brought up as naturally as possible whenever related topics arise, rather than to have special, regular, rather intense presentations at set times. There is a certain scariness about watching film strips in darkened rooms that might tend to make sex education more severe than it deserves to be. Unfortunately, according to Michigan's Attorney General, sex education may not be integrated with the rest of the curriculum since parents may legally have their children excluded from sex education discussions. We ask our school system not only to lobby actively against restrictive rulings of this sort, but also to trust the judgment of teachers in including the reproduction of life as an integral part of the nature of living things.

It would be desirable, too, if teachers from kindergarten through high school were counseled to spot cases of sexual difficulty in children which interfere with their own and with other children's well-being. Hopefully, our schools have diagnostic and counseling facilities which will help children to attain personal comfort at as early an age as possible.

It is also essential that students in classes for the mentally and physically handicapped be treated as fully human beings and be given appropriate access to sex education.

Among the aims of an enlightened sex education program should certainly be the following:

1. Adolescents should be sympathetically made aware of the overwhelming and perhaps frightening sexual changes and urges that may overtake them at this sensitive age, and should be imbued with the need for control over their own bodies and for exercising great responsibility not to hurt or to molest other people, particularly younger ones who cannot defend themselves. The state guidelines stress that elementary

grade children be forewarned so that they will not become the victims of molestation. We suggest that youngsters be helped not to become the perpetrators of child molestation as well.

2. Young people, *female as well as male*, frequently have great need to feel that their bodies and their feelings are within the range of normality, since these are types of topics they may feel reticent to discuss with others. A survey of the material brought home by a fifth-grader, for example, gave no indication that *girls* have external genitalia. Since size and shape of sexual organs seem to be of critical concern, often, to young people, then an understanding sex education program should consider these needs and emphasize human variability as well as similarity.

3. A good sex education program must never make a student feel criminal, dangerous, profoundly guilty, or hopelessly deviant for his or her habits, feelings, and thoughts (although Michigan's guidelines would seem to encourage these feelings). In the sex education classes of a major city, when homosexuality is discussed, boys are led into a darkened auditorium and shown a film in which a sinister figure in a black cape appears as the homosexual tempter. In view of the fact that a great number of young people, particularly young teenagers, have crushes on teachers, coaches, and students of the same sex, and frequently feel different from other children, any act which serves to frighten students with respect to homosexuality will tend to make those having such proclivities feel increasingly abnormal or "deviant," may make them unable to discuss these feelings with others, and may drive them to lives of street solicitation and unhappy promiscuity.

Since "Personal Adjustment" textbooks seem not to mention the word homosexuality (except to discourage students from "deviance"), the topic should certainly be discussed openly and unmoralistically in class. There should be a trustworthy, sensitive staff member at junior high and high schools with whom students can discuss matters pertaining to homosexuality and who can inform the student of resources in the city which will make him or her feel acceptable. Our school system should pressure the State Education Department in its guidelines to deemphasize the stress laid on "socially deviant behavior" when, for example, homosexuality is discussed. It would be better to have no sex education program at all than to ostracize students for the nature of their sexuality.

4. And last, an outstanding difficulty imposed upon our schools by clearly outlandish state laws, is the inability to teach openly about birth control. Below are two seemingly contradictory laws related to the teaching of Health and Physical Education:

> Section 782 of the General School Laws, based on Public Act 266
> of 1949: Provided, however, That it is not the intention or purpose

of this act to give the right of instruction in birth control and it is
hereby expressly prohibited to any person to offer or give any instruction in said subject of birth control or offer any advice or information with respect to said subject.

Section 789b, part (d) of Act No. 44 of the Public Acts of 1968:
d. Recommend and provide leadership for sex education instruction established by the local school district, including guidelines 'for
family planning information.

This second act seems to suggest that sex education classes may discuss
"family planning," but this according to the State Department of Education's guidelines may include such topics as "the values of marital love
and stability," "responsible parenthood," "job prospects and continuing
education for parents," and so on, and so on. *The current legislation still
prohibits "the teaching of birth control or providing any information in
regard to birth control."* (The above quotations and references are from
Sex Education and Family Information, the Michigan Department of
Education's guidelines to sex education.)

One of the ultimate aims of sex education is surely the teaching
of birth control—that is, the conception and production of children who
are planned, wanted, and loved. It is vital, therefore, that students (who
in far greater numbers than heretofore imagined, are having sexual
relationships) be equipped with the knowledge of the prevention of
unwanted pregnancies. It may seem surprising in these modern times
to learn that the great majority of youthful, unwed mothers had no
reliable knowledge of birth-control techniques before becoming pregnant.

In view of the fact that there is no more stigmatizing, handicapping
occurrence in a young girl's life than the birth of an illegitimate child,
we ask the administration to lobby at the state level for the repeal of
obnoxious laws that work only to the detriment of students, and, if
necessary, to break these laws in order to bring about a test case. There
are lawyers in Ann Arbor who are willing to take up this challenge.

Although the laws do not specifically refer to abortion, this is, we
are told, also a forbidden topic in Michigan's schools (although our
newspapers are full of news items about abortion law reform). Preventing
schools from teaching about birth control may force them to have to
counsel girls about abortion!

If our schools are unwilling to instruct students in any matters pertaining to birth control or abortion, then sex education teachers must at the very
least be permitted to refer students to agencies which can give counseling
in these topics. (The law permits the presentation of information regarding "the religious and medical resources for family planning available in
the community.") We ask our school system to acquaint students with

the services of Planned Parenthood (which may soon open a teen clinic) and the Crisis Walk-In Center, at every indicated opportunity.

Undue familiarity rule

We ask that counselors be counseled to avoid inflicting double standards of morality on students, for example, where the so-called "undue familiarity rule" is involved. Students must not be made to feel that girls alone are responsible for amorous acts (including hand holding) and their outcomes. Adolescent boys must not be encouraged to think of themselves as creatures of excusable, unbridled lust, and adolescent girls divided into the "good girls" and the "temptresses." For adolescents to grow into responsible adults, even more socially responsible than some of their parents, both boys and girls must be accountable for their behavior, with due concern for the welfare of the parties with whom they are interacting.

We have been informed of instances even in elementary school in which young boys, holding each other's hands or putting arms around each other's shoulders, were requested to stop this "ungentlemanly" display of affection.

It has been suggested by some counselors that a specific discipline policy be added to the handbook, indicating how "undue familiarity" problems are to be handled. We ask that such a policy be included, and that it be an unmoralistic, humane policy which recognizes the affectional needs of young people.

Recognition of single parent and nonconforming households

At a time when more than 10 percent of America's families are headed by a woman (according to Department of Labor statistics), and at a time when many children are growing up in a variety of nonconforming family constellations, there is a distinct lack of consideration in the Ann Arbor schools for the feelings and the problems encountered by children and adults living in these situations. It is no doubt humiliating for many children, for example, never to see a working mother or divorced parents in their books. (In one school with a high incidence of single-parent families, favorable charts were noted which contained a variety of family settings.) In some schools there is still a "Fathers' Night," at which children proudly show off their accomplishments to their fathers. All too frequently, mothers are expected to be home and available in the daytime to attend school events, to meet with teachers, or to serve lunch to their children. Ann Arbor's traditional school lunch program in many instances causes children with working mothers to feel "highly unusual."

(The only children living within a mile of the school who may bring their lunch are those who are poverty stricken or those with "highly unusual circumstances," such as having a working or a student mother.) Even sex education classes for elementary children invariably show two happy, cooperative parents in a household and do not touch on the possibility of divorce.

We would ask that these difficulties be remedied in at least the following ways:

a. Reading and supplementary books must be sought which will make children from atypical family settings feel more normal.

b. The Ann Arbor schools will have to become sensitive to the fact that many children live with only one adult, who cannot necessarily be available for school functions at times when the schools might wish them to be. Fathers' Nights (and Mothers' Mornings) should be eliminated, parent conferences should be made at night if need be, and school lunch programs should be available to any child wishing to partake. Also, sex education classes must allude in a normal fashion, without pity or moral judgment, to the existence of many types of family relationships.

Discrimination against ethnic and racial minority female students

According to Labor Department statistics, in 1967 the median incomes by race and sex for full-time, year-round workers were:

White men	$7518
Black men	$4837
White women	$4380
Black women	$3268

Furthermore, 44 percent of nonwhite women were in service occupations. And believe it or not, the full-time, year-round median income for private household workers, 47 percent of whom were nonwhite (44 percent Black), was $1298! These figures strongly suggest that our schools, as well as the rest of society, are failing the bulk of our minority women students. The Ann Arbor schools had better ask themselves some important questions concerning their contribution to the perpetuation of these miserable statistics.

What are our schools doing to challenge the interests, abilities, and potentialities of our female students of racial and ethnic minority heritage?

Into what programs are they being guided?

What attempts are being made to guide the learning experiences of our racial and ethnic minority female students?

Is our Multi-Ethnic Program taking into account the specific problems of ethnic-minority females?

Is any attempt being made to encourage these students to aspire to lives of personal accomplishment?

Are they being given guidance toward attaining personal competence in potentially rewarding skills and knowledge?

Are efforts being made to secure books and other materials which help to establish heroines with whom these students may identify?

Are our schools hiring ethnic-minority women in sufficient numbers in administrative, teaching, and counseling positions?

Studies have shown that of all students participating in extracurricular activities, Black females are the least involved. And if textbooks stereotype, discriminate against, and overlook females in general, they greatly compound these problems when dealing with minority females, who are rigidly stereotyped into traditional female roles. In a study performed by a group of Puerto Rican women (*Feminists Look at the 100 Books: The Portrayal of Women in Children's Books on Puerto Rican Themes*), they conclude that "A Puerto Rican girl faced only with the prospects presented in these books might reasonably choose not to grow up at all."

What must our schools do to remedy these problems? Teachers and counselors must exert all effort to recognize and to challenge the abilities and aspirations of minority female students from the earliest grades. Books, films, and other materials must be utilized which emphasize the accomplishments of racial and ethnic minority women. And every effort must be made to develop extra- (and intra-) curricular athletic and nonathletic programs to capture the interest and imagination of these young women and to make them feel like vital members of the school community. Also, career, college, and vocational counseling must be undertaken to equip them to enter rewarding future lives. Affirmative action must be used in securing excellent minority female personnel at administrative, teaching, and counseling levels.

References

1. JUDSON T. LANDIS and MARY G. LANDIS, *Personal Adjustment, Marriage, and Family Living* (Englewood Cliffs, N.J.: Prentice-Hall, 1970), pp. 104–106.
2. HELEN G. WESTLAKE, *Relationships, a Study in Human Behavior* (Boston: Ginn and Company, 1960), p. 207.

PART 3

Books: Propaganda and the Sins of Omission

WOMEN IN CHILDREN'S LITERATURE

Some of my best and most adventurous girl friends are between the covers of books. They range from *Alice in Wonderland* to *Harriet the Spy.* In between are *Caddie Woodlawn, Heidi,* Laura of *The Little House* books, and Arriety of *The Borrowers.* Because of these friends, I was shocked last May to read Elizabeth Fisher's article in the *New York Times* which charged that children's books were unfair to girls. Her strongest claim was that books for our youngest and therefore most impressionable children not only fail to represent the real world of today, but also combine into "an almost incredible conspiracy of conditioning. Boys' achievement drive is encouraged; girls' is cut off. Boys are brought up to express themselves; girls to please. The general image of the female ranges from dull to degrading to invisible."

As I said, my first reaction was shock. This was followed by skepticism and finally by reluctant agreement. I took my first step between skepticism and agreement when I remembered some advice I received in a course entitled "Writing for Children." The instructor told us that the wise author writes about boys, thereby ensuring himself a maximum audience, since only girls will read a book about a girl, but both boys and girls will read about a boy. At the time that I heard this, I felt nothing but gratitude for being let in on a trade secret. Since then, I have heard that Scott O'Dell, who wrote the prize-winning *Island of the Blue Dolphins,* tells how the book was initially rejected by a publisher who wanted him to rewrite it, changing the heroine to a hero.

I took my second step when I sat down in front of the fifty-eight picture books which happened to be on the display cart for use by the children's literature teachers at Eastern Michigan University. As I thumbed through the books looking specifically at the way women and girls were pictured, I was struck by what appears to be a cult of the apron. Of the 58 books, 25 had a picture of a woman somewhere in them. And of these 25 books, all but four had a picture of a woman wearing an apron. Ets and Labistida showed women wearing their aprons to the public market in Mexico, and Robert McCloskey had a woman wearing an apron to the public gardens in Boston. Within these 58 books, I also found a mother alligator, a mother rabbit, a mother donkey, and a mother cat all wearing aprons. In the four books which showed women without aprons, the leading characters included a teaching sister whose habit had a long white frontispiece, a queen who was knitting, an Indian squaw who was stirring a pot of food, and a mother who was taking her children on an outing.

This was enough to convince me that the matter was worthy of additional study. Knowing that I could never look at all children's books, I decided on a rather modest sampling, the winners and runners-up of the Caldecott Award [1] during the last 20 years. These books are fairly representative of the best that we have in picture books, and once a book gets on this exclusive list it is ordered by practically every children's librarian in the country. Hence these are books that reflect our adult values and at the same time influence the formation of early child values. People have told me that if I had looked at books written for junior high school students my findings would have been different. Perhaps so. It's certainly an area that needs investigation. But my reason for concentrating on picture books rather than on those for independent readers (children age eight and above) is that the illustrated books are the ones influencing children at the time they are in the process of developing their own sexual identity. Children decide very early in life what roles are appropriate to male and female. Last summer in our own family, we had a striking example of this. My sister was accepted into medical school. Naturally there were congratulations and comments from neighbors, friends, and relatives. After a few days of this, she found her son (age six) and her daughter (age five) crying real tears for no apparent reason. When she at last got to the cause of their grief, she found that they thought if she were going to become a doctor, she would first have to turn into a man and they wouldn't have a mother.

But on to the survey of the 80 books—I will start by giving some very quick comparisons. First, just going through the titles of the stories, I found 14 males (13 boys and one man), but only four females (two girls and two women) listed by name. In counting the characters pictured in the illustrations, I found a total of 386 females and 579 males. Of the 80 books, there was not a single one that did not have a male (human or animal), but there were six books in which females were completely absent. In a larger group of books—in fact, one fourth of the entire sample —there were only what I would call token females. Seven of these token females were mothers who sewed on the buttons and packed the lunches so that, for example, "The Fool of the World" could go away in his "flying ship," and Si could get a job as "Skipper John's Cook." I expected this, but I was surprised to notice how often women and girls were pictured looking out at the action. They stand in doorways (*The Storm Book*), they look through windows (*The Two Reds*), and they sit on the porch in rocking chairs (*The Day We Saw the Sun Come Up*). Most of the token females were very unobtrusive, such as the princess who is only mentioned as a marriage objective in *The Fool of the World and the Flying Ship* and *Puss In Boots*. In *Why the Sun and Moon Live in the Sky*, we see the moon as the sun's wife who helps build the house, but says nothing. In *Alexander and the Wind-up Mouse* the male characters happen to be in Annie's room. We never see Annie, but she turns out to be the villain because she throws away the old toys. In *One Wide River to Cross*, we see male and female animals, but not male and female people. In *Wave*, the only mention of females is a statement that even the women and babies climbed the mountain. In *May I Bring a Friend*, the queen knits and is swung in a swing. She frowns when they all go fishing and she sits on a cushion in the background when a golden trumpet is brought and all the males take a turn playing. In *Judge*, one of the five prisoners is a woman who is declared a "nincompoop," and in *Mr. T. W. Anthony Woo*, the whole plot is how the lovable Mr. Woo can get rid of his meddlesome sister and her bothersome parrot, who is also female. There is one book in this group that I think is the epitome of male chauvinism. It is an alphabet book called *Ape in a Cape*. It is dedicated to Timmy and it pictures 36 male animals and two females. It begins with the ape who wears a definitely male military cape. When we come to the "Dove in Love" page, we see two identical doves so I assume that one is female. The only other female is a ridiculous "fat lady" hippopotamus in the background of a circus scene. When I came to the "M" page and read "Mouse in a Blouse," I was certain I would see a female animal, but no! The author-artist pictures a mouse in a middy blouse and to make sure there is no mistake he adds a sailor hat labeled U.S. Navy.

But even this book I would not make a special effort to keep away from my daughter. In fact, there was not a single book in the survey that I would want her not to read. On the other hand, I would be very distressed if these books were the only books available to her. If a girl is continually faced with books where the boy does all the explaining while the girl does all the listening, where the boy does all the traveling while the girl does all the waving, where the boy does all the complaining while the girl does all the smiling, and worst of all, where the boy does all of everything and the girl isn't even visible, then I think it reasonable to predict that the girl might have problems in finding her own identity. If she accepts the placid role of the female as shown in some recent picture books, then she runs the risk of becoming an anachronism as well as an unhappy person. I think what is more likely is that if she has a fair amount of energy, ambition, and intelligence, she will reject the placid female role and will instead identify with the male. This too—as most of us know —brings its share of frustration. Rather than dwelling on this point, I will assume that we are in agreement that there is a real need for books presenting models which show accurately and realistically ways in which women and girls can successfully function as individuals.

In the rest of my paper, then, I will change my focus and look behind the statistics to see if we can see the reasons for what truly does look like a prejudice against girls. I am in hopes that if we understand some of the reasons, then perhaps we can be more efficient as we go about trying to ameliorate the situation.

Some people have already suggested that publishers are plotting against women and girls. I find this highly unlikely—at least on a conscious level—because the field of children's literature is one in which women have at least a numerical majority in the control of children's books as they go about their roles of being mothers, teachers, librarians, booksellers, critics, and children's editors. And if the Caldecott books are typical, then women are at least equally represented among the authors, although they are in the minority among the artists. There were 38 male authors or author-artists, as compared with 40 women; however among the free-lance artists there were 25 men as compared to 12 women. The other reason why I do not think that the publishers are intentionally ignoring girls, is that I can see no way in which it would profit either their businesses or society. Until only very recently, it may have been thought best for the world as a whole if girls were not encouraged to do other than focus their lives around being housewives and mothers. But with our longer life expectancies and with the biggest single problem in the world being that of the population explosion, this viewpoint can no longer go unchallenged. I am not saying that we should go about de-emphasizing the traditional female roles, but I am saying that we need to provide dozens or even hundreds of models for young girls so that there is room for selection and individual differences. If women are really going to have smaller families, then they must be allowed additional ways to fulfill themselves. It's because we have such a need for both quantity and quality, that I think we should do all we can to get the commercial publishers to see the possibilities for presenting many roles for children of both sexes. My second reason for feeling that we must work through the commercial publishers is that we must reach all children—not just our own daughters. For example, it isn't going to profit us very much if we convince a little girl that she should become a doctor if we do not also persuade her future husband, neighbors, friends, teachers, counselors, and admissions committee, as well as all the men in the world who now think it unmanly to go to a woman doctor.

When the creator of the Barbie Doll was questioned about the values being promoted through the doll, she stated flatly that her company was a reflection of the culture, not a maker of it. When the time comes that little girls will really grow up to be doctors, then she will manufacture Barbie doctor kits, in addition to Barbie boyfriends and Barbie fashion shows. I don't think that anyone in the field of children's literature would have answered a question about books in this way. People have always recognized that books set standards of behavior and publishers have looked on this as both an obligation and an opportunity— witness the recent flood of Black books.

If it is not a purposeful plot, and if I am correct in assuming that people working with children's books are genuinely people of good will who desire to be fair and to promote honest values, then why do we have a problem?

One reason is the English language. As linguists point out, English is perhaps defective in not having singular pronouns equivalent to the plurals: *they, their,* and *them.* Having no neuter in the singular form means that any animate being must be referred to as either *he* or *she.* Many books, particularly those about animals,[2] are dominated by males simply because the author is forced to choose between masculine and feminine pronouns. An author usually chooses masculine because it is easy and he (or she) has been taught that masculine can stand for both men and women, although not the other way around. A book which illustrates this point is *Feather Mountain.* This is a make-believe story of how the birds of the world first got their feathers. None of the birds have names and the author refers to all of them with the masculine pronouns even though some of them look very feminine as they stitch, and sew, and ruffle and paint. We might compare this to Taro Yashima's treatment of a group of children in *Seashore Story,* where he uses such phrases as "One asked," "Another asked," and "A young teacher answered." For a writer to do what Yashima does rather than referring to everyone as *he,* takes both greater awareness and greater skill in writing. The unadorned indefinite pronoun *one* is too stiff and formal to be appropriate for the intimate style of most picture books. It is no more a part of children's language than is the concept that *he* can stand for girls as well as boys.

Also, children interpret language quite literally. When they hear such expressions as *chairman, brotherly love, ten-man team,* and *fellow-man,* they think of men, not of the whole human race. Another language-related problem is that names are based on the male form and to show a relationship, we often take the male form and then add a feminine suffix, such as *-ess, -ine,* or *-ette.* The *-ette* suffix is what Eve Titus used in naming Anatol's children so that we have *Paul and Paulette, Claude and Claudette,* and *George and Georgette.* It is unfortunate that *-ette* not only indicates feminine, but also smallness and sometimes falseness or insignificance as in *cassette, cigarette,* or *leatherette.* This same linguistic principle applies not only to proper names, but also to other designations such as *god–goddess, host–hostess, major–majorette,* etc. In all these examples the second term simply does not seem as important as the first.

Another problem is related to the artists. Sometimes a book, such as *A Tree is Nice,* is slanted toward boys strictly by the artist. There is nothing in the text of this book to suggest that it is a boy's book, but the illustrator drew 27 males compared to 13 females. He put 11 of the boys and only three of the girls in the branches of trees. The three girls are on the very lowest branches. The other girls are pictured in such poses as waving to a boy who is high in a tree, dragging a little boy through the leaves, helping another little boy into a tree, standing with a sprinkling can, and standing dejectedly alone while the boys climb a magnificent tree. In spite of all this, I think a girl might have been able to identify with the story which is written in the second person and all the way through talks to *you.* But alas, on the final page, the artist shows that *you* is a boy who is pictured planting a tree.

As you perhaps remember, the only real difference between the ratio of male and female authors and artists was in the number of free-lance artists who illustrated books. If these figures are typical, then we can assume that free-lance artists are more than twice as likely to be men as women. And because of the living conditions of New York artists, I think the men are unlikely to have intimate acquaintance with children. They base their drawings on what they can remember from their own childhood, which naturally enough centered around boys.

Out of the 80 books, I found ten modern and original picture-book stories which had girls as the leading characters,[3] compared to 24 stories having boys as the leading characters. There were 12 individual authors and artists involved in the production of these ten books. Nine of these 12 were women. The three men were Ludwig Bemelmens with his *Madeline's Rescue,* Robert McCloskey with both *One Morning in Maine* and

Time of Wonder, and Taro Yashima with *Umbrella.* I think it significant that all three of these men have daughters of their own and the Yashima and McCloskey books are specifically about the artists' own daughters. Perhaps this means that it takes a special acquaintance before a man feels comfortable in picturing girls. Even McCloskey seems shy about drawing girls other than his own. In his two books, the only females he drew were his wife and his two daughters, as compared to 25 different males. It is also interesting that in *Time of Wonder,* his two girls are tremendously adventurous, even sailing across the bay by themselves, but when they get in a crowd of six boys who are diving from rocks, and swimming and surfing, the girls suddenly become very feminine as they play in the sand and sunbathe. Among the authors and artists, I found 13 women who did books specifically about boys. Perhaps this indicates that women, through being mothers, teachers, or librarians—all roles where they observe both boys and girls—feel perfectly at ease in writing about boys and in drawing their pictures.

Now by looking at note three, under Notes, which lists ten books written especially for and about girls, and by noticing the dates (publication was one year prior to the given date of the award), we come to what I think is my most significant finding. If the Caldecott books are representative, then we can conclude that there has been a steady decrease of illustrated books written for, or about, girls. Nine of the ten "girl" books were written during the fifties. The only one written during the sixties is about a girl named Samantha and called Sam. I strongly suspect that the choice of her name was influenced by a desire to attract boys to the book which is entitled *Sam, Bangs and Moonshine.* Further evidence pointing to the fact that girls are losing, rather than gaining, a place in books for the very young is a comparison of the number of girls and the number of boys pictured in the survey books calculated at five-year intervals.[4] From 1951 to 1955, the percentage of girls pictured in the books was 46. By 1956 to 1960, the percentage of girls had shrunk to 41, and by 1961 to 1965, it was down to 35. In the most recent period, 1966 to 1970, only 26 percent of the characters were girls.

Why should girls be losing out? To answer this we have to go beyond the survey books and look at certain developments that I think have influenced all children's books in the last two decades. If publishers are guilty, I think it's not individually, but collectively. In striving to compete, they let themselves be pulled along in certain movements which in combination have served to harness some of the creative variety that is naturally present in authors and artists. These movements grew out of the placid fifties when the wars (including Korea) were over, the soldiers were home, and the women seemed perfectly happy to return to their kitchens and leave the working world to the veterans. Probably other factors also contributed to what was a general emphasis on motherhood and homemaking skills such as gourmet cooking and fancy needlework. Anyway, during the fifties, the feeling was very strong that "A Woman's Place is in the Home!" Suddenly in the fall of 1957, the Russians' Sputnik burst into the picture and we were all caught up in the education explosion which followed. We became interested in science and math and foreign languages, and in 1961 Congress passed the National Defense Education Act which specified that federal funds could be used to purchase science books for school libraries. Publishers stumbled over each other in trying to fill their catalogues with books that would not only qualify for purchase under this Act, but would also excite children enough so that they would read them, and perhaps even purchase them, on their own. In the United States, science has always been thought of as a field appropriate to males. The producers of the new science books had their hands full in breaking new ground. Never before had anyone succeeded in writing informative books that great numbers of children would love to read. Writers could hardly be expected to compound their difficulties by attempting at the same time to break down centuries-old sex barriers. The science books proved to be so popular that publishers expanded into social studies books, mostly centering around great events and great people. This was another natural for male orientation since women have always been practically absent from history books. Examples of this type are the Random House Landmark books which are described and advertised as "colorful and dramatic chapters in American history." However, of the 165 books now in print, there are only five of them about individual American women. Last month when I asked a Random House representative about this, he candidly said that they thought if they got the boys interested, the girls would follow. Even ten years ago, I doubt that he would have dared to say, "If we get the White kids interested, the Blacks will follow."

The results of the National Defense Education Act might be summarized in Remy Charlip style: children can now go to the library and find a wealth of high-quality informative books about every conceivable subject. What good luck! But these thousands of informative books are highly male-oriented and male-dominated. What bad luck!

Another significant part of the education explosion was that people began discovering and paying attention to a fact that we females—both teachers and students—had long known, but been too polite to mention. Little boys did not learn to read nearly as fast or nearly as well as little girls did. Someone said that Johnny couldn't read because the textbooks were dull and were full of feminine values. This claim was widely publicized and Dr. Seuss started a new word game which turned the writer's craft inside out. The object was to find interesting and exciting situations to fit words from the basic reading lists, rather than the usual writing method of finding words to fit situations. This in itself is questionable. But the important point about these books as they relate to this paper is that they were written to answer a specific need. They were written to help *Johnny*—not Joanie, or Janet, or Jeannie—learn how to read. They were purposely and openly defeminized. Dick and Jane, Jack and Janet, Alice and Jerry, and Tom and Betty were replaced by Cowboy Sam, Sailor Jack, Dan Frontier, and such other males as Harold, Tom, Max, Bob, Mr. Pine, Morris, and the Binky brothers. Even the animals were made masculine. Standing next to Little Bear, who is of course a male, we see Chester the Horse, Harry the Dirty Dog, Sam the Firefly, Zeke the Raccoon, Julius the Gorilla, and Albert the Albatross. Many of these books turned out to be delightfully creative and children of both sexes are reading and enjoying them. What good luck! But they are equally, or even more, male-oriented than the science and social studies books. What bad luck!

It is ironic that in recent years, little girls lost out in two different ways. Boys are the dominant figures in the nonfiction section of the library because they are thought to be *more* able than girls in such fields as math, science, and statesmanship. Then they are the dominant figures in the beginning-to-read books for just the opposite reason. They are thought to be *less* able than girls in the field of language arts.

Once the producers of children's books began thinking in terms of boys, nothing happened in the sixties to make them think otherwise. Probably the most significant development of the sixties was the large number of books about Black children, but here again, we see mostly boys. Going back to the survey, in *Lion*, William Pène du Bois pictured the 104 artists who designed the earth. There was one with dark skin, but there was not a single female. In Leo Lionni's *Swimmy*, I'm sure children are quick to see that Swimmy is brave and bright and Black, but they are probably just as quick to see that he is a *he*. The hundreds of other fish are given no sex distinction. Ezra Jack Keats, who was one of the first to produce really quality picture books about Black children, has created a charming and very modern individual named Peter. But in *The Snowy Day*, Peter's mother is seen only as a stereotyped Negro "mammy." In *Goggles*, the only female is Peter's sister who sits on the sidewalk with a baby, drawing pictures while all the excitement of a miniature gang war rages around her.

Another development in the sixties is related to inflation and spiraling production costs. As publishers seek ways to cut their expenses, they look increasingly to the world's folktales where there is no need to pay an author's royalty or double copyright. Perhaps my sampling was weighed in this direction, since the Caldecott Award is given mainly on the basis of the illustrations, and folktales are a favorite with many artists. Out of the 80 Caldecott books, 19 were based on folktales. Folktales are set several hundred, or even thousand, years ago when almost any activity required brute strength. Hence it was by necessity that the men were the doers and the women were the onlookers.

In summary, what is it that I'm asking for? Certainly not that we involve children in our adult male–female quarrels or that we take from the library shelves any of the books that I've talked about. But I am asking for fair play. If we have an alphabet book strictly for boys, let's recognize it as a book teaching male roles rather than the alphabet, and then let's provide something equally interesting which teaches female roles.

I doubt that we can add a new pronoun to the English language, but with a little bit of effort, a good writer can avoid referring to every animal or every character as *he*. And when a book is addressed to the second person *you*, artists can be careful that their illustrations do not restrict this nondefinite pronoun to one sex or the other. Artists can also take a second look at their crowd scenes. What earthly purpose does it serve to draw seven males for every female, which is the ratio that one of my students found in Dr. Seuss's books? I have nothing against artists looking for folktales to illustrate, but I hope that in the future they will look a little deeper. The theme of many folktales is the triumph of the small and the weak through cleverness or perseverance. This was often a female. I am making a plea that we look for some of the most interesting of these stories, and reproduce them to serve as a balance to the many male-oriented folktales now in print. And in the field of social studies and biography, we must also look a little deeper. Surely a firm with all of the resources of Random House can find more than five interesting women in the history of America. And can't we be more realistic when we draw pictures of mothers? Let's show them driving cars, playing guitars, typing letters, and even going to work. When over 40 percent of the mothers in the United States hold jobs I think we should do what we can to help children develop pride in their mothers' accomplishments, rather than a sense of shame or embarrassment in feeling that their mothers *have* to work.

In the easy-to-read books I am all for keeping a low vocabulary combined with action and a high interest level. But I think we are obligated to remember that little girls still read faster and better than little boys, and it is very likely that the easy-to-read books are read by many more girls than boys. Girls like action too. Let's not stop it; let's just include the girls as part of it.

I guess that what I'm asking for is that we stop accepting as a fact the idea that boys will not read books about girls. I think that many of us have been guilty of playing both sides of this coin because at the same time that we were lamenting and prophesying that boys wouldn't read books about girls, we were taking many unnecessary steps to see that they never got the chance. I want a *Harriet the Spy* for preschool and primary age children. This is a book "discovered" by sixth-grade boys. The sex of the leading character is immaterial. What is important is the action and the humor. I think we can have books like this for younger children just as soon as we quit predicting their failure, which in the past has served to frighten away much of the best talent, and start producing books about real little girls—not the stiff, stilted, and placid creatures that we see in so many picture books. The lesson that we should have learned when we began looking at the elementary reading texts in the fifties was that boys wouldn't read books about dull children—male or female.

Notes

1. This award is presented annually by the Children's Service Committee of the American Library Association for the most distinguished picture book of the year. Including the runners-up, 80 books received citations within the last 20 years.
2. There were 15 books in the survey which had animals as the characters. Not one of these had female animals as the main characters.
3. *The Egg Tree*, 1951; *The Most Wonderful Doll in the World*, 1951; *One Morning in Maine*, 1953; *Madeline's Rescue*, 1954; *Play With Me*, 1956; *One is One*, 1957; *Time of Wonder*, 1958; *Umbrella*, 1959; *Nine Days to Christmas*, 1960; and *Sam, Bangs and Moonshine*, 1967.
4.

Years	Boys	Girls
1951–55	273	228
1956–60	148	100
1961–65	66	29
1966–70	92	29

SEX-ROLE SOCIALIZATION IN PICTURE BOOKS FOR PRESCHOOL CHILDREN[1]

An examination of prize-winning picture books reveals that women are greatly underrepresented in the titles, central roles, and illustrations. Where women do appear their characterization reinforces traditional sex-role stereotypes: boys are active while girls are passive; boys lead and rescue others while girls follow and serve others. Adult men and women are equally sex stereotyped: men engage in a wide variety of occupations while women are presented only as wives and mothers. The effects of these rigid sex-role portraits on the self image and aspirations of the developing child are discussed.

Introduction

Sex-role socialization constitutes one of the most important learning experiences for the young child. By the time the child enters kindergarten, he or she is able to make sex-role distinctions and express sex-role preferences. Boys already identify with masculine roles, and girls with feminine roles (Brown, 1956). They also learn the appropriate behavior for both boys and girls and men and women. Hartley (1960) reports that, by the time they are four, children realize that the primary feminine role is housekeeping, while the primary masculine role is wage earning.

In addition to learning sex-role identification and sex-role expectations, boys and girls are socialized to accept society's definition of the relative worth of each of the sexes and to assume the personality characteristics that are "typical" of members of each sex. With regard to relative

Note: By Lenore J. Weitzman, Deborah Eifler, Elizabeth Hokada, and Catherine Ross. Copyright © 1972 by The University of Chicago Press. Reprinted with permission from *The American Journal of Sociology*, May 1972, 77:6.

Publisher's Note: Throughout this article superscript numbers refer to notes listed at the end of the text. The name and date citations refer to the bibliography.

status, they learn that boys are more highly valued than girls. And, with regard to personality differences, they learn that boys are active and achieving while girls are passive and emotional. Eight-year-old boys describe girls as clean, neat, quiet, gentle, and fearful, while they describe adult women as unintelligent, ineffective, unadventurous, nasty, and exploitative (Hartley, 1959). Indeed, Maccoby finds that, although girls begin life as better achievers than boys, they gradually fall behind as they become socialized (Maccoby, 1966).

In this paper we wish to concentrate on one aspect of sex-role socialization: the socialization of preschool children through picture books. Picture books play an important role in early sex-role socialization because they are a vehicle for the presentation of societal values to the young child. Through books, children learn about the world outside of their immediate environment: they learn about what other boys and girls do, say, and feel; they learn about what is right and wrong; and they learn what is expected of children their age. In addition, books provide children with role models—images of what they can and should be like when they grow up.

Children's books reflect cultural values and are an important instrument for persuading children to accept those values. They also contain role prescriptions which encourage the child to conform to acceptable standards of behavior. The Child Study Association (1969), aware of the socialization potential of books, states that a book's emotional and intellectual impact on a young reader must be considered. Therefore it recommends that children's books present positive ethical values.

Because books for young children explicitly articulate the prevailing cultural values, they are an especially useful indicator of societal norms.[2] McClelland (1961) used children's books as indicators of achievement values in his cross-cultural study of economic development. In the period prior to increased economic development he found a high incidence of achievement motivation reflected in the children's books. This indicated a strong positive relationship between achievement imagery in children's stories and subsequent economic growth. McClelland (1961, p. 71) noted that the stories had provided children with clear "instructive" messages about normative behavior. Margaret Mead also commented that "a culture has to get its values across to its children in such simple terms that even a behavioral scientist can understand them."[3]

Study Design

Our study focuses on picture books for the preschool child. These books are often read over and over again at a time when children are in the process of developing their own sexual identities. Picture books are read to children when they are most impressionable, before other socialization influences (such as school, teachers, and peers) become more important at later stages in the child's development.

We have chosen to examine how sex roles are treated in those children's books identified as the "very best": the winners of the Caldecott Medal. The Caldecott Medal is given by the Children's Service Committee of the American Library Association for the most distinguished picture book of the year. The medal is the most coveted prize for preschool books. Books on the list of winners (and runners-up) are ordered by practically all children's libraries in the United States. Teachers and educators encourage children to read the Caldecotts, and conscientious parents skim the library shelves looking for those books that display the impressive gold seal which designates the winners. The Caldecott award often means sales of 60,000 books for the publisher, and others in the industry look to the winners for guidance in what to publish (Nilsen, 1970).

Although we have computed a statistical analysis of all the Caldecott winners from the inception of the award in 1938, we have concentrated our intensive analysis on the winners and runners-up for the past five years. Most of the examples cited in this paper are taken from the 18 books in this latter category.[4]

In the course of our investigation we read several hundred picture books and feel that we can assert, with confidence, that our findings are applicable to the wide range of picture books. In fact, the Caldecott winners are clearly less stereotyped than the average book, and do not include the most blatant examples of sexism.

In order to assure ourselves of the representativeness of our study, we have also examined three other groups of children's books: the Newbery Award winners, the Little Golden Books, and the "prescribed behavior" or etiquette books.

The Newbery Award is given by the American Library Association for the best book for school-age children. Newbery books are for children who can read, and are therefore directed to children in the third to sixth grades.

The Little Golden Books we have sampled are the best sellers in children's books, since we have taken only those Little Golden Books that sold over three million copies.[5] These books sell for 39 cents in grocery stores, Woolworth's, Grant's, and toy and game stores. Consequently, they reach a more broadly based audience than do the more expensive Caldecott winners.

The last type of book we studied is what we call the "prescribed behavior" or etiquette book. Whereas other books only imply sex-role prescriptions, these books are explicit about the proper behavior for boys and girls. They also portray adult models and advise children on future roles and occupations.[6]

If we may anticipate our later findings, we would like to note here that the findings from the latter three samples strongly parallel those from the Caldecott sample. Although the remainder of this paper will be devoted primarily to the Caldecott sample, we will use some of the other books for illustrative purposes.

The Invisible Female

It would be impossible to discuss the image of females in children's books without first noting that, in fact, women are simply invisible. We found that females were underrepresented in the titles, central roles, pictures, and stories of every sample of books we examined. Most children's books are about boys, men, and male animals, and most deal exclusively with male adventures. Most pictures show men—singly or in groups. Even when women can be found in the books, they often play insignificant roles, remaining both inconspicuous and nameless.

A tabulation of the distribution of illustrations in the picture books is probably the single best indicator of the importance of men and women in these books. Because women comprise 51 percent of our population, if there were no bias in these books they should be presented in roughly half of the pictures. However, in our sample of 18 Caldecott winners and runners-up in the past five years we found 261 pictures of males compared with 23 pictures of females. This is a ratio of 11 pictures of males for every one picture of a female. If we include animals with obvious identities, the bias is even greater. The ratio of male to female animals is 95:1.[7]

Turning to the titles of the Caldecott Medal winners since the award's inception in 1938, we find that the ratio of titles featuring males to those featuring females is 8:3.[8] Despite the presence of the popular *Cinderella, Snow White, Hansel and Gretel,* and *Little Red Riding Hood* in the sample of Golden Books that have sold more than three million copies, we find close to a 3:1 male/female ratio in this sample.[9] The 49 books that have received the Newbery Award since 1922 depict more than three males to every one female.[10]

Children scanning the list of titles of what have been designated as the very best children's books are bound to receive the impression that girls are not very important because no one has bothered to write books about them. The content of the books rarely dispels this impression.

In close to one third of our sample of recent Caldecott books, there are no women at all. In these books, both the illustrations and the stories reflect a man's world. *Drummer Hoff* (Emberley, 1967*a*) is about a group of army officers getting ready to fire a cannon; *Frog and Toad* (Lobel, 1970) relates the adventures of two male animal friends; *In the Night Kitchen* (Sendak, 1970) follows a boy's fantasy adventures through a kitchen that has three cooks, all of whom are male; *Frederick* (Lionni, 1967) is a creative male mouse who enables his brothers to survive the cold winter; and *Alexander* is a mouse who helps a friend transform himself.

When there are female characters, they are usually insignificant or inconspicuous. The one girl in *Goggles* (Keats, 1969) is shown playing quietly in a corner. The wife in *The Sun and the Moon* (Dayrell, 1968) helps by carrying wood but never speaks. There are two women in *The Fool of the World* (Ransome, 1968): the mother, who packs lunch for her sons and waves goodby, and the princess whose hand in marriage is the object of the Fool's adventures. The princess is shown only twice: once peering out of the window of the castle, and the second time in the wedding scene in which the reader must strain to find her. She does not have anything to say throughout the adventure, and of course she is not consulted in the choice of her husband; on the last page, however, the narrator assures us that she soon "loved him to distraction." Loving, watching, and helping are among the few activities allowed to women in picture books.

It is easy to imagine that the little girl reading these books might be deprived of her ego and her sense of self. She may be made to feel that girls are vacuous creatures who are less worthy and do less exciting things than men. No wonder, then, that the child psychologists report that girls at every age are less likely to identify with the feminine role, while boys of every age are more likely to identify with the masculine role (Brown, 1956).

Although there is much variation in plot among the picture books, a significant majority includes some form of male adventure. The fisherman in *Seashore Story* (Yashima, 1967) rides a turtle to a hidden world under the sea. After an encounter with a lion, Sylvester is transformed into a rock in *Sylvester and the Magic Pebble* (Steig, 1969). *Goggles* (Keats, 1969) tells of the adventures of Peter and his friends escaping from the big boys. In *Thy Friend, Obadiah* (Turkle, 1969), Obadiah rescues a sea gull; the Spider Man outfoxes the gods in *A Story, a Story* (Haley, 1970). A boy rescues his girl friend from the moon god in *The Angry Moon* (Sleator, 1970). The male central characters engage in many exciting and heroic adventures which emphasize their cleverness.

In our sample of the Caldecott winners and runners-up in the last five years, we found only two of the 18 books were stories about girls.[11]

In one of these stories, *Sam, Bangs and Moonshine* (Ness, 1967), the girl has a boy's name. In the second, *The Emperor and the Kite* (Yolen, 1967), the heroine is a foreign princess.

Each of these girls does engage in an adventure. Sam's adventure takes place in her daydreams, while the adventure of the princess Djeow Seow occurs when her father's kingdom is seized by evil men. Like the male central characters who engage in rescues, Djeow Seow manages to save her father, but she accomplishes this task only by being so tiny and inconspicuous that the evil men do not notice her. Although Djeow Seow is one of the two women central characters, the message conveyed to readers seems to be that a girl can only triumph by playing the traditional feminine role. Women who succeed are those who are unobtrusive and work quietly behind the scenes. Women who succeed are little and inconspicuous—as are most women in picture books. Even heroines remain "invisible" females.

The Activities of Boys and Girls

We can summarize our first findings about differences in the activities of boys and girls by noting that in the world of picture books boys are active and girls are passive. Not only are boys presented in more exciting and adventuresome roles, but they engage in more varied pursuits and demand more independence. The more riotous activity is reserved for the boys. Mickey, the hero of *In the Night Kitchen* (Sendak, 1970), is tossed through the air and skips from bread to dough, punching and pounding. Then he makes an airplane and flies out into the night and dives, swims, and slides until he is home again. Similarly, Archie and Peter race, climb, and hide in the story of *Goggles* (Keats, 1969). Obadiah travels to the wharf in the cold of Massachusetts winter, and Sylvester searches for rocks in the woods.

In contrast, most of the girls in the picture books are passive and immobile. Some of them are restricted by their clothing—skirts and dresses are soiled easily and prohibit more adventuresome activities. In *The Fool of the World and the Flying Ship* (Ransome, 1968), the hero, the Fool, is dressed in a sensible manner, one which does not inhibit his movement in the tasks he has to accomplish. The princess, however, for whom all the exploits are waged, remains no more than her long gown allows her to be: a prize, an unrealistic passive creature symbolizing the reward for male adventuresomeness.

A second difference between the activities of boys and girls is that the girls are more often found indoors.[12] This places another limitation on the activities and potential adventures of girls. Even Sam, in *Sam, Bangs,*

and Moonshine (Ness, 1967), stays inside as she directs the activity of
the book. Sam constructs a fantasy world and sends Thomas, a little boy,
on wild goose chases to play out her fantasies. It is Thomas who rides
the bicycle and climbs the trees and rocks in response to Sam's fantasy.
Sam, however, waits for Thomas at home, looking out the windows or
sitting on the steps. Similarly, in *The Fool of the World* (Ransome, 1968),
the princess remains peering out the window of her castle, watching all
the activities on her behalf. While boys play in the real outdoors, girls
sit and watch them—cut off from that world by the window, porch, or
fence around their homes. This distinction parallels Erik Erikson's (1964)
conception of the masculine outer space and the feminine inner space.

Our third observation deals with the service activities performed by
the girls who remain at home. Even the youngest girls in the stories play
traditional feminine roles, directed toward pleasing and helping their
brothers and fathers. Obadiah's sisters cook in the kitchen as he sits at
the table sipping hot chocolate after his adventures. In *The Emperor and
the Kite* (Yolen, 1967), the emperor's daughters bring food to the
emperor's table, but their brothers rule the kingdom.

While girls serve, boys lead.[13] Drummer Hoff, although only a boy,
plays the crucial role in the firing of the cannon. Lupin, the Indian boy
in *The Angry Moon* (Sleator, 1970), directs the escape from the moon
god. He leads Lapowinsa, a girl exactly his size and age, every step of
the way. Even at the end of the story, after the danger of the Angry
Moon is past, Lupin goes down the ladder first "so that he could catch
Lapowinsa if she should slip."

Training for a dependent passive role may inhibit a girl's chances
for intellectual or creative success. It is likely that the excessive dependency encouraged in girls contributes to the decline in their achievement
which becomes apparent as they grow older. Maccoby (1966, p. 35) has
found that "For both sexes, there is a tendency for more passive-dependent
children to perform poorly on a variety of intellectual tasks, and for
independent children to excel."

The rescues featured in many stories require independence and
self-confidence. Once again, this is almost exclusively a male activity.[14]
Little boys rescue girls or helpless animals. Lupin saves a crying
Lapowinsa from the flames. Obadiah saves the seagull from a rusty
fishhook, and Alexander saves Willie, the windup mouse, from the fate
of becoming a "tossed-out toy." In *Frederick*, Frederick's creativeness
helps to spare his companions from the worst conditions of winter. In
Sam, Bangs, and Moonshine (Ness, 1967), Sam does not play the role of
the rescuer although she is the central character. Rather, her father must
step in and rescue Thomas and Bangs from drowning. In the end, Sam

herself "must be" saved from the potential consequences of her fantasy.

Finally, we want to note the sense of camaraderie that is encouraged among boys through their adventures. For example, *The Fool of the World* depends upon the help and talents of his male companions. In *Goggles* (Keats, 1969), the two male companions together outwit a gang of older boys. Similarly, the bonds of masculine friendship are stressed by Alexander, Frederick, and Frog and Toad.

In contrast, one rarely sees only girls working or playing together. Although in reality women spend much of their time with other women, picture books imply that women cannot exist without men. The role of most of the girls is defined primarily in relation to that of the boys and men in their lives.[15] It is interesting to note that Sam turns to a boy, not a girl, to accomplish all of the activity of her fantasies. Her dreams would have no reality without Thomas.

The sex differences we have noted are even more apparent in the prescriptive or etiquette books. An excellent example is found in a pair of matched books: *The Very Little Boy* (Krasilovsky, 1962a) and *The* by banging on a pan with a spoon. In contrast, the first page of *The* same author, follow the same format, and teach the same lesson: that little children grow up to be big children. However, the maturation process differs sharply for the very little boy and the very little girl.[16]

As we open to the first pages of *The Very Little Boy* (Krasilovsky, 1962a)we find the boy playing on the living room floor by the fireplace. He has already discarded a big rubber ball and is now making a racket by banging on a pan with a spoon. In contrast, the first page of *The Very Little Girl* (Krasilovsky, 1962b) shows the little girl sitting quietly in a big chair. There is no activity in the picture: the little girl is doing nothing but sitting with her hands folded in her lap. This is our introduction to an angelic little girl and a boisterous little boy.

In the following pages the author compares the size of the children to the objects around them; we find that the boy is smaller than a cornstalk, his baseball bat, his sled, his father's workbench, and a lawnmower. In contrast, the little girl is smaller than the rosebush, a kitchen stool, and her mother's workbasket. We note that the boy will be interested in sports—in fact, both the basketball and sled are *his*, waiting there for him until he is old enough to use them. The girl has been given no comparable presents by her parents. She can only look forward to conquering the rosebush and the kitchen stool.

Even more important is the way in which each of them relates to these objects. The little boy is in constant motion, continuously interacting with the world around him. He is *jumping* up to touch the scarecrow next to the cornstalk, *unwrapping* his baseball bat (leaving the mess of paper, string, and box for someone else to clean up), *building* blocks on top of his sled, *reaching* up on tiptoe to touch his father's workbench, and *spraying* the lawn (and himself) with the garden hose. In contrast, the little girl relates to each of the objects around her merely by *looking* at them.

Similarly, when the author indicates what each child is too small to do, we find that the little boy is too small to engage in a series of adventures. The little girl, however, is too small to *see* things from the sidelines. Thus, we are told that the little boy is too small to *march* in the parade, to *feed* the elephant at the zoo, and to *touch* the pedals on his bike. But the little girl is too small to *see* over the garden fence and to *see* the face on the grandfather clock. Even when the little girl is trying to see something she appears to be posing, and thus looks more like a doll than a curious little girl.

The little girl's clothes indicate that she is not meant to be active. She wears frilly, starchy, pink dresses, and her hair is always neatly combed and tied with ribbons. She looks pretty—too pretty to ride a bike, play ball, or visit the zoo.

Little girls are often pictured as pretty dolls who are not meant to do anything but be admired and bring pleasure. Their constant smile teaches that women are meant to please, to make others smile, and be happy. This image may reflect parental values. In a study of the attitudes of middle-class fathers toward their children, Aberle and Naegele (1960, pp. 188–198) report that the parent satisfaction with their daughters seemed to focus on their daughters being nice, sweet, pretty, affectionate, and well liked.

If we follow the little boy and little girl as they grow up, we can watch the development of the proper service role in a little woman. We are shown that the girl grows big enough to water the rosebush, stir the cake batter, set the table, play nurse, and help the doctor (who is, of course, a boy), pick fruit from the trees, take milk from the refrigerator, prepare a baby's formula, and feed her baby brother. Conveniently enough for their future husbands, girls in storybooks learn to wash, iron, hang up clothes to dry, cook, and set the table. Of course, when the boy grows up, he engages in more active pursuits: he catches butterflies, mows the lawn, marches in the parade, visits the zoo to feed the elephants, and hammers wood at the workbench.

One particularly striking contrast between the two children is illustrated by the picture of both of them with their dogs. In discussing how both have matured, the author tells us that both have grown up to be bigger than their pets. The picture of the little girl, however, makes us seriously doubt any grown-up self-confidence and authority. She is shown being pulled by a very small dog, whom she obviously cannot control. The little boy, in contrast, is in firm command of a much bigger dog, and does not even need a leash to control him.

It is easy to see why many little girls prefer to identify with the male role (Hartup, 1962; Brown, 1956). The little girl who does find the male role more attractive is faced with a dilemma. If she follows her desire and behaves like a tomboy, she may be criticized by her parents and teachers. On the other hand, if she gives up her yearnings and identifies with the traditional feminine role, she will feel stifled. Girls who wish to be more than placid and pretty are left without an acceptable role alternative. They must choose between alienation from their own sex of assignment, and alienation from their real behavioral and temperamental preferences.

The rigidity of sex-role stereotypes is not harmful only to little girls. Little boys may feel equally constrained by the necessity to be fearless, brave, and clever at all times. While girls are allowed a great deal of emotional expression, a boy who cries or expresses fear is unacceptable.[17] Just as the only girls who are heroines in picture books have boys' names or are foreign princesses, the only boys who cry in picture books are animals—frogs and toads and donkeys.

The price of the standardization and rigidity of sex roles is paid by children of both sexes. Eleanor Maccoby (1966, p. 35) has reported that analytic thinking, creativity, and general intelligence are associated with cross-sex typing. Thus, rigid sex-role definitions not only foster unhappiness in children but they also hamper the child's fullest intellectual and social development.

Role Models: Adult Men and Women

Adult role models provide another crucial component of sex-role socialization. By observing adult men and women, boys and girls learn what will be expected of them when they grow older. They are likely to identify with adults of the same sex, and desire to be like them. Thus, role models not only present children with future images of themselves but they also influence a child's aspirations and goals.

We found the image of the adult woman to be stereotyped and limited. Once again, the females are passive while the males are active. Men predominate in the outside activities while more of the women are inside. In the house, the women perform almost exclusively service functions, taking care of the men and children in their families. When men lead, women follow. When men rescue others, women are the rescued.[18]

In most of the stories, the sole adult woman is identified only as a mother or a wife. Obadiah's mother cooks, feeds him hot chocolate, and goes to church. The wife of the Sun God carries wood to help him build the house, but she never speaks. Sylvester's mother is shown sweeping, packing a picnic lunch, knitting, and crying. And Mrs. Noah, who had an important role in the biblical story of the flood, is completely omitted from the children's book version.

The remaining three roles that women play are also exclusively feminine roles: one is a fairy, the second a fairy godmother, and the third an underwater maiden. The fairy godmother is the only adult female who plays an active leadership role. The one nonstereotyped woman is clearly not a "normal" woman—she is a mythical creature.

In contrast to the limited range in women's roles, the roles that men play are varied and interesting. They are storekeepers, housebuilders, kings, spiders, storytellers, gods, monks, fighters, fishermen, policemen, soldiers, adventurers, fathers, cooks, preachers, judges, and farmers.

Perhaps our most significant finding was that *not one* woman in the Caldecott sample had a job or profession. In a country where 40 percent of the women are in the labor force, and close to 30 million women work, it is absurd to find that women in picture books remain only mothers and wives (U.S. Department of Labor, 1969). In fact, 90 percent of the women in this country will be in the labor force at some time in their lives.

Motherhood is presented in picture books as a full-time, lifetime job, although for most women it is in reality a part-time 10-year commitment. The changing demographic patterns in this country indicate that the average woman has completed the main portion of her childrearing by her mid-thirties and has 24 more productive years in the labor force if she returns to work once her children are in school. Today even the mothers of young children work. There are over 10 million of them currently in the labor force (U.S. Department of Labor, 1969, p. 39).

As the average woman spends even less time as a mother in the future, it is unrealistic for picture books to present the role of mother as the only possible occupation for the young girl. Alice Rossi (1964, p. 105) has noted that today the average girl may spend as many years with her dolls as the average mother spends with her children.

The way in which the motherhood role is presented in children's books is also unrealistic. She is almost always confined to the house, although she is usually too well dressed for housework. Her duties are not portrayed as difficult or challenging—she is shown as a household servant who cares for her husband and children. She washes dishes, cooks, vacuums, yells at the children, cleans up, does the laundry, and takes care of babies. For example, a typical domestic scene in *Sylvester and the Magic Pebble* shows the father reading the paper, Sylvester playing with his rock collection, and the mother sweeping the floor.

The picture books do not present a realistic picture of what real mothers do. Real mothers drive cars, read books, vote, take children on trips, balance checkbooks, engage in volunteer activities, ring doorbells canvassing, raise money for charity, work in the garden, fix things in the house, are active in local politics, belong to the League of Women Voters and the PTA, etc.[19]

Nor do these picture books provide a realistic image of fathers and husbands. Fathers never help in the mundane duties of child care. Nor do husbands share the dishwashing, cooking, cleaning, or shopping. From these stereotyped images in picture books, little boys may learn to expect their wives to do all the housework and to cater to their needs. These unreal expectations of marriage will inevitably bring disappointment and discontent to both the male and the female partners.

Lonnie Carton's two books, *Mommies* (1960*b*) and *Daddies* (1960*a*) are excellent examples of the contrasting lives to which boys and girls can look forward if they follow the role models provided by the adult characters in picture books. As the books begin, Mommy puts on her apron to prepare for a day of homemaking, while Daddy dashes out of the house with his briefcase on the way to work. The next two pages show the real differences between the woman's world and the man's world. Daddies are shown as carpenters, executives, house painters, mailmen, teachers, cooks, and storekeepers. They are also the bearers of knowledge.

> Daddies drive the trucks and cars,
> The buses, boats and trains.
> Daddies build the roads and bridges,
> Houses, stores and planes.
>
> Daddies work in factories and
> Daddies make the things grow.
> Daddies work to figure out
> The things we do not know (1960).

On the corresponding two pages (in *Mommies*), we learn that, although the mother supposedly does "lots and lots," her tasks consist of washing dishes, scrubbing pots and walls, cooking, baking, tying shoes, catching balls, and answering questions (which seems to be her most "creative" role so far). Mommy does leave the house several times but only to shop for groceries or to take the children out to play. (She does drive a car in this book, however, which is unusual.)

In contrast, when Daddy comes home he not only plays in a more exciting way with the children but he provides their contact with the outside world. While Mommies are restrictive, and "shout if you play near the street," Daddies take you on trips in cars, buses, and trains; Daddies take you to the circus, park, and zoo; buy you ice cream; and teach you to swim. Daddies also understand you better because they "know you're big enough and brave enough to do lots of things that mommies think are much too hard for you." Mothers, however, are useful for taking care of you when you are sick, cleaning up after you, and telling you what to do. Mommies do smile, hug, comfort, and nurture, but they also scold and instruct in a not altogether pleasant manner. They tell you to be quiet, and to "Sit still and eat!" Ironically, this negative image of the nagging mother may be a result of an exclusive devotion to motherhood. As Alice Rossi has observed: "If a woman's adult efforts are concentrated exclusively on her children, she is likely more to stifle than broaden her children's perspective and preparation for adult life. . . . In myriad ways the mother binds the child to her, dampening his initiative, resenting his growing independence in adolescence, creating a subtle dependence which makes it difficult for the child to achieve full adult stature" (1964, p. 113).

In addition to having a negative effect on children, this preoccupation with motherhood may also be harmful to the mother herself. Pauline Bart (1970, p. 72) has reported extreme depression among middle-aged women who have been overinvolved with and have overidentified with their children.

We have already noted that there are no working women in the Caldecott sample. It is no disparagement of the housewife or mother to point out that alternative roles are available to, and chosen by, many women and that girls can be presented with alternative models so that they, like boys, may be able to think of a wide range of future options.

Because there are no female occupational role models in the Caldecott books, we will turn to the prescribed role books to examine the types of occupations that are encouraged for boys and girls. For this analysis we will compare a very popular pair of Hallmark matched books: *What Boys Can Be* (Walley, n.d., *a*) and *What Girls Can Be* (Walley, n.d., *b*). Both books follow the same format: each page shows a boy or a girl playing an occupational role. We are told that boys can be:

> *a fireman* who squirts water on the flames, and
> *a baseball player* who wins lots of games.
> *a bus driver* who helps people travel far, or
> *a policeman* with a siren in his car.

> *a cowboy* who goes on cattle drives, and
> *a doctor* who helps to save people's lives.
> *a sailor* on a ship that takes you everywhere, and
> *a pilot* who goes flying through the air.
> *a clown* with silly tricks to do, and
> a pet tiger owner who *runs the zoo.*
> *a farmer* who drives a big red tractor, and
> on TV shows, if I become *an actor.*
> *an astronaut* who lives in a space station, and
> someday grow up to be *President* of the nation
> [Emphasis added; Walley, n.d., *a*]

The second book tells us that girls can be:

> *a nurse,* with white uniforms to wear, or
> *a stewardess,* who flies everywhere.
> *a ballerina,* who dances and twirls around, or
> *a candy shop owner,* the best in town.
> *a model,* who wears lots of pretty clothes,
> *a big star* in the movies and on special TV shows.
> *a secretary* who'll type without mistakes, or
> *an artist*, painting trees and clouds and lakes.
> *a teacher in nursery school* some day, or
> *a singer* and make records people play.
> *a designer of dresses* in the very latest style, or
> *a bride,* who comes walking down the aisle.
> *a housewife,* someday when I am grown, and
> *a mother,* with some children of my own
> [Emphasis added; Walley, n.d., *b*]

The two concluding pictures are the most significant; the ultimate goal for which little boys are to aim is nothing less than the president of the nation. For girls, the comparable pinnacle of achievement is motherhood!

Many of the differences in the occupations in these two books parallel the male/female differences we have already noted. One is the inside/outside distribution. Eleven of the female occupations are shown being performed inside, while only three are outside. Indeed, none of the female occupations listed necessitates being performed outdoors. The ratio for the male occupations is exactly reversed: three are inside, 11 outside.

We already observed that little girls are encouraged to succeed by looking pretty and serving others. It should therefore not be surprising to find that the women are concentrated in glamorous and service occupations. The most prestigious feminine occupations are those in which a girl can succeed only if she is physically attractive. The glamour occupations of model and movie star are the two most highly rewarded among the female choices. Since few women can ever achieve high status in these glamorous professions, the real message in these books is that women's true function lies in service. Service occupations, such as nurse, secretary, housewife, mother, and stewardess, reinforce the traditional patterns to feminine success.

Although some of the male occupations also require physical attractiveness (actor) and service (bus driver), there is a much greater range of variation in the other skills they require: baseball players need athletic ability, policemen are supposed to be strong and brave, pilots and doctors need brains, astronauts need mechanical skills and great energy, clowns must be clever and funny, and presidents need political acumen.

If we compare the status level of the male and female occupations, it is apparent that men fill the most prestigious and highly paid positions. They are the doctors, pilots, astronauts, and presidents. Even when men and women are engaged in occupations in the same field, it is the men who hold the positions which demand the most skill and leadership. While men are doctors, women are nurses; while men are pilots, women are stewardesses. Only one of the women is engaged in a professional occupation: the teacher. It is important to note, however, that the authors carefully specified that she was a *nursery school teacher.*

Similarly, most of the occupations that require advanced education are occupied by men. Four of the males have apparently gone to college, compared with only one of the women.

It is clear that the book *What Boys Can Be* encourages a little boy's career ambitions. He is told that he has the potential for achieving any of the exciting and highly rewarded occupations in our society.

In contrast, the book *What Girls Can Be* tells the little girl that she can have ambitions if she is pretty. Her potential for achieving a prestigious and rewarding job is dependent on her physical attributes. If she is not attractive, she must be satisfied with a life of mundane service. No women are represented in traditional male occupations, such as doctor, lawyer, engineer, or scientist. With women comprising 7 percent of the country's physicians and 4 percent of its lawyers, surely it is more probable that a girl will achieve one of these professional statuses than it is that a boy will become president.

The occupational distribution presented in these books is even worse than the real inequitable distribution of employment in the professions. Picture books could inspire children to strive for personal and occupational goals that would take them beyond their everyday world. Instead, women are denied both the due recognition for their present achievements and the encouragement to aspire to more broadly defined possibilities in the future.

Conclusion

Preschool children invest their intellects and imaginations in picture books at a time when they are forming their self-images and future expectations. Our study has suggested that the girls and women depicted in these books are a dull and stereotyped lot. We have noted that little girls receive attention and praise for their attractiveness, while boys are admired for their achievements and cleverness. Most of the women in picture books have status by virtue of their relationships to specific men— they are the wives of the kings, judges, adventurers, and explorers, but they themselves are not the rulers, judges, adventurers, and explorers.

Through picture books, girls are taught to have low aspirations because there are so few opportunities portrayed as available to them. The world of picture books never tells little girls that as women they might find fulfillment outside of their homes or through intellectual pursuits. Women are excluded from the world of sports, politics, and science. Their future occupational world is presented as consisting primarily of glamour and service. Ironically, many of these books are written by prize-winning female authors whose own lives are probably unlike those they advertise.[20]

It is clear that the storybook characters reinforce the traditional sex-role assumptions. Perhaps this is indicative of American preferences for creativeness and curiosity in boys and neatness and passivity in girls. Many parents want their sons to grow up to be brave and intelligent and their daughters to be pretty and compliant.

In the past, social theorists have assumed that such strongly differentiated sex roles would facilitate a child's identification with the parent of the same sex. For example, Talcott Parsons (1955) has commented that "if the boy is to identify with his father there must be discrimination in role terms between the two parents" (1955, p. 80). More recently, however, Philip Slater (1964) has argued that adult role models who exhibit stereotyped sex-role differentiation may impede, rather than facilitate, the child's sex-role identification. Children find it easier to identify with less differentiated and less stereotyped parental role models. It is easier for them to internalize parental values when nurturance (the typically feminine role) and discipline (the typically masculine role) come from the same person.

Not only do narrow role definitions impede the child's identification with the same sex parent, but rigid sex-role distinctions may actually be harmful to the normal personality development of the child. In fact, Slater (1964) has postulated a negative relationship between the child's emotional adjustment and the degree of parental role differentiation.

Some evidence, then, suggests these sex roles are rigid and possibly harmful. They discourage and restrict a woman's potential and offer her fulfillment only through the limited spheres of glamour and service. More flexible definitions of sex roles would seem to be more healthful in encouraging a greater variety of role possibilities. Stories could provide a more positive image of a woman's potential—of her physical, intellectual, creative, and emotional capabilities.

Picture books could also present a less stereotyped and less rigid definition of male roles by encouraging boys to express their emotions as well as their intellect. Books might show little boys crying, playing with stuffed toys and dolls, and helping in the house. Stereotypes could be weakened by books showing boys being rewarded for being emotional and supportive, and girls being rewarded for being intelligent and adventuresome.

Although Zelditch (1955, p. 341) has noted the cross-cultural predominance of males in instrumental roles and females in expressive roles—like the patterns we found in children's books—Slater (1964) suggests that the ability to alternate instrumental and expressive role performance rapidly—what he calls interpersonal flexibility—is coming to be more highly valued in our society.

This argues for less stereotyped adult roles. Fathers could take a more active role in housework and child care. And, similarly, the roles of adult women could be extended beyond the limited confines of the home, as in fact they are. When women are shown at home, they could be portrayed as the busy and creative people that many housewives are. For example, the woman in *Pop Corn and Ma Goodness,* the single exception to the Caldecott norm, equally shares diversified activities with her husband.

If these books are to present real-life roles, they could give more attention to single parents and divorced families. Stories could present the real-life problems that children in these families face: visiting a divorced father, having two sets of parents, not having a father at school on father's day, or having a different name than one's mother.

The simplified and stereotyped images in these books present such a narrow view of reality that they must violate the child's own knowledge of a rich and complex world.[21] Perhaps these images are motivated by the same kind of impulse that makes parents lie to their children in order to "protect" them.[22] As a result, the child is given an idealized version of the truth, rather than having his real and pressing questions answered. Not only are the child's legitimate questions ignored, but no effort is made to create a social awareness which encompasses the wider society. Picture books actually deny the existence of the discontented, the poor, the ethnic minorities, and the urban slum dwellers.

Stories have always been a means for perpetuating the fundamental cultural values and myths. Stories have also been a stimulus for fantasy imagination and achievement. Books could develop this latter quality to encourage the imagination and creativity of all children. This would provide an important implementation of the growing demand for *both* girls and boys to have a real opportunity to fulfill their human potential.

Notes

1. We are indebted to William J. Goode, Kai Erikson, Alice Rossi, and Erving Goffman for their insightful comments on an earlier draft of this paper which was presented to the 1971 meeting of the American Sociological Association, Denver, Colorado.
2. Erving Goffman has questioned the direct relationship we have postulated between the themes in children's literature and societal values. He suggests that literary themes may provide alternative cultural norms or irrelevant fantasy outlets. Unfortunately, we do not know of any research other than McClelland's (1961) supporting either our own formulation or Goffman's.
3. As quoted in McClelland (1961, p. 71).
4. The Caldecott winners and runners-up for the past five years are: 1967 winner (Ness, 1967), 1967 runner-up (Emberley, 1967b); 1968 winner (Emberley, 1967a), 1968 runners-up (Lionni, 1967; Yashima, 1967; Yolen, 1967); 1969 winner (Ransome, 1968), 1969 runner-up (Dayrell, 1968); 1970 winner (Steig, 1969), 1970 runners-up (Keats, 1969; Lionni, 1969; Preston, 1969; Turkle, 1969; Zemach, 1969); 1971 winner (Haley, 1970), 1971 runners-up (Sleater, 1970; Lobel, 1970; Sendak, 1970).
5. We wish to thank Robert Garlock, product manager of Little Golden Books, for his help with this information and for furnishing many of the books themselves.
6. The Dr. Seuss books, although popular among preschool audiences, were not included as a supplementary sample because they represent only one author and one publisher rather than a more broadly based series. They do, however, conform to the general pattern of sex-role portrayal that we found among the Caldecott winners.
7. The illustrations of Caldecott winners and runners-up since 1967 included 166 male people, 22 female people, and 57 pictures of both males and females together. The animal illustrations included 95 of male animals, one of a female animal, and 12 of both male and female animals together. Together, this resulted in a total male/female ratio of 11:1. There were also 14 illustrations of characters without a sex.

8. The statistics for titles of the Caldecott winners from the inception of the award in 1938 show eight titles with male names, three with female names, one with both a male and a female name together, and 22 titles without names of either sex. This resulted in an 8:3 male/female ratio. The statistics for titles of recent Caldecott winners and runners-up (since 1967) show eight titles with male names, one with a female name, one with both together, and 10 titles without names of either sex. This resulted in an 8:1 male/female ratio.

9. The statistics for the titles of the Little Golden Books selling over three million copies show nine titles with male names, four with female names, one with both together, and 14 titles without the names of either sex. This resulted in a 9:4 male/female ratio.

10. The statistics for the titles of Newbery winners since the inception of the award in 1922 show 20 titles with male names, six titles with female names, none with both, and 23 titles without the names of either sex. This resulted in a 10:3 male/female ratio.

11. The statistics for central characters in the Caldecott winners since 1938 show 14 males, ten females, six males and females together, and four central characters without a sex. This results in a 7:5 male/female ratio. It is important to note that the situation is becoming worse, not better. During the last five years the ratio of male to female central characters has increased. The statistics for central characters in Caldecott winners and runners-up during the last five years show a 7:2 male/female ratio in contrast to an 11:9 male/female ratio for the years prior to 1967. The statistics for central characters in the Newbery winners since 1922 show 31 males, 11 females, four males and females together, and three central characters without a sex. This results in a 3:1 male/female ratio. The statistics for central characters in the Little Golden Books selling over three million copies show an 8:3 ratio of male/female people, a 5:2 ratio of male/female animals, and a 5:3 ratio of all males and females together.

12. The statistics for activities of boys and girls in Caldecott winners since 1967 show 48 male characters indoors, 105 male characters outdoors, 15 females indoors, and 26 females outdoors. This means that 32.6 percent of the males are shown indoors, while 36.5 percent of the females are shown indoors.

13. The statistics for activities of boys and girls in Caldecott winners and runners-up since 1967 show a 0:3 ratio of males/females in service functions, and a 3:2 ratio of males/females in leadership functions.

14. The statistics for activities of boys and girls in Caldecott winners and runners-up since 1967 show a 5:1 ratio of males/females in rescue functions.

15. This problem is not confined to children's books. As Virginia Woolf pointed out over 40 years ago, women in literature are rarely represented as friends: "They are now and then mothers and daughters. But almost without exception they are shown in their relation to men. It was strange to think that all the great women of fiction were, until Jane Austen's day, . . . seen only in relation to the other sex. And how little can a man know even of that when he observes it through the black or rosy spectacles which sex puts upon his nose. Hence, perhaps the particular nature of women in fiction; the astonishing extremes of her beauty and horror" (1929, p. 8).

16. We gratefully acknowledge Barbara Fried's imaginative analysis of these two books in her paper, "What Our Children Are Reading," written for Sociology 62a, Yale University, fall term, 1970.

17. But Hartley (1959) also discovered that as a corollary the boys felt extreme pressure as a result of the rigid masculine role prescriptions which they saw as demanding that they be strong, intelligent, and generally successful. The boys believed that adults liked girls better because the girls were cute and well behaved.

18. Among the Caldecott winners and runners-up for the past five years, we found that women were engaged in a much narrower range of activities than men. The ratio of male to female adults engaged in service activities was 1:7, while the ratio of male to female adults in leadership activities was 5:0, and the ratio of the male to female adults in rescue activities was 4:1. In addition, 40 percent of adult females, but only 31 percent of adult males, were pictured indoors.

19. Only one of the Caldecott winners presents the woman as an active equal to her husband. It is Edna Mitchell Preston's *Pop Corn and Ma Goodness* (1969).

20. A tabulation of the percentage of female authors indicates that 41 percent of the Caldecott and 58 percent of the Newbery Medal winners were written by women. However, women authors appear to be more positive than male counterparts. The pre-1967 Caldecotts, which had a larger percentage of female central characters, also have a larger percentage of female authors: 48 percent compared with 33 percent.

21. We are indebted to William J. Goode for this insight.

22. This is not to deny the value of fantasy. As Margaret Fuller wrote in 1855: "Children need some childish talk, some childish play, some childish books. But they also need, and need more, difficulties to overcome, and a sense of the vast mysteries which the progress of their intelligence shall aide them to unravel. This sense is naturally their delight . . . and it must not be dulled by premature explanations or subterfuges of any kind" (pp. 310–313). Alice Rossi brought this work to our attention.

Bibliography

ABERLE, DAVID F., and KASPER D. NAEGELE. 1960. "Middle-Class Fathers' Occupational Role and Attitudes towards Children." In *A Modern Introduction to the Family*, ed. by Norman W. Bell and Ezra F. Vogel. New York: Free Press.

BART, PAULINE. 1970. "Portnoy's Mother's Complaint." *Trans-Action*, November/December.

BROWN, DANIEL G. 1956. "Sex Role Preference in Young Children." *Psychological Monograph* 70, no. 14.

CARTON, LONNIE C. 1960a. *Daddies*. New York: Random House.

CARTON, LONNIE C. 1960b. *Mommies*. New York: Random House.

CHILD STUDY ASSOCIATION. 1969. *List of Recommended Books*. New York: Child Study Association.

DAYRELL, ELPHINSTONE. 1968. *Why the Sun and the Moon Live in the Sky*. Boston: Houghton Mifflin.

EMBERLEY, BARBARA. 1967a. *Drummer Hoff*. Englewood Cliffs, N.J.: Prentice-Hall.

EMBERLEY, BARBARA. 1967*b*. *One Wide River to Cross*. Englewood Cliffs, N.J.: Prentice-Hall.

ERIKSON, ERIK H. 1964. "Inner and Outer Space: Reflections on Womanhood." *The Woman in America*, edited by Robert Jay Lifton. Boston: Houghton Mifflin.

FULLER, MARGARET. 1855. "Children's Books." In *Women in the Nineteenth Century*, ed. by John J. Jewett, Boston.

HALEY, GAIL E. 1970. *A Story, a Story: An African Tale Retold*. New York: Atheneum.

HARTLEY, RUTH E. 1959. "Sex-Role Pressures and the Socialization of the Male Child." *Psychological Reports* 5:457–468.

HARTLEY, RUTH E. 1960. "Children's Concepts of Male and Female Roles." *Merrill-Palmer Quarterly* 6:83–91.

HARTUP, WILLARD W. 1962. "Some Correlates of Parental Imitation in Young Children." *Child Development* 33:85–96.

KEATS, EZRA JACK. 1969. *Goggles!* Toronto: Macmillan.

KRASILOVSKY, PHYLLIS. 1962*a*. *The Very Little Boy*. Illustrated by Ninon. New York: Doubleday.

KRASILOVSKY, PHYLLIS. 1962*b*. *The Very Little Girl*. Illustrated by Ninon. New York: Doubleday.

LIONNI, LEO. 1967. *Frederick*. New York: Random House.

LOBEL, ARNOLD. 1970. *Frog and Toad Are Friends*. New York: Harper & Row.

MCCLELLAND, DAVID C. 1961. *The Achieving Society*. New York: Free Press.

MACCOBY, ELEANOR E. 1966. "Sex Differences in Intellectual Functioning." In *The Development of Sex Differences*. Stanford, Calif.: Stanford University Press.

NESS, EVALINE. 1967. *Sam, Bangs, and Moonshine*. New York: Holt, Rinehart & Winston.

NILSEN, ALLEEN PACE. 1970. "Women in Children's Literature." Paper presented at workshop on Children's Literature, Modern Language Association Meeting, December 27, New York.

PARSONS, TALCOTT. 1955. "Family Structure and the Socialization of the Child." In *Family, Socialization and Interaction Process*, ed. by Talcott Parsons and Robert F. Bales. New York: Free Press.

PRESTON, EDNA MITCHELL. 1969. *Pop Corn and Ma Goodness*. New York: Viking.

RANSOME, ARTHUR. 1968. *The Fool of the World and the Flying Ship*. New York: Farrar, Straus & Giroux.

ROSSI, ALICE. 1964. "Equality between the Sexes." In *The Woman in America*, ed. by Robert Jay Lifton. Boston: Houghton Mifflin.

SENDAK, MAURICE. 1970. *In the Night Kitchen*. New York: Harper & Row.

SLATER, PHILIP. 1964. "Parental Role Differentiation." In *The Family: Its Structure and Functions*, ed. by Rose L. Coser. New York: St. Martin's.

SLEATOR, WILLIAM. 1970. *The Angry Moon*. Boston: Little, Brown.

STEIG, WILLIAM. 1969. *Sylvester and the Magic Pebble*. New York: Simon & Schuster.

TURKLE, BRINTON. 1969. *Thy Friend, Obadiah*. New York: Viking.

U.S. DEPARTMENT OF LABOR. 1969. *1969 Handbook on Women Workers*. Washington, D.C.: Government Printing Office.

WALLEY, DEAN. n.d., *a*. *What Boys Can Be*. Kansas City: Hallmark.

WALLEY, DEAN. n.d., *b. What Girls Can Be.* Kansas City: Hallmark.

WOOLF, VIRGINIA. 1929. *A Room of One's Own.* New York: Harcourt, Brace & World.

YASHIMA, TARO. 1967. *Seashore Story.* New York: Viking.

YOLEN, JANE. 1967. *The Emperor and the Kite.* Cleveland: World.

ZELDITCH, MORRIS, JR. 1955. "Role Differentiation in the Nuclear Family." In *Family, Socialization, and Interaction Process,* ed. by Talcott Parsons and Robert F. Bales. New York: Free Press.

ZEMACH, HARVE. 1969. *The Judge.* New York: Farrar, Straus & Giroux.

DICK AND JANE AS VICTIMS:
SEX STEREOTYPING IN CHILDREN'S READERS—
EXCERPTS

The Second-Sex Themes: Nice Girls Finish Last

Explicitly or implicitly, consciously or unconsciously, the stories we are going to examine illustrate the negative of active mastery. Dependency and Pseudo-dependency. Passivity. Incompetence. Fearfulness. People who have these traits—people who are docile, fearful, dependent—cannot conceive of themselves becoming responsible for their own lives or taking the active role in a situation. They are denied the dignity of solving their own problems. They see themselves as the Other,[1] one who supports those who act or one who provides the background against which the action takes place. Their goals are painfully limited. If they do act, it is usually stupidly. Naturally, they have mishaps. Inevitably, they turn away from the frightening, punishing, overwhelming outside world and focus on the friendly, familiar terrain of the home. Naturally they are victims and targets for ridicule. Could anyone seriously hold up such narrow, unenviable, life-denying traits for our children to model themselves on? The answer is yes and no. No, if you're referring to boys. Yes, if you're speaking of girls.

More subtle indoctrination, equally unhealthy for little girls, is the insistence on self-abnegation and the womanly "virtues" of domesticity. The message clearly written between the lines for even the slowest reader to read is for girls to be obedient and comply uncomplainingly—even happily—with the wishes of others. What happens to a girl who is told repeatedly to minister to others' needs and comforts and to put others first? She gets in the habit of putting herself last. Behind the stove where she is told she belongs.

Passivity, docility, dependency (pseudo- and real)

Always it is the female of the species who exhibits this mild, soft, spiritless behavior within the pages of the readers. By our count, over six to one—or 119 girls to 19 boys. Mothers move through these pages like so much ectoplasm. Little girls endlessly play with dolls, cry over dolls, give tea parties, look on helplessly or passively or admiringly while boys take action. Tommy, on the other hand, doesn't play house—he builds one. Sally's role in the same sorry tale is clear—she puts on her bonnet and admires the results.

In story after story, girls like Sally are shown as spectators of life. They are given things, told things, provide a ready-made audience and instant admiration for whatever's going on. In illustration after illustration, as well as in the stories themselves, girls look on with hands behind their backs. They look on while boys play cowboy, look on while boys make carts, look on while boys rescue animals, look on while boys save the day. And they admire, oh, how they admire what they see: "Oh, Raymond, boys are much braver than girls!" When one girl merely reports a forest fire—what anyone breathing might be expected to do under similar circumstances—the author is so overcome that he pours praise on her as if she had put out the blaze single-handedly at the risk of her life.

Girls often depend on boys when they are quite capable of handling the situation themselves. One finds she can only skate when she has Mark to lean on; another can only reach a jar if a boy brings a stepladder. Almost without exception females in the readers are subordinate to males. Girls, small and large, are helped out of one difficulty after another by their brothers, older or younger. On a trip to the store two boys, symbolically enough, walk in front; two girls follow meekly behind.

Altruism, kindness, and the womanly "virtues"

Altruism is admirable. Everybody knows that. Yet in the readers, the altruism of girls is always tinged with self-abnegation. Girls' frequent efforts to help others are motivated by very generous and noble impulses, but such efforts always require a personal sacrifice, which is presented as a normal and positive thing. Girls in the readers are good by definition. Mary is a kind, thoughtful, industrious sister. When Sam eats up the cake, when Walter reveals the secret, the girls understand—and forgive. But these splendid virtues are called up exclusively in the circumscribed arena of the female world.

Boys, when *they're* good give up some time and energy for others but there is no sense of sacrifice. They are creating something new not taking something away from themselves. They are *civic*-minded like the fellow who figured out how to utilize sidewalk space for play space or like the boys who raised money for a hospital. They use initiative in carrying out their good impulses. Since their time is valuable, they can rarely stop and help on a one-to-one basis; boys' help is provided on a whole-sale basis, to whole neighborhoods or villages or groups of people. Altruism is a positive characteristic for benevolent boys, 55 times; a self-effacing one for "good" girls, 22 times.

Goal constriction and sex-role stereotyping

Girls in the readers rehearse their domestic roles continuously—166 times to boys' 50. Girls are found cooking 33 times, cleaning 27 times. The most popular room in any given house, for a girl, is the kitchen. This could be true because the refrigerator is an acknowledged mecca for all small people, but the reader's girl is in her kitchen for other reasons. She is reinforcing her major sex-dictated stereotype. Domestic. These girls make lunch, fix dinner, prepare sandwiches or a salad and fill a picnic basket (while the boy-picnickers play), or bake cookies for a coed party. They stand at sinks high with pots and pans, scoop up broken eggs, set the table, scrub floors, wash laundry, wash dinner dishes, while their brothers scoot out to play. They're incorrigible, these girls, One of them insists on helping cook, clean, and serve supper, though she has just succeeded in rescuing a drowning fisherman. What boy could equal her? Or would want to? One young girl who longed to go out to play Jack-in-the-Box had to clean up after dinner since she was the only girl in the family. But she is an exception; some reader girls are known to be happy only when cleaning and we quote: ". . . she never thought of anything but dusting, washing, rubbing, and scrubbing."

When they leave the kitchen, what do little girls do? They go marketing. Once a girl who wants to do "something different" is offered a shopping trip to buy her brother some t-shirts. Girls are also pictured as addicted to sewing and mending, but nowhere is one shown making a new dress. Creativity, even in the domestic ghetto where they are purportedly sovereign, is still out of reach for girls.

Except for these domestic chores at which girls are sometimes as expert as their mothers (a girl's inborn aptitude for drudgery is presented in the same spirit as a Black person's "natural rhythm"), only rarely are girls permitted to be at the center of the action. In one such real life instance when a girl succeeds outside her domestic role, her success is explained as exceptional: "Amelia Earhart was different from the beginning from the other girls." In order to be popular, Katie, a genuine achiever, takes care to disguise her prowess. What price success for a girl?

Where boys are concerned, domestic chores are performed grudgingly in order to assist their mothers and sisters, whose proper province it is to cope with such matters. Now and again a boy might help with the dishes or do heavy work such as waxing a floor or clearing out a woodsman's cabin. There are very few instances of boys scrubbing, cleaning, or scouring in the ordinary course of things as their share in the common domestic responsibility, just as a girl is never depicted changing tires or sawing and hammering. If a boy cooks, it is to make a mustard sandwich for himself or to cut ham with a big knife. A boy may eat cookies, but he mustn't bake them. Not on the pages of the readers. Only once is a boy required to act as a babysitter, which he does reluctantly, whereas this is a common occupation for girls. But even here the achievement and learning aspect for boys is not forgotten. In the course of his term as sitter he is required to use his ingenuity to get his foolish sister out of a locked closet.

In the readers, gender terminology is often used as a means of indicating or underlining characteristics in animals or inanimate things. Soft, delicate fluffy kittens are usually female. So is the lazy magpie. Boisterous, playful dogs are male. Old people who are mean and ugly are female (possibly an unconscious carryover of the wicked old witch syndrome, but where is the equally infamous bogey man?). Wise old people are without exception male, and a human being of any stature is male by definition. Thus, hieroglyphologists are "men" who study Egyptian writings, and elsewhere we meet "sayings of Wise Men." We don't want to be unreasonable and hold the readers responsible for the sexism built into the English language, which symbolically has handed over the entire world to the men, with pronouns like the bisexual "he" for he-and-she, and words like "mankind" that stand for all of us. But the readers don't have to extend this practice by defining archeologists as "men" who dig. Archeologists are also women. Why not, simply, "people" who dig? A preponderantly female Red Cross Unit is referred to as "brothers." Why not as "one family"? The built-in sexism of our common language is loud and clear in a comment made to the young Oliver Perry on these pages: "You're certainly not up to a man's work, so you'll start as a scrubwoman."

Incompetency and mishaps

Both boys and girls have mishaps with equal frequency, but girls' mishaps come about while carrying out domestic responsibilities or through simply being female (hence foolish). Boys' accidents come about through roughhousing or adventuring. Thus, one kind of mishap results from stupidity, the other from curiosity and enthusiasm. One girl manages to get dirty simply by sitting down whereas an active boy soils his clothing by playing with a dog. There are often stories about girls who have ripped and spoiled their clothing, and, in one rare instance, when this happens to a boy, the school principal appoints his assistant, a woman, to do the mending. Boys' mishaps are thoroughly mitigated because they are part of an adventurous experience from which they profit. If a boy is temporarily incompetent, say in putting a toy together, the ineptitude doesn't last long and he soon fixes it. Girls had better make it on the first chance as they are not given a second try. They don't. A girl falls from stilts on her first attempt and that is her final downfall; she gets no other chance. All too typically, a girl's failure is often in tandem with a boy's success. A boy solves a problem that a mother and daughter cannot unravel. A girl who mistakes a stick for a snake is shown the light and reassured by a boy. Boys are seldom conned. That's for girls. A foolish princess believes every word she hears, just as Red Riding Hood believes the wolf. In one amazing story the author, by some Freudian slip, changes the sex of the stupid *female* kitten in time for "him" to outwit the fox!

Victimizing and humiliating the opposite sex and excessive aggression

We discovered close to 100 stories that condoned meanness and cruelty as part of the story line. This figure would be far higher if we had included fantasy and animal stories in our statistical count. There were 67 stories in which one sex demeaned the other: 65 of these were directed against girls, only two against boys. This particular aspect of cruelty would be greatly swelled if fantasy tales were included as well. Girls are attacked as a class. The negative behavior always goes unpunished and is never commented upon as such. The way to gain a sense of superiority albeit a highly immature one, is to make someone else seem unimportant. Possibly this is a misguided attempt on the part of the readers to co-opt the boys, since they have more difficulty learning to read and girls usually outstrip them in this all-important area in the early school years. More likely, however, it reflects the way society unconsciously views females.

There is also a slightly higher frequency and less subtle onslaught of these stories in the early grades when children are young and impressionable. Since we find this fault such a serious one, we would like to point out that series of books published by Sullivan, Harper and Row, Houghton Mifflin, and Macmillan, in that order, are the chief offenders, although the other series follow closely behind.

In the stories of excessive aggression, it is notable that males are usually the aggressors and that females are only one of several types of victims. But girls as well as boys join in the sport of demeaning girls in their anxiety to please the power faction. You can hear them put themselves down with remarks like: "I'm just a girl but I know enough not to do that." or, "Even I can do it and you know how stupid I am." The readers give boys the ammunition, if society hasn't done so already, to attack girls as foolish, vain, silly, dumb, boring, no good at games and sports, etc. ad nauseum. To be in the company of girls lowers one's status, children learn at age six, as they are learning to read. Boys are never ridiculed as members of the group "male." In the 65 stories in which the readers ridicule and demean girls, girls are excluded from groups, rejected from gangs, deliberately shown up as scaredy-cats and made fun of for their domesticity. A boy ridicules some girls who are cooking by remarking: ". . . but who wants to eat dinner with a lot of girls anyway?", ". . . good thing for a girl to learn to cook," ". . . women sure are funny!" One girl gets into a baseball team but the other team laughs at her and at the team since "They must be terrible if they have a girl pitcher." "Don't be silly," says a small boy to his older sister when she points out his error, "Girls never understand anything."

Not only do boys tease girls for their stupidity when they make mistakes, they show them up repeatedly by succeeding where girls fail. They charitably "allow" girls to do things "even though" they are girls, but the smartest girl in the class is not smart enough to get on the passenger list of a time machine in a reader story—space is reserved for the smartest boy.

It is important to note that while boys are being given permission to vent a twisted type of aggression and sadism, girls are being told not only to suppress their natural aggressive urges but to accept their role as victims and passive foils without a struggle. Quite often, animal stories offer a mask behind which aggressive tricks can be played, as in the case of Mr. Fox who tricks Mr. Crow by flattery until Mr. Crow opens his mouth and loses his food to the fox. Aggression of the excessive type is shown twice as often by male children as they shoot animals to prove their strength; trick girls, animals, and other boys in a sadistic manner. Now and then a girl hits or strikes back at a boy, or is rude to another girl, but she has to become a witch before a female may be permitted any real wickedness. And witches usually get it in the end. Of all the areas studied, girl-baiting and belittling have the most pernicious potential for lowering the self-esteem of females, too young yet to assess the truth of the claims that they are the inferior sex.

Feeling and expressing emotion

Neither girls nor boys in the readers exhibit any realistic range of human emotions, but even the few permitted are off-limits to boys. Emotions belong to the lesser sex, something that weak, foolish people alone experience. Boys must fight back fears and tears, while girls succumb without a struggle to irrational terrors and foolish weeping. Only on the pages of a reader does a girl weep nonstop from morning to night over a broken doll. Only on the pages of a reader does a boy remain impassive while his canoe proceeds out of control through the rapids. Gender determines these things. Other natural emotions such as anger, joy, compassion, sadness, even love, make only brief appearances in the entire series. Spontaneous and honest expression of feelings is a rare thing indeed, here or in life, but its absence in the readers is the more lamentable because it reinforces unreasoning cultural taboos against expressing emotions, and reduces those that can be expressed into mere sex-role stereotypes. It is cruel to urge young boys to suppress all feelings and to stunt little girls by urging them to vent immature ones. One emotion, however, is dwelt on almost obsessively in the readers. Fear. For this reason, we are discussing it as a separate entity.

Fear

The chief stereotype for boys has to do with the maintenance of a facade of bravery and dauntlessness, like the boy who has to face a moral decision about whether to sustain his sister's flattering image of him as a pillar of strength or to tell her the truth about his feelings. The image of girls as fearful and inadequate serves only too well to further enhance boys' aura of success, and shore up the male ego. Girls are used to making such sacrifices.

In the readers, girls are heard to express fears three times more often than boys. Girls are fearful of woods, older boys, snakes, insects, the dark, animals, and sometimes, alas, "just everything" and are allowed, even encouraged, to hang on to their fears. For boys, a recurrent theme is overcoming fear through suppression or perseverance. Take the fear of water. Little boys fight it; little girls hang their clothes on a hickory limb and don't go near it. Boys struggle with and subdue fears of horses, heights, crawly things, the dark, and even of a buffalo stampede. One boy overcomes his fear of horses and rides on in an emergency. When two little girls stand on chairs and shriek for their younger (!) brother to rescue them from a frog, it is in the best feminine tradition.

Comedy and humor

There is little in the readers to relieve the deadly seriousness. What passes for humor has already been hinted at in "Victimizing . . . the Opposite Sex." That a girl bakes a cake and forgets to serve it can only be funny if you think girls are foolish. The other attempts at humor come through animal escapades, such as a hen who lays square eggs. Again, the females of the species are the silly ones as epitomized by Mrs. Goose who takes a bath without water. Just like a woman!

Loneliness, boredom, and aimless activity

Only a handful of stories take up loneliness and boredom but quite a few stories of the filler type have to do with aimless activity. These latter stories seem to have no point to make, as if they were put in between acts to give the real actors time to change their clothes. And so it will come as no surprise that girls predominate in these stories two to one, standing around, watching television, sitting in the sandbox or getting new clothes. The same ratio holds for loneliness and boredom. A girl who is lonely and bored on a rainy day is resigned to her fate (while her mother and sister who are busy with the cleaning are apparently resigned to theirs), but a boy who finds himself bored in school devises an imaginary journey through Dictionopolis and amuses himself with new words. Boys are rarely described as lonely.

The motivation gap

Rarely are we offered an explanation of why people behave as they do. Why do boys tease girls? Why are women mean to animals or mothers cross with children? Why are children so unkind and even cruel to newcomers in their midst? People, simply, come in two styles—good and bad. To present the world in this motivationless way implies the even more insidious idea that all these traits and more are inborn, not subject to change. The same is true for sex-role stereotypes. They are presented as *given*, not *created*.

On the rare occasions when the readers do try to explain these "phenomena," their rationale seldom accords with any existing theory of behavior. It appears to be derived intact from "common knowledge" which could more properly be called common ignorance (most of it collected and preserved and passed along from reader to reader till it reaches our children). An example of such "motivation explanation" appears in a story about a bully. His abominable behavior is attributed solely to the fact that his mother works in contrast to the good boy whose mother is home all day. What kind of idea is this, we wonder, to instill in the minds of millions of school children whose mothers work outside the home, and whose families are dependent on that income?

Physical appearance

Boys never seem to care how they look, but girls have a great need to be beautiful and well-groomed. Do the readers attempt to correct this imbalance? On the contrary. Girls are encouraged to dress up and play, to covet clothes and to preen, whereas clothing or physical attractiveness is virtually ignored in relation to boys.

Everybody knows a princess is always beautiful. Again, by definition. Is she also interesting, intelligent, humorous or witty, kind, adventurous—they seldom say. We assume so since beauty notoriously fades so fast and princesses live happily ever after. But what about the prince? He's usually handsome but that's rarely his only claim to fame.

Size is frequently mentioned. Any illustrator of readers knows that girls are invariably smaller than boys. If a visitor from Outer Space picked up one of these books, he or she would have to assume from the illustrations that girls as a species come smaller and younger than boys on planet Earth.

The reader girls are indeed stunted . . . in *all* ways. Nice girls finish last!

Adult Role Models

In the readers, there are many role models for boys to shop among, from which to select a skill, a trade, a profession. Men are shown in almost every conceivable role; for girls, the Reader Seal of Approval is reserved for one form of service or another, with wife or mother the overwhelming favorite. A girl with any other designs on the future must consider herself some kind of misfit, even though one indomitable woman does slip through and succeed in becoming a doctor. It is hardly enough to give back perspective. Painter, lawyer, lighthouse keeper, baker, whaler, naturalist—girls need not apply. Architect, scientist, mathematician, engineer, professor—it's a closed union unless you have the right sex. Technicians, factory workers, sales personnel and other occupations, in reality open to both sexes on a large scale, are 100 percent male in the readers. To be more exact, there are 147 different possibilities suggested for boys. For girls, a mere 26. Adult males are job holders and fathers. Adult females are either job holders or mothers, rarely both. Only direct necessity drives mother to work, never mere desire or special skill or burning talent. The entire reader study of 134 books unearths only three working mothers, though the United States Office of Labor statistics tell us that 38 percent of all working women have children under 18.[2] A young girl is constantly being "sold" on nursing over doctoring, stenography over business administration, teaching over school administration, and on motherhood over all other alternatives. The little lamb asks her mother what she can be, and Mother says: "You can be a sheep. A mother sheep, just like me." The message is rarely this explicit; it doesn't have to be.

The reader mother is a limited, colorless, mindless creature. She wants nothing for herself you have to assume, since her needs are mentioned only once in this entire study when she treats herself to some earrings on a shopping trip. She is what we have all been looking for all our lives, the perfect servant. Not only does she wash, cook, clean, nurse, and find mittens; these chores constitute her only happiness. In illustrations she frequently appears in the classic servant's posture, body slightly bent forward, hands clasped, eyes riveted on the master of the house or the child. She is perpetually on call, perpetually available, perpetually a reproach to any female who might aspire to anything more than waiting on others. Says Jack in a retelling of "Jack and the Beanstalk": "Mother, get me my ax." And mother gets the ax.

The mother in the readers is more remarkable for what she *doesn't* do than for what she *does* do. She is never shown making something of her own or working at some task unconnected with domestic duty. Children never hush to allow her to concentrate. They never help with chores in order for her to have some time of her own. They never bring her cups of tea while she relaxes with the papers. They never meet her at the station or the airport as she returns from some independent expedition. Her unlucky son sits up on a tree for hours waiting for father to come home and rescue him with the ladder. Clearly, one needs masculine resourcefulness to think of such an ingenious solution.

Wives and mothers are not only dull; sometimes they are actually unpleasant! One mother chases the children with a rolling pin and a wife nags her husband until he misses his three wishes. Mom spanks, yells, gets mad. She hates fun and spontaneity almost as much as she hates dirt. In fantasy stories, women are sometimes extremely cruel to animals.

Father is the "good guy" in the family. He's where the fun is. He builds things with his children, and takes them hunting, fishing, and up in planes. He solves the problems. No wonder he's allowed to rest and relax in his favorite chair so often. If mother isn't, could it mean what it

TABLE 1
STATISTICS

	Allyn & Bacon	American Book Co.	Bank Street	Ginn	Harper and Row	D. C. Heath	Houghton Mifflin	Laidlaw	Lyons & Carnahan	Macmillan	Open Court	Science Research Associates	Scott, Foresman	New S.F. Reading System	Singer/Random House	Sullivan	Totals
Number of books read	3	6	7	10	6	7	9	5	9	9	2	10	13	12	5	21	134
Total number of stories	85	175	116	361	130	176	151	81	100	165	81	221	321	110	94	393	2,760
Featuring boys	31	42	43	107	40	49	63	10	34	48	4	62	116	28	30	116	823
Featuring girls	7	25	17	31	13	12	24	1	6	13	3	17	42	11	0	99	319
Featuring adult males	1	10	7	7	8	3	21	4	3	12	7	24	0	2	8	2	119
Featuring adult females	0	2	2	7	4	2	9	0	0	1	2	5	1	2	0	0	37
Boy and girl	8	16	18	79	6	20	5	3	10	15	4	13	76	9	3	105	390
Male animal	2	6	1	12	1	20	3	21	4	8	24	2	1	6	14	1	126
Female animal	3	0	2	14	2	7	1	2	1	5	7	5	1	1	3	1	55
Male folk fantasy	7	17	2	34	16	21	9	22	6	16	14	15	6	7	12	6	210
Female folk fantasy	1	4	1	6	2	4	3	6	3	0	15	4	1	0	4	3	57
Male biography	16	11	1	9	18	12	6	7	13	17	0	15	22	16	6	0	169
Female biography	3	3	0	3	4	0	0	0	0	5	0	2	5	1	1	0	27
Other: Science, neuter animal, social, etc.	6	39	22	52	16	26	7	5	20	25	1	57	50	27	13	60	426
Occupations shown for men	22	25	24	24	26	30	29	14	13	33	Not listed	21	33	35	13	25	
Occupations shown for women	7	7	5	2	2	3	9	3	2	5	Not listed	5	5	11	2	7	

seems to mean—that she does no "real" work and therefore doesn't *deserve* a rest?

Responsibility in the home is rigidly defined. The inside jobs go to Mom, the outside jobs to Pop, along with all the mechanical failures. Father's the fixer, even though Mother actually uses most of the domestic equipment. For mother to change a tire would be as blasphemous as if father were to whip up the supper. Sooner would the readers have children witness a little violence and cruelty than such unsettling social patterns. In one little attempted comedy, a husband and wife change roles with disastrous results. The moral is clear: we must each be content with what we are meant to be.

Sometimes we wondered during this study why all the marriages shown in the readers are so joyless. There's no closeness between husband and wife—all the interaction is between parent and child. There's virtually no touching between adults. Fathers rarely give wives a hug. Mothers never kiss husband or anybody else. Outside of sad-happy waves from a doorway, and food offering, demonstrations of affection are out-of-bounds. Yet marriage is presented not only as the happy ending but as the only ending. Single parents, in real life a sizable statistic in this country, are rarely permitted on stage in the readers (as if they had a communicable disease). In one reader story they come right out and say it: "It's so good to have a man around the house," though the man in question is an out-of-work relative who is invited to move in with the struggling widow and her two children. This cliché is not inevitably wrong; but used in a situation like this, it has the effect of belittling the survival skills which the woman has already demonstrated.

Parents never "have words," let alone conflicts with each other. Now and then a wife will nag her husband into doing something foolish, or give him bad advice which he quite properly ignores, as the story proves. Any less-than-perfect marriages are projected onto animals, like the cat and dog who set up house together, she (cat) to do the housekeeping and he (dog) the rest. When he finds her asleep one day, he accuses her of laziness and they fight like, well, cats and dogs, ever after.

Single females don't hang around the readers very long; they are in the marketplace, quite frankly, like the girl who attended the king's birthday party because "it might be a good place to catch a husband." One backward 19-year-old daughter is prodded by her mother and told she ought to be thinking of getting married. No mother is in a hurry to unload a son, and never are males casting about in search of a wife as their ultimate goal—unless, of course, she has a kingdom attached. If love is woman's *whole* life, it is because her life is, perforce, an incomplete one.

Victorian children's morality tales that picture the most sadistic punishments for the mildest crimes—such as bad table manners—have been routed from our children's libraries and exiled to the curio shelves. They are no longer considered suitable for impressionable young minds. Yet Victorian modes of living and Victorian casts of thought throw a long shadow over the readers. Because these are no longer applicable to the present situation (if they ever were more than a middle-class delusion) and immoral besides in the bias and strictures against women's participation in life, it is time we reexamined these attitudes and let the sun shine in.

Notes

1. SIMONE DE BEAUVOIR in *The Second Sex* (New York: Bantam, 1961), p. 129, discusses the implications of this term.
2. See *Women at Work,* United States Government Publications, 1969, comparative tables.

RUN, MAMA, RUN:
WOMEN WORKERS IN ELEMENTARY READERS

Though method and philosophy may vary from school to school and even from teacher to teacher within a school, exposure to basic readers is an educational constant for almost every elementary school child. From these sets of readers he derives his first systematic "scholarly" view of the world beyond the schoolroom, beyond the home, beyond his immediate community of friends, neighbors, and relatives. What is the occupational nature of that outer world? Tennyson and Monnens [5] studied the presentation of workers in elementary readers and concluded that the world of work as shown in readers differed from that shown in the *Occupational Outlook Handbook* in being composed more of professional and service occupations at the expense of other kinds of work. These results substantiated those obtained earlier by Lifton [2]. The interest of these researchers was in the worker as such, undifferentiated by sex, and they were not concerned with the accuracy of the presentation of woman's multiple roles.

The present study looks only at adult women in elementary readers and asks, "To what extent are women shown as workers?" Do these fictional or historical working women have husbands and children in the same proportion that women workers have them in real life? What occupations are these working women employed in and are they distributed among the various occupations in the same way that they are, in fact, distributed in the present labor market?

Note: By Buford Stefflre. Copyright © 1969 by the National Vocational Guidance Association. Reprinted with permission from *Vocational Guidance Quarterly*, December 1969, 99–102.

Method

The primers and basic texts, first through sixth grade, currently being sold by the following publishers were examined: Economy; Ginn; Harper Row; Houghton Mifflin; Scott, Foresman; and John C. Winston. Because the sets of readers from the various publishers differ in their intended target groups, the number of readers in each set varied from a high of 13 (John C. Winston) to a low of nine (Scott, Foresman, and Houghton Mifflin). These readers were analyzed in order to specify for each of the 1,028 adult women depicted in these readers, her marital status (married, single, or unstated), her maternal status (children, no children, or unknown), and her vocational status (working in an occupation classifiable according to *Dictionary of Occupational Titles* [D.O.T.]; working in an unclassifiable occupation; occupational status not given or clearly not working). Adult men were classified only as working, not working, or unknown.

Much difficulty was encountered in doing these analyses and it was apparent that the authors did not write these books with a view to ease occupational research. It was sometimes impossible to know whether "Mrs. Brown" and "Tommy's mother" (mentioned three pages earlier) and "the lady who sold gingerbread" (mentioned four pages later) constituted three people, two, or one. Frequently no clear reference was made to marital, maternal, or occupational status and, therefore, the number in the unknown classifications tended to be large. Some rather arbitrary decisions were made: That woman selling the gingerbread—was she a saleslady, a baker, or a manager? A saleslady. How do I know? I just know—that's all! Finally, the D.O.T. taxonomy simply had no proper label for a few of the occupations, so they were dropped from the analysis. Witch, lady-in-waiting, and queen are all honorable and socially valuable callings but they are impossible to classify.

Results

The first analysis—that of the percentage of women who were employed—showed little variation by publisher with a high of 24 percent in the Harper Row books and a low of 16 percent in the Scott, Foresman, and in John C. Winston books with an overall average of 19 percent. Because, in fact 40 percent of adult women are employed [3] and because of the gross nature of the analyses, these differences among publishers did not seem great enough to merit a continued examination of inter-publisher variation, and subsequent data were pooled across publishers. Since 87 percent of the men were identified as workers, the message in these basic readers seems clear—practically all men work but few women work! The reality—practically all men work and nearly half of the adult women work! Put another way, in the labor force as it now exists, 37 percent of the workers are women [1] but in the labor force as depicted in elementary school readers, only 7 percent of the workers are women.

Taylor [4] says that 60 percent of all working women are married and living with their husbands but in the readers, if we count only those women whose marital status is clearly identifiable, we find that only 39 percent of the working women are married.

The overall percentage of married women who are working varies from a high of 44 percent at ages 45–54 to a low of 31 percent at ages 55–64 [6]. In the basic readers, 5.5 percent of married women are identified as workers. The message—women are either married or working; the reality—a large percentage of women are married and working.

In one area the readers closely resemble reality. Forty-eight percent of married working women have no children [5] and in the readers 44 percent of married working women are childless.

On the contrary, while the percentage of mothers in the labor force is difficult to determine, it is clearly much larger than the basic readers suggest. Of the white mothers with children under three, 29 percent work while 42 percent of white mothers with children between six and 17 work. The percentages are slightly higher for nonwhite mothers [1]. In the elementary readers examined, 3.3 percent of mothers work. The message—practically no mothers work; the reality—a sizable minority of mothers work.

Finally, what do these working women do and what is the relationship between women's occupations in elementary readers and their occupations in the real world of work? To answer these questions certain assumptions had to be made to equate U.S. Census data with the D.O.T. classification system as shown in Table 1. The 5.8 percent from the Census data in the "occupations not reported" category were disregarded for this part of the analysis as were the 9 percent "unclassifiable" in the data from the readers.

The discrepancies between the composition of the women's real labor force and the labor force as shown in the readers are great and obvious. The percentage of women working at the professional level is shown in the readers to be four times greater than it actually is. Seven times as many women work at factory type jobs than is indicated by the distribution of women workers in elementary readers. Finally, three times as many women work at clerical and sales jobs than is indicated by the distribution of women workers in elementary readers. The message—two thirds of women workers are employed at the professional level; the reality—more women work at clerical sales occupations, at factory manual occupations, than at professional occupations which account for only one sixth of employed women.

Individual occupational discrepancies are, of course, numerous but the most significant one concerns teachers. The readers show 33 percent of women workers to be teachers but in fact only 7 percent of women workers are so employed [1].

Few women in elementary readers work at "masculine" jobs. Dick and Jane rarely see a woman engineer.

Discussion

Because elementary school readers do not have as one of their purposes the dissemination of accurate occupational information, the authors and publishers of these readers cannot be faulted for the discrepancies between their portrayal of the working woman and present reality. However, this discrepancy does call for supplementary actions by the counselor and teacher to give a more accurate picture of the place of work in the life of the modern woman.

Surely it is incontrovertible that the child should have a chance to learn that practically all women work at some time in their adult lives, that nearly half are working at any one time, that over a third of all workers are women, that most working women are married and half of these have children, that over a third of mothers are working at any one time, that women work in a variety of occupations but particularly at clerical and sales occupations, factory manual occupations, and at service occupations. Such information not only acquaints the child with society as it exists but prepares the young girl for the multiple roles—wife, mother, worker—that she probably will play and prepares the young boy to understand the multiple roles of his future wife.

Exposure to role models of working women other than the ubiquitous teacher seems needed—through the use of consultants from the community, through visits showing women at work, and through the resources of literature. The counselor may be particularly useful at stimulating and coordinating these activities particularly since the evidence suggests that elementary school teachers are not well acquainted with the total scope of occupations [2].

Finally, although the methods used in this study were "loose"—that is, one person, not a panel of judges, classified jobs and no chi-squares were committed—the results are so clear and consistent that it seems most likely that they do represent the current status of the woman worker in the elementary reader.

TABLE 1

DISTRIBUTION OF WOMEN WORKERS IN ELEMENTARY
SCHOOL READERS AND IN REALITY

U.S. Census 1960 Categories *	D.O.T. 1965 Occupational Categories †	% of Women Workers	
		In Elementary Readers	In Reality
Professional, technical, and kindred workers	Professional, technical and managerial occupations	63	17
Managers, officials, and proprietors, except farm			
Clerical and kindred workers	Clerical and sales occupations	13	38
Sales workers			
Private household workers	Service occupations	18	21
Service workers, except private household			
Farmers and farm managers	Farming, fishery, forestry, and related occupations	3	2
Farm laborers and foremen			
Craftsmen, foremen, and workers	Processing occupations	3	22
	Machine trade occupations		
Operatives and kindred workers	Bench work occupations		
Laborers, except farm and mine	Structural work occupations		
	Miscellaneous occupations		
	Total	100	100

* U.S. Census of Population 1960, United States Summary, Detailed Characteristics, Table 201, pages 1–522 to 1–527.

† *Dictionary of Occupational Titles* 1965, Vol. II, Occupational Classification, page 1. (This method of equating census data and D.O.T. categories was suggested in a personal communication from Robert Halbisen, Supervisor Occupational Information Unit, State of Michigan, Department of Labor.)

References

1. G. E. HARBESON, *Choice and Challenge for the American Woman* (Cambridge: Schenkman Publishing Company, 1967).
2. W. M. LIFTON, "Vocational Guidance in the Elementary School," *Vocational Guidance Quarterly*, 8 (Winter 1959–1960): 79–82.
3. B. S. MARTIN, *Working Women—Who Are They?*, Institute of Life Insurance, April 1968.
4. L. TAYLOR, *Occupational Sociology* (New York: Oxford University Press, 1968).
5. W. W. TENNYSON and L. P. MONNENS, "The World of Work Through Elementary Readers," *Vocational Guidance Quarterly*, 12 (Winter 1963–1964): 85–88.
6. S. L. WOLFBEIN, *Occupational Information* (New York: Random House, 1968).

LIBERATED CHINESE PRIMERS (LET'S WRITE SOME TOO)

A year ago, we ordered four children's books from China: *I Am on Duty Today; Flowers in Full Bloom; The Little Doctor;* and *Secret Bulletin.*[1] I want to describe these chiefly as possible models for books our children need.

"The Little Doctor" is a girl. She treats her younger sister's sick doll, then her younger brother's teddy bear, and a rocking horse whose "leg" is broken. Without any help from brothers—big or small—the doctor mends the rocking horse with a hammer and nails.

On the cover of another primer, *I Am on Duty Today,* a girl puts on a red armband, and inside she says:

> I am on duty today
> Helping in our nursery
> I get up with the sunrise
> And go to work happily.

In the following pages, a boy joins her and the two perform identical tasks: they tidy the schoolroom, feed pet animals, greet the other children as they arrive, check them for cleanliness, until they are the last to leave at the end of the day and the teacher thanks them for their work. The illustrations contribute to the lesson in sexual equality. All children are dressed in plain, comfortable, bright-colored clothing that consists of trousers and a shirt. Only small details—a pigtail or a hair ribbon—distinguishes girls from boys.

Flowers in Full Bloom, a somewhat more advanced primer, continues the lesson in sexual equality. The book's scheme is simplicity itself:

Note: By Florence Howe. Reprinted with permission from *Women: a Journal of Liberation,* Fall 1970, 2:1, 33–34. Copyright © 1970 by *Women: a Journal of Liberation* (3028 Greenmount Avenue, Baltimore, Maryland 21218).

21 illustrations of children in adult work roles, each picture accompanied by a poem. On the first page, for example, a girl mends a fishing net:

> I am mending the net for our commune.
> When it is finished, I'll put out to sea
> Where shoals of fish with glittering scales,
> Both large and small will swim into my net.

The book includes more pictures of girls than of boys, and while we might expect boys to ride buffalo and sharpen sickles, we do not expect girls to steer banana boats, or to put out to sea in fishing boats. Nor do we expect to find boys and girls washing clothes or performing identical farm tasks.

The title page of the book offers additional instruction. Wearing a long yellow sash, bracelets, hair ribbons and flowers, a girl plaits her hair before a mirror:

> This little girl can arrange her hair,
> Decorating her ebony plaits
> with red silk bands.
> She dances at the harvest gathering,
> Like a butterfly fluttering among the flowers.
> With a carrying-pole she shoulders
> two baskets which touch the ground;
> She carries a hoe taller than herself.
> She sings a song about pineapples & bananas,
> Which makes our mouths water.
> The audience clap her,
> And she nods back to them.

The lesson is clear: work does not defeminize women. The flower in full bloom is strong enough to wield a hoe and carry heavy baskets from the fields.

Unlike the others, *Secret Bulletin* is a complicated and suspenseful story written for older children. Two children, a boy and a girl, who seem to be between ten and 12 years old, are attempting to operate a primitive mimeograph machine in a secret place. They have been assigned the printing of handbills announcing "that the People's Liberation Army had crossed the Yangtse River and that Shanghai was soon to be liberated." There is some dispute about the preparation of mimeo ink. The boy stubbornly insists upon his own knowledge of inks and nearly wrecks the stencil before he listens to Hsiao-Fen's information about thinning the ink with kerosene. Later, as they are trying to carry the leaflets—hidden in their clothing—across the spy-filled city, he foolishly greets someone he should not have recognized, and they are both stopped for searching. To get them out of trouble, Hsiao-Fen hides all the leaflets in her clothes and then pretends she's crying about a sick relative.

The story is deliberately the boy's: he tells it in a consistent reportorial style that includes his own feelings but imposes none on Hsiao-Fen. "Though we were the same age," he reports on page one, "I always used to think of myself as the older, and I wanted her to listen to me." By page 30, however, his experiences have transformed that view: "Suddenly I began to feel that Hsiao-Fen was really the older of us. Certainly she understood things better than I." He admires her for her brains, her wit, and her courage.

The books *our* children read also provide instruction in sexually-ascribed social roles and in the sexual basis of power relationships. Many stories focus on children's relationships, and significantly, in most U.S. primers, brothers are older (and wiser) than sisters.

In our children's books women are mommies and mommies do not work. If women appear rarely as workers, it is in stereotyped white-collar jobs—receptionist, telephone operator, secretary. Mostly, their "career" is marriage, and that lesson is taught early.

Clearly, we need new books. The Chinese ones offer some helpful models—women are doctors, lawyers, and factory workers. But we can also work out our own models. We can tell our daughters and sons about our own lives and the lives of women we've known or are beginning to learn about. Let's write primers that will liberate our children.

Notes

1. These books are available through China Books and Periodicals, 2929 24th St., San Francisco, Calif. 94110. They were published by the Foreign Language Press of the Peoples Republic of China, the first two in 1966, the last in 1965. Inexpensively produced in paper cover, they are attractive and readable.

THE NEGATIVE IMAGE OF WOMEN IN CHILDREN'S LITERATURE

> There was an old woman who lived in a shoe;
> She had so many children she didn't know what to do.

Recently the Women's Liberation Front has tried to take the old woman out of her shoe, to provide day care centers for her many children while she competes with men for jobs, to change the abortion laws so that she won't have any more children—thus freeing her erotic zones. The growing militant movement of emancipated women is no longer content to be the passive implement of men. Picketing beauty contests, condemning *Playboy* magazine, lobbying for legislative reform, today's woman is sensitive to any reference that might indicate her inferiority to a man. In their struggle for equality, women are fighting centuries of tradition, a tradition that has continually relegated women to an inferior position. They've been omitted from history books. In literature they have been denigrated, as evidenced by these "quotable quotes":

> The man's desire is for the woman, but the woman's desire is rarely other than for the desire of the man. *Samuel Taylor Coleridge*
>
> Most women have no character at all. *Alexander Pope*
>
> The Germans are like women, you can scarcely ever fathom their depths. They haven't any. *Friedrich Wilhelm Nietzsche*

Even in the traditional classics that children read is embedded the underlying assertion that women are inferior.

No one can deny the deep impressions that nursery rhymes and folk tales make upon young minds. Since folk materials are a reflection

217

of the culture from which they grow, it would be curious to see how a young child may be influenced by their prevalent values. By examining female types recurrent throughout children's literature, one discovers that the passive female is portrayed sympathetically; whereas the assertive female is portrayed unsympathetically.

When one examines nursery rhymes and folk tales for sympathetic female characters, he finds two recurring types—the sweet, little old lady and the beautiful young heroine—both of whom are lovably incompetent.

The little old lady usually exhibits one or more characteristics that indicate her ineffectuality: eccentricity, befuddlement, and imperceptiveness.

Regarding eccentricity—or weirdness—consider the nursery rhyme about the old woman who sweeps the cobwebs from the sky:

> There was an old woman tossed up in a basket,
> Seventeen times as high as the moon;
> Where she was going I couldn't but ask it,
> For in her hand she carried a broom.
>
> Old woman, old woman, old woman, quoth I,
> Where are you going to up so high?
> To brush the cobwebs off the sky!
> May I go with you? Aye, by-and-by

This old woman has clearly departed from earthiness. She is wonderfully whimsical and her mission to the sky—seventeen times as high as the moon—is an expression of infinity, phrased in language the child can understand. Yet, she functions in a world that departs from reason—and is, consequently, eccentric. Equally eccentric is Mother Goose:

> Old Mother Goose,
> When she wanted to wander,
> Would ride through the air
> On a very fine gander.

Her flights through the air are as wondrously eccentric as the missions to the sky. It appears doubtful, however, that either of these old ladies, stripped of their magical powers, could function effectively, for society does not tolerate too much eccentricity.

Grounded, old women are befuddled by life:

> There was an old woman who lived in a shoe;
> She had so many children she didn't know what to do;
> She gave them some broth without any bread;
> She whipped them all soundly and put them to bed.

As the rhyme indicates, the old woman, overrun by children, is unable to cope with life. Her only control measures—feeding, beating, and sending to bed—lack both imagination and humanity. Also befuddled is the old woman who falls asleep on the king's highway, enroute to sell her eggs:

> There was an old woman, as I've heard tell,
> She went to market her eggs for to sell;
> She went to market all on a market day,
> And she fell asleep on the king's highway.
>
> There came a peddler whose name was Stout,
> He cut her petticoats all round about;
> He cut her petticoats up to the knees,
> Which made the old woman shiver and freeze.

Awakening from her sleep, shivering with cold, the woman illustrates her dazed confusion by saying, "O deary, deary me, this is none of I!" It would appear inconceivable, even to a small child, that anyone could remain asleep while some interloper cuts her clothes away. To further exemplify her befuddlement, the old lady, shorn of petticoats, unable to recognize herself, depends on her dog to identify her:

> Home went the little woman all in the dark,
> Up got the little dog, and he began to bark;
> He began to bark; so she began to cry,
> "O! deary, deary me, this is none of I!"

The implication in this rhyme—that a dog may have intelligence equal to or greater than an old woman's—is echoed in "Old Mother Hubbard":

> Old Mother Hubbard
> Went to the cupboard
> To get her poor dog a bone;
> But when she came there
> The cupboard was bare,
> And so the poor dog had none.
>
> She went to the baker's
> To buy him some bread;
> But when she came back
> The poor dog was dead.
>
> She went to the joiner's
> To buy him a coffin;
> But when she came back
> The poor dog was laughing.

If one interprets the lines literally, the woman's intelligence is dwarfed by the dog's. In the course of the rhyme, the old woman runs twelve errands for this precocious canine, who, in addition to other talents smokes a pipe, reads the news, and plays the flute. Indeed the old woman mutters a truth when, bowing before the dog, she says, "Your servant." Befuddlement in the extreme is evidenced in the cumulative folk tale, "The Old Woman and Her Pig." An old woman is confronted with a simple task: "As she was coming home, she came to a stile; but the piggy wouldn't go over the stile." Rather than carry the pig, she enlists the aid of numerous passersby—not without difficulty. The entire preposterous sequence is described in the tale's final paragraph:

> As soon as the cat had lapped up the milk, the cat began to kill the rat; the rat began to gnaw the rope; the rope began to hang the butcher; the butcher began to kill the ox; the ox began to drink the water; the water began to quench the fire; the fire began to burn the stick; the stick began to beat the dog; the dog began to bite the pig; the little pig in a fright jumped over the stile; and so the old woman got home that night.

In addition to being eccentric and befuddled, old ladies in children's literature tend to be imperceptive. The grandmother in "Little Red Riding Hood" is unable to distinguish between her granddaughter's voice and the wolf's imitation. Consequently, she gives the wolf complete instructions about how to open the door. The result: She is devoured. The old woman's murder is vividly described: "He leaped on to the poor old woman and ate her up in less than no time, for he had been three days without food." Equally imperceptive is the grandmother in the Czechoslovakian folk tale "Budelinik." For each of three days, the grandmother leaves a young boy alone in the house with instructions to let no one in. During the first two evenings a smart fox (1) tricks the boy into opening the door, (2) devours the boy's dinner, and (3) leaves the boy in tears, hungry. Granny, knowing the dangers inherent in the boy's first two experiences with the fox, unwisely leaves him alone on the third day. That evening the fox kidnaps the boy. Upon discovering her grandson gone, "Granny just cried and cried, she was so lonely and sad."

Examined collectively, these old ladies are a ludicrous bunch—with their brooms, flying geese, hysterics, and inane rituals. As ineffectual human beings, they pose no threat to men. They are at best lovable; at worst, ignorant. They are, in fact, easily condescended to. They lack dignity, intelligence; they certainly command no respect.

Another recurring female type, portrayed with disguised condescension, is the beautiful, young heroine, who is, above all, helplessly dependent upon men. Classic children's heroines are either dull-witted, spiritless, passive, naive, or amoral.

Snow White, for example, is fairly dull-witted. Her life-death struggle against her wicked stepmother involves perilous situations with which Snow White cannot cope. Consequently, males, more clever than she, come forward to save her. When the queen first orders Snow White's death, a huntsman takes the girl into the forest and frees her. Cleverly, to assuage the queen's suspicions, "as a token, he brought back the heart of a wild boar and the wicked queen thought it was Snow White's." Snow White is again saved by men as she is granted asylum at the home of the seven dwarfs. The dwarfs are also clever and warn Snow White about the queen: "One of these days she'll find out that you are here. So be careful, child, and don't let anyone into the house." Despite the dwarfs' continual warnings, Snow White demonstrates her dull-wittedness three times. The queen comes, disguised, three times to kill her—as a peddler, as an old peasant lady, and as an apple seller. Each time Snow White is "taken in." The dwarfs save her the first two times, but it takes a handsome prince to dislodge the poisoned apple from her throat.

Just as Snow White is dull-witted, Cinderella is spiritless. Rather a simpleton, Cinderella allows herself to be bullied by two incredibly selfish stepsisters. Assigned hard tasks, beaten, deprived of decent food and shelter, Cinderella could "soon [forget] their tongues and bruises." Always happy, for some unexplainable reason, Cinderella never seems to improve her station but merely accepts what life gives her: "From morning to night she sat stitching and stitching till she could scarcely see out of her young eyes or hold her needle. The harder she worked and the more she tried to please them, the worse they fumed and flustered." As in Snow White's case, a prince saves the day: "When Cinderella was brought to the King and the Queen, they received her as if she were a long-lost daughter."

A third heroine, Rapunzel, is passive. She submits to being Mother Gothel's tower prisoner, obediently lowering her braids on command from the witch:

"Rapunzel, Rapunzel,
Let down your hair."

As soon as Rapunzel heard this, she took her long braids, wound them once or twice around a hook outside the window, and let them fall twenty ells downward toward the ground. This made a ladder for the witch to climb, and in that way she reached the window at the top of the tower.

Again, it is the prince who attempts to free Rapunzel, unassisted by any active spirit of rebellion on her part. Later, pregnant, Rapunzel submits to the most dehumanizing treatment:

> [The witch] grabbed Rapunzel's golden hair, twisted it once or twice around her left hand, snatched a pair of scissors with her right, and ritsch, rotsch, the beautiful braids lay on the floor. And she was so heartless after then that she dragged Rapunzel to a waste and desolate place, where the poor girl had to get along as best she could, living in sorrow and want.

Sleeping Beauty, a fourth heroine, is naive. Unaware of the Fairy Woman's curse, the young princess mistakes the old spinner as a friend who will soon teach her to spin: "She span with such skill and ease, her right hand drawing the strands from the cleft stick or distaff, while her left twisted and stayed, twisted and stayed, that the Princess longed to try too." She consequently smuggles the poisoned spindle into her room and, while practicing with it, pricks her thumb; she then goes to sleep for 100 years. As in the other cases, a handsome prince comes to the aid of the helpless heroine. After struggling through the overgrowth surrounding the castle, torn and bleeding, he comes to her bedchamber: "Then, remembering the tale that had been told him, he stopped, crossed himself, and gently kissed the sleeper, then put his hunting-horn to his lips, and sounded a low, but prolonged, clear blast upon it, which went echoing on between the stone walls of the castle."

Most dependent upon men is a fifth heroine, the miller's daughter in "Rumpelstiltskin." The girl is incapable of moral judgment, her life being determined by the actions and personalities of three men—none of whom are particularly admirable. First of all, her father is a braggart: "It happened one day that he came to speak with the king, and, to give himself consequence, he told him that he had a daughter who could spin gold out of straw." Second, the king is greedy; he imprisons the young girl: "Now set to work, and if by the early morning thou hast not spun this straw to gold thou shalt die." Third, Rumpelstiltskin, himself an opportunist, agrees, for a price, to spin gold from straw on three occasions, in attempts to sate the king's increasing avarice. On the third occasion, Rumpelstiltskin demands as payment the girl's firstborn child (the king, having seen the girl as a source of wealth, promises to marry her, "although she is but a miller's daughter"). One year after the marriage, the little man returns to claim his child. But the queen, saddened by Rumpelstiltskin's refusal to accept riches, is given one chance to keep the child: "The little man had pity upon her." She must, within three days, guess his name. The queen guesses the name and Rumpelstiltskin, in a sense the story's most sympathetic character, meets an unfortunate demise: "In his anger he stamped with his right foot so hard that it went into the ground above his knee; then he seized his left foot with both his hands in such a fury that he split in two, and there was the end of him." What appears most ironic is that the queen feels no compassion for the unfortunate little man who has helped her; yet not once does she express any disapproval of her father's shameful pomp nor the king's ruthless greed. It's as if she is immune to morality.

The five heroines have common characteristics. First, they possess great physical beauty. Second, they are subjected to unfortunate circumstances—poverty or the threat of death—from which they are saved by aggressive males of royal lineage. Third, although the heroes in all five tales are definitely attracted to the heroines, there is little or no explication of the heroines' feelings for their "lovers." Even Rapunzel's motivation for marriage is dubious: "I am sure he will be much kinder to me than Mother Gothel." Fourth, and most important, all five heroines function in a moral vacuum. They are not expected to choose between right and wrong. Their moral decisions are precluded by the decisive actions of aggressive men to whom they submit passively.

Little old ladies and beautiful, young heroines—both types ineffectual in an active social context—are portrayed sympathetically. But what about the independent woman—the woman who attempts to control her own destiny—who doesn't rely on male heroics? She is portrayed unsympathetically—either as an evil witch or as a hateful housewife.

The witch figure in children's literature, a woman whose outward ugliness is a reflection of her inward evil, is portrayed as excessively competent, usually able to control her environment. She is normally more shrewd than her female victims, but usually less intelligent than her male antagonists. Witches display detestable flaws in character: cannibalism, sadism, and revengefulness.

The clever witch in "Hansel and Gretel" is cannibalistic. Her tasty house is an ingenious trap to snare innocent children, whom she intends to eat. The physical appearance of this cannibal is awesome: "Her sharp nose bent down to meet her bristly chin. Her face, all folds and wrinkles, looked like an old shriveled pear; and she had only three teeth, two above and one below, all very long and narrow." The old witch, however, is outsmarted on two occasions—not by Gretel, but by Hansel and a little white bird, a *he*. First, Hansel, taking advantage of the old crone's nearsightedness, never extends his finger through the cage: "He always poked out a dry old bone, and the Old One, because of her red eyes, never knew the difference . . . and wondered why it was that he did not get fat." Second, as the impatient witch makes plans to bake Gretel as well as Hansel, a little white bird warns Gretel about the stove: "Beware, beware,/Don't look in there." Gretel, subsequently, dispatches the witch.

Mother Gothel in "Rapunzel" personifies a most hideous trait: sadism. First, the old woman's lush garden tortures her neighbor, a hungry young woman:

> But when [the woman's] glance fell upon a fine big bed of rampion (which in that country is called *rapunzel*) a strange feeling came over her. She had always been fond of rampion salad, and these plants in the witch's garden looked so fresh, so tempting, that she felt she must have some, no matter what the cost.

The husband, falling prey to his wife's ill-fated attraction to the rampion, vows to steal it—to save her from starvation. The witch, then, has the couple trapped, for as the wife's need for rampion increases, so does their indebtedness to the witch: "When your first child is born, you must give it to me." The witch's second sadistic act occurs when she locks the child away in a tower: "When she was twelve years old, the witch took her off to the woods and shut her up in a high tower. It had neither door nor staircase, but at its very top was one tiny window." Despite the child's intense sadness, the witch keeps her imprisoned. Her third sadistic act occurs when she corners the prince in the tower: "'Aha!' she cried mockingly. 'You have come to get your dear wife. Well, the pretty bird is no longer in her nest and she'll sing no more. The cat has taken her away, and in the end that same cat will scratch out your eyes.'" Grieved, the prince leaps from the tower and is blinded.

In "Sleeping Beauty" the witch, "a bent-up old Fairy Woman—the oldest and most potent of them all," is revengeful. Not having been invited to the infant princess' christening, she utters a curse:

> Plan as you may, the day will come,
> When in spinning with spindle, she'll prick her thumb.
> When in dreamless sleep she shall slumber on
> Till years a hundred have come and gone.

Years later, the evil woman returns to the castle, disguised, to ensure the fulfillment of the spiteful curse: "Then the old woman, laying her bony fingers that were cold as a bird's claws on the Princess's hand, showed her how to hold the [poisoned] spindle, and at last bade her take it away and practice with it. . . ."

Aggressive females, unlike the incompetent old ladies and the equally ineffectual young heroines, pose a threat to men. Consequently, the witch metaphor is effective, since, from a man's point of view, "liberated" women are a danger to society. Consider the common characteristics of the three witches. All three are cruel. All three defy rationality. All three are without sexual attraction. But most important, all three seem determined to destroy innocence and beauty. Perhaps in the destruction of the witch—man can coexist with the little old ladies and dominate the young heroines—man eliminates a threat to his superiority. In "Hansel and Gretel," outsmarted by Hansel and the male bird, the witch is incinerated in her own trap. In "Rapunzel," the witch's power cannot overcome the prince's sexual potency. In "Sleeping Beauty," the witch's curse is ineffective, for after the prince saves Beauty—incidentally, a significant allegorization—life resumes where it left off.

Another aggressive female type is the domineering housewife, who functions in one or more roles; wife, mother, and stepmother. As a wife, she is a nag; as a mother she is a shrew.

In "The Fisherman and His Wife," the woman is a nag in the extreme. In contrast to her contented husband, Ilsebill is unhappy with their life in a vinegar jug. Exploiting her husband's close relationship with a magic fish, she insists her husband get her a better house. When this is accomplished, her demands increase in number and value: a stone mansion, a kingship, the position of Emperor, the Papacy, and finally God-liness. Her lust for power has, thus, become insatiable.

In "Hansel and Gretel," the wife is selfish: "She was a hard-hearted woman and did not much care what became of the children." Like the fisherman's wife, she controls her husband with her most effective weapon: nagging. When her husband refuses to desert his children in the forest, "she nagged and scolded until the poor man, not knowing what else to say, consented." When the children, through trickery, return home, the wife begins to nag again: "As before, the father tried to talk her out of it, but the hard-hearted stepmother wouldn't listen to him. He who says A must also say B, and because the father had given in the first time, he had to give in this time as well."

What happens to wives who try to take over? According to these two folk tales, they are eminently unsuccessful. Ilsebill, after requesting to be God, is returned to the vinegar jar by the magic fish, a male. The stepmother, getting no satisfaction from her husband, packs "up her things in a large red handkerchief and [runs] away." In both cases, women are "put down" by men. However, their demands, examined in realistic terms, are not unreasonable. No woman can long tolerate a static existence inside a "sour" house. Nor can she abide insufficient food for the house-hold. Yet, these demands, in the hands of the tale spinners—whoever they may be—are distorted by the portrayal of concerned wives as harridans. Ironically, then, the husbands, whose ineffectuality as providers has caused the crisis situations, remain endeared to the reader.

Another household figure pejorated in children's literature is the mother. She is often portrayed a shrew, being either cruel, vain, greedy, or demanding.

In "Brother and Sister," the witchlike mother is cruel. Making life unbearable for her two stepchildren, she drives them away into the forest. Subsequently, she uses her magical powers to cast a spell on the brooks, turning her stepson into a fawn: "Now the wicked stepmother . . . never dreamed but that the sister had been eaten up by wild beasts in the forest, and that the brother, in the likeness of a fawn, had been slain by the hunters." When her expectations prove false and she finds that her stepdaughter is queen, she demonstrates her ultimate cruelty: she puts a spell on the queen and substitutes her own ugly daughter in the queen's bed. She "gave [her daughter] also the Queen's form and countenance, only she could not restore the lost eye. So, in order that the King might not remark it, she had to lie on the side where there was no eye."

In "Snow White and the Seven Dwarfs," the stepmother is vain: "Indeed, her only wish in life was to be fairest in the land." A magic mirror—the spirit of truth—keeps her informed as to her status. Her one competitor, she discovers, is her own stepdaughter: "Queen, thou art of beauty rare/But Snow White with ebon hair/Is a thousand times more fair." The Queen, then, tries four separate plots, all designed to kill Snow White: (1) she orders a royal huntsman to murder the girl in the forest, (2) she tries to strangle Snow White with a girdle, (3) she tries to poison her with a comb, and (4) she drugs her with a specially prepared apple. Her vanity, then, leads the queen into a fruitless existence of jealousy and treachery.

In "Toads and Diamonds," the mother is greedy. She has two daughters: "The elder was so like her mother in temper and face that to have seen the one was to have seen the other. . . . The younger . . . was as beautiful a girl as one could see." Needless to say, the mother favors the older daughter. When the younger girl comes home with precious stones dripping from her mouth—a reward for her kindness to an old fairy —the mother promptly sends out her favored daughter to get *her* share. The old fairy sends back the ill-tempered girl spitting up lizards and snakes, rather than precious stones.

In "The Twelve Months," a tale parallel to "Toads and Diamonds," the stepmother is demanding. As in "Toads and Diamonds," a woman has two daughters, one of whom, the stepdaughter Marushka, possesses great beauty and is, consequently, hated by both the mother and her own daughter and turned into a household slave. The woman's rapacity is realized in her exploitation of her daughter's relationship with the all-powerful Twelve Months, a group of men that inhabit a mountain top. She and her daughter Holena send Marushka, under threat of death, on impossible errands—to find violets, strawberries and apples—in the midst of winter. Impressed by the "treasures" Marushka brings home, Holena, followed by her mother, sets out in search of the Twelve Months: "[Marushka] waited for them [at home], but they didn't come. She cooked dinner for them, but still they didn't come. In fact they never came, for they both froze to death on the mountain."

Just as nagging wives are forcefully defeated, so are wicked mothers, and usually by men. In "Brother and Sister," the witch-stepmother is burned at the stake on command from the king. In "Snow White and the Seven Dwarfs," the wicked queen "was given a pair of red hot shoes with which she had to dance out her wicked life." In "Toads and Diamonds," the mother drives her own daughter from the house and is left alone. In "The Twelve Months," the stepmother is killed by a powerful male, Great January.

In considering select nursery rhymes and folk tales, one can see that women are portrayed somewhat negatively, either as ineffectual creatures who need to be dominated by men or as aggressive monsters who must be destroyed by men. One can assume that these folk materials were born in and perpetuated by societies that maintained the "natural inferiority of women." However, today, when women are seeking liberation and equality, a young child's image of what is read to him may be in sharp contrast to what he sees. On the other hand, liberated women may unwittingly be perpetuating the "monster" image; after all, one of the liberation organizations was called W.I.T.C.H.

"SOME DAY MY PRINCE WILL COME":
FEMALE ACCULTURATION THROUGH THE
FAIRY TALE

In a review of children's stories for a Christmas issue of *The New York Review of Books,* Alison Lurie praised traditional fairy and folk tales as

> one of the few sorts of classic children's literature of which a radical feminist would approve. . . . These stories suggest a society in which women are as competent and active as men, at every age and in every class. Gretel, not Hansel, defeats the Witch; and for every clever youngest son there is a youngest daughter equally resourceful. The contrast is greatest in maturity, where women are often more powerful than men. Real help for the hero or heroine comes most frequently from a fairy godmother or wise woman, and real trouble from a witch or wicked stepmother. . . . To prepare children for women's liberation, therefore, and to protect them against Future Shock, you had better buy at least one collection of fairy tales. . . .[1]

Radical feminists, apparently, bought neither Ms. Lurie's ideas nor the collections of fairy tales. It is hard to see how children could be "prepared" for women's liberation by reading fairy tales; an analysis of those fairy tales that children actually read indicates instead that they serve to acculturate women to traditional social roles.

Ms. Lurie has now repeated her argument in a recent article, in which she objects to the opinion that feminists actually have of such stories as "Cinderella" and "Snow White":

> It is true that some of the tales we know best, those that have been popularized by Disney, have this sort of heroine. But from the

Note: By Marcia R. Lieberman. Copyright © 1972 by the National Council of Teachers of English. Reprinted by permission of the publisher and the author from *College English,* December 1972, 383–395.

> point of view of European folklore they are a very unrepresentative selection. They reflect the taste of the refined literary men who edited the first popular collections of fairy tales for children during the Victorian era. Andrew Lang, for instance, chose the tales in his *Blue Fairy Book* (first published in 1889) from among literally thousands known to him as a folklorist; and he chose them . . . partly for their moral lesson. Folk tales recorded in the field by scholars are full of everything Lang leaves out: sex, death, low humor, and female initiative.
>
> In the other more recent collections of tales—as well as in Lang's later collections—there are more active heroines. . . .[2]

No one would disagree with Ms. Lurie that Andrew Lang was very selective in choosing his tales, but to a feminist who wishes to understand the acculturation of women, this is beside the point. Only the best-known stories, those that everyone has read or heard, indeed, those that Disney has popularized, have affected masses of children in our culture. Cinderella, the Sleeping Beauty, and Snow White are mythic figures who have replaced the old Greek and Norse gods, goddesses, and heroes for most children. The "folk tales recorded in the field by scholars," to which Ms. Lurie refers, or even Andrew Lang's later collections, are so relatively unknown that they cannot seriously be considered in a study of the meaning of fairy tales to women.

In this light, *The Blue Fairy Book* is a very fruitful book to analyze, for it contains many of the most famous stories, and has perhaps been the best-known and hence most influential collection of tales. It was compiled by Andrew Lang and first published by Longmans Green, and Co. in London in 1889. It was followed by *The Red Fairy Book*, and then the *Green*, and then by many others, the *Yellow*, the *Brown*, the *Rose*, the *Violet*, etc. In the preface to *The Green Fairy Book*, in 1892, Lang noted that the stories were made not only to amuse children, but also to teach them. He pointed out that many of the stories have a moral, although, he wrote, "we think more as we read them of the diversion than of the lesson." [3] The distinction that Lang drew between diversions and lessons is misleading, for children do not categorize their reading as diverting or instructive, but as interesting or boring. If we are concerned, then, about what our children are being taught, we must pay particular attention to those stories that are so beguiling that children think more as they read them "of the diversion than of the lesson"; perhaps literature is suggestive in direct proportion to its ability to divert. We know that children are socialized or culturally conditioned by movies, television programs, and the stories they read or hear, and we have begun to wonder at the influence that children's stories and entertainments had upon us, though we cannot now measure the extent of that influence.

Generations of children have read the popular fairy books, and in doing so may have absorbed far more from them than merely the outlines of the various stories. What is the precise effect that the story of "Snow White and the Seven Dwarfs" has upon a child? Not only do children find out what happens to the various princes and princesses, woodcutters, witches, and children of their favorite tales, but they also learn behavioral and associational patterns, value systems, and how to predict the consequences of specific acts or circumstances. Among other things, these tales present a picture of sexual roles, behavior, and psychology, and a way of predicting outcome or fate according to sex, which is important because of the intense interest that children take in "endings"; they always want to know how things will "turn out." A close examination of the treatment of girls and women in fairy tales reveals certain patterns which are keenly interesting not only in themselves, but also as material which has undoubtedly played a major contribution in forming the sexual role concept of children, and in suggesting to them the limitations that are imposed by sex upon a person's chances of success in various endeavors. It is now being questioned whether those traits that have been characterized as feminine have a biological or a cultural basis: discarding the assumptions of the past, we are asking what is inherent in our nature, and what has become ours through the gentle but forcible process of acculturation. Many feminists accept nothing as a "given" about the nature of female personality; nearly all the work on that vast subject is yet to be done. In considering the possibility that gender has a cultural character and origin we need to examine the primary channels of acculturation. Millions of women must surely have formed their psychosexual self-concepts, and their ideas of what they could or could not accomplish, what sort of behavior would be rewarded, and of the nature of reward itself, in part from their favorite fairy tales. These stories have been made the repositories of the dreams, hopes, and fantasies of generations of girls. An analysis of the women in *The Blue Fairy Book* presents a picture that does not accord with Ms. Lurie's hypothesis.

Certain premises and patterns emerge at once, of which only the stereotyped figure of the wicked stepmother has received much general notice. The beauty contest is a constant and primary device in many of the stories. Where there are several daughters in a family, or several unrelated girls in a story, the prettiest is invariably singled out and designated for reward, or first for punishment and later for reward. Beautiful girls are never ignored; they may be oppressed at first by wicked figures, as the jealous Queen persecutes Snow White, but ultimately they are chosen for reward. Two fundamental conventions are associated here: the special destiny of the youngest child when there are several children in a family (this holds true for youngest brothers as well as for youngest sisters, as long as the siblings are of the same sex), and the focus on beauty as a girl's most valuable asset, perhaps her only valuable asset. Good temper and meekness are so regularly associated with beauty, and ill temper with ugliness, that this in itself must influence children's expectations. The most famous example of this associational pattern occurs in "Cinderella," with the opposition of the ugly, cruel, bad-tempered older sisters to the younger, beautiful, sweet Cinderella, but in *The Blue Fairy Book* it also occurs in many other stories, such as "Beauty and the Beast" and "Toads and Diamonds." Even when there is no series of sisters (in "Snow White and Rose Red" both girls are beautiful and sweet) the beautiful single daughter is nearly always noted for her docility, gentleness, and good temper.

This pattern, and the concomitant one of reward distribution, probably acts to promote jealousy and divisiveness among girls. The stories reflect an intensely competitive spirit: they are frequently about contests, for which there can be only one winner because there is only one prize. Girls win the prize if they are the fairest of them all; boys win if they are bold, active, and lucky. If a child identifies with the beauty, she may learn to be suspicious of ugly girls, who are portrayed as cruel, sly, and unscrupulous in these stories; if she identifies with the plain girls, she may learn to be suspicious and jealous of pretty girls, beauty being a gift of fate, not something that can be attained. There are no examples of a crossed-pattern, that is, of plain but good-tempered girls. It is a psychological truth that as children, and as women, girls fear homeliness (even attractive girls are frequently convinced that they are plain), and this fear is a major source of anxiety, diffidence, and convictions of inadequacy and inferiority among women. It is probably also a source of envy and discord among them. Girls may be predisposed to imagine that there is a link between the lovable face and the lovable character, and to fear, if plain themselves, that they will also prove to be unpleasant, thus using the patterns to set up self-fulfilling prophecies.

The immediate and predictable result of being beautiful is being chosen, this word having profound importance to a girl. The beautiful girl does not have to *do* anything to merit being chosen; she does not have to show pluck, resourcefulness, or wit; she is chosen because she is beautiful. Prince Hyacinth chooses the Dear Little Princess for his bride from among the portraits of many princesses that are shown to him because she is the prettiest; the bear chooses the beautiful youngest daughter in "East of the Sun and West of the Moon"; at least 20 kings compete to win Bellissima in "The Yellow Dwarf"; the prince who penetrates the jungle of thorns and briars to find the Sleeping Beauty does so because he had heard about her loveliness; Cinderella instantly captivates her prince during a ball that amounts to a beauty contest; the old king in "The White Cat" says he will designate as his heir whichever of his sons brings home the loveliest princess, thereby creating a beauty contest as a hurdle to inheriting his crown; the prince in "The Water-Lily or The Gold-Spinners" rescues and marries the youngest and fairest of the three enslaved maidens; the King falls in love with Goldilocks because of her beauty; the enchanted sheep dies for love of the beautiful Miranda in "The Wonderful Sheep"; Prince Darling pursues Celia because she is beautiful; the young king in "Trusty John" demands the Princess of the Golden Roof for her beauty, and so on. This is a principal factor contributing to the passivity of most of the females in these stories (even those few heroines who are given some sort of active role are usually passive in another part of the story). Since the heroines are chosen for their beauty (*en soi*), not for anything they do (*pour soi*), they seem to exist passively until they are seen by the hero, or described to him. They wait, are chosen, and are rewarded.

Marriage is the fulcrum and major event of nearly every fairy tale; it is the reward for girls, or sometimes their punishment. (This is almost equally true for boys, although the boy who wins the hand of the princess gets power as well as a pretty wife, because the princess is often part of a package deal including half or all of a kingdom). While it would be futile and anachronistic to suppose that these tales could or should have depicted alternate options or rewards for heroines or heroes, we must still observe that marriage dominates them, and note what they show as leading to marriage, and as resulting from it. Poor boys play an active role in winning kingdoms and princesses; Espen Cinderlad, the despised and youngest of the three brothers in so many Norwegian folk tales, wins the Princess on the Glass Hill by riding up a veritable hill of glass. Poor girls are chosen by princes because they have been seen by them.

Marriage is associated with getting rich: it will be seen that the reward basis in fairy and folk tales is overwhelmingly mercenary. Good, poor, and pretty girls always win rich and handsome princes, never merely handsome, good, but poor men. (If the heroine or hero is already rich, she or he may marry someone of equal rank and wealth, as in "The White Cat," "Trusty John," "The Sleeping Beauty," etc.; if poor, she or he marries someone richer.) Since girls are chosen for their beauty, it is easy for a child to infer that beauty leads to wealth, that being chosen means getting rich. Beauty has an obviously commercial advantage even in stories in which marriage appears to be a punishment rather than a reward: "Bluebeard," in which the suitor is wealthy though ugly, and the stories in which a girl is wooed by a beast, such as "Beauty and the Beast,"

"East of the Sun and West of the Moon," and "The Black Bull of Norro-way."

The bear in "East of the Sun and West of the Moon" promises to enrich the whole family of a poor husbandman if they will give him the beautiful youngest daughter. Although the girl at first refuses to go, her beauty is seen as the family's sole asset, and she is sold, like a commodity, to the bear (the family does not know that he is a prince under an enchantment). "Beauty and the Beast" is similar to this part of "East of the Sun," and the Snow White of "Snow White and Rose Red" also becomes rich upon marrying an enchanted prince who had been a bear.[4] Cinderella may be the best-known story of this type.

Apart from the princesses who are served out as prizes in competitions (to the lad who can ride up a glass hill, or slay a giant, or answer three riddles, or bring back some rarity), won by lucky fellows like Espen Cinderlad, a few girls in *The Blue Fairy Book* find themselves chosen as brides for mercantile reasons, such as the girl in "Toads and Diamonds" who was rewarded by a fairy so that flowers and jewels dropped from her mouth whenever she spoke. In "Rumpelstiltskin," the little dwarf helps the poor miller's daughter to spin straw into gold for three successive nights, so that the King thinks to himself, " 'She's only a miller's daughter, it's true . . . but I couldn't find a richer wife if I were to search the whole world over,' " consequently making her his queen.[5] The system of rewards in fairy tales, then, equates these three factors: being beautiful, being chosen, and getting rich.

Alison Lurie suggests that perhaps fairy tales are the first real women's literature, that they are literally old wives' tales: "throughout Europe . . . the storytellers from whom the Grimm Brothers and their followers heard them were most often women; in some areas they were all women." [6] She wonders if the stories do not reflect a matriarchal society in which women held power, and she mentions Gretel as an example of an active, resourceful young heroine (I will set aside the problem of the power of older women for the moment). An examination of the best-known stories shows that active resourceful girls are in fact rare; most of the heroines are passive, submissive, and helpless. In the story of "Hansel and Gretel" it is true that Gretel pushes the witch into the oven; Hansel is locked up in the stable, where the witch has been fattening him. At the beginning of the story, however, when the children overhear their parents' plan to lose them in the forest, we read that "Gretel wept bitterly and spoke to Hansel: 'Now it's all up with us.' 'No, no, Gretel,' said Hansel, 'don't fret yourself, I'll be able to find a way of escape, no fear' " (p. 251). It is Hansel who devises the plan of gathering pebbles and dropping them on the path as they are led into the forest.

> Later, in the dark forest, Gretel began to cry, and said: "How are
> we ever to get out of the wood?" But Hansel comforted her. "Wait
> a bit," he said, "till the moon is up, and then we'll find our way sure
> enough." And when the full moon had risen he took his sister by the
> hand and followed the pebbles, which shone like new threepenny
> bits, and showed them the path. (p. 252)

After they get home, they overhear their parents scheming to lose
them again. Gretel weeps again, and again Hansel consoles her. Gretel
does perform the decisive action at the end, but for the first half of the
story she is the frightened little sister, looking to her brother for comfort
and help.

Even so, Gretel is one of the most active of the girls, but her company is small. The heroines of the very similar "East of the Sun" and "The
Black Bull of Norroway" are initially passive, but then undertake difficult
quests when they lose their men. The heroine of "East of the Sun" suc-
cumbs to curiosity (the common trap for women: this story is derived
from the myth of Cupid and Psyche), and attempts to look at her bear-
lover during the night, and the second heroine forgets to remain motion-
less while her bull-lover fights with the devil (good girls sit still). The
lovers disappear when their commands are broken. The girls travel to the
ends of the earth seeking them, but they cannot make themselves seen or
recognized by their men until the last moment. The Master-maid, in a
story whose conclusion resembles these other two, is concealed in a back
room of a giant's house. A prince, looking for adventure, comes to serve
the giant, who gives him tasks that are impossible to accomplish. The
Master-maid knows the giant's secrets and tells the prince how to do the
impossible chores. She knows what to do, but does not act herself. When
the giant tells her to kill the prince, she helps the prince to run away,
escaping with him. Without her advice the escape would be impossible,
yet apparently she had never attempted to run away herself, but had been
waiting in the back room for a prince-escort to show up.

Most of the heroines in *The Blue Fairy Book*, however, are entirely
passive, submissive, and helpless. This is most obviously true of the Sleeping Beauty, who lies asleep, in the ultimate state of passivity, waiting for
a brave prince to awaken and save her. (She is like the Snow White of
"Snow White and the Seven Dwarfs," who lies in a deathlike sleep, her
beauty being visible through her glass coffin, until a prince comes along
and falls in love with her.) When the prince does penetrate the tangle of
thorns and brambles, enters the castle, finds her chamber, and awakens
her, the princess opens her eyes and says, " 'Is it you, my Prince? You have
waited a long while' " (p. 59). This is not the end of the story, although it
is the most famous part. The Sleeping Beauty, who was, while enchanted,

the archetype of the passive, waiting beauty, retains this character in the second part, when she is awake. She marries the prince, and has two children who look savory to her mother-in-law, an Ogress with a taste for human flesh. While her son is away on a hunting trip the Ogress Queen orders the cook to kill and serve for dinner first one child and then the other. The cook hides the children, serving first a roast lamb and then a kid, instead. When the Ogress demands that her daughter-in-law be killed next, the cook tells her the Queen-mother's orders. The young Queen folds up at once: "'Do it; do it' (said she, stretching out her neck). 'Execute your orders, and then I shall go and see my children . . . whom I so much and so tenderly loved'" (p. 62). The compassionate cook, however, decides to hide her too, and the young King returns in time to save them all from the Ogress' wrath and impending disaster.

Cinderella plays as passive a role in her story. After leaving her slipper at the ball she has nothing more to do but stay home and wait. The prince has commanded that the slipper be carried to every house in the kingdom, and that it be tried on the foot of every woman. Cinderella can remain quietly at home; the prince's servant will come to her house and will discover her identity. Cinderella's male counterpart, Espen Cinderlad, the hero of a great many Norwegian folk tales, plays a very different role. Although he is the youngest of the three brothers, as Cinderella is the youngest sister, he is a Cinderlad by choice. His brothers may ridicule and despise him, but no one forces him to sit by the fire and poke in the ashes all day; he elects to do so. All the while, he knows that he is the cleverest of the three, and eventually he leaves the fireside and wins a princess and half a kingdom by undertaking some adventure or winning a contest.

The Princess on the Glass Hill is the prototype of female passivity. The whole story is in the title; the Princess has been perched somehow on top of a glass hill, and thus made virtually inaccessible. There she sits, a waiting prize for whatever man can ride a horse up the glassy slope. So many of the heroines of fairy stories, including the well-known Rapunzel, are locked up in towers, locked into a magic sleep, imprisoned by giants, or otherwise enslaved, and waiting to be rescued by a passing prince, that the helpless, imprisoned maiden is the quintessential heroine of the fairy tale.

In the interesting story of "The Goose-Girl," an old Queen sends off her beautiful daughter, accompanied by a maid, to be married to a distant prince. The Queen gives her daughter a rag stained with three drops of her own blood. During the journey the maid brusquely refuses to bring the Princess a drink of water, saying "'I don't mean to be your servant any longer.'" The intimidated Princess only murmurs, "'Oh! heaven, what am I to do?'" (p. 266). This continues, the maid growing ruder, the Princess meeker, until she loses the rag, whereupon the maid rejoices, knowing that she now has full power over the girl, "for in losing the drops of blood the Princess had become weak and powerless" (p. 268). The maid commands the Princess to change clothes and horses with her, and never to speak to anyone about what has happened. The possession of the rag had assured the Princess' social status; without it she becomes *déclassée*, and while her behavior was no less meek and docile before losing the rag than afterwards, there is no formal role reversal until she loses it. Upon their arrival the maid presents herself as the Prince's bride, while the Princess is given the job of goose-girl. At length, due solely to the intervention of others, the secret is discovered, the maid killed, and the goose-girl married to the Prince.

The heroine of "Felicia and the Pot of Pinks" is equally submissive to ill-treatment. After their father's death, her brother forbids her to sit on his chairs:

> Felicia, who was very gentle, said nothing, but stood up crying quietly; while Bruno, for that was her brother's name, sat comfortably by the fire. Presently, when suppertime came, Bruno had a delicious egg, and he threw the shell to Felicia, saying:
> "There, that is all I can give you; if you don't like it, go out and catch frogs; there are plenty of them in the marsh close by." Felicia did not answer but she cried more bitterly than ever, and went away to her own little room. (p. 148)

The underlying associational pattern of these stories links the figures of the victimized girl and the interesting girl; it is always the interesting girl, the special girl, who is in trouble. It needs to be asked whether a child's absorption of the associational patterns found in these myths and legends may not sensitize the personality, rendering it susceptible to melodramatic self-conceptions and expectations. Because victimized girls like Felicia, the Goose-girl, and Cinderella are invariably rescued and rewarded, indeed glorified, children learn that suffering goodness can afford to remain meek, and need not and perhaps should not strive to defend itself, for if it did so perhaps the fairy godmother would not turn up for once, to set things right at the end. Moreover, the special thrill of persecution, bordering at once upon self-pity and self-righteousness, would have to be surrendered. Submissive, meek, passive female behavior is suggested and rewarded by the action of these stories.

Many of the girls are not merely passive, however; they are frequently victims and even martyrs as well. The Cinderella story is not simply a rags-to-riches tale. Cinderella is no Horatio Alger; her name is partly synonymous with female martyrdom. Her ugly older sisters, who are jealous of her beauty, keep her dressed in rags and hidden at home. They order her to do all the meanest housework. Cinderella bears this ill-treatment meekly: she is the patient sufferer, an object of pity. When the older sisters go off to the ball she bursts into tears; it is only the sound of her weeping that arouses her fairy godmother. Ultimately, her loneliness and her suffering are sentimentalized and become an integral part of her glamor. "Cinderella" and the other stories of this type show children that the girl who is singled out for rejection and bad treatment, and who submits to her lot, weeping but never running away, has a special compensatory destiny awaiting her. One of the pleasures provided by these stories is that the child reader is free to indulge in pity, to be sorry for the heroine. The girl in tears is invariably the heroine; that is one of the ways the child can identify the heroine, for no one mistakenly feels sorry for the ugly older sisters, or for any of the villains or villainesses. When these characters suffer, they are only receiving their "just deserts." The child who dreams of being a Cinderella dreams perforce not only of being chosen and elevated by a prince, but also of being a glamorous sufferer or victim. What these stories convey is that women in distress are interesting. Fairy stories provide children with a concentrated early introduction to the archetype of the suffering heroine, who is currently alive (though not so well) under the name of Jenny Cavilleri.

The girl who marries Blue Beard is a prime example of the helpless damsel-victim, desperately waiting for a rescuer. She knows that her husband will not hesitate to murder her, because she has seen the corpses of his other murdered wives in the forbidden closet. The enraged Blue Beard announces that he will cut off her head; he gives her 15 minutes to say her prayers, after which he bellows for her so loudly that the house trembles:

> The distressed wife came down, and threw herself at his feet, all in tears, with her hair about her shoulders.
> "This signifies nothing," said Blue Beard: "you must die": then, taking hold of her hair with one hand, and lifting up the sword with the other, he was going to take off her head. The poor lady, turning about to him, and looking at him with dying eyes, desired him to afford her one little moment to recollect herself.
> "No, no," said he, "recommend thyself to God," and was just about to strike. . . . (p. 295)

"At this very instant," as the story continues, her brothers rush in and save her.

It is worth noticing that the one Greek legend that Lang included in *The Blue Fairy Book* is the Perseus story, which Lang entitled "The

Terrible Head." It features two utterly helpless women, the first being Danae, who is put into a chest with her infant son, Perseus, and thrown out to sea, to drown or starve or drift away. Fortunately the chest comes to land, and Danae and her baby are saved. At the conclusion of the story, as the grown-up Perseus is flying home with the Gorgon's head, he looks down and sees "a beautiful girl chained to a stake at the high-water mark of the sea. The girl was so frightened or so tired that she was only prevented from falling by the iron chain about her waist, and there she hung, as if she were dead" (p. 190). Perseus learns that she has been left there as a sacrifice to a sea monster; he cuts her free, kills the monster, and carries her off as his bride.

Few other rescues are as dramatic as that of Blue Beard's wife or of Andromeda, but the device of the rescue itself is constantly used. The sexes of the rescuer and the person in danger are almost as constantly predictable; men come along to rescue women who are in danger of death, or are enslaved, imprisoned, abused, or plunged into an enchanted sleep which resembles death. Two well-known stories that were not included in *The Blue Fairy Book*, "Snow White and the Seven Dwarfs" and "Rapunzel," are notable examples of this type: Snow White is saved from a sleep which everyone assumes is death by the arrival of a handsome prince; Rapunzel, locked up in a tower by a cruel witch, is found and initially rescued by her prince.

Whatever the condition of younger women in fairy tales, Alison Lurie claims that the older women in the tales are often more active and powerful than men. It is true that some older women in fairy tales have power, but of what kind? In order to understand the meaning of women's power in fairy tales, we must examine the nature, the value, and the use of their power.

There are only a few powerful good women in *The Blue Fairy Book*, and they are nearly all fairies: the tiny, jolly, ugly old fairy in "Prince Hyacinth," the stately fairies in "Prince Darling," "Toads and Diamonds," and "Felicia," and of course Cinderella's fairy godmother. They are rarely on the scene; they only appear in order to save young people in distress, and then they're off again. These good fairies have gender only in a technical sense; to children, they probably appear as women only in the sense that dwarfs and wizards appear as men. They are not human beings, they are asexual, and many of them are old. They are not examples of powerful women with whom children can identify as role models; they do not provide meaningful alternatives to the stereotype of the younger, passive heroine. A girl may hope to become a princess, but can she ever become a fairy?

Powerful, bad, older women appear to outnumber powerful, good ones. A certain number of these are also not fully human; they are fairies, witches, trolls, or Ogresses. It is generally implied that such females are wicked because of their race: thus the young king in "The Sleeping Beauty" fears his mother while he loves her, "for she was of the race of the Ogres, and the King (his father) would never have married her had it not been for her vast riches; it was even whispered about the Court that she had Ogreish inclinations, and that, whenever she saw little children passing by, she had all the difficulty in the world to avoid falling upon them" (p. 60). Either extra-human race or extreme ugliness is often associated with female wickedness, and in such a way as to suggest that they explain the wickedness. The evil Fairy of the Desert in "The Yellow Dwarf" is described as a "tall old woman, whose ugliness was even more surprising than her extreme old age" (p. 39). The sheep-king in "The Wonderful Sheep" tells Miranda that he was transformed into a sheep by a fairy "'whom I had known as long as I could remember, and whose ugliness had always horrified me'" (p. 223). The bear-prince in "East of the Sun" is under a spell cast by a troll-hag, and the fairy who considers herself slighted by the Sleeping Beauty's parents is described as being old: the original illustration for Lang's book shows her to be an ugly old crone, whereas the other fairies are young and lovely.

In the case of wicked but human women, it is also implied that being ill-favored is corollary to being ill-natured, as with Cinderella's stepmother and stepsisters. Cinderella is pretty and sweet, like her dead mother. The stepmother is proud and haughty, and her two daughters by her former husband are like her, so that their ill temper appears to be genetic, or at least transmitted by the mother. The circumstances in "Toads and Diamonds" are similar: the old widow has two daughters, of whom the eldest resembles her mother "in face and humour. . . . They were both so disagreeable and so proud that there was no living with them. The youngest, who was the very picture of her father for courtesy and sweetness of temper, was withal one of the most beautiful girls ever seen" (p. 274).

Powerful good women are nearly always fairies, and they are remote: they come only when desperately needed. Whether human or extra-human, those women who are either partially or thoroughly evil are generally shown as active, ambitious, strong-willed and, most often, ugly. They are jealous of any woman more beautiful than they, which is not surprising in view of the power deriving from beauty in fairy tales. In "Cinderella" the domineering stepmother and stepsisters contrast with the passive heroine. The odious stepmother wants power, and successfully makes her will prevail in the house; we are told that Cinderella bore her ill-treatment patiently, "and dared not tell her father, who would have rattled her off; for his wife governed him entirely." The wicked maid in "The Goose-Girl" is not described as being either fair or ugly (except that the Princess appears to be fairer than the maid at the end), but like the other female villains she is jealous of beauty and greedy for wealth. She decides to usurp the Princess' place, and being evil she is also strong and determined, and initially successful. Being powerful is mainly associated with being unwomanly.

The moral value of activity thus becomes sex-linked.[7] The boy who sets out to seek his fortune, like Dick Whittington, Jack the Giant-Killer, or Espen Cinderlad, is a stock figure and, provided that he has a kind heart, is assured of success. What is praiseworthy in males, however, is rejected in females; the counterpart of the energetic, aspiring boy is the scheming, ambitious woman. Some heroines show a kind of strength in their ability to endure, but they do not actively seek to change their lot. (The only exceptions to this rule are in the stories that appear to derive from the myth of Cupid and Psyche: "East of the Sun" and "The Black Bull of Norroway," in which the heroines seek their lost lovers. We may speculate whether the pre-Christian origin of these stories diminishes the stress placed on female passivity and acceptance, but this is purely conjectural.) We can remark that these stories reflect a bias against the active, ambitious, "pushy" woman and have probably also served to instill this bias in young readers. They establish a dichotomy between those women who are gentle, passive, and fair, and those who are active, wicked, and ugly. Women who are powerful and good are never human; those women who are human, and who have power or seek it, are nearly always portrayed as repulsive.

While character depiction in fairy tales is, to be sure, meager, and we can usually group characters according to temperamental type (beautiful and sweet, or ugly and evil), there are a couple of girls who are not portrayed as being either perfectly admirable or as wicked. The princesses in "The Yellow Dwarf," "Goldilocks," and "Trusty John" are described as being spoiled, vain, and willful: the problem is that they refuse to marry anyone. The Queen in "The Yellow Dwarf" expostulates with her daughter:

> "Bellissima," she said, "I do wish you would not be so proud. What makes you despise all these nice kings? I wish you to marry one of them, and you do not try to please me."
>
> "I am so happy," Bellissima answered: "do leave me in peace, madam. I don't want to care for anyone."
>
> "But you would be very happy with any of these princes," said the Queen, "and I shall be very angry if you fall in love with anyone who is not worthy of you."

But the Princess thought so much of herself that she did not consider any one of her lovers clever or handsome enough for her; and her mother, who was getting really angry at her determination not to be married, began to wish that she had not allowed her to have her own way so much. (p. 31)

Princess Goldilocks similarly refuses to consider marriage, although she is not as adamant as Bellissima. The princess in the Grimms' story, "King Thrushbeard," which is not included in this collection, behaves like Bellissima; her angry father declares that he will give her to the very next comer, whatever his rank: the next man to enter the castle being a beggar, the king marries his daughter to him. This princess suffers poverty with her beggar-husband, until he reveals himself as one of the suitor kings she had rejected. Bellissima is punished more severely; indeed, her story is remarkable because it is one of the rare examples outside of H. C. Andersen of a story with a sad ending. Because Bellissima had refused to marry, she is forced by a train of circumstances to promise to marry the ugly Yellow Dwarf. She tries to avoid this fate by consenting to wed one of her suitors at last, but the dwarf intervenes at the wedding. Ultimately the dwarf kills the suitor, whom Bellissima had come to love, and she dies of a broken heart. A kind mermaid transforms the ill-fated lovers into two palm trees.

These princesses are portrayed as reprehensible because they refuse to marry; hence, they are considered "stuck-up," as children would say. The alternate construction, that they wished to preserve their freedom and their identity, is denied or disallowed (although Bellissima had said to her mother, " 'I am so happy, do leave me in peace, madam.' ") There is a sense of triumph when a willful princess submits or is forced to submit to a husband.

The Blue Fairy Book is filled with weddings, but it shows little of married life. It contains 30 stories in which marriage is a component, but 18 of these stories literally end with the wedding. Most of the other 12 show so little of the marital life of the hero or heroine that technically they too may be said to end with marriage. Only a few of the stories show any part of the married life of young people, or even of old ones. The Sleeping Beauty is a totally passive wife and mother, and Blue Beard's wife, like the Sleeping Beauty, depends on a man to rescue her. Whereas the Sleeping Beauty is menaced by her mother-in-law who, being an Ogress, is only half-human, Blue Beard's wife is endangered by *being* the wife of her ferocious husband. (Her error may be ascribed to her having an independent sense of curiosity, or to rash disobedience.) This widely known story established a potent myth in which a helpless woman violates her husband's arbitrary command and then is subject to his savage, implacable fury. It is fully the counterpoise of the other stock marital situation containing a scheming, overbearing wife and a timid, hen-pecked husband, as in "Cinderella"; moreover, whereas the domineering wife is always implicitly regarded as abhorrent, the helpless, threatened, passive wife is uncritically viewed and thus implicitly approved of. As Andromeda, Blue Beard's wife, or the imperiled Pauline, her function is to provide us with a couple of thrills of a more or less sadistic tincture.

The other peculiar aspect of the depiction of marriage in these stories is that nearly all the young heroes and heroines are the children of widows or widowers; only five of the 37 stories in the book contain a set of parents: these include "The Sleeping Beauty," in which the parents leave the castle when the hundred-year enchantment begins, and the two similar tales of "Little Thumb" and "Hansel and Gretel," in both of which the parents decide to get rid of their children because they are too poor to feed them. (In "Little Thumb" the husband persuades his reluctant wife, and in "Hansel and Gretel" the wife persuades her reluctant husband.) Cinderella has two parents, but the only one who plays a part in the story is her stepmother. In general, the young people of these stories are described as having only one parent, or none. Although marriage is such a constant event in the stories, and is central to their reward system, few marriages are indeed shown in fairy tales. Like the White Queen's rule, there's jam tomorrow and jam yesterday, but never jam today. The stories can be described as being preoccupied with marriage without portraying it; as a real condition, it's nearly always offstage.

In effect, these stories focus upon courtship, which is magnified into the most important and exciting part of a girl's life, brief though courtship is, because it is the part of her life in which she most counts as a person herself. After marriage she ceases to be wooed, her consent is no longer sought, she derives her status from her husband, and her personal identity is thus snuffed out. When fairy tales show courtship as exciting, and conclude with marriage, and the vague statement that "they lived happily ever after," children may develop a deep-seated desire always to be courted, since marriage is literally the end of the story.

The controversy about what is biologically determined and what is learned has just begun. These are the questions now being asked, and not yet answered: to what extent is passivity a biological attribute of females; to what extent is it culturally determined? Perhaps it will be argued that these stories show archetypal female behavior, but one may wonder to what extent they reflect female attributes, or to what extent they serve as training manuals for girls? If one argued that the characteristically passive behavior of female characters in fairy stories is a reflection of an attribute inherent in female personality, would one also argue, as consistency would require, that the mercantile reward system of fairy stories reflects values that are inherent in human nature? We must consider the possibility that the classical attributes of "femininity" found in these stories are in fact imprinted in children and reinforced by the stories themselves. Analyses of the influence of the most popular children's literature may give us an insight into some of the origins of psychosexual identity.

References

1. ALISON LURIE, "Fairy Tale Liberation," *The New York Review of Books*, December 17, 1970, p. 42.
2. ALISON LURIE, "Witches and Fairies: Fitzgerald to Updike," *The New York Review of Books*, December 2, 1971, p. 6.
3. ANDREW LANG, ed., *The Green Fairy Book* (New York: McGraw-Hill, 1966), pp. ix–xi.
4. In these stories, the girl who marries a beast must agree to accept and love a beast as a husband; the girl must give herself to a beast in order to get a man. When she is willing to do this, he can shed his frightening, rough appearance and show his gentler form, demonstrating the softening agency of women (as in the story of Jane Eyre and Mr. Rochester). These heroines have an agentive role, insofar as they are responsible for the literal reformation of the male.
5. ANDREW LANG, ed., *The Blue Fairy Book* (New York: McGraw-Hill, 1966), p. 98. All quotations are from this edition.
6. ALISON LURIE, "Fairy Tale Liberation," *loc. cit.*
7. RUTH KELSO's *Doctrine for the Lady of the Renaissance* (Urbana: University of Illinois Press, 1956) demonstrates that "the moral ideal for the lady is essentially Christian . . . as that for the gentleman is essentially pagan. For him the ideal is self-expansion and realization. . . . For the lady the direct opposite is prescribed. The eminently Christian virtues of chastity, humility, piety, and patience under suffering and wrong, are the necessary virtues" (p. 36).

Louisa May Alcott:
THE AUTHOR OF "LITTLE WOMEN" AS FEMINIST

"I believe that it is as much a right and duty for women to do something with their lives as for men; and we are not going to be satisfied with
such frivolous parts as you give us." [1] It is a quote that might be found in
the works of one of the leaders of the struggle for women's liberation in
the late nineteenth and early twentieth centuries. Actually it is Rose
Campbell, the heroine of two of Louisa May Alcott's books for girls, *Eight
Cousins* and *Rose in Bloom*. This quote is a keynote to any analysis of the
works of Alcott.

The obvious question is, of course, why bother to analyze Louisa
May Alcott at all? Her name has become a byword for everything re-
pellent in middle-class culture—it conjures up sweet, starched little girls
docilely reading the books their mothers and grandmothers had read
years before. She would seem a prime example of everything hip culture
scorns, literati ignore, and feminists detest.

But the image of Alcott is derived from people who have never read
her, or have long forgotten what they *did* read. The fact is that, as a writer
of children's books she is superb (and who is to say that this literature is
any less important than that written for adults?), and that, while in no
way a radical, she is very much a humanist, very much a feminist, and
very much to be considered in our own time.

Basic to Alcott's work is a profound humanism. Her biographer,
Cornelia Meigs, cites her tremendous admiration for Dickens,[2] and this is
evident throughout her work—the Pickwick Club formed by the sisters in
Little Women, the references to Dickens in many of the books, and the
scenes from the lives of the poor much like those of Dickens, though less

Note: By Karen Lindsey. Reprinted with permission from *Women: a Journal
of Liberation,* Fall 1970, 2:1, 35–37. Copyright © 1970 by *Women: a Journal of
Liberation* (3028 Greenmount Avenue, Baltimore, Maryland 21218).

brutal than his. Both writers felt deeply the wretchedness of poverty and
the unequal class system, and both failed to make the next step and reject
the morality of class, finding solutions only in individual virtue. But unlike Dickens, Alcott was a woman—limited by her womanhood to a narrower view of life, but also aware, because of those limits, of something
Dickens could ignore—the oppression of women.

She saw this oppression in terms of the upper- and middle-class
women, and Rose Campbell is an excellent example. In *Eight Cousins,*
Rose is a pretty, weak teenage heiress, newly orphaned, who is adopted
by her uncle and lives surrounded by uncles, aunts, and seven boy
cousins. *Eight Cousins* follows her growth until her eighteenth birthday,
and the story is picked up a year later in *Rose in Bloom.* It is in this book
that Rose declares her independence. Rejecting the frivolous life of a
belle, she invests her wealth and time in philanthropic endeavors—despite
the ridicule of many of her friends and of her handsome cousin Charlie.
People warn her that this kind of life will repel suitors; Rose declares that
she will then remain a spinster. When she does in fact marry, it is not
the fashionable Charlie she chooses, but homely Mac, who has succeeded
in his own worthy endeavors and has encouraged hers.

Rose does eventually marry; many Alcott heroines do not. It is
interesting that in almost every one of her books there is a major female
character who remains single, willingly, for the freedom to do the work
she feels important: in *An Old Fashioned Girl,* Maud remains a "busy,
lively spinster," [3] in *Jack and Jill,* Molly "remained a merry spinster all her
days, one of the independent, brave, and busy creatures of whom there is
such need in the world to help take care of other people's wives and children, and to do the many useful jobs that married folk have no time for." [4]
Perhaps most important is Nan, of *Little Men* and *Jo's Boys*—an attractive
girl who becomes a doctor, opting to remain single despite the ardent
courtship of Tommy Bangs. She is, she declares, "very glad and grateful
that my profession will make me a useful, happy and independent spinster." [5] Useful, lively, independent, happy—these are the adjectives Alcott
uses for her spinsters. An unmarried woman is not an old maid to be
pitied; she is free and happy in herself, and useful to her fellows.

Alcott's most famous character, of course—the beloved Jo of *Little
Women, Little Men,* and *Jo's Boys,* does marry, but she rejects romantic
Laurie and later marries the older, wiser Professor Bhaer. Their marriage,
while full of love, is less romantic than companionable. And it is to Jo,
alone of all her woman characters, that she allows a combination of marriage and career: Jo and her professor run a school for boys, Professor
Bhaer teaching classes and Jo raising the boys—a mother still, but in a
special and singular way. Later, Jo becomes a famous author, returning

to her resemblance to Alcott herself. It is in any case an ideal marriage, one that Alcott may very well have dreamed of. She never did marry, and was very clear about her feelings on marriage. In her diary, she said of her sister Anna's wedding: "Mr. Emerson kissed Anna; and I thought that honor would make even matrimony endurable." Later, visiting Anna's new home, she wrote: "Very sweet and pretty; but I would rather be a free spinster and paddle my own canoe." [6]

More important than her feelings about marriage is her emphasis on feminine friendship. She hated the kind of backbiting, frivolous friendships so common among women, and emphasized always the deep, sincere, simple love of genuine friendship: the relationship of the sisters in *Little Women;* of Rose and Phoebe in *Eight Cousins* and *Rose in Bloom;* and the almost bohemian friendship emphasized in a short but significant chapter of *An Old Fashioned Girl.* "Help one another, is part of the religion of our sisterhood, Fan," says Polly in this chapter, and the four women—sculptor, painter, writer, and music teacher—live this religion.

In this same chapter, we see clearly Alcott's ideal of womanhood. Polly, who has brought her rich, bored friend Fanny to see her other friends and learn what richness women can bring to each other's lives, shows Fanny a statue being made by the sculptor. It is a model of Woman, as she should be.

". . . See what a fine forehead, yet the mouth is both firm and tender, as if it could say strong, wise things, as well as teach children and kiss babies. We couldn't decide what to put in the hands as the most appropriate symbol. What do you say?"

"Give her a sceptre; she would make a fine queen," answered Fanny.

"No, we have had enough of that; women have been called queens for a long time, but the kingdom given them isn't worth ruling," answered Rebecca. . . .

"Put a man's hand in hers, to help her along then," said Polly . . .

"No; my woman is to stand alone, and help herself," said Rebecca decidedly.

"She's to be strong-minded, is she?" and Fanny's lips curled as she uttered the misused words.

"Yes, strong-minded, strong-hearted, strong-souled and strong-bodied; that is why I made her larger than the miserable, pinched-up woman of our day. Strength and beauty must go together. Don't you think these broad shoulders can bear burdens without breaking down, these hands work well, these eyes see clearly, and these lips do something besides simper and gossip?"

> "Put a child in her arms, Becky."
> "Not that even, for she is to be something more than a nurse. . . ." [7]

Friendship, strength, and independence—these are the qualities Alcott demands in the women of her books, and in women everywhere.

With the kind of perception Alcott had, one is forced to wonder why she never criticized the institutions responsible for the evils she despised. Suffering for the poor, she never questioned the capitalist class system that produced such conditions. Admiring, and personally preferring spinsterhood, she never criticized the institution of marriage. Demanding of women that they be independent, she failed to demand that men share the domestic tasks and thus allow women that independence. I think there are two major reasons for this: the limits of her mind, and her personal family life. Alcott was a sensitive writer, and a talented one, but not, I think a truly imaginative one. She drew from her own experience, and did it brilliantly, but she lacked the insight to imagine possibilities beyond that experience. She passionately loved her family; it could not have occurred to her to question the validity of the family as a social unit.

It is this love of family, ironically, that probably accounts both for her art and for her limits as a social observer. She lived for them; except for a month working as a nurse during the Civil War, she worked only to keep her family comfortable and together. She worshiped her father, Bronson Alcott, or so Cornelia Meigs tells us; yet even Meigs, painting the family in as rosy a light as Alcott herself would have done, cannot quite conceal the true picture of what Bronson Alcott must have been: brilliant, compassionate—and filled with a remarkably selfish dedication which allowed him, while fighting for social improvements in the world, to keep his wife working herself nearly to death for him. A typical scene in Meigs's biography occurs when the Alcotts begin to live communally at Fruitlands. They gather together in the evening:

> Bronson would get out the beloved book (*Pilgrim's Progress*) and read aloud . . . he would put down the book . . . and ask: "What is God's noblest work?" They must all answer . . . the older philosophers . . . and also the children . . . Abba Alcott, who had toiled without ceasing since daylight, would be sitting by the single lamp sewing as though her life depended on it. She was the only woman there, and hers was the only able pair of hands for the tasks of preparing food, sweeping, washing and keeping all this household clothed. The questions went round from one to another, but she did not answer. It was agreed that she was to be excused, that she had other things of which to think.[8]

Despite Meigs's prettifying, it isn't a nice picture: Abba, worn from working for her own family, must now take on the housework for a group of strangers, and, while she is excused from answering questions, it seems fairly clear that the men are all excused from helping her in any of the domestic tasks foisted on her.

This selfishness of Bronson's is consistent throughout Meigs's book. Bronson was often not working (he was too idealistic for most jobs), and Abba was forced to work for a time as well as to keep house. How could Louisa, then, admit the tyranny of marriage without admitting the tyranny of her beloved father? One wonders if she was ever aware of this conflict, if she ever felt any resentment toward Bronson Alcott. That she felt resentment, at least unconsciously, seems clear in a striking way; in her most famous, and directly autobiographical book, *Little Women*, she all but ignores his existence. There was no way to excuse Bronson Alcott, but neither could Louisa ever condemn him—so, in her book (though hardly in her life) Louisa simply ignored him.

That Alcott's perceptions as a feminist were regrettably limited is all too apparent. She sensed only what woman should achieve, and not what changes were needed before that achievement could be possible. But when we consider much of today's children's literature or the kiddie shows on television, Alcott appears far advanced indeed. Our daughters could do worse than to read Louisa May Alcott—to cry with Jo over Beth's young death, to rejoice with Rose over Phoebe's success, to feel the beauty and dignity of friendship that pervades the books. In her perception she does not go far enough, but what she does explore she does beautifully, and with a love, a compassion, a dignity that are certainly worthy of our admiration and enjoyment.

References

1. LOUISA MAY ALCOTT, *Rose in Bloom* (New York: A. L. Burt Co., 1918), p. 10.
2. CORNELIA MEIGS, *Invincible Louisa* (Boston: Little, Brown and Co., 1933), p. 184.
3. LOUISA MAY ALCOTT, *An Old-Fashioned Girl* (New York: Grosset and Dunlap, 1911), p. 327.
4. LOUISA MAY ALCOTT, *Jack and Jill* (New York: Grosset and Dunlap, 1928), p. 303.
5. LOUISA MAY ALCOTT, *Jo's Boys* (New York: Grosset and Dunlap, 1949), p. 15.
6. MEIGS, p. 129.
7. *An Old Fashioned Girl*, pp. 226–228.
8. MEIGS, p. 59.

A FEMINIST LOOK AT CHILDREN'S BOOKS

Is the portrayal of females in children's books sexist? That is, are girls and women assigned only traditional female roles and personalities? And when the female foot fails to fit that often too-tight shoe, is the girl or woman then seen as an unfortunate, troubled human being?

These questions were the basis of a group effort to scrutinize some of the more highly praised children's books. In our view, a nonsexist portrayal would offer the girl reader a positive image of woman's physical, emotional, and intellectual potential—one that would encourage her to reach her own full personhood, free of traditionally imposed limitations.

In selecting books to examine, we consulted a number of influential lists. These were the *Notable Books of 1969* (American Library Association), the Child Study Association's annual recommendations for that same year, and the Newbery Award winners.

It was a shock to discover almost immediately that relatively few of the books on these lists even feature female characters—let alone what we would consider *positive* female characters. Of all 49 Newbery Award winners, books about boys outnumbered books about girls by about three to one. On that score, the years have brought little improvement. The ALA list for 1969 gave us a ratio of over two to one.

The Child Study Association list for the same year proved more difficult to analyze. It is very long, divided into innumerable categories, and many of the books can't yet be found in the libraries. However, we made a separate check of several categories. Under the heading of "Boys and Girls" we found a male to female ratio of two to one. "Growing Up" the ratio was over three to one. And "Sports," of course, like certain bars

Note: By Feminists on Children's Media. Reprinted with permission from *School Library Journal,* January 1971, 17:5, 19–24. Copyright © 1971 by the Xerox Corporation.

we could formerly name, was 100 percent male. The rest of the book list may not follow the pattern of this sampling, but suspicion runs high!

The thoughtful introduction to the Child Study Association list makes the following statement: The books a child reads "should not shield him from knowledge of destructive forces in the world, but rather help him to cope with them." We agree, for the most part. But why does the sentence read "shield *him*" and "help *him*"? Sexism is such a destructive force in the world, that we feel the implicit sexism in this sentence should not be overlooked.

The introduction states also that a book's "possible emotional and intellectual impact on a young reader" must be considered. Right on! Not even a problem of gender there. The CSA continues: "from its inception, it has been aware of the mental health aspects of reading and asks that books for children present basically honest concepts of life, positive ethical values, and honest interpersonal relationships."

We ask no more than that. The CSA has clearly been struggling to encourage greater sensitivity toward racism in books for children. If only their future book selections could be made with an equally growing sensitivity to the impact of sexism? Many of the present selections fail to realize the promise of their own introduction. The list is guilty of sexism—if only through indifference.

Of course, a greater sensitivity to sexism would greatly curtail the current lists of recommended children's books—at least for the next few years. Yet, a scrupulous attitude on the part of prestigious organizations would surely serve powerfully in raising the general feminist consciousness of the children's book world, making forever obsolete Eve Merriam's recent and accurate comment that "sex prejudice is the only prejudice now considered socially acceptable." Habit dies hard.

We'd like to apologize for seeming to pick on CSA. It's just that such a praiseworthy introduction deserved attention in terms of its implications for the female image. Nor were we being picky in our examination of specific books: checking the prevalence of so virulent a disease as sexism requires the isolation of even potential carriers.

What would we like to see in children's books? What were our criteria? We wanted to see girl readers encouraged to develop physical confidence and strength without the need to fear any corresponding loss of "femininity." We would have liked to see the elimination of all those tiresome references to "tomboys." Why can't a girl who prefers baseball to ballet simply be a girl who prefers baseball to ballet?

Many women have to—or simply prefer to—earn a living. Can't we encourage girls to find satisfaction and fulfillment in work, and lay forever the suspicion that work outside the home for a *woman* is primarily proof of her inability to love a man, or to land a sufficiently lucrative one? Women do study seriously, work with enjoyment—or at least pride in their competence—get promoted, and (of course) fight sexism at work and in their families in order to progress. Let's show them as no less "feminine," despite the assertiveness and firm sense of self required in this untraditional role.

Margaret Mead has written that "man is unsexed by failure, woman by success." That's another brutal truth we'd like to see changed. And while we're about it, let's not overlook the fact that boys, too, are denigrated and cramped by sexism. Our current rigid role definitions require that a boy be all that a girl should not be: unafraid, competent at "male" jobs, strong. A weeping boy is a "sissy." Words like "sissy"— and "hero," too—should be dissected and exposed for the inhuman demands they make on growing boys. Children's books could help.

We object to a woman's being defined by the man she marries, or the children she bears, or the father she once obeyed. Let's see women who are people in their own right—independent of such compensatory affiliations. And if a woman doesn't want children, or even a husband, must this be seen as peculiar? Why not encourage girls in a search for alternate life styles? Give a girl all the possible options you give a boy for her future life choices, all his freedom to inquire and explore and achieve. Her options don't have to be slanted toward certain current socially imposed preferences.

There are books on superwomen. Okay. Superwomen do exist. But many more books are needed on women who simply function very well and freely wherever they choose—or are forced—to apply their abilities.

We are bitterly tired of seeing depictions of the woman as castrator. Even a well-known writer, whose portrayal of girls we frequently admire, slipped badly in some recent picture books. In one of these, the mother reproves her son for spilling the mud he is playing with—even though the scene is outdoors! In another, little sister (and we know where she learned *her* lesson) reproves brother for accidentally spilling paint off his easel. Little girls are as capable of making a casual mess and as freely lost in creative play as little boys. A picture book that does that beautifully is *Rain Rain Rivers* by Uri Shulevitz (Farrar, 1969) which we were delighted to find on both the ALA and CSA lists. (We were as pleased to find the two previously mentioned books ignored by both lists.)

And when, as must sometimes happen if books portray real life, there is an overcontrolling or too-bossy woman, she should not be made a fool or villain. A little understanding—of her problem, her frustration at not being allowed to play an equal role in her family or her world, and her consequent misuse of energy to project her ideas and ego through the lives of others—is long overdue.

How about books showing more divorced and single-parent families? And, for heaven's sake, every divorced or widowed mother does not solve her problems through remarriage—or even wish to do so. (Few do, you know!) Maybe she can start on that career she never had—and discover a new concept of herself. The difficulties and the loneliness are real, as are the child-care problems. But let the woman find a new self-reliance in fighting her own battles—and joy in winning at least some of them.

There is also the question of language. No more automatic use of "he" to mean "child," or "mankind" to mean "humankind." If at first the alternatives seem forced—and they will—they won't sound that way for long.

Despite our criticism of socially assigned roles, we don't mean to diminish or ignore the mother or housewife. She is often a strong, wonderfully rich human being. Her role can be vital, and sometimes she finds satisfaction in it. But let's not insist on that as *her* role. Men can also cope skillfully with household tasks—and not necessarily look for a woman or daughter to take them off the hook.

Sexist Books

The books we read—most from the lists mentioned earlier—fell, or were pushed by our merciless analysis, into several categories. One, plain and simple, was the sexist book, in which girls and women are exclusively assigned traditional female roles—although the material may, unhappily, be fairly true to life.

We were forcibly struck by the purposeful sexist propaganda between the covers of some of the recommended children's books.

Young women who have found it an uphill struggle to identify with the popular female image will recognize it as propaganda—and not simply as a natural reflection of life. Unfortunately the girl reader is not yet so experienced. Books that outline a traditional background role for women, praising their domestic accomplishments, their timidity of soul, their gentle appearance and manners, and—at the same time—fail to portray initiative, enterprise, physical prowess, and genuine intellect deliver a powerful message to children of both sexes. Such books are a social poison.

Take, for a horrible example, the attitude exemplified in the following line: "Accept the fact that this is a man's world and learn how to play the game gracefully." Those words fell from the lips of a *sympathetic* male character in Irene Hunt's 1967 Newbery winner *Up a Road Slowly* (Follett, 1966). Or take this juicy bit from the 1957 winner *Miracles on Maple Hill* by Virginia Sorenson (Harcourt, 1956).

> For the millionth time she was glad she wasn't a boy. It was all right for girls to be scared or silly or even ask dumb questions. Everybody just laughed and thought it was funny. But if anybody caught Joe asking a dumb question or even thought he was the littlest bit scared, he went red and purple and white. Daddy was even something like that, old as he was.

Does that passage describe real life? Indeed it does! But a good book for children should comment and leave the child feeling something is wrong here. This one does not. In fact, we voted it our supreme example of the most thoroughly relentless type of sexism found in children's literature. The girl, Marly, never overcomes her hero worship of brother Joe or her comparative inferiority. And it certainly would have been relevant to explore the toll that maintaining hero status takes on Joe's character.

Such perfect examples, of course, are not the rule. But there was a surplus of books whose thesis might seem less obvious, but whose refrain was predictably the same. A little girl in the 1955 Newbery winner *The Wheel on the School* (Harper, 1954) asks her boy playmate: "Can I go, too?" And the response is "No! Girls are no good at jumping. It's a boy's game." Meindert DeJong leaves it at that—and another eager little girl reader is squelched.

Those fictional girls who join the prestigious ranks of male adventurers often do so at the expense of other members of their sex. And small wonder, the tomboy-turned-token-female is simply the other side of the coin. The message is clear: if a girl wishes to join the boys in their pranks and hell-raising, or to use her imagination and personality in leading them, she renounces all claim to supposedly feminine characteristics—tears and fears and pink hair ribbons. The line between traditionally assigned sex roles is drawn sharp and clear. The girl who crosses that line is forced to desert her sex rather than allowed to act as a spokeswoman for a broader definition.

Take *Lulu's Back in Town* (Funk & Wagnall, 1968). The proof provided by author Laura Dean to show Lulu's final acceptance by the boys is the clubhouse sign: "FOR BOYS ONLY. No Girls Allowed. (Except Lulu.)" This is seen by the author, who unfortunately happens to be a woman, as a satisfactory ending. But our committee was not so pleased. (Except to find that neither ALA nor CSA had listed it.)

Cop-Outs

The cop-out book is often the most insidious. At its worst, it promises much and delivers nothing. But the better ones are the most infuriating, for often they are only a step away from being the exact kind of literature we'd like to see for girls *and* boys *about* girls. The actual cop-out may be only a crucial line, a paragraph, the last chapter. But somewhere a sexist compromise is made, somewhere the book adjusts to the stereotyped role of woman, often for the sake of social pressure and conformity. The compromise brings with it a change, and this change is not only disturbing, but often distorts the logical development of the character herself. Suddenly her development is redirected—or, rather, stunted.

The many cop-out books we found are probably a fair reflection of the social uncertainties and inner conflicts of writers, publishers, and reviewers in our sexist society.

Caddie Woodlawn by Carol R. Brink (Macmillan, 1935) is a Newbery winner. Not a recent one, but still extremely popular. Caddie is a young pioneer girl, allowed to run free with her brothers. She is happy and strong in her so-called tomboy role. Though her mother pressures her to become more of a "lady," the reader feels serenely certain that Caddie will remain her own person. Alas, as the book draws to a close, Caddie's father pleads: "It's a strange thing, but somehow we expect more of girls than of boys. It is the sisters and wives and mothers, you know, Caddie, who keep the world sweet and beautiful. . . ." Thus subdued, she joins the insipidly depicted girls at the weaving loom. True, the boys do ask her to teach them how to weave. Apparently they may choose to join women at their work, but no longer may Caddie choose to run free in the woods. And we are left feeling cheated. Why should it be the *right* choice for her obediently to join the "sweet and beautiful" women of the world on their pedestals? Why shouldn't she continue to struggle for a life in which she might fulfill some inner potential?

The linking of a girl's growing up to the abandoning of her "tomboy" ways is a depressingly frequent theme in these books. As a stage in growing up, tomboy behavior appears to be acceptable. But the girl must in the end conform to more socially approved behavior. In a widely used bibliography compiled by Clara Kirchner in 1966 entitled *Behavior Patterns in Children's Books* there is an entire section called "From Tomboy to Young Woman." Here are two random descriptions:

> *A Girl Can Dream* by Betty Cavanna (Westminster, 1948): Loretta Larkin, tops in athletics but poor in social graces and jealous of a classmate who shines socially, finds out that being "just a girl" can be fun.

Billie by Esphyr Slobodkina (Lothrop, 1959): Billie, who wore faded jeans and played boys' games because she didn't like being a girl, came to think differently after she took ballet lessons to limber up a sprained ankle.

These books fit into the following categories: Womanliness, Growing Up, and Popularity.

Young readers of such grievous cop-outs are forced to believe that the spunk, individuality, and physical capability so refreshingly portrayed in tomboy heroines must be surrendered when girls grow up—in order to fit the passive, supposedly more mature image of a young woman. But where is that earlier energy to be spent? Is depression in the adult woman perhaps linked to the painful suppression of so many sparks of life?

In a way we could call the cop-out book the "co-op" book, for it permits the tomboy reader to believe she can pass comfortably over into that other world at a safely future date. Real life is rarely like that.

A new book recommended on both the ALA and the CSA lists is Constance Green's *A Girl Called Al* (Viking, 1969). The main character comes across as a nonconformist who truly enjoys her individuality, and throughout most of the book she eschews traditional female worries—how she looks, hooking boyfriends, etc. Wonderful. But the ending is a neat little all-American package. Al gets thin, gets pretty, and now she will be popular. All these sudden switches hit the reader in the last few pages. Her pigtails make room for a feminine hairdo. Her closest friend explains: "Her mother took her to the place she gets her hair done and had the man wash and set Al's hair, and now she wears it long with a ribbon around it. It is very becoming, my mother says. She is right. But I miss Al's pigtails. I wanted her to wear it this way but now that she does I'm kind of sorry. She looks older and different, is all I know."

Again, we are led to believe that another character in our long line of individual heroines will conform to the role society has rigidly defined for her. We find it hard to buy the sudden change in Al. And we also miss the pigtails.

Sometimes it is the focus of a book that makes it a cop-out. When we read the 1959 Newbery winner, Elizabeth Speare's *The Witch of Blackbird Pond* (Houghton Mifflin, 1958), we praised Kit's independent spirit, her rejection of bigoted values, and her truly striking courage at a time when women were burned for witchcraft. From a feminist standpoint, the book is marred only by the plot's revolving around the standard question. "Whom shall Kit marry?" In too many books we find the male character worrying about *what* shall he be—while the female character worries about *who* shall he be.

Only a few hairs are out of place in *Next Door to Xanadu* by Doris Orgel (Harper, 1969), also listed by ALA and CSA. The main character faces the too-often very real hatred of preteen boys toward girls. She meets it with strength, earning respect. The only boy-crazy girl in the book is deemphasized. But one scene allows our society's pervasive sexism to come shining through.

At a going-away party for one of the girls, a woman parades as a fortune-teller. "She took out a bowl, put it on the table, filled it with all sorts of strange little things. Then she said 'Who among you dares to delve into the secrets the future holds in store?'" Here were the fortunes of the girls: The girl who pulled out two safety pins would be "the mother of a fine pair of twins." Chalk meant another would be a teacher. The one who picked a little sack of soil would be "a farmer's wife." One pulled a penny: she would be very rich. One picked a little plastic boy doll and she would meet a "fine young man." "Great happiness" was in store for the one who got a bluebird's feather. When one of the girls pulled out a jack, the fortune teller chanted: "Butcher, baker, candlestick-maker; tailor, sailor, teacher, preacher; doctor, lawyer, carpenter, smith— she would have kept it up, but Helen guessed it. Betsy would marry a jack-of-all-trades."

Not *be* a jack-of-all-trades, but *marry* one. Not *be* a farmer, but be a farmer's wife. The only vocation predicted was that of teacher. Unfortunately, fortune-tellers will be like that, until we have feminist fortune-tellers. That would certainly bring brighter futures.

At the risk of carping, we felt that such a fine book as *A Wrinkle in Time* by Madeline L'Engle (Farrar, 1962), the 1963 Newbery winner, had a hint of acceptance of woman's second-class status. This is almost the only science fiction book in which a girl is the main character. We even find a mother who is a scientist, perhaps one of the only scientist moms in juvenile fiction. But why did father have to be a super scientist, topping mom by a degree or two?

Positive Images

Happily, if not of course, there are some books for children which show female characters in flexible, diverse roles. They allow for character development beyond the stereotype, and do not disappoint us in the end.

At first we tried calling these "non-sexist." But we found many books were not precisely either sexist or cop-out, though somehow they did not quite fit our exacting feminist standards, usually because they did not deal with the questions they posed in a sufficiently clear, real, and affirmative way. The rare book that did succeed, even in this, is our positive-image book.

Certainly, these categories overlap a bit. *A Wrinkle in Time* really belongs among the positive-image books. We just couldn't resist putting down papa's degrees. Unfair, we admit, because of the especially fine, honest relationship between Calvin (the boy who is a friend, as opposed to Boy Friend) and the girl protagonist. They respect each other's heads, and his ego does not stand in the way of her saving the day with an act of courage that rescues her little brother. We also applauded the image of the mother as a brilliant scientist who instills pride in her children.

Another Newbery we salute is the 1961 winner, *Island of the Blue Dolphins* by Scott O'Dell (Houghton Mifflin, 1960), one of the rare books showing a girl with strong physical skills. She kills wild dogs, constructs weapons, kills a giant tentacled sea fish, and hauls a six-man canoe by herself. The Indian girl protagonist, Karana, spends 18 years alone on a bleak and lonely island. And there we are indeed tempted to ask why such a marvelous heroine can only be encountered alone on an island— and never in the midst of society?

While on the subject of positive images, there is a new book we hope will appear on the 1970 recommended lists. *Rufus Gideon Grant* by Leigh Dean (Scribners, 1970) is about a boy, but we were taken by the following reference to a woman: "There inside this magazine was this lady, climbing giant trees and playing with wild chimpanzees. . . ." And Rufus asks: "Can a boy be a zoologist?"

If we had time we would also like to discuss such essentially positive-image books as *Strawberry Girl* by Lois Lenski (Lippincott, 1945), *From the Mixed-Up Files of Mrs. Basil E. Frankweiler* by E. L. Konigsburg (Atheneum, 1967), Vera and Bill Cleaver's *Where the Lilies Bloom* (Lippincott, 1969), and *Pippi Longstocking* by Astrid Lindgren (reissued in paper by Viking, 1969). Padding our Positive-Image list a bit we might add commendable classics like Lewis Carroll's *Alice in Wonderland* (first published in 1865), *Anne of Green Gables* by Lucy M. Montgomery (Grosset & Dunlap, 1908), and *Rebecca of Sunnybrook Farm* by Kate Douglas Wiggin (Macmillan, 1903). Of course there are some positive books that escaped our notice, just as some of the negative ones may have slipped by, but we wanted to cover a fourth and extra category that seems to overlap all the others.

Especially for Girls

This category appears on a number of publishers' lists and on lists of recommended books. It's called "especially for girls." The reason advanced by librarians and publishers for having such a category at all is that while girls are perfectly happy to read "boys'" books, no self-respecting boy will read books about girls.

In our male-dominated society, unfortunately, this is probably true. But listing a separate group of books for girls provides boys with a list of books *not* to read, further polarizing the sexes.

There seems only one possible justification for a separate category of books for girls: to spot and recommend those books which, according to our highest, most stringent feminist standards are not sexist. Pursuing this logic, when children's literature no longer supports sexism, there will no longer be any reason to list books "especially for girls."

The current lists of girls' books promoted by publishers, show a preponderance of stories about love, dating, and romance. And there are the companion books about young girls with problems like shyness, overweight, glasses, acne, and so on, that are supposed to interfere with romance. Certainly, problems facing young girls should be dealt with in the books they read, but we resent the implication forced on young girls that romance is the only fulfilling future for them. Boys, too, are involved in romance, but their books are about other things.

The lists for girls also include career books about nurses, secretaries, ballet dancers, stewardesses. Why not more female doctors? Bosses? Pilots? Aquanauts? Present books simply reinforce the sex roles imposed by society—and even then virtually all the careers end in a cop-out. When the girl marries she gives up the career. But *must* marriage and career be mutually exclusive? These books are justified by their publishers in terms of the market—they are meant to sell rather than to edify. We happen to believe that career books that edify will also sell, and far more lastingly, as women gain in the struggle for their freedom.

But what about those lists of currently recommended books that *are* intended to edify? In 1969, for example, the Child Study Association listed eight books "Especially for Girls." Of all of these, we were disheartened to find that only one was free—or almost free—of sexism. Two more were cop-out books. The rest were middling to very bad.

Let's start with the best. *The Motoring Millers* by Alberta Wilson Constant (Crowell, 1969) not only shows delightful girls and women behaving responsibly and delightfully—and doing many things the men do—but the question of sex roles is specifically aired. In the story, the winner of an auto race turns out to be a young girl. When the wife of a college president says to her: "I want you to know that I am highly in favor of your driving in this race. Women should advance their cause in every field," the winner replies, "I didn't think about that. I just love to drive. Taught myself on our one-cylinder Trumbull when I was ten." We welcome both reactions.

Two more books on this list, *A Girl Called Al* and *Next Door to Xanadu,* have already been described above as cop-outs, though we did consider them both *almost* commendable. To those three acceptable books, we would also add *Julie's Decision* by Rose A. Levant (Washburn, 1969) except that we were disturbed by what seemed a paternalistic white attitude especially inappropriate in a book about a black girl.

But after these titles, the CSA girls' list deteriorates into sexism. It is shocking to find "recommended for girls" a book like *The Two Sisters* by Honor Arundel (Meredith, 1969), which not only reinforces the stereotype of girls as romantic, clothes-crazy, and spendthrift, but whose moral says that, when all is said and done, love is a woman's proper vocation and her future ought to be subordinated to her husband's. The young heroine in *The Two Sisters* has just told her father that she may abandon her university scholarship to follow her husband who has gone off to find a better job in another city. Her father says gently: "Geoff's quite right to be ambitious and you're right not to stand in his way. A man who doesn't get a chance to fulfill his ambition makes a terrible husband." It doesn't occur to either that a woman who sacrifices her potential can also end up making a terrible wife.

John Rowe Townsend's *Hell's Edge* (Lothrop, 1969) is just as bad. The motherless teenage heroine cooks all the meals and does the housework for her teacher-father, whose domestic ineptitude is paraded as one of his endearing qualities. A pair of sisters in the book are set up with mutually exclusive stereotyped female traits—and then shot down for them. One is described as a "half-wit" for being concerned with looks and clothes; the other sister, a bookworm, is denigrated for not caring about her looks or clothes. Damned if you do and damned if you don't.

In another CSA recommendation, the boys in the family are considered more important than the girls, even though the book is supposedly for girls. (Well, it happens in real life too!) The name of that prize is *One to Grow On* by Jean Little (Little, Brown, 1969).

In *A Crown for a Queen* by Ursula Moray Williams (Meredith, 1969), the plot revolves around—get ready—a *beauty* contest with the boys as judges! The most memorable (and most offensive) line occurs when the heroine, Jenny, finally gets the beauty crown. As we might predict, she "never felt happier in her life." This is scarcely the positive female image we'd be looking for, even if we could all be beauty queens.

As our consciousness of "woman's place" changes, our recommendations of books for girls must change. As must books themselves. Eventually, we will have no more need for any list recommended "Especially for Girls."

THE SKIRTS IN FICTION ABOUT BOYS:
A MAXI MESS

What do the books that are known to be popular with boys tell them about girls and women? To determine this, I read and re-read some prize-winning novels and some books by noted and prolific authors. These titles were published during the past 18 years and focus on modern Americans. Two things struck me: the sweeping, sometimes contradictory (and often condemnatory) nature of the authors' statements about the female sex that get dropped into dialogue or inserted as undeveloped asides; and the fact that the girl friends and mothers are almost always unrealized or unpleasant characters—one-dimensional, idealized, insipid, bitchy, or castrating—while sexually neutral characters, such as little sisters and old ladies, are most often well conceived and likable.

For example, consider two unusually insightful, well-written books by Nat Hentoff: *Jazz Country* and *I'm Really Dragged But Nothing Gets Me Down*. Despite their perceptive analyses of youthful malaise, both are markedly flawed by the treatment accorded girl friends. In *Jazz Country*, jazz freak Tom Curtis likes Jessica, a briefly visible blonde. Jessica is the girl about whom narrator Tom says: "She wasn't like most of the girls I knew. You asked her a question and she answered. Straight. No fencing or teasing." The quality of honesty that Tom considers unique to Jessica isn't really, of course, and it's a disservice to imply to boys that it is. In fact, there is nothing in Jessica's actions or responses that makes her a special, individual person in any way; she's merely a mouthpiece to relate information about other characters in the book and a sounding board for their ideas and problems.

In the more episodic *I'm Really Dragged But Nothing Gets Me*

Note: By Diane Gersoni-Stavn. Reprinted with permission from *School Library Journal,* January 1971, 17:5, 66–70. Copyright © 1971 by the Xerox Corporation.

Down, confused high school senior Jeremy Wolf has a crush on a girl, Tracy—another bland, inadequately fleshed out, rarely seen blonde. It's interesting that both of these books feature militant Black girls who are much more striking characters. And Jessica's mother, Veronica, a jazz aficionado and patron, 50 years old and ". . . hipper than the kids I knew who *thought* they were so hip," is also a more solid character. Boys will at least get a hint of what a workable marriage can involve from the description of Veronica's: Jessica's father " '. . . liked Mother so much that he was always trying to get with the music . . . even began reading *Down Beat* so he could make some intelligent conversation with them about jazz.' " But Veronica, and the Black girls Mary (*Jazz Country*) and Chris, play "character" roles in these books. The two most important girls in terms of a boy's development—the potential (in *Jazz Country*) and actual (in *I'm Really Dragged . . .*) romantic interests—are flimsy creations.

Boys read a lot of sports books, and William E. Butterworth is the author of many. His *Fast and Smart, Grand Prix Driver,* and *Stock-Car Racer* all concern young men in their late teens whose main interest is the racing circuit. In *Fast and Smart* and *Grand Prix Driver,* women are essentially unimportant to the plots. However, each hero digs a brash-but-honest-blonde; in *Fast and Smart,* she's a reporter, and in *Grand Prix Driver,* she's a pit bunny. These tinny girls pop up very occasionally but have absolutely no substance or interest as characters in and of themselves. In *Stock-Car Racer,* 20-year-old Dave interacts with an over-protective mom and an equally overprotective busybody of an aunt, as well as with an honest-blonde girl friend. (Dave's mother and aunt, as seems to be the wont of women in auto racing fiction, want him to stop racing because it's ". . . dangerous, unprofitable, and unfitting"; the male relatives are of course racing enthusiasts). Butterworth does raise a valid point regarding the male role: "[Dave] wondered then why a man had to be ashamed of being afraid, why it was necessary to conceal from everyone the fact that you had considered all the facts and were scared. But he was doing it, just as everybody else did it." But one wonders why the author doesn't extend some understanding of the follies of sexual stereotypes to matters concerning females, many of whom thrill to auto racing—*driving* as well as onlooking—and to cars in general. In his girl's book, *Susan and Her Classic Convertible,* Butterworth does allow his heroine to be a gung-ho car fancier. But he has her drop her high school mechanics class (which she had taken to recondition her 1947 Caddy) in response to pressure from her parents and school administrators, who don't consider it fitting for a girl to take such a course.

If Nat Hentoff's and even more so William Butterworth's leading ladies are paper thin, James L. Summers', in *The Iron Door Between* and *You Can't Make It by Bus,* are made of the stuff of angels. Both of these books concern moody, rebellious, tough boys—one a J.D., the other a chicano—who are emotionally propped by strictly supportive, positively and wholly idealized, sweet young things. Summers at least attributes intelligence to his girls but also states generally that "The girls . . . by their very nature were good students, gentle, feminine . . . fairly quiet. . . ." In short, they're doomed to being unreal in his books, and if boy readers take them as examples of what girls should or will be, they'll be greatly disillusioned with the human specimens they'll meet.

Can a boy in a boy's book like a substantial girl character who isn't nicey-nice? Yes, but usually only if she's brittle and superficial. In Annabel and Edgar Johnson's *Count Me Gone,* mixed-up teen Rion tells his story and that of his brother Doug and Doug's "bohemian" fiancée, Shirli. Doug wants to convince Shirli: "'That it wouldn't be impossible for her to settle down and want some security and lead a warm, interesting kind of life like Mother does. She'd find it very fulfilling, once she got used to it. . . . She doesn't seem to realize that her romantic side has to come down to earth . . . if I'm being conservative, it's to assure her future, *her* security.'" This is the flip side to a controversial security coin that I'll be referring to again. Here, it's significant to note just what the Johnsons do with Shirli. A potentially interesting, independent girl is depicted as a neurotic, disloyal chick out for kicks—a basically unpleasant character. Shirli is contrasted with the young wife of one of Doug's friends—an uptight sorority type. So, boys have to take a pick of two caricatures, different but equally unflattering.

Paul Zindel, in *I Never Loved Your Mind,* makes another rebellious girl bite the dust. Ingenuous, 17-year-old Dewey pants after shallow Yvette—vegetarian, petty thief, free-living, -loving hippie type. And that's the problem with her—she's a type that the author tries to pawn off as a believable character who happens to be phony and callous. When Yvette dumps Dewey and goes off into the noonday sun one isn't surprised— merely relieved that the exiting of this walking cliché signals the end to a disappointing book.

Well, and what about good old Mom? To Oliver Butterworth, she's an insipid lady who flutters around chronically worrying and inanely commenting. For example, in the fantastical *The Trouble with Jenny's Ear,* Mrs. Pearson (mother of two sons who are electronics nuts and of a sweet daughter, Jenny, who briefly enjoys the ability to hear other people's unspoken thoughts) says to her bachelor brother: "'All you have to do is give them earrings for presents instead of the insides of alarm clocks.'"; "'When you were a kid you used to go around trailing wires and buzzers and things, and all the boys would follow you around, but you never could understand why girls weren't interested in your door-bells and clock springs.'" Mom can never get it straight in her befuddled little mind that the word is "microphone," not "megaphone," and she is completely unnerved by electrical setups.

Even more insipid than Mrs. Pearson is Mrs. Twitchell in *The Enormous Egg*, a fantasy about the hatching of a Triceratops in a rural New Hampshire town. The protagonist, Nate, and his dad both possess some intelligence and curiosity. But Mom, upon the birth of the Tricera-tops, for example, says: "'Goodness gracious! And right here in our back yard. It doesn't seem hardly right. And on a Sunday, too.'" When her hus-band makes a humorous observation regarding a dead relative, Mom pipes up with: "'Walter! He just got a bit crotchety along toward the end. I don't think we should say anything disrespectful of him.'" When a group of visiting, arguing scientists delays dinner because of lengthy dis-cussions, Mom says to Nate: "'Oh, you and your scientific world. I should think the scientific world would know when it was time to go home for supper, instead of hanging around to all hours and making people late for their meals.'" Narrator Nate reflects that "I don't think Mom ever *could* see what was so important about dinosaurs," and readers who take Butter-worth's Moms seriously will never see what's so important about mothers. (It's interesting to note that the author also socks it to the equally stereo-typed scientists he's created: thinks Nate when the scientists are debating over Triceratops' manner of eating—"As far as I could see, Uncle Beazley was just *eating*, but they couldn't let it go at that. Scientists really sound pretty funny when you listen to them talk that way." Scientists *can't* let things go at that, and snickering at their probing, tenacious curiosity is part and parcel of a certain locker room mentality that gibes at women.)

Can a boy in a boy's book have a mother who isn't vapid? Yes, but usually only if she's cruelly domineering or lax in her maternal obliga-tions. In Barbara Wersba's *The Dream Watcher*, for example, there are two important women. One is a poor, alcoholic spinster on welfare whose poetic allusions and fantasized stories of her glorious past on the stage inspire the terribly normal, average Albert Scully to appreciate his own capabilities and potential: ". . . [Mrs. Woodfin] had made *me* feel differ-ent . . . I had seen myself as a person for the first time in my life." But, what about young Albert's mom, the really significant woman in his life? She is a castrator who constantly puts down her unsuccessful hard-drink-ing insurance man of a husband: "'If he [Albert] had a father he could respect, he wouldn't have turned out this way.'" While Wersba treats Mr. Scully sympathetically (he had always wanted to be a pilot but his wife steered him toward business), she has little patience with the wife's own frustrations. *Why* does Mrs. Scully daydream about being a celebrity? If she's emasculated her husband, as it's implied, what in her own background limited *her* ability to relate to people and led her to cope by restructuring her reality? These questions never even come to the fore in this book; boys see only the father as immediate victim, the son as probable, long-range victim, and the mother as vulture.

In Emily Neville's *It's Like This, Cat*, 14-year-old Dave likes Mary, whose intense mother Nina (Mary calls her that) looks like a beatnik (so Dave says) and allows her daughter complete freedom. Herself the child of an artist/father and writer/mother, Nina grew up on Paris' Left Bank. Having given Nina this background, Mrs. Neville could have endowed her with the complex personality, lively intellect, and genuine individualism of a truly memorable character. Instead, she has made her a caricature —a soulful, poetic beatnik who forgets to eat because she's thinking and reading all the time, who scorns science (and thinks Mary is wasting her time when she goes to an aquarium!), and who likes to think of her daughter as ". . . walking alone with the wind in [her] hair, thinking poetic thoughts." Though not insipid, Nina's a cliché of another sort, and just as much of a copout as the Mmes. Pearson, Twitchell, and Scully. Dave's own mother is of the more standard worrywart variety—a nervous, quiet woman who goes into paroxysms of asthmatic wheezing whenever voices are raised around her. Not surprisingly, she's much less colorful than the old woman in the book—weird Kate the cat rescuer, who eats primarily cottage cheese, instinctively knows the right things to say to a kid, and winds up inheriting a million dollars from her detested brother.

There is a mother of another sort in William Corbin's *Smoke*, a popular story about a boy, almost 15, who befriends a wild German shepherd and eventually brings himself to accept his much-resented stepfather. The two females in the book are Chris's little sister Susie and his mother. Susie is a spunky, quick-witted kid, respected and adored by her brother. Ranch wife Mom, though laden down with some artificial dialogue, is refreshingly humorous and gutsy. However, her basic intelligence is somewhat compromised by her stand in a major conflict with Cal, her second husband. Chris runs away to the mountains with the dog Smoke after grievously insulting his mother and Cal. Mom wants to have the authorities locate him; Cal, maintaining that Chris is almost a man, wants to let him come home by himself at a time of his own choosing. Mom says:

> "This *man* business. As if getting to be a man was like joining a *club* or something . . . they've been at it for about a hundred thousand years! At first they'd give a boy a stone ax and say, 'Go bash somebody's brains out and then you'll be a *man*.' Later on they

> did it with swords and called it chivalry. And now, when they have
> to . . . go through the motions of being civilized, they think up a
> lot of *subtle* ways to torture boys, or get them to torture themselves,
> in order to qualify for the club . . . All right, I'll put my faith in
> you . . . But it's *blind* faith. You've been talking man-talk, and I
> don't understand the language."

Mom's historical assessment certainly has some merit, and her inability
to understand he-"man-talk" is to her credit. But the particular situation,
centering on Chris's need to work out his feelings toward his stepfather in
solitude, is explicable in human terms, not "man" terms; Cal is right to
want to allow Chris to return in his own way in his own good time. It's
unfortunate that Mom's thought-provoking observations may seem of
dubious value to readers because her specific application of them is ill
considered.

If the merits of presumed "man-talk" are challenged in *Smoke*, they
are exalted in William Gault's *Quarterback Gamble* and *The Oval Playground*. In *Quarterback Gamble*, there is the observation: "She had her
own female, illusory world and that made her difficult to convert." The
"she" is a young lady who must decide *between* being a quarterback's
wife and having a career in teaching. In *The Oval Playground*, the major
woman is Mom, a librarian, so we're told, and a lady fully cognizant of
her place in the order of things. Says she to her auto-racing son Mark:
" 'You're a man and this is a man's world so I can't even hope to understand it.' " When widowed Mom doesn't want to marry 42-year-old Al because he races, Mark says and thinks, in contrast to Doug's security comments in *Count Me Gone:* " 'Al's what he is. He's not something you can
convert to your specifications . . . The half-men . . . they're all alike
. . . The men who play it safe. The men who think there's nothing in the
world as important as money.' . . . How can you explain to a woman
about being too careful? It's the way they like to live. It's a *thing* with
them, security is; they never seem to feel the need to test themselves.
And they can take over a man and get him to thinking the same way."
(A hint of witchcraft trials—the woman as demonic possessor! Mr. Gault
should realize that such generalizations feed the anger of many women
today. In fact, one way for a woman to test and assert herself is to read
and denounce books like *The Oval Playground*.) Later on, Mom again
alludes resignedly to " 'A world I don't understand. A man's world.' "
Fittingly enough, she therefore spends all her time vocalizing her fears
about racing and packing elaborate lunches for the track-bound men.
What has Mr. Gault really done here? He's constructed a weak, clichéd
woman character and then made her look ridiculous to readers by con-

trasting her with male characters who exhibit superior, supposedly masculine qualities and abilities.

More explicitly than Gault, Joseph Krumgold uses his state-of-the-sexes observations to "explain" the sad state of modern society. His . . . *And Now Miguel,* a capably written book, concerns a farm-dwelling family and particularly the next to the youngest son. Miguel's mother and sisters seem to exist only because the author assumed the men of the family would have to come into contact with women sometimes. They're alluded to primarily in terms of their familial roles: e.g., Miguel wonders "'. . . what there could be for supper.'" His father: "'That's for Mama and the girls to figure out. Their worry. What we got to worry about is the flock.'" Given the farm setting, such role delineation is realistic enough. Krumgold begins to slide with *Onion John,* a dull book that touts the glories of rugged individualism by focusing on the antics of a superstitious old man who is befriended by 12-year-old Andy. Andy's housewife mother is an innocuous, really irrelevant character, visible a little more often than Miguel's mother but just barely. In both of these books, there is some father-son conflict. The fathers—a sheepherder and a Rotarian hardware store owner, respectively—are both strong, basically admirable characters, however, and the differences are satisfactorily resolved.

The author has gone from farm to town, where the men work in the immediate vicinity of their homes. In *Henry 3,* a book set in wealthy suburbia, Krumgold through his characters laments the fact of commuting fathers and tortuously and speciously indicts the presumably eviscerating "matriarchal" suburban values. Henry Lovering is a kid with an embarrassingly high I. Q. His dad during the day is a fawning corporate climber; his mom *likes* life in suburban Crestview. When the Loverings are ostracized because of the bomb shelter they have installed in their home (Mr. Lovering's in the shelter biz), it seems likely that the family will have to leave Crestview. Henry's upset about this, but the old sage of the book, his friend Fletcher's ruggedly individualistic grandfather, tells him to shed no tears; that Crestview's no place for a boy to grow to manhood in because it's

> ". . . a woman's world around here. Crestview is her idea . . .
> these women have to be safe. They have their children to protect.
> Their first big idea is to get enough security to bring up a family.
> And the second, they have to be in fashion. Because in a place
> like this a woman can't grow old . . . the ideas it (Crestview)
> lives by. They're about thirty-five hundred years old. That's how
> far back you'd have to go to find a world anything like Crestview,
> a matriarchy. . . . A society that's ruled by women. And there you
> have it, why Crestview's wrong. . . . Fashion's fine and so is

security, but they're not enough to control a lot of machinery. If we can't find anything better to live by than those two things, we might as well give this particular planet back to the ants."

Now, even so general a source as the *Encyclopaedia Britannica* states: "No peoples on earth are known to be organized matriarchically, nor are there reliable historical records of such societies. If there ever were matriarchates in the very earliest times, there is no trustworthy evidence for their existence . . . the society as a whole has never been found in which women in general have authority over men in general." Given that any intelligent discussion of matriarchy must involve uncertainty, it is revealing that Mr. Krumgold has a sympathetic character impart a rigid theory—the basis of which is emphatically in disfavor—in ringing, pontifical tones to young readers. Even if one were to accept his patently absurd generalizations regarding all women in suburbia, it's difficult to follow Krumgold's logic. Is Crestview the woman's idea? Isn't it just as valid to postulate that suburbia is the status symbol of the rising young executive? *If* women can't grow old in Crestview, is that a situation of their own choosing? Do they enjoy the fashion treadmill? Or must they maintain their youthful, fashionable looks in order to be acceptable assets to their husbands?

Rivaling Mr. Krumgold in misleading use of words and minimal objectivity is Frank Bonham. In Bonham's 1956 title, *The Loud, Resounding Sea,* the most admirable female character is Delphine the Dolphin, with whom the young hero, Skip Turner, enjoys a marvelous rapport based on mutual trust, affection, and respect. Skip's attitude toward pretty, blonde Leslie, with whom he works in a lab during the summer, is a lot less flattering: "Like most girls, she was about as practical as a chicken-wire fishbowl." Bonham does a fair enough job with Skip's mother; she's a hard-working schoolteacher, and the mainstay of her family because her husband, a skilled cook and restaurateur, has advanced wanderlust and is rarely at home. Mr. Turner himself is a basically amiable character, yet Skip does express resentment at the burden he puts on Mrs. Turner. In the end, it's stated that the itinerant chef will undertake a steady business right near home. He tells Skip: " 'I need a woman to tell my plans and troubles to. What man doesn't? An understanding wife to help him into his cardboard armor in the morning, and put him back together at night.' " Very true. How about a woman's right to the same kind of support? Bonham doesn't negate it here, but silence is *not* always affirmative.

In the didactic *The Vagabundos,* his sympathy for roving dads becomes an adulatory obsession, and mom becomes a drag, on both husband and son. Eric Hansen pursues his father to Baja when the retired, wealthy, middle-aged—and bored—Southern Californian, who is believed to have a heart condition, leaves his family behind and sets out to do his thing—whatever that may be. Says a "wise" character in the book, waitress Mabel: " 'Why don't you leave the poor guy alone? Those airline ads showing the wife whining, 'Take me along to the convention'—they turn my stomach. Hasn't everybody got a right to be alone once in a while?' " (Come now, Mabel. At a convention?). Later, shades of Krumgold: "Eric . . . suddenly perceived that the whole Ranch Sereno game—parties, clubs, feuds, hobbies—was a sort of complex machine designed and manufactured by women—but very inexpertly—so that it took all the time of every man on the Ranch to keep it from flying apart . . . He fantasied the reunion with his father on the beach . . . No drying stockings, hair curlers, and other woman-stuff for a while. Just camping, skin-diving, living in the sun." It is never acknowledged that a major part of the Ranch Sereno game was invented by men; that since success in business leads to power, men seeking such power will organize parties, clubs, etc. to make business contacts. As for the beach-side activities, women have been known to indulge happily in camping and such.

Dr. Nestor, another "wise" character whom Eric encounters while tracking down Dad, says: " 'Just because a man's always been a house-cat type doesn't mean there isn't a little wildcat blood left in him. And if that kind of blood is kept bottled up forever, it curdles in the brain. . . . Do you want to know what's the matter? Women in the States, especially in areas like yours, have forgotten how to be women; but they haven't yet learned how to be men. They've turned into harpies, and their men into zombies. God, it's pitiful!' " It's pitiful indeed that all women be held responsible for the lack of integrity and purpose in some men. Eric himself really doesn't need much encouragement in male chauvinist ideas: "He knew that in Mexico a husband was a king; his behavior was not to be questioned by his family. In the abstract, the idea had appeal."

For a short time, Eric takes Dr. Nestor's daughter Polly, a big, beautiful blonde, along on his quest. Her father comments about her: " 'Remember—she's a female, and full of tricks.' " Thinks Eric: "Men [e.g., William Gault] liked to talk about women as though they had some sort of special malignant power, a witchlike ability to control men. But Polly was honest and open, a real sweet kid. Joanie [a girl friend of sorts back home] had some of the witch in her, and would do mean things just to make you burn." However, though Polly is supposedly an unusually fine specimen of female, she later pulls all kinds of teasing tricks and says " 'I'm a witch . . . I *was* being nasty . . . Girls just do those things, I guess. We're really not aware of doing them . . .' " Using girls to damn girls to boys is a remarkably low trick, and Mr. Bonham is at subterranean level here. He has Eric agree with Polly: " 'Even old girls like my mother. If she hadn't torpedoed my father's idea to buy a garage, he might not have taken off.' "

Later, a "wise" Mexican contributes his version of what the score is: " 'The women should run some things. But not all . . . American women . . . They wear pants and shout like boys. Are they men or women? They don't seem to know, and the men don't know enough to tell them to shut up.' " Eric: " 'That's it right there. [Polly] . . . began to think she should run the show. That's where I had to straighten her out. And after I got her straightened out she seemed happier.' "

Given all this, it is not unreasonable to wonder at Mr. Bonham's problems with American women. But it is certainly most reasonable to doubt the fairness of propagandizing young boys in this way. The jacket copy says about this book: ". . . it has some wise things to say about the role of men and women in each other's lives . . ." I think it has some revealing things to say about the antediluvian concepts and personal conflicts reeling around in Mr. Bonham's head, as well as about the total cynicism of flap copy writers.

Are there books boys can come away from with pretty good feelings about girls and women? A few. Though its mother characters are minimal, *It's Like This, Cat* offers a refreshing romantic interest in Mary, Nina's daughter. Mary is independent (pays her own way on the ferry and at lunch), gracious (accepts a treat pleasantly), and occupationally motivated (she likes snakes, is fascinated by science, and admires the work of a *woman* vet at the zoo). Similarly, in the author's *Berries Goodman,* a couple of good characterizations help to counter an occasional stereotype (e.g., a run-of-the-bagel Jewish mother). The protagonist, Berries, is a likable boy. His playmate, Sandra, the girl next door, is a great athlete; sometimes obnoxious (but readers see how *both* of her bigoted parents have conditioned many of her less admirable responses); sometimes goodhearted—in short, human. And, Berries' own mother, bored with domesticity in the suburbs, gets a job selling real estate and does very well at it.

Though Vera and Bill Cleaver for some reason feel compelled to announce in *Grover* that Ellen Grae isn't "like most girls," they do make her an exciting and vibrant one. Ellen Grae is imaginative, intelligent, loyal and exuberant; her friendship with the similarly endowed Grover is one of equals. As Grover tells her one day when they're fooling around: " 'Ellen Grae, you aren't ever going to be anybody's servant and you know it.' "

Like *Grover,* Keith Robertson's *Henry Reed's Big Show* spotlights a friendship of two ingenious, nimble-witted kids: Henry and Midge Glass. It does its share of generalizing along sexual lines: "Midge hasn't been too enthusiastic about putting on a show but then I suppose that's because she's the practical type. It's really men who are the artists in the world—the great painters and writers, directors, and even chefs." But at least the actual characterization of Midge is a good one. She comes up with as many clever ideas as Henry, and she's just as good at executing them. Midge's spirit is excellently exemplified in an episode in which a tophatted Henry drives up in horse-drawn buggy to surprise her: "I should have known nothing would bother Midge. She looked at the buggy and at me and started grinning. 'Wow!' she said. 'Terrific, Henry! That's cool! Can I drive?'"

An equally spunky, much older lady steals a lot of the limelight in Bob Wells's *Five-Yard Fuller.* This book can't be taken seriously: it's completely broad, comic strip, cornpone humor. It's also very popular with kids, so it's fortunate that the incredible fullback's incredible mother has many admirable qualities. Author Wells does have the old girl scold about wet feet, deaths from neglected colds, the virtues of mustard baths, etc. And he hopefully includes a few woman generalizations for doubtful laughs (e.g., about a football coach—"Being married, he knew that the one sure way of losing an argument with a woman was to lose his temper."). But Ma, certainly unlike most fictional mothers, is a goodhearted, highly successful strategist in a "man's" game—and, readers are told on the last page—one hell of a quarterback.

It's good that boys have access to books like the above. But it's unfortunate that the Cleavers and Robertson, for example, by extolling the uniqueness of their girls (numerous authors herald an admirable female character as a welcome freak), imply that such O.K. females are rare. And, it's nice that Ma Fuller does more than kvetch—but why aren't there more equally knowledgeable, sympathetic moms—and girls—in *serious* fiction about boys?

For many of the 51 years of American children's book publishing, authors didn't hesitate to parade minor Black characters of the cotton-pickin'-watermelon-lickin' variety. Nor was there much reticence about showcasing negative stereotypes of Jews, priests, or various nationalities. But since books reflect the general social and human values of their societies, such titles would now be pounced on and rejected by reviewers. There is little doubt today that the "fair" sex has received less than a fair deal in many areas of personal life and work. Hopefully, from January 1971 onward, the women who crowd the children's book field will not continue to buy, promote, and circulate fiction that isn't keeping pace with societal consciousness, that either clearly or subtly sabotages the idea of women as human beings—and even as reasonable people.

Bibliography

BONHAM, FRANK. *The Loud Resounding Sea.* 209 pp. Crowell, 1963.

BONHAM, FRANK. *The Vagabundos.* 222 pp. Dutton, 1969.

BUTTERWORTH, OLIVER. *The Enormous Egg.* illus. by Louis Darling. 188 pp. Atlantic: Little, 1956.

BUTTERWORTH, OLIVER. *The Trouble With Jenny's Ear.* 275 pp. Atlantic: Little, 1960.

BUTTERWORTH, W. E. *Fast and Smart.* 138 pp. Norton: Grosset, 1970.

BUTTERWORTH, W. E. *Grand Prix Driver.* 123 pp. Norton: Grosset, 1969.

BUTTERWORTH, W. E. *Stock-Car Racer.* 208 pp. Norton: Grosset, 1966.

BUTTERWORTH, W. E. *Susan and Her Classic Convertible.* 190 pp. Four Winds Pr.: Scholastic, 1970.

CLEAVER, VERA and BILL CLEAVER. *Grover.* illus. by Frederic Marvin. 125 pp. Lippincott, 1970.

CORBIN, WILLIAM. *Smoke.* 253 pp. Coward, 1967.

GAULT, WILLIAM. *The Oval Playground.* 157 pp. Dutton, 1968.

GAULT, WILLIAM. *Quarterback Gamble.* 137 pp. Dutton, 1970.

HENTOFF, NAT. *I'm Really Dragged But Nothing Gets Me Down.* 127 pp. S. & S., 1968.

HENTOFF, NAT. *Jazz Country.* 146 pp. Harper, 1965.

JOHNSON, ANNABEL and EDGAR JOHNSON. *Count Me Gone.* 188 pp. S. & S., 1968.

KRUMGOLD, JOSEPH. *. . . And Now Miguel.* illus. by Jean Charlot. 245 pp. Crowell, 1953.

KRUMGOLD, JOSEPH. *Henry 3.* illus. by Alvin Smith. 268 pp. Atheneum, 1967.

KRUMGOLD, JOSEPH. *Onion John.* illus. by Symeon Shimin. 248 pp. Crowell, 1959.

NEVILLE, EMILY CHENEY. *Berries Goodman.* 178 pp. Harper, 1965.

NEVILLE, EMILY. *It's Like This, Cat.* illus. by Emil Weiss. 180 pp. Harper, 1963.

ROBERTSON, KEITH. *Henry Reed's Big Show.* illus. by Robert McCloskey. 207 pp. Viking, 1970.

SUMMERS, JAMES L. *The Iron Doors Between.* 206 pp. Westminster, 1968.

SUMMERS, JAMES L. *You Can't Make It By Bus.* 174 pp. Westminster, 1969.

WELLS, BOB. *Five-Yard Fuller.* illus. by Harold Eldridge. 192 pp. Putnam, 1964.

WERSBA, BARBARA. *The Dream Watcher.* 171 pp. Atheneum, 1968.

ZINDEL, PAUL. *I Never Loved Your Mind.* 181 pp. Harper, 1970.

FEMINISTS LOOK AT THE 100 BOOKS:
THE PORTRAYAL OF WOMEN IN CHILDREN'S BOOKS ON PUERTO RICAN THEMES

Sexism might be defined as those attitudes and actions that relegate women to a secondary and inferior status in this society and prevent them from developing into full human beings. Women are expected to find primary fulfillment in marriage and motherhood where they function as servants for other people rather than as people in their own right. A concept of women's mental and physical inferiority is the philosophical underpinning for male supremacy. Among other things, it excludes women from a wide range of occupational pursuits, and makes their value as human beings synonymous with their physical appearance and sex appeal.

Of the 100 books for and about Puerto Rican children analyzed in the Council study, boys are the main characters in 32 books of fantasy and fiction, while only 18 books in this category portray girls as the central characters. This imbalance is an indication of the sexism that pervades the book publishing world. Publishers claim that books about girls are less profitable to produce because boys will not read them (while girls do read about boys). Boys as a rule stay away from books about girls because the authors create girl characters who are dull, uninteresting, and unadventuresome. Authors claim that they are only portraying the reality of femaleness but, as our study will show, this claim is untrue.

While oppressive conditions have undeniably maimed many girls and women, making them passive and adventureless, the books we are talking about are fictional, and in such books authors have the opportunity—and the obligation—to counteract centuries of literary abuse of the

Note: Compiled by Dolores Prida and Susan Ribner in collaboration with Edith Dávila, Irma Garcia, Carmen Puigdollers, and Arlene Rivera. Reprinted by permission of the Council on Interracial Books for Children, Inc. (1841 Broadway, New York, N.Y. 10023) from *Interracial Books for Children,* Spring 1972.

female sex by creating girls in all kinds of exciting roles and by breaking them out of their traditional confines.

The unfortunate finding of our study is that with only a few minor exceptions, the books repeat and reinforce the traditional female stereotypes. Very few of the Puerto Rican girls have any character at all, and their activities are dull. Mothers and other adult women are portrayed as similarly uninteresting. In fact, the non-Puerto Rican authors in depicting their misconceptions of Puerto Rican life—not one of the fiction books about girls was authored by a Puerto Rican—have circumscribed the female role all out of proportion to reality. Not only is the female role in the books more constricted than a comparable Anglo-American girl's would be, but it is even more limited than the Puerto Rican female role is in actual fact. A Puerto Rican girl faced only with the prospects presented in these books might reasonably choose not to grow up at all.

Early Childhood Readers

The training necessary to mold the special female being starts at birth when girls are handled as if they are more passive and fragile than boys. By four and five years of age, their training for housewifery and motherhood has begun, as girls are taught at home how to help mother cook, clean, and take care of baby. At school, during the first couple of grades, both girls and boys are taught how to read and write, but in other ways teachers and books start gearing girls toward the gentle "womanly arts" of doll and house playing, painting, sewing, etc., while the boys are encouraged to avoid these in favor of more active, adventuresome, and challenging pursuits.

There are eight books about Puerto Rican girls in the four-to-seven-year-old category. They present no challenge in either text or illustration to the traditional rearing of young girls.

The eight nice, obedient Puerto Rican girls in these books help their mothers at home and do "female" activities at school. (Being Puerto Rican, they also learn English as a school activity.)

In six of the eight books, girls are pictured playing with dolls, and in three stories, dolls play a major role in the plot. While there is nothing objectionable about girls (or boys) playing with dolls, when it is done to the exclusion of all else, that is harmful. The dolls shown are blond and fair-skinned, while their owners are usually brunette and dark-skinned.

At this young age, girls are often physically active—not yet concerned with the image of fragility that they will later be expected to project. In these eight books, however, the heroines are pictured in dresses, playing girls' games like hopscotch or jumprope. Not one girl, for example, is pictured in an active role in any way similar to the hero of *A Week in Henry's World*—constantly jumping off things, playing baseball, standing on his hands, and racing down streets.

A comparison with four-to-seven-year-old fictional boy characters in the "100 books" reveals in additional ways just how restricted the eight girls are. Not one girl takes a trip out of the neighborhood as does Barto in *Barto Takes the Subway*. Not one girl does anything as heroic as Miguel who "saves a mountain" for the neighborhood children in *Miguel's Mountain*. The authors have consciously restricted the lives of these Puerto Rican girls, even more than is true in real life.

Intermediate Age Books

There are six books with heroines in the eight to twelve age range. Here are some of the stereotypical situations found in them:

The girls give up dolls and begin to rely on girl friends and pets instead.

School takes on increasing significance in their lives, and for a brief period they might excel in certain aspects of reading and writing (or in learning to speak English). It is permissible for girls to be smart at this age, as long as they begin to act as if they were less intelligent by the time they start dating boys.

Fun activities portrayed are playing with girl friends, gardening, sewing, play-acting, and joining the girl scouts.

The girls are homebodies. Rarely do they venture outside the home alone. Even in the company of others they do not go great distances away from home. They are kept busy helping their mothers clean and cook. They always follow the orders of their fathers.

They are generally sweet, responsible, docile, nice.

Several additional stereotypes appear in the six books and seem to be tied directly to the authors' concept of female Puerto Ricanness.

The authors have given four of the six girls older brothers who take care of them, make decisions for them, and order them around. The girls thereby become even more constricted in what they can do.

These older boys are often called *hombrecito*—"little man"—by their families. They take over as head of the family in the father's absence. They order the mother around. No such importance is *ever* given the girls in the same way, and no author ever challenges this concept.

Fathers in these books are depicted as supreme commanders of their particular nuclear families. They are waited on and catered to. Their authoritarianism and leadership position are never challenged by the authors.

While some feminists have recently complained that children's literature often brands the girl who likes physical activity as a "tomboy" (implying that she is acting like a boy instead of like a normal female), these books about Puerto Rican girls don't have even one "tomboy" in them. The authors have apparently decided that Puerto Rican girls uniformly don't go in for sports and other strenuous physical activities. All six of the heroines wear dresses at all times. (In reality, Puerto Rican girls do not wear dresses 100 percent of the time.)

Possibly because the girls are Puerto Rican, the authors feel compelled to have them be the smartest kids. Candita becomes the best new English speaker in her class (*Candita's Choice*). Rosita enters 6-1 (the top) class after she learns English (*A Present from Rosita*). Magdalena reaches an IGC (Intellectually Gifted Children) class (*Magdalena*). The racist implication is that when you're Puerto Rican you must be above average to prove yourself.

What are boys' activities at this age in the Puerto Rican fiction books? They learn how to deep-sea dive (*I Am from Puerto Rico*); they camp out alone at Bear Mountain (*The Silver Cart*); and they go by themselves to Coney Island (*Antonio's World*). They secretly get jobs (*José's Christmas Secret*). They hide sisters in abandoned buildings and scavenge food for them (*Tomás Takes Charge*). They play basketball (*City High Five*), baseball (*Baseball Flyhawk*), chess (*A Guy Can Be Wrong*), and run clubhouses (*The Clubhouse*). Girls of this age are just not allowed any such exciting activity. Is it any wonder that boys don't want to read books about girls?

Teenagers—Early and Late

There are two books about younger and two about older Puerto Rican teenagers. In the two early teenage books, the heroines become interested in boys and are strongly influenced by them. They make decisions according to what their boyfriends think, and they take orders from them. As would be expected, appearance becomes more important.

The authors have done their own racist thing on the early teenage girls. At a time when girls of most backgrounds begin to exert a certain independence from home, the only action the authors see Puerto Rican girls engaged in is joining predatory gangs. To limit the alternatives for independent action as a female to "deviant" behavior is a good example of the close affinity of sexism and racism.

The girls in the two late teenage books finally get down to where it's at—marriage and "career." In the latter case, since the authors have made the girls "poor Puerto Ricans," they are involved in supporting their families, yet they are relegated exclusively to very low positions in the job market, as waitresses and babysitters. "Careers" above this level are never seriously considered.

Of course, the books end with the girls planning marriage. While the author of *Don't Look at Me That Way* happily doesn't see marriage as her heroine's only purpose for being, it is nonetheless her destiny. No alternative is presented.

Males in the Puerto Rican fiction books for boys fare not much better than the girls. The boys are not concerned with romance in these books (*The World of Carlos* and *Moncho and the Dukes*), but being subject to racist attitudes of the authors, the boys all turn out to be juvenile delinquents. And at the same time, subject to the authors' sexist attitudes, the boys are more proficient than the girls in crime, and as gang leaders they tell the wayward girls what to do.

How Mothers Are Portrayed

Of the 18 books, nine depict mothers exclusively as housewives; six are housewives who also work at low-skilled jobs in factories, hospitals, or as cleaning ladies, and all cook, clean, and mother after work. In two books no mother is depicted, and in one we don't know what the mother does.

What this says to a Puerto Rican girl is that if she decides to become a mother, the odds are close to 100 percent that she will be a housewife or a combined housewife and low-income, low-skilled worker. Not a single alternative is presented. No group of people is so limited in role.

In addition, mothers are usually portrayed as characterless and vague, especially in stories where the father is present. (Magdalena's grandmother proves the one exception to this stereotype.) Mothers are also presented as weak. They are the ones who cling most to tradition (a weakness from the authors' point of view), who miss Puerto Rico the most (another weakness from the authors' point of view), and who have the most trouble adjusting to the United States (still another weakness from the authors' point of view).

These stereotypes are contrary to reality in which Puerto Rican mothers are so frequently strong figures in the home.

Other Adult Women

Are there no interesting, skilled, creative, dashing Puerto Rican women for young girls to dream about and emulate? Not in these books.

Take a look, for example, at the jobs assigned to the women who are not mothers. There is not a single woman in all the 18 books who is clearly defined as a Puerto Rican and who holds a position outside the home other than a low-skilled uninteresting job. A few possible Puerto Rican professionals appear in minor roles: Spanish-speaking Carolla Santos owns a dress store in *Rosaria;* a Spanish-speaking teachers' aide helps out in *I Am Here;* and the classroom teacher in *A Surprise for Carlotta* is named Mrs. Lopez, although there is no indication that she is anything other than Pure Americana. These are the only possible Puerto Rican professional or semiprofessional women mentioned in the books. All Puerto Rican women neighbors and friends in these fiction books have jobs similar to the mothers.

Is this the reality for Puerto Rican women—the reality the authors and editors feel so compelled to write about? Hardly. The authors' middle-class values keep them from discussing the true realities of ghetto life—the reality of drugs, the reality of prostitution, and all the other realities poor women are oppressed by every day. The authors' politics won't allow them to show the reality of the increasing number of Puerto Rican activist and revolutionary women. The authors' racism won't allow them to show Puerto Rican women as skilled professional lawyers, teachers, and doctors, few though these may be. And their racism and sexism and lack of imagination keep them from showing women in fantasy situations, as astronauts, Puerto Rican fairy-godmothers, or whatever.

A number of non-Puerto Rican professional women, however, are portrayed in the books: teachers, nurses, social workers, and librarians. One white girl wants to be a doctor (*Candita's Choice*); one white woman is a school principal (*Magdalena*); one black woman is a judge (*Gang Girl*); one black woman is a teacher's aide (*What Do I Do?*); and one Asian-American woman is a teacher (*What Is a Birthday Child?*).

It is interesting to note that other than the principal, judge, and would-be doctor, all these jobs are women's traditional "professional" roles—mostly service jobs and jobs dealing with young children. And in the fiction, they're minor walk-on parts at that (except for the teachers and the social workers who are constantly trying to take over for the Puerto Rican adult women).

The 18 fictional books in which girls are the central characters are reviewed in the paragraphs that follow.

Early Childhood Readers

What Is a Birthday Child? by Ruth M. Jaynes, photos by Harvey Mandlin (Bowman).

Dear Uncle Carlos, by Seymour Reit, photos by Sheldon Brody (McGraw-Hill).

These two early childhood readers are uninspiring Dick and Jane books with Puerto Rican characters. The first depicts the events that take place in a middle-class school on the birthday of five-year-old Juanita (of undetermined Latin origin). Juanita does the following female sex-stereotyped activities: listens passively to singing, records, and stories; cuts flowers from the beautiful outdoor garden; dresses up in adult women's clothes; plays with the big blond doll; and eats punch and cookies with her classmates.

In *Dear Uncle Carlos* (one of the three male-authored fictional books), the Puerto Rican girl, Wanda—also about five years old—writes a birthday letter with the help of her parents to an uncle in Puerto Rico. As usual, Spanish words are misspelled. "Feliz Cumpleaños" (Happy Birthday) is incorrectly spelled "Feliz Compleaños." The book is unimaginatively done, and the child isn't even allowed to write her own letter, but some adult's imitation of a child's writing appears.

What Do I Do? by Norma Simon and Joe Lasker (Whiteman).

This book has the virtue of being the only one of the 18 fictional books that is bilingual. Unfortunately, Spanish is given a secondary position by being put under the English in smaller print.

The book portrays with some humor and liveliness the events in the day of a young Puerto Rican girl (about five years old) who lives in a housing project and goes to school in a neighborhood that is mixed black, brown, and white (majority nonwhite).

Once again, there are gross mistakes in Spanish. For example, the heroine's name is Consuela. Consuelo is the correct spelling.

The book will win no feminist prize since nice, obedient Consuela does mostly "girl things"—helping with the baby at home, setting the table, etc. Physically, however, she is active, and one picture of her sprawling on the floor in school, playing with a wagon, is good and unusual. For some unknown reason the father looks like Frankenstein, and for once, the housewife-mother looks realistically exhausted at the end of the day.

(In a companion bilingual book—*What Do I Say?*—the main character is a boy, and this book has more going for it. The black school teacher is not an aide, as she is in *What Do I Do?*, and the Spanish text is, for a change, correct.)

Carmen, by Bill Binzen (Coward).

Sex stereotyping is heavy in this ghetto-adjustment photograph book (male authored). Carmen (four or five years old) is the empty-headed female who has no inner resources for amusing herself on a rainy day. Her brother, of almost the same age, is shown absorbed in his cars, "as usual," not at all troubled by the rain. Carmen needs externals to save her. As only a "female" would do, she puts on her brightest dress hoping to cheer herself up. Then she looks out the window and notices a new girl in a window across the street, to whom she proceeds to display her doll. Later the two girls meet on the street and play that girl's game, hopscotch. Next day they play together again, wearing their best dresses, with their dolls and Teddy bears.

There are also problems of story continuity in this book. The setting is a cold and rainy day in February, yet when the rain stops, the girls play outdoors in cotton dresses, without coats, on a dry pavement. One cannot help noticing that Carmen's blond friend is better and more expensively dressed.

Maria, by Joan M. Lexau, illustrated by Ernest Crichlow (Dial).

Although the book appears on recommended lists of books about Puerto Ricans, there is no mention in the text that Maria is Puerto Rican. She comes from an Hispanic culture, however.

A lack of understanding of Hispanic cultural background is evident in this book. The parents sell an antique doll that was a family relic in order to obtain money for food, shoes, and a cheaper doll for their child. It is doubtful, however, that Spanish parents would do such a thing since it is a cultural tradition to respect and cherish objects that belonged to one's great-grandmother and that have been passed on to each generation.

The book is also negative from a feminist viewpoint. As in many of the stories, there is a big brother who knows it all, makes the decisions, and protects the girl. Even more offensive is that, once again, the dominant object in Maria's life is a doll (again of lighter skin color than the little girl).

Maria is another adapt-yourself-to-America book, with the father always talking about "When we are rich." And what might seem "practical" from one standpoint—selling a doll in order to have more money— is, in the context of this story, something else: the selling of one's culture in order to make it in a different society.

I Am Here—Yo Estoy Aquí, by Rose Blue, illustrated by Moneta Barnett (Watts).

This is a well-written, nicely illustrated, and a rather touching story, but it has serious flaws.

It is the story of Luz's first day in a U.S. kindergarten. Luz has just come from Puerto Rico, misses home, is afraid of the new school, and doesn't speak English. A white teacher, and a Spanish-speaking teacher's aide, sympathize with Luz's language difficulties and give her multilingual lessons. By the end of the day, with the added help of seeing her first snowfall, Luz adjusts, and she learns to say in English, "I am here."

Pattern one: This is an adjustment-to-America book, with the moral being "All you have to do is learn English, and everything will be all right."

Pattern two: Aside from the welcome addition of the female Spanish-speaking teacher's aide, sex stereotyping is strong in this book. The classroom illustrations show girls, exclusively, playing with dolls. Both boys and girls are playing with paints and blocks. Boys, exclusively, are playing with peg boards, trains, and planes. The text has Luz in the following actions: crying, being upset, sitting, eating, and gradually adjusting. Except for learning a little English and playing in the snow, she is passive and meek all day—a traditionally "feminine" approach to a difficult situation.

Pattern three: The book lacks authenticity. When Luz is given a hot dog for lunch she acts as if she never saw one before. Most U.S. foods and pseudo-foods—like hot dogs—are well known in Puerto Rico.

Angelita, by Wendy Kesselman, photos by Norma Holt (Hill & Wang).

This book has aroused heated controversy. It has been described as a "beautiful" and "touching" story, with excellent photographs. One reviewer felt that this story of a young girl's move from Puerto Rico to New York is portrayed with "that touch of fantasy and beauty that all lives, no matter how poor they appear, contain." Other reviewers consider this book an "overly romantic," "abominable concoction of saccharine sentimentality."

To *Angelita*'s credit, while a major portion of the book concerns a girl and her doll, it shows her in a much wider scope of activities than any of the other early childhood books about Puerto Rican girls. We see Angelita in Puerto Rico climbing mountains, playing with a crab on the beach, riding horses, swimming, and even being self-sufficient enough to "go off by herself into the hills." Aside from Rosa-Too-Little, of the book by that name, Angelita is the only Puerto Rican girl pictured in shorts, also underpants, without a top—allowing her that freedom of movement to be an active, physical person.

Of all the early childhood books, *Angelita* comes closest to portraying the starkness of the contrast between rural and ghetto living conditions. In some ways, this story patterns itself after the other books. It is a story in which the heroine eventually adjusts to ghetto, U.S.A., and does so with the help of that first-seen snowfall (". . . for the first time she was happy in New York"). Puerto Rico is portrayed as overly romantic, overly beautiful, even though the father does admit that it's hard to make a living there.

In an otherwise quite authentic book, it is unfortunate that the authors chose to substitute the term "coquille bird" for coqui. A coqui is a tree frog, indigenous to Puerto Rico, and in many ways a national symbol. The authors tell us they deliberately changed it because coquille bird would be better understood in the United States than coqui.

Rosa-Too-Little, by Sue Felt (Doubleday).

This well-known, extensively used book (published in 1950) is found on all lists of books for Puerto Rican children. It is about a young girl, Rosa (nowhere in the book is it stated that she is Puerto Rican), who desperately wants a library card and learns to write her name for that express purpose. Views on this book range from Good to Poor, from a "nothing, boring, uninteresting, uninspiring" book to a "nice, simple, motivational" story.

There is little that is Puerto Rican about the book and, aside from a few Spanish words and her darker skin, Rosa could be an Anglo-American child living in a city neighborhood.

Rosa's being "too little" for various activities is objectionable to Puerto Ricans who are always being told that their country is ten or one hundred times smaller than every other place, and that their physical stature is too little for certain jobs (police work, for example).

Most of the reviewers agree that the only positive aspect of the story is Rosa's keen interest in books and her diligent effort to learn how to write her name. While this is a positive action, it in no way challenges stereotypes. Those who recommended *Rosa-Too-Little* for the Liberated Child's Library in the first issue of *Ms.* magazine should take a closer look at the stereotypes portrayed in this book.

Rosa, too small for most things, is big enough to help her mother cook, and the mother is always depicted with her apron on. On the streets the girls play their usual games of jumprope (wearing dresses of course), while the boys play with live things and train pigeons on the roof. Sometimes the girls and boys all play in the fire hydrant water, but in the illustrations the boys actually *play,* while the girls stand passively, somewhat frightened, in the spray. The only adult women presented, other than the mother, are the librarians (a female occupation), and even this is denied to Rosa, since they are all pictured as very Anglo-American. To the book's credit, Rosa does *not* play with a doll, and sometimes she is pictured wearing shorts.

Some reviewers liked the illustrations, while others found them depressing and dull. One felt Rosa looked like an American Indian and saw this as indicative of the general confusion in the United States about ethnic groups.

Intermediate Age Books

A Surprise for Carlotta, by Nellie Burchardt, illustrated by Ted Lewin (Watts).

An outrageous book. For one thing, the author confuses Spanish with Italian. "Com' un' angelina!" (p. 43) is misspelled Italian. Spanish words are often misspelled and misused in the book; Carlotta and Francesca are not Spanish names.

The heroine, Carlotta (who is about eight), is portrayed as "the other" type of female—the competitive, jealous, classical brat. She is terribly nasty and hostile, yet no particularly good explanation is offered for her behavior other than that she is short for her age. Her major action in the book is falling in love with a duck at school and taking care of him for a weekend (motherhood training?). Her one creative act is to name the duck "Dandelion."

Carlotta actually does some nonfeminine things, such as touching snakes before boys dare to, and helping to construct a duck cage in school. As boys will do, she hits people physically when she's mad. She is not actually a tomboy—she's not at all athletic and is always pictured in her darling little skirts. But as she grows up physically, we are given to understand that she will grow up mentally, i.e., she will give up her outrageous behavior and act her sex.

The men in her family are clearly The Unchallenged Rulers. Her brother is the *hombrecito* of the house; the father makes all major decisions, and he is served meals first "not just so he could get to his job on time, but also because that was the way it had always been in Puerto Rico" (p. 71).

My House Is Your House, by Tony Talbot, illustrated by Robert Weaver (Cowles).

A slicker-than-usual book about moving out of the ghetto. Eleven-year-old Juana's family moves from their "condemned" slum neighborhood to Islip, New York, after their tenement and all their belongings are destroyed in a fire.

Juana, like Carmen of *Spider Plant,* doesn't want to move from her Puerto Rican neighborhood (roosters, botanicas, bodegas, etc.), nor does she want to part with her possessions which she sees as extensions of herself. After the fire, Juana convinces herself that what counts are "their lives, not the objects that were ready to be discarded." The family then moves with not one possession to their new empty house and are "ready for a new start." What sounds like American practicality in Juana's attitude is, in this case (as in *A Present from Rosita* and *Maria*) something else, for the objects and the neighborhood they so willingly relinquished really symbolize their Puerto Ricanness. It is presented more subtly in this book, but the moral is still: if you want to make it in America, then you'd better leave your old culture behind—burn it—and start clean.

Because Juana is a girl, her mother prohibits her from packing cartons. "It's man's work," she says. The book is concerned mostly with Juana's emotions about moving (female) rather than her actions (male). The only future she sees for herself is in vague terms of "weddings and babies." She takes some initiative, however, in curing her sick dog, and she does wander around her neighborhood by herself.

An unwary reader might easily be deceived by this book because it does have touches of solid realism, such as the girl wetting her bed from anxiety and her 14-year-old brother smoking marijuana (but also causing the fire with it). The excellent illustrations and the correct use of Spanish might also make people feel that the book has something going for it, but these are just fancy coverings for the same old female stereotypes and assimilationist themes.

Magdalena, by Louisa R. Shotwell, illustrated by Lilian Obligado (Viking).

The best book in this particular age group, *Magdalena* is about a sixth-grade girl and her grandmother. For a change, this is not predominantly about suffering and ghetto adjustment. It has welcome touches of fantasy, magic, and adventure. The writing is better, wittier, and more poetic than most, and the illustrations are exceptional.

This is in some ways a real Women's Book. Adult male authority figures are notably absent, and the females have true character and strength. The all-wise, warm, dignified grandmother, who is into spiritualism and herbal remedies, is unforgettable, and even the school principal is a woman (white, of course). The emphasis in the book is on people and their humanity, not on the social environment.

Magdalena herself does some mildly courageous and adventuresome things—for example, actually going out on her own to visit an eccentric old woman. Magdalena and her girl friend Spook are the best writers in their IGC class, and they consciously choose to write about the memorable *women* in their life. Unfortunately, one dominant theme in the book concerns Magdalena's braids—i.e., her appearance, a female concern.

The book is consciously interracial with one white, eccentric woman and one memorable, very wise black male sixth-grader, Sam, as important characters.

A Present from Rosita, by Celeste Edell, illustrated by Elton C. Fax (Messner).

The Spider Plant, by Yetta Speevack, illustrated by Wendy Watson (Atheneum).

These two books were written by New York City teachers. They are both rather dull adjustment-to-the-ghetto books that skirt the edges of real problems and present unreal solutions to unreal situations.

The heroines, Rosita and Carmen, are both 12 years old with older brothers, and with mothers who find it hard to adjust to the United States. Both attend what seem to be totally unreal, nonghetto type schools where the teachers are loving and the classes calm and pleasant. Adjustment to school and learning English are unrealistically easy for both girls. Their major problem is in overcoming prejudices that are blocking their chances for friendship with other children. The burden of proof is placed on the girls; that is, they must prove their worth through exemplary conduct.

Carmen of *The Spider Plant* has been stigmatized for the crime of digging up dirt twice in Central Park, and to redeem herself she must give cuttings of her spider plant to every kid in the class, as well as put on an allegorical play proving her innocence. In the second book, Rosita is faced with anti-Puerto Rican prejudices and must learn English, be in the top of her class, paint beautiful scenes for a school play, constantly salute the flag, and remodel her mother's hand-sewn wedding gown to fit her blonde, beautiful girl friend who needs a costume for a school play. Then, and then only, are the two girls accepted and loved (as evidence, according to the authors, that racism is easily overcome!)

The Spider Plant has the distinction of being recommended by some feminist groups, yet it portrays Carmen washing dishes after dinner while her brother, the "hombrecito," begins his homework (although she has homework as well). She also joins the girl scouts where she will learn homemaking and gardening. Is this a feminist book?

A Present from Rosita, written in stilted English, is practically an outright propaganda book and claims that it is not only good to become an "American," but that this is easy to accomplish.

Candita's Choice, by Mina Lewiton, illustrated by Howard Simon (Harper).

This well-known old-timer (1959) is not only written in stilted English but utilizes several of the grosser themes pervading the adjustment-to-New York-from-Puerto Rico books.

Eleven-year-old Candita has The Language Problem. Rather than be humiliated for not knowing English in school, she refuses to speak at all until she has learned it perfectly. Secretly she learns to read "Bushy Tail the Squirrel," and eventually she speaks perfect English in school and is destined to win honors for her excellent language adjustment.

White paternalism has a field day in this book. Candita's white girl friend is *the* one who always makes her feel better, and *the* one whose father gets Candita's sculptor father a job sweeping floors in a museum, for which he is overwhelmingly grateful.

As a female, Candita is allowed to resist and then learn English, read, baby-sit, get appendicitis, and dream of being with her father, "to live in his house and learn his work, and then to cook and to sew for him." Carving and modeling figures would be fine for her to learn, but she won't have much time for that after taking care of her father.

Early Teenage Books

Rosaria, by Susan Thaler, illustrated by Genia (McKay).

Gang Girl, by H. Samuel Fleischman, illustrated by Shirley Walker (Doubleday).

These two are probably the most dangerous of the fictional books. Both are about teenage Puerto Rican "good girls" who turn "bad." Disillusioned with American ghetto life, they join gangs, take part in robberies (directed by male gang members), and are rehabilitated by white social workers and boy friends who teach them that they can make it by staying within the American mainstream. The onus for all "deviant" behavior in these books is on the individual girls. The moral of both books is: there is no good reason for being disgruntled by society—it is all your own wrong attitude that gets you in trouble.

An outrageous incident in *Gang Girl* has one of the boy gang leaders shot and killed by cops while running from an attempted burglary. No one, not even the dead boy's girl friend, Maria—the 14-year-old heroine—is particularly angry with the police, or upset about the boy's murder. They all blame themselves instead. They have "learned their lesson," and The Spanish Ladies, the fighting gang that Maria heads, must be reformed. In the process, the male author reforms the gang, in some respects, from "bad" to worse. While the girls do stop beating up on other neighborhood girls, they change from an active, independent female group to a passive social club with the most frivolous of "female" interests. As a start, the social worker suggests: "It's fun to learn how to fix yourselves up. I could get a friend of mine who works in a beauty parlor to come and show you how to do your hair and put on makeup."

The reviewers feel that this carefully "researched" book—publisher's blurb—has absolutely no veracity, and no relation to the reality of Puerto Rican ghetto life—except, of course, for the intrusion of social workers and the brutality of the police.

Rosaria (there is no such Spanish name—the correct spelling is Rosario) is a slightly more realistic, more Puerto Rican, more "hip" and hence more dangerous book. Rosaria, a brilliant teenage writer drops out of school and joins her brother Carlo's gang because of a clearly defined (and correct) anger at a society that has destroyed her father through racist union practices. Directed by male gang members, she helps rob a jewelry store, and after being arrested, speaks eloquently of American injustice, refusing to accept guilt, and stating that she knows only of "the crime of being poor, the sin of going hungry."

While Carlo (Italian spelling of Charles, in Spanish it is Carlos) serves five years in prison, the heroine is rehabilitated in Project Step-Ahead as a teacher's aide in a summer school where she meets a handsome blond Yale-bound boy who "saves her," with the help of the social worker. (The author does not allow a Puerto Rican girl to "save" herself or be saved by another Puerto Rican woman, or by any Puerto Rican, for that matter. Anglo-American arrogance assumes that only Anglo-Americans know the answer for the "poor Puerto Ricans.") Together, this all-American team convinces Rosaria that her bitterness is unfounded. . . . "You can't blame others for your own mistakes," says her blond boyfriend (meaning that if a union discriminates against you, it's your own mistake, etc., etc.)

As in *Candita's Choice,* the father of the Anglo boy gets Rosaria's father a job, and from then on, everything is fine.

Older Teenage Books

> *The Girl from Puerto Rico,* by Hila Colman (Morrow).

> *Don't Look at Me That Way,* by Caroline Crane (Random House).

Here are two more books with remarkably similar story lines. Two Puerto Rican teenage girls, both high school dropouts, must find jobs to help support their large, fatherless families, run by docile and "backward" mothers. The girls' lives are complicated by the presence of younger brothers who have run-ins with the police. The girls get jobs as waitresses and baby-sitters, and in the latter position, both are presented with almost identical problems: they baby-sit for well-off white patronizing liberal women. These women, in turn, have neighbors or nephews who are eligible white college boys and who are interested in the girls, but treat them in heavy racist and sexist stereotyped ways. A central question in each book is how the girls will relate to these patronizers and their middle-class values.

Eighteen-year-old Rosa of *Don't Look at Me That Way* discovers the latent racism of American liberals, and she rejects them and their values. She is the only protagonist in all the 18 fiction stories who is offered the rags-to-riches American dream by white benefactors (free car and free college) but rejects the offer as degrading and patronizing.

Of all the stories, *The Girl from Puerto Rico*'s 15-year-old Felicidad is the only female protagonist to return to Puerto Rico to live, finding the United States unsatisfactory. She goes back, however, only because she had wanted very much to be an "American," but found that Americans didn't want *her.* This theme might be interesting if handled correctly, but the author is unsure of what position to take on the issue and so she equivocates and contradicts herself.

The ending, for example, is utterly mystifying. Although everything in the book reveals to Felicidad that New York City and white liberals really *are* racist, she, for no apparent reason, leaves for Puerto Rico stating that her patronizers are "her two good friends" and that New York was truly a "wonderful city."

These two teenage books discuss heretofore taboo subjects and offer truths about ghetto living that are usually avoided. From both stories the reader learns that not all Puerto Ricans are fair-skinned (even though the heroines usually appear to be very fair). From *Don't Look at Me That Way*, the reader learns that poor children often eat paint off walls and get poisoned; that cops aren't liked; and that people don't believe prisons rehabilitate. That women get pregnant, sometimes without husbands, and that they sometimes die in childbirth (Rosa's mother).

That marriage is not usually bliss and that men do abuse women. From *The Girl from Puerto Rico,* the reader learns that men (Felicidad's father) sometimes die from trying to uphold the image of their masculinity. And that Puerto Ricans sometimes take out their frustrations at ghetto living on their natural allies, their black neighbors, and vice versa.

While Felicidad is to a degree strong and willful and engaged in meaningful activities, she is more often wishy-washy, inconsistent, and concerned with dating problems. Her major concern in the book is whether to marry Fernando and have children in Puerto Rico or to stay in New York, date white American· boys, and go shopping on Fifth Avenue. She ends up, as expected, in Fernando's arms, swooning as he proposes to her.

Don't Look at Me That Way, on the other hand, comes closer to being a feminist book than any of the 18. In an interview, the author told us that she does deliberately write from a feminist viewpoint. The book shows, in the treatment of Rosa's mother, just how badly poor women in America are oppressed by society and by men, and the way in which younger women, especially Puerto Ricans, are considered sex objects for men's enjoyment.

As an individual, Rosa is strong, practical, smart, and she is not dependent on male opinion for her own ideas. Toward her boyfriend and her white suitors she is unusually tough. In a semi-rape scene she wounds her attackers with cut glass. She will probably marry her Puerto Rican boyfriend Julio, but she knows that this is not *the* answer to life, and she is not all that excited about marital prospects.

Don't Look at Me That Way undoubtedly has the most going for it in the teenage category. It is fairly authentic, good reading, and avoids the traditional sell-out to Americana. Although the girl is *not* particularly Puerto Rican as a person, she stands apart as one of the only characters in these books verbally to affirm proudness in being Puerto Rican.

REDUCING THE "MISS MUFFET" SYNDROME: AN ANNOTATED BIBLIOGRAPHY

Last January *SLJ* featured two articles pointing up the indisputable negative stereotyping of women and girls in children's books ("A Feminist Look at Children's Books") by the Feminists on Children's Media, pp. 19–24; *LJ*, January 15, 1971, pp. 235–240; and my own critique, "The Skirts in Fiction About Boys: a Maxi Mess," pp. 66–70; *LJ*, January 15, 1971, pp. 282–286). Are things getting better? We wanted to see and so decided this January to publish a list of 1971 and available Spring 1972 titles which depict women and girls realistically and fairly. Some 100 publishers were invited to submit for consideration those titles they thought to be suitable, and we received 21 picture books, 36 nonfiction titles, and 83 novels.

The above numbers reveal that writers' difficulty in finding worthwhile real women to showcase is superseded only by illustrators' inability to actually *show* nonstereotyped females. Of the relatively few picture books submitted, several do depict little girls with guts, imagination, athletic skill, take-charge ability, and just plain likability. Some, moralizing strenuously for female freedom, are too message-riddled for success (e.g., one title builds up a sloppy little girl at the unwarranted expense of a neat little boy). A good many just happen to have female protagonists, undoubtedly because females are "in" now. Only a few of these girls are capably characterized and attractively visualized.

Most of the nonfiction titles received were biographies. The publishers seem to have a penchant for hovering over a few stars: e.g., there are three books on Mary Cassatt and two apiece on Golda Meir and Shirley Chisholm. As is par for the course generally, the upper-grade

Note: By Diane Gersoni-Stavn. Reprinted with permission from *School Library Journal*, January 1972, 18:5, 32–35. Copyright © 1972 by the Xerox Corporation.

289

biographies are superior out of all proportion to the painfully dull, heavily fictionized works hacked out for the lower and middle grades. (Out of at least 10 submitted lower/middle-grade biographies of famous women, only one merits placement on the recommended list). As is also true generally, the biographers—especially those dealing with persons still living—show a distinct disinclination to offer even the minutest criticism of their subjects. Nor do many of them successfully combine information about their subjects' professional and personal lives (let alone, God forbid, cite faults). Like it or not, even young readers want to know just what kind of a social/romantic/sexual/familial life notable women of the past and present were and are able to maintain, given the pressures of their times.

As for the ample number of fiction titles submitted: many of the stories are mysteries (adolescent superwomen resolving untrue-to-life situations) and sci-fi/fantasy (extraterrestrial and just plain extraordinary heroines with life experiences well beyond the reach of average earthling understanding). There are numerous family/adventure stories—e.g., of the English variety—in which the characterizations of both males and females tend to be secondary to complex plotting, snappy dialogue, and brisk pace. Geared toward the middle grades, these are at least more entertaining to read than are the heavy first-person narratives for junior high and high school readers which rely extensively, uninterestingly, and self-consciously on their protagonists' unoriginal cerebral processes. Several of the girls met in the books of this type are runaways and on the road; many have parents who are (1) divorced (-cing), (2) dead, (3) lushes, (4) markedly obtuse. There are a few girl-and-animal stories for both grade levels, and the usual melodramatic teen-discovers-romance-and-sex sagas. Several of the novelists thoughtfully kill two birds with one stone by presenting protagonists who are both female and black. Even the best of the stories rarely have all valid female characters. An adequately fleshed-out girl is countered by a stereotyped, batty old lady; another believable kid is contrasted with her stereotyped hip mother and their stereotyped uptight neighbor.

Whether due to a genuine sense of social responsibility or canny calculation of the profits and glory accruing to those who publicize social/controversial issues, publishers are nothing if not topical. Vibrating to the pitch of the times they go aloft with space-flight/moon books that are as numberless as the stars, eye the occult in covens of texts, or scrutinize our damaged ecosystems and life interdependencies in a never depleting supply of ecology books. Similarly, they have been reforming their lists in accord with the women's liberation fervor of the times. Though most of their female-conscious efforts are hack bandwagon entries (some proclaim contemporaneity with one-sentence allusions to the Movement), others are of good quality and genuinely nonsexist. Their existence tends to take wind out of the sails of revolutionary feminist juvenile publishing ventures which so far lack the finances and the talent stables to produce superior nonsexist books with visual/physical appeal. When no books are available on a socially significant subject, mediocre and even moralistic titles are rightfully considered better than nothing. But juvenile nonsexist literature, as proffered by the Establishment publishers, is past the embryonic stage.

Inevitably, the spate of female-conscious books recalls the rush of "black" books which began to hit the market in the mid-sixties. Black fiction for children has achieved artistic distinction with such works as Hamilton's *The Planet of Junior Brown* and Jordan's *His Own Where*. Though fiction for children centering on women and girls has produced no *Golden Notebook* yet, it should soon; more women with enlightened minds and literary talents are now starting to write about women and girls, and we can expect great things from capable authors who can bring to bear powers of both empathy and recall.

But the vital difference at this point between juvenile books featuring Blacks and female-conscious juvenile books is that good novels about Blacks don't have to play for audience laughs—and their authors wouldn't dare to. Even the unexceptional titles are straightforward, serious stories about average black kids. Conversely, even the good books about white women and girls still rely heavily on humor, stock chortle-producing characters, and those extraordinary heroines—suffragists, unusually precocious little girls, "spunky" problem solvers—to snare a readership. Humor is certainly not a bad thing, and children's books were and often are pompous, grim, and boring without it. But real females' childhoods just aren't all that funny, and there is a great need for excellent, girl-centered juvenile novels which fall between humor and melodrama, for a juvenile *Death of a Salesman.*

Of the 140 titles submitted to us, then, as books which treat women and girls realistically and fairly, the best—10 picture books, 12 nonfiction titles, 18 novels—are annotated below. The list includes no ugly, pointless picture books; grossly fictionized, fawning biographies; badly characterized, unevocatively written novels; nor preachy, rhetoric-splattered propaganda for the Movement.

The picture books chosen are unusually solid as a group. One title treats cleverly the mutual aversion which, for whatever reasons of conditioning, often does exist between small boys and girls. There is a clever concept book, a title with a blissfully diabolical little heroine, a thoroughly engaging animal fantasy, and a spoofy take-off on the fairy tale genre. The rest of the books simply offer warm, substantial stories with believable heroines, and they're good to look at, as picture books should be.

The saddest—and most criminal—lack on the recommended list is of those topnotch lower- and middle-grade biographies, for true accounts of striking individualists can go where honest fiction about average people must often hesitate to tread. The upper-grade biographies are very good; a few have some minor fictionizing which doesn't negate their overall worth. There's a useful, if not dynamite, book on acting written by a great practitioner of that art, as well as a compendium of famous ghostly/ ghastly stories conceived by women. Also, there are two really good books on the history and evolution of the Movement.

As for the fiction: even good writers seem unable to treat real late-adolescent females. The heroines of the eight upper-grade titles include a Cockney superwoman, a suffragist, a Russian noblewoman, an Inter-planetary Federation agent, and an earthy, earthly recluse—hardly Every-girls. And, look at that middle-grade fiction list—at least six out of the ten titles owe their success to the kind of amusing but stock humor cited above. Of the four which don't, two are about black girls.

To return to an earlier question: are things getting better for non-sexist juvenile literature? (1) Yes. They're getting better slowly. (2) They should be getting better faster. (3) The only reason they've gotten better at all is because concerned women knowledgeable about children and their books have made themselves and their ample stockpile of sup-portive facts heard.

Picture Books, Kindergarten–Grade 3

Abramovitz, Anita. *Winifred.* color illus. by Carroll Dolezal. 32pp. Steck-Vaughn, 1971.

Bright color paintings carry this story about a handy little girl who learns that signs made to order prevent neighborhood havoc.

Bonsall, Crosby. *The Case of the Scaredy Cats.* color illus. by author. 64pp. (I Can Read Mysteries). Harper, 1971.

It's boys vs. girls but fair shakes for all; little Annie runs away, frightened only because the boys, vanquished in battle by the girls, had fled: "They looked scared to me. . . . So I hid, too."

Conford, Ellen. *Impossible, Possum.* color illus. by Rosemary Wells. 32pp. Little, 1971.

As a (tail) swinger Randolph Possum's a loser till his sister, a witty Wunderkind, teaches him how to hang loose.

Gauch, Patricia Lee. *Christina Katerina and the Box.* illus., some color, by Doris Burn. unpaged. Coward, 1971.

The box becomes a castle becomes a clubhouse becomes a racing car becomes a dance floor when imaginative Christina Katerina rescues it from a mundane fate as a trash bin.

Hirsh, Marilyn and Narayan, Maya. *Leela and the Watermelon.* color illus. by Marilyn Hirsh. unpaged. Crown, 1971.

Leela swallows more than a watermelon seed when she believes her brother's story that a melon will now grow in her stomach. A very simple, natural tale, illustrated by striking watercolors.

Miles, Betty and Blos, Joan. *Just Think!* color illus. by Pat Grant Porter. 40pp. Knopf, 1971.

It's old folks at home and young ones too: the mrs. sculpts while her husband brings coffee; dad walks his son to school while mother works in a lab; girls and boys together jump rope, play cowboys, dolls, and baseball. An egalitarian grab-bag of bright words, concepts, and busy-day activities.

Ness, Evaline. *Do You Have the Time, Lydia?* color illus. by author. unpaged. Dutton, 1971.

Lydia, who sews and bakes but also hammers nails and builds racing cars, learns to include her unhappy little brother in her hyperactive daily routine.

Preston, Edna Mitchell. *Horrible Hepzibah.* illus. by Ray Cruz. 48pp. Viking, 1971.

The only person meaner and uglier than Hepzibah Smith is her hideous old aunt for whom she's named. Funny/nasty pen-and-ink drawings follow the evil twosome as they cow a Horrible Ugly, unnerve Mr. and Mrs. Smith, and vanquish painfully prissy Beautiful Vanilla.

Shulman, Alix. *Finders Keepers.* color illus. by Emily McCully. unpaged. Bradbury, 1971.

Hawk-eyed Lisa always finds lost toys and new trifles in the playground for her friends; one day, she stumbles on an old wagon and, with a healthy display of ego, decides to keep it for herself.

Williams, Jay. *The Silver Whistle.* color illus. by Friso Henstra. unpaged. Parents' Magazine Pr., 1971.

Prudence is constitutionally blasé but her ample spunk, quick thinking, and clever use of a magic whistle enable her to save a kingdom and wed a very likable prince.

Biography, Grades 3–6

McKown, Robin. *Marie Curie.* illus. by Karl W. Swenson. 96pp. (World Pioneer Biographies) Putnam, 1971.

Abridged and simplified from McKown's 1959 biography of Curie, this palatably fictionized book details the scientist's radium-centered achievements and successful collaboration-marriage with Pierre.

Biography, Grade 7 Up

Hicks, Nancy. *The Honorable Shirley Chisholm: Congresswoman from Brooklyn.* 123pp. index. Lion Bks., 1971.

The Honorable Shirley is nobody's fool and many people's hope for constructive, creative, do-something government. There's minimal fictionizing and lots of brisk, succinct writing here.

Hollander, Phyllis. *American Women in Sports.* 128pp. photogs. Norton: Grosset, 1972.

Terse, refreshingly objective glimpses at such stars as Eleanora Sears, Kathy Kusner, Gertrude Ederle, Florence Chadwick, Wilma Rudolph, Billie Jean King, Maureen Connolly, Althea Gibson, Carol Heiss, Babe Didrikson, Debbie Meyer, and many others.

Klein, Mina C. and Klein, H. Arthur. *Kathe Kollwitz: Life in Art.* 192pp. photogs. reprods. bibliog. index. Holt, 1972.

A truly excellent, nonfictionized biography of the great German graphic artist whose powerful renderings of poverty and rejection of militarism and fascism ("Der Hitler ist ein Esel!") catapulted her into Nazi disfavor.

McKown, Robin. *The World of Mary Cassatt.* 224pp. photogs. (Women of America Series) Crowell, 1972.

Another fine biography of another noteworthy artist, this describes the talents, illumines the friendships (e.g., with Degas), and even points up the limitations of the French Impressionist-affiliated portrait painter, Mary Cassatt.

Ross, Pat, comp. and intro. by. *Young and Female: Turning Points in the Lives of Eight American Women.* 118pp. photogs. bibliog. Random, 1972.

A very useful collection of excerpts from the adult autobiographies of Shirley MacLaine, Shirley Chisholm, Dorothy Day, Emily Hahn, Margaret Sanger, Althea Gibson, Margaret Bourke-White, and Edna Ferber.

> Shulman, Alix. *To the Barricades: the Anarchist Life of Emma Goldman.* 255pp. photogs. sel. bibliog. index. (Women of America Series) Crowell, 1971.

A very inclusive, lively biography of the remarkable woman whose support of anarchism, birth control, free love, women's suffrage, and a whole host of other unpopular causes put her years ahead of her time—the first half of the twentieth century—and made her anathema to most Americans.

> Vipont, Elfrida. *Towards a High Attic: the Early Life of George Eliot, 1819–1880.* 145pp. photogs. reprods. index. Holt, 1971.

This very well written biography shows how the homely girl from a conservative Victorian family went on to live with a man outside of marriage and create such classics as *Adam Bede, Silas Marner,* and *Middlemarch.*

Literature and the Arts, Grade 7 Up

> Harris, Julie with Barry Tarshis. *Julie Harris Talks to Young Actors.* 192pp. photogs. index. Lothrop, 1971.

One of America's most respected actresses speaks informally on the need to cultivate discipline and good physical health, "method" acting, ways of breaking into the theater or films, and places at which to study the theater arts.

> Manley, Seon and Lewis, Gogo, sels. *Ladies of Horror: Two Centuries of Supernatural Stories by the Gentle Sex.* 288pp. photogs. reprods. biog. notes. Lothrop, 1971.

Despite the coy title, this offers splendid spookery served up by such mistresses of the macabre as Agatha Christie, Mary Shelley, E. Nesbit, Shirley Jackson, Daphne du Maurier, and nine others.

The Women's Movement, Grade 7 Up

> Harris, Janet. *A Single Standard.* 144pp. index. McGraw, 1971.

A single standard for male and female behavior and achievement has always been the goal of those advocating women's liberation, and in this thoughtful work Harris traces the work and philosophies of several such reformers: Mary Wollstonescraft, Thomas Paine, John Stuart Mill, the Grimkés, etc.

Komisar, Lucy. *The New Feminism.* 181pp. index. Watts, 1971.

For older readers, this excellent title concentrates less on the historical and more on the psychological and current legal aspects of the women's liberation struggle. It includes student dialogues and a particularly good chapter on such noteworthy misogynists as Freud, Strindberg, Hitler, Rousseau, etc.

Fiction, Grades 3–6

Burton, H. *The Henchmans at Home.* illus. by G. V. Ambrus. 192pp. Crowell, 1972. Gr 5–8.

A family saga that really commands attention; readers follow feisty Rob, independent Ellen, and ambitious William through childhood fun and games, adolescent aspirations, post-adolescent disillusionments, and adulthood compromises.

Corcoran, Barbara. *This Is a Recording.* illus. by Richard Cuffari. 168pp. Atheneum, 1971. Gr 5–8.

Her parents are marital rifting, so pistol-packing Marianne's packed off herself to Montana and an actress-grandmother she doesn't remember. Her first-person narrative, ostensibly a tape-recorded diary, is amusing and comparatively unself-conscious.

Mathis, Sharon Bell. *Sidewalk Story.* illus. by Leo Carty. 73pp. Viking, 1971. Gr 3–6.

The ends are all neatly and predictably tied together in this story about a black girl who saves her friend's family from eviction, but Lilly Etta's a believable character and her *Sidewalk Story* capably evokes urban life.

Murray, Michele. *Nellie Cameron.* illus. by Leonora E. Prince. 185pp. Seabury, 1971. Gr 4–6.

A simple but effective story about nine-year-old, black Nellie whose self-image is solidly boosted when sympathetic Miss Lacey teaches her how to read.

Raskin, Ellen. *The Mysterious Disappearance of Leon (I Mean Noel).* illus. by author. Dutton, 1971. Gr 4–6.

A wacky heiress would be in the soup if not for the efforts of her two young traveling companions: earnest, well-meaning—if indecisive—Tony and terribly clever, cool-headed Tina.

Sachs, Marilyn. *The Bears' House.* illus. by Louis Glanzman. 81pp. Doubleday, 1971. Gr 4–6.

Fran Ellen's an anti-heroine; she sucks her thumb, smells, disgusts her classmates, and lives happily only in a dreamworld inhabited by Goldilocks and the three bears. But she herself is very real, and Sachs limns her with warmth, humor, and total understanding.

Sharmat, Marjorie Weinman. *Getting Something on Maggie Marmelstein.* illus. by Ben Shecter. 101pp. Harper, 1971. Gr 3–6.

Thad finally does get something on Maggie, but by the time he's ready to use it the two kids have called a grudgingly respectful truce. A lighthearted story about a boy and a girl who are both equal parts softies and one-uppers.

Streatfeild, Noel. *Thursday's Child.* illus. by Peggy Fortnum. 275pp. Random, 1971. Gr 5–8.

A good British orphanage story complete with mistreated children, a tyrannical matron, an angel-of-mercy gentlewoman—and indomitable heroine Margaret Thursday, who refuses both to be cowed by Matron and eased into a do-nothing, aristocratic life: "'I'm going to make my name famous.'"

Symons, Geraldine. *The Workhouse Child.* illus. by Alexy Pendle. 221pp. Macmillan, 1971. Gr 5–7.

In this witty bit of Victoriana, the workhouse child is helped by socially concerned Pansy who herself is extricated from a tight situation by her steely-minded friend Atalanta.

Udry, Janice May. *Angie.* illus. by Hilary Knight. 64pp. Harper, 1971. Gr 4–6.

In a brisk, funny series of chapter-episodes, Angie outmaneuvers an obnoxious schoolmate, fools a couple of big-shot boys, goes into business selling rides, and even befriends her school principal.

Fiction, Grade 7 Up

Aiken, Joan. *The Cuckoo Tree.* illus. by Susan Obrant. 314pp. Doubleday, 1971. Gr 6–9.

Eighteenth-century Cockney heroine Dido Twite doesn't just fight off a baddie or two but saves Richard IV's crown for him in this preposterous, merry adventure.

Almedingen, E. K. *Anna.* 192pp. Ariel: Farrar, 1972. Gr 7 up.

A romantic but atmospheric novel about Almedingen's Russian great-grandmother Anna, whose learning and knowledge of languages dazzled even Catherine the Great.

Bolton, Carole. *Never Jam Today.* 241pp. Atheneum, 1971. Gr 8–11.

A solid, often humorous novel about an early twentieth-century suffragist who defies her family to join the picket line and then opts for college, apartment, and career over early marriage.

Crawford, Deborah. *Somebody Will Miss Me.* 215pp. Crown, 1971. Gr 9 up.

Abby's an average girl passing through worse-than-average hard times; her depression and maturation blues are skillfully evoked in this finely written novel.

Embry, Margaret. *Shádi.* 92pp. Holiday, 1971. Gr 7 up.

A memorable story about a poor Navajo family and big sister Emma, their chief mainstay. Emma's a real-world heroine whose heroics consist of surviving and keeping her family together.

Engdahl, Sylvia Louise. *The Far Side of Evil.* illus. by Richard Cuffari. 292pp. Atheneum, 1971. Gr 7–10.

Sentimentality certainly doesn't influence the decisions of Interplanetary Federation agent Elana, whose refusal to interfere in the affairs of—and thereby possibly save—a planet on the verge of nuclear war pits her against a male agent who's been distracted by his love for one of the planet's women.

Jordan, June. *His Own Where.* 89pp. Crowell, 1971. Gr 7 up.

An urban teen-age love story that's never maudlin; Angela and Buddy, absorbed exclusively in and buoyed only by each other, make love in a cemetery and hope for a child to share their joy.

Renvoize, Jean. *A Wild Thing.* 248pp. Atlantic: Little, 1971. Gr 9 up.

A British girl runs away to live in the wilderness, takes a lover so she can bear a daughter to share her life, then dies in childbirth, alone in the wild. It's unsettling, compelling reading; though Morag finally loses to death, she commands attention throughout.

ALL PREGNANT GIRLS HAVE BOY BABIES

Teen-age pregnancy has now been admitted to the narrow circle of subjects deemed fit for the teen-age reader. I suppose that these novels will appeal to girls who like the general run of teen-age fiction: they can be certain that here they will find a strong story line (both author and reader know at every step exactly what's got to come next) fleshed out with realistic details (though one would never gather from these books that not every pregnant woman suffers from morning sickness). They can enjoy the comfort of reading about a troublesome event in the ambience of a cosy status quo.

One suspects that the books serve a further purpose: to convince the juvenile publisher that by providing a category called "teen-age pregnancy" he's facing up to life today and being more honest and informative than he used to be. If he believes that, he's kidding himself. The times have changed, and the publishers have moved along; but on the evidence of these books they're still bringing up the rear, as distant from the vanguard as they ever were.

I've read six of these novels, three from a year or more back and three just coming out this fall; the six were so alike that I found the chief difficulty in reviewing them to be remembering which was which. Let's take the three new ones. They are called *Phoebe* by Patricia Dizenzo (McGraw-Hill), also available in paperback (Bantam); *Yesterday's Child* by Ann Victor (Lippincott) and *The Longest Weekend* by Honor Arundel (Nelson). They have an awful lot in common. To wit: they are each explicit about the symptoms of pregnancy, the panic of the girl, her loneliness upon finding herself pregnant. Each girl is her parents' only child

Note: By Carolyn G. Heilbrun. In *The New York Times Book Review*, November 8, 1970. Copyright © 1970 by The New York Times Company. Reprinted by permission.

and has trouble communicating. Each is a "good" girl, and each book
makes the point that it's the "good" girls who get caught. Obviously we
are meant to believe that here we have the story of your daughter and
mine. Why is it then that the heart sinks at the contemplation of these
explicit and not ill-written books?

The reason is that the girls who are at the heart of the books, like
slaves, like once-loved animals pathetic in their suffering, are acted upon.
There is not one of them with the smallest sense of destiny, of herself as a
specially valuable human being rather than as a host of female organs,
not one of them who could imagine herself as an autonomous being. If we
are going to continue telling young readers that women are not much
more than throbbing wombs, then we will continue to have trouble unless
we lock them up until they marry. If, however, we wish to have a world
occupied by female youngsters who are also human beings, then we must
give them a sense that they have a destiny and that their sexual life should
be seen as part of that destiny. In each of these books the girl dreams her
way through school bored. In each, her status derives from the attentions
of boys. In each, while the boy considers what he might become and looks
on fatherhood as one aspect of these plans, the girl thinks of nothing but
shame, what the neighbors will think, when her clothes will fit again and
how she will return to her previous life. What life? is a question not asked.

The Longest Weekend, a British book, is the slickest and best written of the lot and not really a teen-age pregnancy story at all. The father
is soon to graduate from medical school, is witty and attractive; in love
with the girl, thinks she is using the pill, and ends up marrying her and
claiming their three-year-old child. It's a pleasant story with a good deal
of truth about the difficulties of spending whole days in the exclusive
company of a three-year-old, and plenty of romance. Since it all ends
happily, it hasn't very much to do with the problems of pregnancy, but
rather of a girl who decides to let the nice man love her. Probably just the
thing to read after a hard day studying American history.

Of the other two, *Phoebe* is regrettably the better, "regrettably" because its excellence so clearly derives from the sex education film that
was its previous incarnation. One can see the film as one reads, and it is
certainly to be recommended to anyone who wonders what it's like to discover yourself pregnant, what follows the discovery if you can have an
abortion (they are illegal in this book) and what are the difficulties of
talking to one's parents about the matter.

Yesterday's Child complicates itself with argumentative parents, a
drinking father who manages to understand, and one of those impossible
mothers who never understands anything. The story carries the heroine
through the institution where she has the baby (a boy, of course; teen-age

heroines who enter these homes always have boys); and if any girl ever wondered about these homes, she need wonder no longer.

Well, what did I want? Assuming that the authors and publishers are really trying to explore a very difficult and complex problem and not just titillate their readers while delivering a terrible warning, what could these books present that would touch with some profundity upon the problems of teen-age sexuality?

We have achieved—and it has been the struggle of centuries—some degree of enlightenment and tolerance about sexual relations unsanctified by matrimony. Victorian authors took their lives in their hands writing about such a subject. George Eliot had to hang her unmarried mother; Mrs. Gaskell suffered for not trying to send hers to coventry; and even in our own century, when H. G. Wells allowed his heroine to have a baby with her lover and then marry someone else, he raised such a storm that we have to shoot down college students to match it today.

We don't think that because a girl has had an illegitimate baby she ought to be treated like a criminal; but neither do we come right out and *tell* girls the facts of life, the chief of which is that if a girl has sexual intercourse without contraceptives she may get pregnant (and life being what it is, she probably will). Only *The Longest Weekend* makes this point explicitly, though the others refer vaguely to contraceptive problems that the girls never really face up to. We have now provided places where unmarried girls can go to have their babies and adoption agencies that will find homes for them. Is this what the problem is all about? Things were certainly easier for Samuel Johnson who, when Boswell tried to defend an adulterous woman, said: "My dear Sir, never accustom your mind to mingle virtue and vice. The woman's a whore, and there's an end on't."

At least the poor woman knew where she stood. Today, the girl is told that looks are all, that popularity with boys is central, that not to be cute enough to be picked out by an adolescent boy is death. But she is never told about her own sexual development or her own identity.

What of the teen-ager who has lifted *Phoebe* from the fiction shelves of the library? She will never learn from this or any other teen-age fiction that with the population problems today she *must* not look to pregnancy as the major event in her life, but as one among several major events, just as a boy looks to fatherhood. She must learn that her life, like the boy's, can be ordered toward work she finds absorbing, rewarding, or simply necessary, that her sexuality must follow a pattern that is hers and not only a response to a boy's sexuality.

The sexuality of boys is continuous. As they grow to sexuality and reach, very soon, the most sexually demanding period of their lives, sex with a woman will be similar to the sexual experience they have already had. Not so with a girl. For her, according to all studies, sex begins with intercourse, not before it. For her, sex is an initiation, because only then does she discover her sexual self. Girls grow to full sexuality after experience with a boy for whom they feel affection at the least, at best love and a sense of communion. Therefore the tension between a boy who will demand sex in the rear of a car with a girl whose name he does not know, and a girl who wishes to awaken to true sexuality is a real tension and must be faced. The double standard, the "virginity mystique," is still with us and must be discussed and appraised in the light of a new world and new knowledge.

Having read these books, honest in their way but so achingly hollow at the center where a human being is supposed to be, I would like to suggest that the next teen-age book be a discussion by several post-teen-age boys and girls, of the problems I have named. Take it down on tape and edit it. Talk about everything from what Masters and Johnson have discovered about female sexuality to male adolescent needs, from women's lib and whether boys ought to pay on dates to the whole question of femininity. It won't be a novel, it might not even be a book of lasting interest; but we would all learn something, especially teen-agers. If we're not, with S. Johnson, going to call the teen-age mother a whore, let's give her a chance to think of herself as something other than a teen-age mother.

TEXTBOOKS AND CHANNELING

This paper examines the way social studies textbooks present the different roles that men and women play in American society. I chose five texts written for grades one to three. All were published since 1962, four of them since 1964. I deliberately chose texts that look modern. In analyzing the texts for sex roles, I have considered only descriptions of modern times, leaving out descriptions of pioneer or Indian life. I have considered the information conveyed by the pictures as well as the written texts because young children learn much from pictures. One of the books, *People and Their Social Actions*, is almost all pictures.

Work is one of the main concepts in all these books. In the five texts combined, men are shown in or described in over 100 different jobs and women in less than thirty. Almost all of the women's jobs are ones usually associated with women. They are teachers, librarians, and actresses. They serve people or help men to do more important jobs by being stewardesses, nurses, dental assistants, typists, secretaries, or switchboard operators, or by working in their husband's business. Women also do what was once their work in the home. They cut cloth and sew in a dress factory. (Men in the same factory design the clothes and make the patterns.) Women are weavers, or they work in thread factories or as seamstresses. Women also provide food—they grow vegetables (while men work the big farm machinery), work in canneries, package strawberries, and dry grapes. Women package the fish men catch. Women are waitresses in small diners, but men are waiters in fancy restaurants described in the same text.

In the picture book, there are several pages asking which work re-

Note: By Jamie Kelem Frisof. Reprinted with permission from *Women: a Journal of Liberation,* Fall 1969, 1:1, 26–28. Copyright © 1969 by *Women: a Journal of Liberation,* 3028 Greenmount Avenue, Baltimore, Maryland 21218.

quires training. More training is always required by the work being done
by men. One page asks which people are leaders of different organizations—all male leaders of male organizations. On another page the child
is to match the instruments of work with the worker. There is one woman
who is to be matched with a shopping cart.

There are a few jobs which both women and men do. These include
working in a factory that makes dollar bills, being a member of Congress
(of course there are only one or two women in Congress and a man is
shown speaking), working in a bank as a teller, working in a candy store,
and painting portraits. In a section on scientists, Rachel Carson is mentioned along with a number of men.

In *Our Working World* women have the role of volunteers. They
can see things that are wrong with society and they try to help poor
people. This is not work for which they are paid; nor is it important
enough for men to do it. Government (men), business (men), and volunteers (women) are the three groups which can solve society's problems!
In another text a community is having trouble collecting enough tax
money for the school. The young woman school teacher agrees to stay
until the end of the year for less pay.

Men have jobs which children are supposed to consider glamorous.
They are firemen, policemen, soldiers, President, astronauts, scientists, TV
cameramen, engineers, baseball players, circus performers, symphony con-
ductors, executives, city councillors, diamond examiners, lifeguards, professional swimmers, forest rangers, loggers, museum guides, cattle ranch-
ers, sheep shearers, and government workers. Men have the jobs of di-
recting people and planning things. They are architects, bank managers,
restaurant managers, pilots, city planning experts, factory owners, and
dress designers. They work in supermarkets where women shop. They
are professional bakers and chefs, though women do these jobs at home.
A woman typist works in a little office on a regular typewriter, but a man
is shown typing on a machine that is surrounded by a complicated com-
puter. Men also have a large number of ordinary jobs—they work in mills,
make wool, do construction work, take tickets at the movie theater; they
are doormen, sanitation workers, ambulance attendants, teachers, bus-
boys, mailmen, carpenters, and factory workers.

Any girl who has not already learned what mommies do and daddies
do will quickly see that men go places, struggle against nature, direct
large enterprises, boss women, make money, and gain respect and fame.
Women, on the other hand, have so few jobs of interest open to them
that they might as well stay home with their children. Their work at
home is not seen as particularly difficult or important. They clean, cook,
sew, shop, and plant flowers. There is no description of how difficult it is

to bake a pie. Nor is there a paragraph on how important it is to be knowledgeable when shopping in order not to be cheated. The picture of American women is one of time spent nonproductively at home while the fathers work. The mother's most important role—raising her children—is played down completely. Mother does not teach or discipline her children. She does not offer them many explanations although occasionally she is responsible for exposing them to new experiences. Her relationship with them is not one which seems to require much effort on her part or theirs. The role of housewife-mother is not considered a job; it is not work for which one is paid. The impression given by these books is not that mothers have important work to do in the home while fathers earn money (a phony view in itself), but that mothers are not capable of doing anything worthwhile, or at least not worth reading about in school.

Four out of five of these books use some family stories to relate social studies information. Because the men work, the families have to move when the father's job is moved or stay in a place because it is near the father's work. If a family wants to go on a vacation, they have to wait until the father can take time off from work. The father is more likely to make the decisions about trips and sightseeing than the mother. He drives the car, reads the maps and deals with hotel clerks, salesmen, and guides. For the most part, father gives the children more factual information about the world than mother does—information about how the government works or how cloth is made, for example. On a trip the mother makes a remark such as "Now we're crossing the Hudson River, children" and the father follows it with a history of the state of New York that covers the next three pages.

At meetings, there are always men speakers. In one book where a new community is formed, men are elected to chair meetings and to be officials of the new community. Women are present at the town meetings, but hardly say a word. They often busy themselves making lemonade or serving cookies. At the voting polls, women may have the job of checking people's names, but they are never the political candidates.

Because the father makes the money, he is the most important member of the family. A house is where "Mr. Brown and his family live." In one story about a sheep ranch first Uncle Ned is mentioned, then we learn that Uncle Ned and his wife go to church in the town, and a few pages later, we discover that Uncle Ned's wife has a name, Aunt Mary. Mrs. Irwin, who takes care of the boy at the local store, is called the "storekeeper's wife." (Isn't she also the storekeeper?) She contributes the longest bit of talking done by a woman in this particular book (*Our Working World*). It is a humorous account of how sheep being herded by men sometimes get loose and she has to run out of her house and yell in order to chase them away from her flower beds. When her story is finished, the boy laughs.

Most of the child characters in these books are boys. Stories sometimes focus on a girl and a boy and, very rarely, on a girl. The boys do the most traveling, ask the most questions, and find the most interesting objects. Boys visit forest workers, construction sites, a sheep ranch, and an Indian reservation, without any girls along to get in the way. The only visit a girl makes unaccompanied by a boy is to a dress factory to see another girl's mother at work. When a family with a boy and a girl visit Washington, D.C., the boy asks more questions. When a similar family visits Florida the boy finds an interesting shell and a coconut. The girl finds nothing. A little boy who decides to set up a store cajoles his little sister into working for him.

In *Living in America* the family has a girl, Kathy, and a boy, Mark. Mark is older and consequently more knowledgeable. He can visit interesting places, have friends, read, and find a wild burro. Kathy, being younger, cries a lot, is afraid of the subway, cannot read, and cannot go to see the river with her father because she must help her mother in the kitchen. She asks many silly questions which Mark answers condescendingly. This was the fifth book I read and, after all the others, I got the impression that the girl *had* to be younger because it would never do for her to have adventures and leave her brother at home.

These books give the distinct impression that, even at an early age, boys are allowed to and able to do more than girls, to get out of the house more freely, and to see more. Since boys are going to have more interesting and varied jobs when they grow up, they have ambitions. They fantasize about working on a train, working in a broom factory, being President. Boys grow up to be doctors and to work in airplane factories. A girl's ambition is presented by only one statement, "Maybe I'll design fabrics when I grow up," made by Betsy after design printing has been explained to her by her father. (In the factory she visits, however, only men are shown doing designing.)

The first story about a girl in the SRA book is about Wendy Wheat, a smiling face on a wheat stalk. Wendy's ambition is to be made into puffed wheat. She is harvested, sold, bought, stored in a grain elevator, put on a train, sold again, and stored in a ship. Finally, she is processed into puffed wheat, packaged, and sold again. A picture shows her smiling as she slides out of a cereal box into a bowl of milk, ready to be consumed. I hardly need mention that all along the way men are responsible for her fate.

These books all lack interesting and competent female characters with which girls in the primary grades can identify. It may be true that girls do better than boys in elementary school because they identify with women teachers and/or are more obedient, but they are quickly taught that their futures are limited. They can learn all the facts about the interesting jobs their male classmates will have some day, but nothing is said of their own wide horizons. The boys' jobs probably do not turn out to be so interesting, but at least the boys have something to look forward to and are expected to define themselves in some way other than who they belong to or who they possess.

These books also do not show an accurate proportion of working mothers. (Only one is included in a story.) Therefore, even if a girl's mother works at an interesting job, the child is given the impression that her mother is not a normal mother (and maybe does not love her children?). On top of the fact that the girl may resent her mother's working, she is taught that her mother's work is less important than her father's or that her mother works only because there is no father in the family and therefore she is doubly deprived.

The pictures, which are very important in children's books, show only men or boys more than seven times as often as only women or girls (in four of the five texts, not counting pictures of Indians). There are 398 pictures of only males compared with 256 pictures of males and females together. I have not broken down these pictures with both sexes into categories, but many of them are women being served or helped by men, boys and girls playing together, or families. Rarely are men and women working together or seen in equally competent roles. *People and Their Social Actions*, the picture book, has 117 pictures of men and boys, 15 pictures of women and girls, and 31 pictures of both sexes.

The use of the word "men" to mean "mankind" or "people" reinforces the idea that men accomplish things. This seems like a minor point, but to a seven-year-old child the word "men" may very likely mean "adult males" and no more. For example, we learn that "Men ask questions about nature. The more men learn about nature, the better they can protect themselves." Maybe the writers of the text do mean adult males. According to their book, men are more likely than women to ask questions, to learn, and to protect themselves.

The saddest statistic is that seven of the eleven authors of these books are women who obviously do work. However, the four male authors always have their names listed first.

Social studies textbooks are a relatively small and insignificant aspect of the socialization of girl children. Nonetheless, they do their part in preparing girls to accept unquestioningly their future as unimportant, nonproductive, nonadventurous, and unintelligent beings.

Textbooks Examined

CUTRIGHT, PRUDENCE; CLARK, MAE KNIGHT; and NEWELL, BERNICE. *Living in America Today and Yesterday*. New York: The Macmillan Co., 1962.

PRESNO, VINCENT, and PRESNO, CAROL. *People and Their Social Actions, Man in Action Series*. Englewood Cliffs, N.J.: Prentice-Hall, Inc., 1967.

PRESTON, RALPH C., and CLYMER, ELEANOR. *Communities at Work*. Health Social Studies Series. Boston: D. C. Heath and Co., 1964.

SENESH, LAWRENCE. *Our Working World: Neighbors at Work*. Chicago: Science Research Associates, Inc., 1965.

WANN, KENNETH; VREELAND, JANE D.; and CONKLIN, MARGUERITE A. *Learning About Our Country*. Boston: Allyn & Bacon, Inc., 1964.

WOMEN IN U.S. HISTORY HIGH SCHOOL TEXTBOOKS

Early in our history, enterprising groups of English gentlemen attempted to found all-male colonies. The attempts were failures, but the idea of a society without women appears to have held extraordinary appeal for the descendants of those early colonists. Throughout our history, groups of intrepid males have struck off into the wilderness to live in bachelor colonies free from civilization and domesticity.

The closing of the frontier and the presence, even from the earliest days, of equally intrepid females ended these dreams of masculine tranquility. Yet, the hopeful colonists may have had their revenge. If women have had their share in every stage of our history, exactly what they did and who they were remains obscure. Ask most high school students who Jane Addams, Ida Tarbell, or Susan B. Anthony were, and you may get an answer. Ask about Margaret Sanger, Abigail Duniway, or Margaret Brent, and you will probably get puzzled looks. Sojourner Truth, Frances Wright, Anna Howard Shaw, Emma Willard, Mary Bickerdyke, Maria Mitchell, Prudence Crandall, and scores of others sound like answers from some historian's version of Trivia.

Interest in the fate of obscure Americans may seem an esoteric pursuit, but this is not the case. History, despite its enviable reputation for presenting the important facts about our past, is influenced by considerations other than the simple love of truth. It is an instrument of the greatest social utility, and the story of our past is a potent means of transmitting cultural images and stereotypes. One can scarcely doubt the impact of

Note: By Janice Law Trecker. Reprinted by permission of the National Council for the Social Studies and Janice Law Trecker from *Social Education,* March 1971, 249–61+.

history upon the young in the face of recent minority groups' agitation for more of "their history."

Minority groups are perhaps not the only ones with a complaint against the historians and the schools, nor are they the only ones to show the effects of stereotypes. Consider the most recent reports of the President's Commission on the Status of Women. According to the 1968 report of the Commission, *American Women,* in the fall of 1968 only 40 percent of entering college freshmen were women. The lag in female participation in higher education is even more noticeable at the graduate level. Statistics from the Commission's 1968 report indicated that women earned only one in three of the B.A. degrees and M.A. degrees granted and only one in ten of the doctorates. It is seldom noted that this represents a percentage decline from the 1930s when women received two in five B.A. degrees and M.A. degrees, and one in seven Ph.D. degrees. The loss of potential talent this represents is clear from the Commission's information that among the top 10 percent of our high school seniors, there are twice as many girls as boys with no college plans.

Able girls are not entering science and mathematics in any great number, and, according to the *Conant Report,* they fail to take courses and programs commensurate with their abilities. There seems to be a clear need for an examination of the factors which permit the loss of considerable amounts of female talent.

The Education Committee of the President's Commission on the Status of Women was concerned about this loss, noting that:

> Low aspirations of girls are the result of complex and subtle forces. They are expressed in many ways—even high achievement—but accompanied by docility, passivity, or apathy. The high motivation found in the early school years often fades into a loss of commitment and interest, other than in the prospect of early marriage.

The Committee found some of the reasons for this loss of motivation are the stereotypes of women in our culture and in the lingering ideas of female inferiority.

Educators should be aware that the school is one of the means by which the stereotypes of women and their capacities are transmitted. As one of the main cultural forces in the society, the school shares a responsibility for the diminished aspirations of its female students. Looking at the position of women in our society, one would have to be very sanguine to say that the education of American girls needs no improvement. Something is wrong when women are concentrated in a relatively few, lower-paid positions; when there are few women represented in the upper levels of government and industry; and when the symptoms of discontent and frustration are all too clearly manifesting themselves among militant young women.

Something is indeed wrong, and educators should begin a rigorous investigation of their programs and practices in order to discover if they are reinforcing the cultural pressures which discourage talented girls.

Analysis of High School Textbooks

A reasonable place to start, considering the admitted obscurity of most women in American history, is the United States history text. Are the stereotypes which limit girls' aspirations present in high school history texts?

The answer is *yes*. Despite some promising attempts to supplement the scant amount of information devoted to women in American history texts, most works are marred by sins of omission and commission. Texts omit many women of importance, while simultaneously minimizing the legal, social, and cultural disabilities which they faced. The authors tend to depict women in a passive role and to stress that their lives are determined by economic and political trends. Women are rarely shown fighting for anything; their rights have been "given" to them.

Women are omitted both from topics discussed and by the topics chosen for discussion. For example, while only a few women could possibly be included in discussions of diplomacy or military tactics, the omission of dance, film, and theater in discussions of intellectual and cultural life assures the omission of many of America's most creative individuals.

Women's true position in society is shown in more subtle ways as well. While every text examined included some mention of the "high position" enjoyed by American women, this is little more than a disclaimer. Wherever possible, authors select male leaders and quote from male spokesmen. Even in discussions of reform movements, abolition, labor—areas in which there were articulate and able women leaders—only men are ever quoted. Even such topics as the life of frontier women are told through the reminiscences of men. When they are included, profiles and capsule biographies of women are often introduced in separate sections, apart from the body of the text. While this may simply be a consequence of attempts to update the text without resetting the book, it tends to reinforce the idea that women of note are, after all, optional and supplementary. Interestingly enough, the increase in the amount of space devoted to black history has not made room for the black woman. In these texts black history follows the white pattern, and minimizes or omits the achievements of the black woman. Like the white woman, she is either omitted outright, or is minimized by the topics selected.

These assertions are based upon the examination of over a dozen of the most popular United States history textbooks. Most were first copyrighted in the sixties, although several hold copyrights as far back as the early fifties, and one text is copyrighted back to 1937. Included are the following:

Textbooks

Baldwin, Leland D., and Warring, Mary. *History of Our Republic*. Princeton: D. Van Nostrand Co., Inc., 1965.

Bragdon, Henry W., and McCutchen, Samuel P. *History of a Free People*. New York: The Macmillan Company, 1965.

Brown, Richard C.; Lang, William C.; and Wheeler, Mary A. *The American Achievement*. New Jersey: Silver Burdett Company, 1966.

Canfield, Leon H., and Wilder, Howard B. *The Making of Modern America*. Boston: Houghton Mifflin Company, 1964.

Frost, James A.; Brown, Ralph Adams; Ellis, David M.; and Fink, William B. *A History of the United States*. Chicago: Follett Educational Corporation, 1968.

Graff, Henry E., and Krout, John A. *The Adventure of the American People*. Chicago: Rand McNally, 1959.

Hofstadter, Richard; Miller, William; and Aaron, Daniel. *The United States—The History of a Republic*. Englewood Cliffs: Prentice-Hall, Inc., 1957.

Kownslar, Allan O., and Frizzle, Donald B. *Discovering American History*. 2 Vols., New York: Holt, Rinehart and Winston, 1964.

Noyes, H. M., and Harlow, Ralph Volney. *Story of America*. New York: Holt, Rinehart & Winston, 1964.

Todd, Lewis Paul, and Curti, Merle. *Rise of the American Nation*. (1 Vol. and 2 Vol. editions) New York: Harcourt, Brace & World, 1966. 2 Vol. edition includes selected readings.

Williams, T. Harry, and Wolf, Hazel C. *Our American Nation*. Ohio: Charles E. Merrill Books, Inc., 1966.

Collections of documents

Hofstadter, Richard. *Great Issues in American History*. 2 Vols., New York, Vintage, 1958.

Meyers, Marvin; Kern, Alexander; and Carvelti, John G. *Sources of the American Republic*. 2 Vols., Chicago: Scott, Foresman & Company, 1961.

All entries indexed under "Women" were examined and various other sections and topics where information about women might reasonably be expected were examined. Particular attention was paid to women in colonial and revolutionary times, education, the women's rights movement and suffrage, reform movements, abolition, the Civil War, labor, frontier life, the World Wars, family patterns, the present position of women, and all sections on intellectual and cultural trends. The resulting picture is a depressing one.

On the basis of information in these commonly used high school texts, one might summarize the history and contributions of the American woman as follows: Women arrived in 1619 (a curious choice if meant to be their first acquaintance with the new world). They held the Seneca Falls Convention on Women's Rights in 1848. During the rest of the nineteenth century, they participated in reform movements, chiefly temperance, and were exploited in factories. In 1923 they were given the vote. They joined the armed forces for the first time during the Second World War and thereafter have enjoyed the good life in America. Add the names of the women who are invariably mentioned: Harriet Beecher Stowe, Jane Addams, Dorothea Dix, and Frances Perkins, with perhaps Susan B. Anthony, Elizabeth Cady Stanton, and, almost as frequently, Carrie Nation, and you have the basic "text." There are variations, of course, and most texts have adequate sections of information on one topic, perhaps two, but close examination of the information presented reveals a curious pattern of inclusions and neglects, a pattern which presents the stereotyped picture of the American woman—passive, incapable of sustained organization or work, satisfied with her role in society, and well supplied with material blessings.

1. Revolutionary and early federal periods

There is little information available in most texts concerning the colonial woman, or on her daughters and granddaughters in the revolutionary and early federal periods. The amount of information ranges from one textbook's two paragraphs on women's legal and social position to another textbook's total absence of anything even remotely pertaining to women during the early years of American history. Most texts fall in between. Some attention is commonly paid to the legal disabilities inherited from English law, although one textbook limits itself to "tobacco brides" and a note about William Penn's wife. Usually, little is said about the consequences of the social, political, and legal disabilities of the colonial woman, although the sharp limitations of the nineteenth century and the exploitation of the working-class women in the early industrial age were a direct result of woman's lack of political influence and her gradual exclusion from "professional" and skilled jobs. The texts are especially insensitive to the problem of religious and clerical prejudices against women. The long opposition of most American religious groups to women's rights is almost never suggested.

The perfunctory notice taken of women's education in the early period is discussed below. It should be noted, however, that few texts take any note of sectional differences in women's education or in other aspects of the position of women.

Although a number of texts mention the high regard in which the colonial woman was held, few are named and only one gives much information about the amount of work done outside the home by colonial women. Women mentioned are Pocahontas and Anne Hutchinson. Sections on Pocahontas tend to favor discussion of such questions as "Did Pocahontas really save John Smith?", rather than on any information about her life or the lives of other Indian women. Anne Hutchinson is almost always subordinated to Roger Williams. In one book, for example, she is described as another exile from Massachusetts. In more generous texts, she may receive as much as a short paragraph.

In general, the treatment of the early periods in American history stresses the fact that the America of the colonies, and early republic, was a "man's world." The authors wax eloquent over the "new breed of men." Any doubt that this might be merely linguistic convention is soon removed. The colonial farmer is credited with producing his own food, flax, and wool, in addition to preparing lumber for his buildings and leather goods for himself and his family. What the colonial farmer's wife (or the female colonial farmer) was doing all this time is not revealed, although plenty of information exists. Such passages also convey the unmistakable impression that all the early planters, farmers, and proprietors were male.

Education is important in consideration of the position of women because, as Julia Cherry Spruill points out in *Women's Life and Work in the Southern Colonies*, lack of opportunities for education finally ended women's employment in a variety of areas as technology and science made true "professions" of such occupations as medicine. In the early days, women, despite stringent legal restrictions, participated in almost all activities save government, the ministry of most religions, and law (although the number who sued and brought court cases is notable).

Usually, if any notice at all is taken of the education of girls and women, it is limited to a bland note that ". . . girls were not admitted to college" or "Most Americans thought it unnecessary or even dangerous to educate women." These statements are presented without explanation.

A mention of the existence of the dame schools completes the information on women and education.

After the colonial-revolutionary period, it is rare for more than one paragraph to be devoted to the entire development of education for women. Often, none of the early educators are mentioned by name. The facts that women literally fought their way into colleges and universities, that their admission followed agitation by determined would-be students, and that they were treated as subservient to male students even at such pioneering institutions as Oberlin, are always absent. The simple statement that they were admitted suffices.

2. Sections on rights and reforms

The most information about women appears in two sections, those on women's rights and suffrage and general sections on reform. Yet a full page on suffrage and women's rights is a rarity and most texts give the whole movement approximately three paragraphs. The better texts include something on the legal disabilities which persisted into the nineteenth century. These sections are sometimes good, but always brief. Most of them end their consideration of the legal position of women with the granting of suffrage, and there is no discussion of the implications of the recent Civil Rights legislation which removed some of the inequities in employment, nor is there more than a hint that inequities remained even after the Nineteenth Amendment was passed.

Leaders most commonly noted are Susan B. Anthony, Elizabeth Cady Stanton, and Lucretia Mott. Aside from passage of the Nineteenth Amendment, the only event noted is the Seneca Falls Convention of 1848. Even less space is devoted to the later suffrage movement. Anna Howard Shaw is seldom mentioned and even Carrie Chapman Catt is not assured of a place. The western ladies like Abigail Duniway are usually absent as are the more radical and militant suffragettes, the members of the Woman's Party. Alice Paul, leader of the militants, is apparently anathema.

This is perhaps not too surprising, as the tendency in most texts is to concentrate on the handicaps women faced and to minimize their efforts in their own behalf. One textbook, which dutifully lists Seneca Falls, Stanton, Mott, Wright, Anthony, Stone, and Bloomer, tells very little about what they did, noting "the demand for the right to vote made little headway, but the states gradually began to grant them more legal rights." The text mentions that by 1900 most discriminatory legislation was off the books and describes the post-Civil War work of the movement in these terms: "the women's rights movement continued under the leadership of the same group as before the war and met with considerable success." Later two lines on suffrage and a picture of a group of suffragettes complete the story. Lest this be considered the most glaring example of neglect, another textbook devotes two lines, one in each volume, to suffrage, mentioning in volume one that women were denied the right to vote and returning to the topic in volume two with one line on the Nineteenth Amendment in the middle of a synopsis of the twenties. This book actually includes more information on the lengths of women's skirts than on all the agitation for civil and political rights for women.

Other texts show a similar lack of enthusiasm for the hundred years of work that went into the Nineteenth Amendment. One places woman suffrage fifth in a section on the effects of the progressive movement. Catt, Anthony, and Stanton are mentioned in a line or two, while whole columns of text are devoted to Henry Demarest Lloyd and Henry George.

At times there appears to be a very curious sense of priorities at work even in textbooks which give commendable amounts of information. One book uses up a whole column on the Gibson Girl, describing her as:

> . . . completely feminine, and it was clear that she could not, or would not, defeat her male companion at golf or tennis. In the event of a motoring emergency, she would quickly call upon his superior knowledge . . .

The passage goes on to point out that this "transitional figure" was politically uninformed and devoted to her traditional role. One would almost prefer to learn a little more about the lives of those other "transitional figures," the feminists, yet there is almost no mention of their lives, their work, or their writings.

Only one text quotes any of the women's rights workers. It includes a short paragraph from the declaration of the Seneca Falls Convention. The absence in other texts of quotes and of documentary material is all the more striking, since a number of the leaders were known as fine orators and propagandists. Books of source materials, and inquiry method texts, are no exception; none of those examined considers woman suffrage worthy of a single document. One book is exceptional in including one selection, by Margaret Fuller, on the topic of women's rights.

The reformers and abolitionists are slightly more fortunate than the feminists. Three women are almost certain of appearing in history texts, Harriet Beecher Stowe, Jane Addams, and Dorothea Dix. Addams and Stowe are among the few women quoted in other source books or regular texts and, along with the muckraking journalist Ida Tarbell, they are the only women whose writings are regularly excerpted. Addams and Dix are usually given at least one complete paragraph, perhaps more. These are sometimes admirably informative as in certain sections on Dix. Other reformers, including the women abolitionists, both white and black, are less fortunate. The pioneering Grimké sisters may rate a line or two, but just as often their only recognition comes because Angelina eventually became Mrs. Theodore Weld. None of the female abolitionists, despite their contemporary reputations as speakers, is ever quoted. Interest in black history has not made room for more than the briefest mention of Harriet Tubman, whose Civil War services are deleted. Sojourner Truth and the other black lecturers, educators, and abolitionists are completely absent. The texts make little comment about the nineteenth century's intense disapproval of women who spoke in public, or of the churches' opposition (excepting always the Quakers, from whose faith many of the early abolitionists came).

Women journalists are given even less notice than the early lecturers. The women who ran or contributed to newspapers, periodicals, or specialized journals and papers for abolition, women's rights, or general reform are rarely included.

The reform sections of these high school texts frequently show the same kind of capriciousness that in sections on the twenties assigns more space to the flapper than to the suffragette. In discussions on reform movements, they give more prominence to Carrie Nation than to other more serious, not to say more stable, reformers. The treatment of temperance is further marred by a failure to put women's espousal of temperance in perspective. Little stress is placed on the consequences for the family of an alcoholic in the days when divorce was rare, when custody of children went to their father, and when working women were despised. Nor is there much mention of the seriousness of the problem of alcoholism, particularly in the post-Civil War period.

3. Neglected areas

The most glaring omission, considering its impact on women and on society, is the absence of a single word on the development of birth control and the story of the fight for its acceptance by Margaret Sanger and a group of courageous physicians. The authors' almost Victorian delicacy in the face of the matter probably stems from the fact that birth control is still controversial. Yet fear of controversy does not seem a satisfactory excuse. The population explosion, poverty, illegitimacy—all are major problems today. Birth control is inextricably tied up with them as well as with disease, abortion, child abuse, and family problems of every kind. Considering the revolution in the lives of women which safe methods of contraception have caused, and the social, cultural, and political implications of that revolution, it appears that one important fact of the reform movement is being neglected.

A second, largely neglected area is the whole question of woman's work and her part in the early labor movement. Although the American woman and her children were the 'mainstays of many of the early industries, for a variety of social and political reasons she received low wages and status and was virtually cut off from any hopes of advancement. The educational limitations that gradually forced her out of a number of occupations which she had held in preindustrial days combined with prejudice to keep her in the lowest paid work. Whether single, married, or widowed, whether she worked for "pin money" or to support six children, she received about half as much as a man doing the same or comparable work.

Obviously under these conditions, women had exceptional difficulties in organizing. Among them were the dual burden of household responsibilities and work, their lack of funds, and in some cases their lack of control over their own earnings, and the opposition of male workers and of most of the unions.

Despite these special circumstances, very little attention is paid to the plight of the woman worker or of her admittedly unstable labor organizations. Information on the early labor leaders is especially scanty; one textbook is unique with its biographical information on Rose Schneiderman. On the whole, the labor story is limited to the introduction of women workers into the textile mills in the 1840s. As a caption in one book so concisely puts it, "Women and children, more manageable, replaced men at the machines." Others note the extremely low pay of women and children, one text calling women "among the most exploited workers in America." Anything like a complete discussion of the factors which led to these conditions, or even a clear picture of what it meant to be "among the most exploited," is not found in the texts.

Several things about women and labor are included. Lowell mills receive a short, usually complimentary, description. The fact that the Knights of Labor admitted women is presented. There then follows a hiatus until minimum wage and maximum hour standards for women workers are discussed. The modern implications of this "protective legislation" is an area seldom explored.

Despite the fact that abundant source material exists, the sections on labor follow the familiar pattern: little space is devoted to women workers, few women are mentioned by name, and fewer still are quoted.

Most texts content themselves with no more than three entries of a few lines each.

The absence of information on the lives of women on the frontier farms and settlements is less surprising. In the treatments of pioneer settlements from the colonial era on, most texts declare the frontier "a man's world." This is emphasized by the importance the authors place on descriptions and histories of such masculine tools as the Pennsylvania rifle and the ax, the six-shooter, and the prairie-breaker plow. One textbook is perhaps the most enthralled with these instruments, devoting five pages to the story of the six-shooter. Scarcely five lines are spent on the life of the frontier woman in this text, and most other works are also reticent about the pioneer woman.

Only "man's work" on the frontier is really considered worthy of description. This is particularly puzzling, since there was little distinction in employment, and marriage was a partnership with lots of hard work done by each of the parents. On pioneer farms, typical "woman's work" included, in addition to all the housework, the care of poultry; the dairy— including milking, feeding, tending to the cows, and making butter and cheese; the care of any other barnyard animals; the "kitchen" or vegetable garden; and such chores as sewing, mending, making candles and soap, feeding the hired hands, and working in the fields if necessary.

Considering these chores, it is hard to see why discussions of pioneer farming content themselves with descriptions of the farmer's struggles to plow, plant, and harvest. The treatments of the frontier period also omit mention of the women who homesteaded and claimed property without the help of a male partner. According to Robert W. Smuts in *Women and Work in America*, there were thousands of such women. Information about the women on the frontier tends either to short descriptions of the miseries of life on the great plains frequently quoted from Hamlin Garland or to unspecific encomiums on the virtues of the pioneer women. One text states: ". . . [the women] turned the wilderness into homesteads, planted flowers and put curtains in the windows. It was usually the mothers and school teachers who transmitted to the next generation the heritage of the past."

The relationship between women's exertions on the frontier and their enlarged civil and political liberties in the Western states and territories is often noticed. Their agitation for these increased privileges is generally unmentioned.

With little said about women's life in general, it is not surprising that few are mentioned by name. Sacajawea, the Indian guide and interpreter of the Lewis and Clark expedition, shares with Dix, Stowe, and Addams, one of the few solid positions in United States history texts.

Occasionally the early missionaries to Oregon territory, like Nerissa Whitman and Eliza Spaulding, are included, and one book even adds a "profile" of Nerissa Whitman. Most, however, only mention the male missionaries, or include the fact that they arrived with their wives.

4. Civil War period

Like the frontier experience, the Civil War forced women from all social strata into new tasks and occupations. In *Bonnet Brigades,* a volume in the *Impact of the Civil War Series,* Mary Elizabeth Massey quotes Clara Barton's remark that the war advanced the position of women by some 50 years. Great numbers of women dislocated by the war were forced into paid employment. The war saw the entry of women into government service, into nursing, and into the multitude of organizations designed to raise money and supplies for the armies, to make clothing, blankets, and bandages. The result of this activity was not only to force individual women outside of their accustomed roles, but to provide the experience in organization which was to prove valuable for later suffrage and reform movements. The war helped a number of women escape from the ideas of gentility which were robbing women in the East of much of their traditional social freedom, and brought women of all classes into the "man's world." In addition to the few women who served as soldiers, women appeared in the camps as nurses, cooks, laundresses, adventurers; they served in the field as spies, scouts, saboteurs, and guides; they worked in the capitals as the "government girls"—the first female clerks, bookkeepers, and secretaries. Women opened hospitals, set up canteens, and developed the first primitive forms of what we know as USO clubs and services. After the war, they served as pension claims agents, worked to rehabilitate soldiers, taught in the freedman's schools, entered refugee work, or tried to find missing soldiers and soldiers' graves.

Of all these activities, women's entry into nursing is the only one regularly noticed in the texts. The impact of the war upon women, and upon the family structure, is barely mentioned, although a few texts include a paragraph or two on the hardships which women faced during the conflict. The only women mentioned by name are Clara Barton and Dorothea Dix, who held the position of superintendent of women nurses. Other women, like Mary Bickerdyke, who was known both for her efforts during the war and for her work for needy veterans afterwards, are omitted. No other women, black or white, are named, nor is there any information on the variety of jobs they held. The special problems of black women in the postwar period rarely get more than a line, and the efforts by black women to set up schools and self-help agencies are omitted.

5. *The Two World Wars*

While women in the Civil War era receive little attention, even less is given to them during the two World Wars. In both cases, their wartime service is glowingly praised, but few details are presented. At least half of the texts examined make no note at all of women's wartime activities during the First World War; in a number of others, the story of women's entry into what were formerly labeled "men's jobs" is dealt with in a captioned picture.

As for social changes between the wars, a number of texts devote several paragraphs to the "liberation of women" and to their changing status. In one textbook there are four paragraphs devoted to these liberated ladies—the only two mentioned being Irene Castle and Alice Roosevelt. Like other texts, this one devotes a considerable amount of space to fashions and flappers and to the social alarm which they occasioned.

There is little about the later stages of the rights movement, although two textbooks note the relationship between women's wartime service and the increasing willingness of the nation to grant rights and privileges to women. One limits itself to three sentences, noting women's work "in factories and fields" and their efforts behind the lines overseas. "Women's reward for war service was the Nineteenth Amendment which granted them the franchise on the eve of the 1920 election." Readers might wish for greater elaboration.

The period from the Depression to the present day receives the same laconic treatment in the texts. The one woman sure of notice in this period is Frances Perkins, Roosevelt's Secretary of Labor. She receives at least a line in most texts and some devote special sections to her. Frances Perkins appears to be the "showcase" woman, for no other American woman is regularly mentioned—this includes Eleanor Roosevelt, who is omitted from a surprising number of texts and who is mentioned only as Roosevelt's wife in quite a few more.

The World War II era marked the beginning of the Women's Military Corps. This fact is invariably mentioned, usually with a captioned picture as an accompaniment. As in World War I, women entered factories, munitions plants, and "men's jobs" in great numbers. This development rarely gets more than a paragraph and the differences between the experience in World War I and the longer exposure to new jobs in World War II are seldom elucidated. The impact of the war on women and specific information about the variety of jobs they held is sketchy or nonexistent.

Information on women in the postwar era and in the present day is hardly more abundant. The history texts definitely give the impression that the passage of the Nineteenth Amendment solved all the problems created by the traditional social, legal, and political position of women. Contemporary information on discrimination is conspicuously absent. The texts are silent on current legal challenges to such practices as discriminatory hiring and promotion and companies' failures to comply with equal pay legislation. They do not take account of agitation to change laws and customs which weigh more heavily on women than on men. There is nothing about recent changes in jury selection, hitherto biased against women jurors, or reform of discriminatory practices in criminal sentences; there is no information on the complex problems of equitable divorce and guardianship, nor on the tangled problem of separate domicile for married women.

A number of texts do, however, provide good information on changes in the structure of the family, or provide helpful information on general social and political changes. The impression, insofar as these sections deal directly with American women, is a rosy picture of the affluence and opportunities enjoyed by women. Many books note the increasing numbers of women employed in the learned professions, but never the percentage decline in their numbers. While women undoubtedly enjoy more rights, opportunities, and freedoms than in many previous eras, the texts give an excessively complacent picture of a complex and rapidly changing set of social conditions.

6. Intellectual and cultural achievements

A final glimpse of the position of the American woman may be gained from sections dealing with intellectual and cultural trends and achievements. Since most texts extol the role of women in preserving culture and in supporting the arts, one might expect women to be well represented in discussions of the arts in America. A number of factors, however, operate against the inclusion of creative women. The first, and one which deprives many creative men of notice as well, is the extreme superficiality of most of these discussions. Intellectual and cultural life in America is limited to the mention of a few novelists and poets, with an occasional musician or playwright. Only a few individuals in each category are ever mentioned, and the preference for male examples and spokesmen, noticeable in all other topics, is evident here as well. In individual texts, this leads to such glaring omissions as Emily Dickinson and Margaret Fuller. To be fair, the text guilty of ignoring Miss Dickinson appears to feel that John Greenleaf Whittier was one of our greatest poets, yet ignorance of American poetry is hardly an acceptable excuse.

Dickinson and Fuller, however, are among the small, fortunate circle including Harriet Beecher Stowe, Willa Cather, and Margaret Mitchell who are usually named. The principles governing their selection and decreeing the omission of other writers like Edith Wharton, Ellen Glasgow, Eudora Welty, and Pearl Buck are never explained. Apparently their presence or absence is determined by the same caprice which decrees Edna St. Vincent Millay the only modern female poet.

Only a handful of texts discuss painters and sculptors, but of those that do make some effort to include the visual arts, only one reproduces a painting by Mary Cassatt. Georgia O'Keeffe is also represented in this text. Other texts, even when including Cassatt's fellow expatriates, Sargent and Whistler, omit her—an exclusion inexplicable on grounds of quality, popularity, or representation in American collections. Contemporary art is totally ignored and everything after the Ashcan School is left in limbo. This omits many painters of quality and influence, including the many women who have entered the arts in the twentieth century.

More serious than the sketchy treatment given to the arts covered by the texts is the omission of arts in which women were dominant or in which they played a major part. Dance is never given as much as a line. This leaves out the American ballerinas, and, even more important, it neglects the development of modern dance—a development due to the talents of a handful of American women like Isadora Duncan, Martha Graham, and Ruth St. Denis.

There is a similar neglect of both stage and screen acting. If film or drama are to be mentioned at all, directors and writers will be noted. It hardly seems necessary to point out that acting is an area in which women have excelled.

Music sees a similar division with similar results. Composers and instrumentalists, chiefly men, are mentioned. Singers, men and women, are omitted. This particularly affects black women. Only one textbook mentions Marian Anderson and Leontyne Price. White classical singers are ignored as are the black women jazz singers.

If intellectual and cultural developments are limited to areas in which men were the dominant creative figures, it is obvious that American women will not receive credit for their contributions. It also seems clear that such superficial accounts of the arts are of questionable value.

Summing Up

Although it is tempting to imagine some historical autocrat sternly decreeing who's in and who's out—giving space to Harriet Beecher Stowe but not to Marianne Moore; to Dorothea Dix but not Mary Bickerdyke; to Pocahontas but not Margaret Brent; to Susan B. Anthony but not

Abigail Duniway—the omission of many significant women is probably not a sign of intentional bias. The treatment of women simply reflects the attitudes and prejudices of society. Male activities in our society are considered the more important; therefore male activities are given primacy in the texts. There is a definite image of women in our society, and women in history who conform to this image are more apt to be included. History reflects societal attitudes in all topics, hence the omission of potentially controversial persons like Margaret Sanger or that militant pioneer in civil disobedience, Alice Paul. Sensitivity to social pressure probably accounts for the very gentle notes about religious disapproval of women's full participation in community life and for omission of contemporary controversies, especially on sexual matters, which would offend religious sensibilities.

Another factor which affects the picture of women presented in these texts is the linguistic habit of using the male pronouns to refer both to men and to men and women. While this may seem a trivial matter it frequently leads to misunderstanding. Discussing the early colonists, for example, solely in terms of "he" and "his" leads to the implication that all early proprietors, settlers, planters, and farmers were men. Given the cultural orientation of our society, students will assume activities were only carried on by men unless there is specific mention of women.

To these observations, authors of high school texts might reasonably respond that their space is limited, that they seek out only the most significant material and the most influential events and individuals; that if dance is omitted, it is because more people read novels, and if such topics as the role of female missionaries or colonial politicians are neglected, it is for lack of space. One is less inclined to accept this view when one notices some of the odd things which authors do manage to include. One feels like asking, "How important was Shays's Rebellion?". Should the Ku Klux Klan receive reams of documentary material and woman suffrage none? Do we want to read five pages on the six-shooter? Is two columns too much to give to Empress Carlotta of Mexico, who lived most of her life in insanity and obscurity? Is the aerialist who walked a tightrope across Niagara Falls a figure of even minor importance in American history? Is Henry Demarest Lloyd more important than Carrie Chapman Catt? Are the lengths of skirts significant enough to dwarf other information about women?

There are other questions as well: How accurate is the history text's view of women and what images of women does it present? The texts examined do very little more than reinforce the familiar stereotypes.

It should be clear, however, that changes in the construction of high-school-level history texts must go beyond the insertion of the names of prominent women and even beyond the "profiles" and "special sections" employed by the more liberal texts. Commendable and informative as these may be, they are only the beginning. Real change in the way history is presented will only come after those responsible for writing it, and for interpreting the finished product to students, develop an awareness of the bias against women in our culture, a bias so smooth, seamless and pervasive, that it is hard to even begin to take hold of it and bring it into clear view. Until this awareness is developed, until the unquestioned dominance of male activities and the importance of male spokesmen and examples are realized, texts will continue to treat men's activities and goals as history, women's as "supplementary material."

One sees this quite clearly in the existence of sections dealing with women's rights, women's problems, and women's position, as if women's rights, problems, and position were not simply one half of the rights, problems, and position of humanity as a whole, and as if changes in women's position and work and attitudes were not complemented by changes in the position, work, and attitudes of men. A sense of the way the lives and duties and achievements of people of both sexes are intermeshed is needed in expositions of life in all periods of American history.

To do this it is clear that material hitherto omitted or minimized must be given more consideration. For example, information about mortality rates, family size, and economic conditions must be included, along with more information on the impact of technological change, on the mass media, and on moral and religious ideas. More information about how ordinary people lived and what they actually did must be included as well as information drawn from the ideas and theories of the educated classes.

This is not to deny that certain developments have had far more effect on women than on men, or that women's experience might be different from men's: for example, the early struggles to form unions. Nor is it to deny that more information on women leaders is needed and more space for their particular problems and achievements. More information on all aspects of women's life, work, and position—legal, social, religious, and political—is needed, but more information alone, no matter how necessary, will not really change histories. What is needed, besides more information, is a new attitude: one which breaks away from the bias of traditional views of women and their "place" and attempts to treat both women and men as partners in their society; one which does not automatically value activities by the sex performing them; and one which does not relate history from the viewpoint of only half of the human family.

GUIDELINES FOR EQUAL TREATMENT OF THE SEXES IN SOCIAL STUDIES TEXTBOOKS

The overwhelming male orientation of most social studies textbooks misrepresents females to young readers and gives them a biased view of over 50 percent of all human beings. It is damaging to the self-image of girls, who learn to underrate themselves and other members of their sex, and burdens young people of both sexes with unrealistic or stereotyped attitudes and expectations concerning themselves and others.

School textbook writers, editors, and publishers do not consciously seek to produce educational literature which is derogatory to females. They have, however, been socialized and educated in the traditions of a male-oriented social structure, language, and literature; and they tend to continue to write and think in those archaic molds. The time has come for those who write and publish textbooks for young people to take a fresh look at the past and present, and at their own assumptions regarding the nature and role of the female human being.

These *Guidelines* have been prepared to assist writers and others who seek to provide equal treatment of the sexes in textbooks. Specific problem areas—each of them facets of the total configuration of male orientation—are identified, and suggestions are given for ways in which writers may provide readers with a balanced view of members of both sexes as individuals. Our discussion focuses primarily on United States history textbooks, but the principles involved are applicable to educational and other literature in a wide range of fields.

Note: Copyright © 1973 by Elizabeth Burr, Susan Dunn, and Norma Farquhar.

I. Male-Oriented Substantive Content

Omissions of females from history

Textbook accounts of historical events frequently omit reference to women's participation in those events, or to the impact of those events upon women. Discussions of such legal milestones as the Magna Carta, the Declaration of Independence, and Homestead Act, and the Fourteenth and Fifteenth Amendments to the Constitution of the United States often fail to make clear their degree of application or lack of application to females. For example, writers generally fail to discuss the problem of whether such phrases as "all men are created equal" and "governments are instituted among Men" were intended to apply to females (or to American Indians or other people of non-European descent). In discussing freed slaves during the post-Civil War period, textbooks may relate that the Fourteenth Amendment made "them" citizens and that the Fifteenth Amendment gave "them" the right to vote, without making it clear that although black females as well as black males became citizens they did *not* gain the right to vote at that time. Textbooks may tell students that the "colonists" of Virginia were the first to "govern themselves," without explaining that female colonists, as well as certain categories of males, were in fact denied that privilege.

Unless textbooks make it clear that from the very beginning of the historical experience which led to the establishment of the United States women were systematically subjected to legal discrimination, students will form a false impression of past American society and will be unprepared to understand subsequent struggles of females to attain equality.

Discussions of economic life in history and geography textbooks characteristically fail to refer to the significant part which women have played—both individually and collectively—in the production of goods and services. "Early American crafts" or "skills that settlers in the New World brought with them from the Old World" are sometimes described so as to include only crafts and skills ordinarily practiced by males; while the crafts and skills typical of females—including the making of such crucial items as candles, soap, cloth, clothing, quilts, and cheese—are often discussed under the heading of "family life" or "social life" if they are considered at all. Statements such as "New Englanders were men of the sea,"[1] and "most men were farmers or merchants, or skilled in such crafts as carpentry or bricklaying," unaccompanied by any discussion of women's participation in economic activities, suggest to young readers (1) that women were neither farmers nor merchants, and (2) that women's economic functions were not vital to the economy. Both of these ideas are fundamentally erroneous.

Textbook writers who wish to provide fair treatment of the sexes must recognize the impact of females in all areas of social, economic, and cultural development, as well as the impact upon females of historical events, of legislation, and of all manner of social phenomena.

Glorification of males

In textbooks one typically finds males referred to as *bold, adventurous, imaginative,* and *foresighted:* "Bold men discovered the New World"; "Adventurous men came to settle in the new lands," etc. Were all the men who sailed with Columbus bold? Were all of the male immigrants adventurous? Were there not some men who were desperate, hesitant, or even unwilling?

Ideas and opinions are also commonly attributed to males: "Foresighted *men* saw the need for . . ."; "*Men* from the North regarded slavery as . . ."; "Some *men* believed that ships could reach the East by sailing west."

Textbook writers should reassess their present estimation of males as characteristically bold, adventurous, imaginative, foresighted, and endowed with the only ideas worth discussing. Unless the authors are in a position to document the idea that women did not have opinions on the matters being discussed, they should avoid giving that impression.

Women's struggles for equal rights

The relegation of women to a separate and lesser status is a theme that runs throughout history. No United States social studies textbook can provide equal treatment of the sexes without making that fact clear, and without including an extensive discussion of women's struggles to obtain equal political, educational, legal, employment, and human rights. The women's movement is comparable in scope and importance to the antislavery movement or the labor movement. To dispose of the problem of discrimination against 50 percent of the population and the long decades of struggle against it in a few short lines or paragraphs, and as a narrow and finite event of America's past, is equivalent to writing the history of medieval Europe with but a passing mention of the rise and decline of the institution of serfdom.

Role assigning

Textbooks commonly describe some work as *"men's work"* and other work as "women's work." While it is true that in the past certain work has tended to be distributed along sex lines, textbooks typically fail to discuss the degree to which sex work-roles have changed and blurred. Men have worked as secretary-typists; women have labored in mines and cotton fields; men have nursed sick people and reared children; women have borne arms. Authors should not leave readers with the impression that certain work is the exclusive province of women and other work the proper domain of males.

Moral disapproval of women who work outside of the home

The view that "women's place is in the home" is commonly reflected in textbooks. Frequent reference is made to women who "had to work" or who went to work "in order to help out" with family finances. Such phraseology suggests on one hand that child care and housekeeping are not "work" and on the other that when a female steps outside of the home to earn money she is engaging in a questionable activity which is not entirely voluntary and which is justifiable only on the basis of pressing economic need. The right of females to be gainfully employed outside of the home should not be questioned, however indirectly. (A widower, even though he be wealthy and need not work, is never expected to stay home and care for his children.)

Fragile women and "man-sized" jobs

Over the past decade writers have become sensitized to the semantics of race prejudice. No contemporary textbook would state that "A black man, George Washington Carver was nevertheless a botanist of genius." Textbook writers should similarly understand the inherent sex bias in a sentence such as, "Beautiful, soft-spoken, and well-bred, she was nevertheless able to manage a large plantation successfully." Writers should eliminate the "fragile women" element from their writing, and learn to suppress their tone of amazement when describing the accomplishments of attractive females. Above all, they should avoid giving the impression that there is normally an inverse relationship between female pulchritude and female competence.

Women as hausfraus

School textbook writers never forget that Anne Hutchinson was the mother of over a dozen children, but they fail to tell us that she was skilled in the preparation and use of pharmaceutical supplies, and that it was she and not her husband who reached the decision that the family should leave England and settle in the Massachusetts Bay Colony.

Similarly, one textbook describes Abigail Adams as hanging up the laundry in an unfinished room of the White House, without mentioning the fact that she was an exceptionally capable and influential human being. Such treatment of individual women in school textbooks emphasizes their most stereotyped aspects and neglects their unique and individual qualities.

Descriptions of "women's work", as largely consisting of household chores ignores the fact that throughout United States history women have (1) managed their own businesses, (2) assumed responsibility in church, school, and civic affairs, (3) farmed, (4) educated themselves when denied access to schools of higher learning, (5) written works of prose, poetry, and nonfiction, and (6) assumed the burden of supporting their families.

Textbook writers who wish to provide equal treatment of the sexes should deal with individual women as individuals and with women collectively in a manner which accurately conveys their occupations and concerns. To fail to make it clear that many women of the past were not *hausfraus* pure and simple is to distort the facts.

Exclusion of illustrations of women

It is not uncommon for textbooks to contain ten or more times as many illustrations of males as of females. Illustrations are of substantial influence in forming impressions in the minds of young readers. The selection of illustrations should be based upon a careful evaluation of the following criteria: (1) the accuracy of the explicit information conveyed; (2) the nature of the illustrations' implicit, subliminal messages; (3) the importance of avoiding stereotyped portrayals of all kinds; and (4) the degree of accuracy with which the illustrations, as a whole, represent the frequency and distribution of males and females in the populations being discussed by the textbook.

"Girl watching" in textbooks

A fifth-grade textbook relates that upon seeing women sent by the King of France to the American colonies to become "wives" for the settlers, one male settler commented that "some were big, some little; some were fat, some were lean," but that all of these women were nevertheless snapped up right away.[2] Nowhere in this textbook is any group of males described in terms of their physical charms or lack of them. Such emphasis on females' physical appearance and neglect of their other qualities should be avoided.

II. The Language of Inequality

A language is not merely a means of communication; it is also an expression of shared assumptions. Language transmits implicit values and behavioral models to all those people who use it. When basic assumptions change, the idioms which express them become obsolete. The pages that follow suggest certain changes in language designed to eliminate phraseology that reflects outdated assumptions concerning females.

Subsuming terminology

For purposes of this paper, subsuming terms are masculine terms which are commonly believed to include or refer to females as well as males but which, in fact, operate to exclude females.

When told that "*men* by the thousands headed west," or that "The average citizen of the United States is proud of *his* heritage," the young reader is unable to form a mental image which includes females. It is of no avail for a parent or teacher to explain that *men* "really means" *both men and women,* or that *he* "really means" *both he and she.* Even an adult is unlikely to picture a group of amicable females when reading about "men of good will."

Similarly, when informed that *man*-made improvements have raised America's standard of living, or that a task required a certain amount of *man*power, a child cannot be expected to develop the concept that females as well as males have participated in the developmental process.

Educational literature which discusses human origins provides many striking examples of the way in which subsuming terminology leads to conceptual distortion. In such literature illustrations of reconstructed skeletons and skulls are generally *identified as being male* and labeled Peking *Man,* Neanderthal *Man,* Java *Man,* Cro-Magnon *Man,* and so on. Although common sense tells us that many prehistoric individuals must have been female, females are virtually never represented as *examples* of a human type. Such unscholarly treatment cannot fail to suggest to young readers that females are a substandard or deviant form of human being— a rib, as it were, taken from "*Man.*"

In the same way, constant reference to "*man's*" inventions, "*man's*" discoveries, and "*man*-made" implements has apparently led illustrators to portray those who are supposed to have discovered the use of fire, those who are supposed to have manufactured stone tools and many other objects, those who built prehistoric structures, and those who are supposed first to have noticed constellations, comets, etc., in the night sky, as *males.* There is no possible way of knowing the sex of the individual who made any given prehistoric object or discovery. Nor is it possible to know the sex of individuals who stenciled outlines of their hands on cave walls, created symbolic or artistic objects and paintings, or constructed shelters. Therefore textbooks should not suggest that only males functioned in the above-described ways.

Sexist ambiguity

Use of the words *man* (without a definite article) and *men* to represent human beings in general or adults in general is also objectionable on the ground that such usage is ambiguous. Since both *man* and *men* are also frequently used to denote males only, it often becomes a matter of making an educated guess as to whether the author means males and females both, or males only. It is moreover possible that such terms are employed by authors to conceal their lack of information concerning females.

Authors and editors alike are so accustomed to the use of subsuming terminology that the greatest care must be taken to ensure its elimination. Subsuming masculine terms must be replaced by clearly inclusive or neutral words such as *citizens, inhabitants, women and men, human beings, people, individuals,* and so on. Phrases such as *manpower* and *man-made* may be replaced by such expressions as *human energy, made by men and women,* or *manufactured;* the words *forefathers* and *fathers* (in the sense of "forefathers") should be replaced by *precursors* or *ancestors;* the word *brotherhood* should be replaced by *amity, unity, community, common humanity,* or some other nonsex-related term; and the indeterminate use of *he* and related pronouns should be discontinued in favor of *he or she,* and the like.[3]

The hypothetical person as male

A frequently occurring case of male orientation in textbooks is the use of hypothetical males as examples:

"If a *man* wanted to travel from South Carolina to Massachusetts in 1750. . . ." "The *man* of tomorrow may live in a totally prefabricated house." "A discontented *man* could move west." In textbooks females seldom participate in hypothetical financial transactions. Thus we find explanations such as: "If a *man* sold a piece of land *he* had to put a two-shilling stamp on the deed." "When a *man* went to the bank to borrow money. . . ." "A *man's* taxes depended upon. . . ."

Unless it has been verified that females never engaged in the mentioned activities, the word *man* should be replaced by the word one or person, or hypothetical persons be portrayed as female in a fair number of instances. Students should not be given the false impression that only males traveled, became discontented, needed to borrow money, paid taxes, etc.

In a similar vein, textbooks habitually picture the "average" and the "typical" person as male: "The average American does not *himself* manufacture most of the things *his* family needs." "The American was a new kind of *man*." Writers should keep in mind the fact that "the average *man*" is not the average "*person*," and that any discussion of national, regional, racial, or cultural traits is one-sided if it refers to males only.

The society as male

Textbook writers should refrain from using phrases that imply that males are the only significant people in the social milieu: "Compared to other *men*, Jefferson was. . . ."; "More than any other *man*, he. . . ." Such phrases should be revised to read: "Compared to *his contemporaries*, Jefferson was. . . ."; "More than any other *person*, he. . . ." The original male-oriented phraseology reflects the attitude that in discussions of comparative excellence women are judged a priori as unqualified for consideration.

Male-oriented quoted material [4]

(1) "*Men* since the beginning of time have sought peace" (General Douglas MacArthur); (2) "The American is a new *man*, who acts upon new principles; *he* must therefore entertain new ideas, and form new opinions" (J. Hector St. John de Crèvecoeur); (3) "These are the times that try *men's* souls" (Thomas Paine); (4) "The New Englander, whether *boy* or *man*, in a long struggle with a stingy or hostile universe, had learned also to love the pleasure of hating; *his* joys were few" (Henry Adams).

The above and similar quotations which are found in textbooks reflect the opinion that females are of no consequence. Such quotations are permissible in textbooks only as examples of contemporary prejudiced attitudes toward females.

Some quotations of documentary material, however, will inevitably be regarded as necessary in spite of the fact that they are couched in male-oriented language. A case in point is the Gettysburg address:

> Fourscore and seven years ago our *fathers* brought forth on this continent a new nation, conceived in liberty, and dedicated to the proposition that all *men* are created equal. . . . and that govern-

ment of *the people,* by *the people,* for *the people,* shall not perish from the earth.

If this or other similarly male-oriented documents are quoted, the textbook must point out the male orientation of the language. Any textbook quoting the Gettysburg address should, for instance, indicate that when President Lincoln spoke of *people* he had in mind *males,* because at the time of his famous speech females were not permitted to vote and were denied many other legal rights enjoyed by males.

Nobody knows her name

Reflecting a time when females were in fact the possessions, under law, first of their fathers and then of their husbands, who were empowered by law to beat them, sell them, or otherwise dispose of them arbitrarily, females are still commonly identified in the obsolete terms of those who "own" them.

In textbooks, females are typically referred to merely as *wives* (Mrs.), *daughters* (Miss), or *mothers of* males who are clearly identified by name and occupation. Such possessive terms of reference deliver the message that in and of themselves females are of no particular interest or importance, and reflect the assumption that marital status is *the* crucial and significant fact of life for women.

Compare, for example, the following two sentences:

1. George Ferris married the daughter of the wealthy Boston banker, Edward Howell.

2. Alice Howell, of Boston, heir to a banking fortune, married George Ferris.

The second sentence permits recognition of Alice as a person in her own right; the first, in which she is *nameless,* suggests that whatever shadowy identity she may have possessed depended upon the identity first of her father and then of her husband. Similarly, phrases such as "the farmer's wife" clearly convey the idea that the female was merely a possession of a male farmer and was not herself a farmer, when in fact women who were married to men who farmed small parcels of land were themselves farmers in every sense of the word.

Textbook writers who wish to give equal linguistic treatment to the sexes should cite females by their complete names and occupations whenever possible. They should eliminate the terms "Miss" and "Mrs." from their writing vocabularies. They should refer to "men and women on farms" or "farming men and women," rather than to "farmers and their wives." Similarly, all references to "men and their wives" should be revised to "men and women" or "husbands and wives."

Sexist generic terminology

Textbooks frequently use generic terms such as those (italicized) in the following sentences: "The *peasants* were oppressed." "The *pioneers* suffered many hardships." "*Beggars* slept in doorways."

In the above examples it is not clear whether the italicized generic terms refer to both men and women or to men exclusively. We know that the terms do *not* refer to women exclusively, because when writers intend to discuss women only, they invariably use language such as the following: "*Peasant women* were oppressed." "*Pioneer women* suffered many hardships." "*Beggar women* slept in doorways." Such usage as the following is rarely encountered: "Peasant *men* were oppressed." "Pioneer *men* suffered many hardships." "Beggar *men* slept in doorways."

From all of the above it must be concluded that authors tend to blur *men* with *people in general*; i.e., they are willing to let *men* stand for *people in general* and to let the deeds and experiences of *people in general* be attributed to *men*. At the same time, they are not willing to blur *women* with *people in general* or to permit *women* to represent *people in general*. A picture of women captioned simply "farmers" or "pioneers" is never to be seen in textbooks. Linguistic failure to permit women to be "people" mirrors a long tradition of male supremacy and a socially induced need to keep women in a separate and unequal category—to keep them "in their place."

The implications of sexist generic terminology can be seen clearly in the following sentence: "*Muslims* resented seeing *their wives and daughters* go unveiled." In a female-oriented version of the language of inequality the sentence would read: "*The husbands of the Muslims* resented seeing *them* go unveiled." If the terminology for males and females were equal, the sentence would read: "*Muslim men* resented seeing *Muslim women* go unveiled."

Writers must make explicit the sexual composition of the groups they are discussing, and in contexts where a group of women cannot be labeled simply "peasants" or "Muslims" or the like, neither should a group of men be so labeled.

Mother's baby but father's heir

Because women in our society have traditionally been expected to assume the full burden of child care, textbooks tend to describe young children who still need care as the mother's but to describe male offspring who are seen as heirs and female offspring of marriageable age as the father's. (1) "Abraham Lincoln, *his* wife, and *his* son . . ." (2) "Mothers could leave *their* young children at Hull House." (3) "Sacajawea carried *her* infant son . . ." (4) "Balboa married *the daughter of an Indian chief.*" (5) "*Anne Hutchinson* had fifteen children . . ."

In (1) the wording should have been "Abraham and Mary Lincoln and *their* son . . ." In (2), unless it had been verified that fathers never left *their* children at Jane Addams' kindergarten at Hull House, the word "parents" should have been used instead of "mothers." In (3) Sacajawea's husband was also present on the expedition that made her famous, so any account should refer to *their* son. In (5) it should have been stated that Anne and William Hutchinson were the parents of 15 children. In short, textbooks should recognize, wherever possible, the relationship of both parents to their children.

Women as luggage

Textbooks commonly describe migrations of human populations in terms such as the following: (1) "The pioneer took his family west in a covered wagon." (2) "Men trekked over the mountains with their wives, children, and cattle." (3) "Some Forty-niners took their families with them." In each of the foregoing examples women are regarded more as luggage than as human beings. Such treatment deprives females of their true status as pioneers, travelers, or seekers-after-gold in their own right.

Unless it has been determined that in such instances the females under discussion were moved involuntarily, authors should write: "Americans moved west . . ."; "Families trekked over the mountains . . . ," and so on. They should never write of "*men*" who "*brought along*" wives. Authors also have a responsibility to make their readers aware of the fact that significant numbers of single women and female heads of family participated in the westward movement and other migrations.

Male-oriented glossing of terms

Textbooks often define or explain words which are applicable to either or both sexes as though they applied exclusively to males. For example, "militia" has been explained as "*men* who . . ."; "dictator" as "a *man* who . . ."; "Forty-niners" as "*men* who . . ."; "monarchy" as a "nation ruled by a *king.*" Students may thus be led incorrectly to believe that women cannot join a militia or be dictators, that women were not also "Forty-niners" and that only males may be monarchs. Such false and misleading explanations and definitions should be avoided.

Neutral occupational terminology

Occupational terms ending in "-man"—airman, fireman, cameraman, anchorman, statesman, workman, iceman, repairman, watchman, salesman, and the like—are objectionable because they suggest that certain fields of endeavor are closed to females. Premodern terms such as bondman or ploughman, used in a discussion of premodern times, may be permissible, but modern sex-affiliated terms should be eliminated. They not only give young people false impressions about their future vocational prospects; they also tend to perpetuate existing discriminatory practices.

Authors who do not want to use or invent new terminology may evade the issue by recasting entire sentences. For example, "Mr. Jones sent for a TV repairman" can be revised to "Mr. Jones called a TV repair service." The ending "-man" is, however, increasingly being replaced by the ending "-person" to form terms like "chairperson." The word "salesperson" is already widely accepted, and other neutral terms will gain acceptance as the decisive influence of language on the attitudes and lives of people becomes more widely understood.

Terms to be avoided

The term *housewife* should never be used because it suggests that domestic chores are the exclusive burden of females. It gives female students the idea that they were born to keep house and teaches male students that they are automatically entitled to laundry, cooking, and housecleaning services from females in their families. The inculcation of such attitudes is inconsistent with the ideal of equal educational and vocational opportunities.

Similarly, where *men* are referred to as *men* rather than *husbands,* but women are referred to as *wives* rather than *women,* the textbook is again treating men as persons (not husbands) and women as wives (not persons). The term *wife* should therefore be used sparingly. The following terms and expressions should be regarded as demeaning and should not be used: *lady* (as synonym for adult female), *girl* (as synonym for adult female), *the little woman, the weaker sex,* and *squaw.*

Such terms as *author, aviator, heir, laundry worker, sculptor, singer, poet, Jew,* and *Negro* are neuter terms which are applicable to both females and males. The use of words ending in "feminine" suffixes—such as *authoress, aviatrix, heiress, laundress, sculptress, songstress, poetess, Jewess,* and *Negress*—is unacceptable. Terms ending in "feminine" suffixes imply that females are a special and unequal form of the correct neuter expression. Thus, to speak of Edna St. Vincent Millay as a "poetess" is to exclude her from the legitimate circle of *poets;* to speak of Amelia Earhart as an "aviatrix" denies her full status as *aviator;* to refer to Golda Meir as a "Jewess" denies her full status as a *Jew;* and so on. In cases where it is regarded as necessary to indicate the sex of the individual, the expressions "female poet," "female Jew," and so on may be used. However, in modifying neuter terms the word "lady" (as in "lady lawyer," "lady doctor") is never acceptable.

In conclusion, authors and publishers who seek to provide a just portrayal of the sexes in textbooks must include material which accurately represents the role of females in history and society and must use language which permits readers to perceive females as whole human beings.

Notes

1. Unless otherwise indicated, the sentences and phrases presented in this paper as examples of language habits or of typical textbook discussion, while not quoted from any particular textbook, are based closely on the actual language used in textbooks.
2. CLARENCE L. VER STEEG, *The Story of Our Country* (California State Textbook), p. 86.
3. Male orientation may also be avoided in such cases by changing the subject of the sentence to a neuter plural.
4. Authors' italics.

LOST HERSTORY: THE TREATMENT OF WOMEN IN CHILDREN'S ENCYCLOPEDIAS

With the women's liberation movement has come a deep concern over the negative, passive self-image acquired by young girls as a result of early sexist upbringing, their resulting low aspirations, and the widening academic and vocational achievement gap between the sexes.

Recently, in Brooklyn, New York, a group of mothers whose children attend a private school formed an organization called the Sex Roles Committee in order to bring to the attention of teachers ways in which children, mostly girls, are limited through social and traditional attitudes passed on or reinforced by schools. Among their concerns are children's reading materials. Other groups and individuals across the country are also vitally concerned, as indicated by the recent appearance of a number of articles and monographs dealing with the images and roles of women in children's materials. Subjects covered range from Mother Goose to high school history textbooks. There is a law in California requiring accurate portrayal of male and female roles in state-approved textbooks by 1975.

It is safe to predict that the roles of women, past and present, will become increasingly important as a classroom topic in elementary and high schools—if they have not already.

Encyclopedias

Among the essential reading and research tools in these schools are encyclopedias. Students turn to them for background material and limited "in-depth" study. It is therefore legitimate for librarians who are specialists

Note: By Linda Kraft. Reprinted with permission from *School Library Journal,* January 1973, 19:5, 26–35. Copyright © 1973 by the Xerox Corporation.

in information, who select reference materials for purchase, and who, in the schools, instruct children in the critical use of research materials, including encyclopedias, to ask the question:

Do the encyclopedias which are intended for use by children provide adequate and accurate information on the roles and problems of women, past and present?

If they fail, not only will girls' negative self-images be reinforced but all children will be denied an accurate account of historical fact as well as current reality once again.

It was with this question in mind that this study was undertaken. My assumption was not that encyclopedia editors and publishers were intentionally conspiring to treat women in a shabby way. Rather, I hypothesized that they, like writers of textbooks, basic readers, and children's fiction may reflect the traditional, prevailing social attitudes toward women's roles.

The encyclopedias surveyed were five of the sets recommended for children's home use by the Reference and Subscription Books Committee of the American Library Association: *Britannica Junior* (Encyclopaedia Britannica, 1972), *Compton's Encyclopedia and Fact Index* (F. E. Compton, 1972), *Merit Students Encyclopedia* (Crowell Collier, 1970), *The World Book Encyclopedia* (Field Enterprises Educational Corp., 1972), and *The New Book of Knowledge: The Children's Encyclopedia* (Grolier, 1971). (Unfortunately, the 1972 revisions of the *Merit Students Encyclopedia* and the *New Book of Knowledge* were not accessible at the time my research was undertaken.)

A natural starting place for investigation might have been the major or longest article on women in each encyclopedia. But, to limit analysis to these articles would not result in a valid answer to the question. Irving Sloan in his study, *The Treatment of Black Americans in Current Encyclopedias* (American Federation of Teachers, 1970), says:

> Whether . . . a particular set of encyclopedias offers a quantitative and qualitative presentation of the black American's life and history is determined neither by how many pages its general article is nor by the eminence of the black historian who writes it. . . . Rather the real measure is how much material about the black American appears within separate entries on other topics.

The same criterion should be applied to the subject of women. Will a student researching early labor activities in the United States find information on women leaders and strikes in the entry on labor, or will that information appear only in the general article on women—if at all?

In addition to general essays on women, articles dealing with the various phases of American history, such as the colonial period, the Revolutionary War, the Civil War and abolition, pioneer life and westward expansion, the labor movement, reform, temperance, and the World Wars, were analyzed, as were cultural articles on dance, theater, art, music, science, black studies; vocational articles such as medicine, nursing, home economics, social work, library science, and occupations in general; and articles on the family and child development. These are articles of interest to many school-age children for curricular or noncurricular reasons, and are also articles likely to contain information about women and their roles. An attempt was made to determine the adequacy of biographical treatment—an important part of any encyclopedia—through a measure of the number of specific entries in the index on individual women of importance.

Methodology

In order to analyze the treatment of women in various articles in children's encyclopedias, a number of content categories were set up. Upon reading a given encyclopedia article, specific examples representative of these categories were identified and recorded. The content categories used were based on specific kinds of bias found in social studies textbooks as reported by Elizabeth Burr, Susan Dunn, and Norma Farquhar in *Equal Treatment of the Sexes In Social Studies Textbooks: Guidelines for Authors and Editors* (The Authors, 1973, mimeo.). The guidelines are intended to help authors and editors conform to the aforementioned California law. The categories were only slightly modified for this study and there is evidence that the principles behind them are applicable to encyclopedias as well as to textbooks. (Definitions of the scope of the content categories are provided in the concluding section of this article.)

Words and sentences from various articles which exemplify certain of the content categories were chosen for inclusion in this article if they clearly indicated discriminatory treatment. My decision to include certain examples and to exclude others for reasons of brevity was often arbitrary. No set was ideal in its treatment and there is no intentional effort to make any set appear to be a more serious offender.

Women—Rights—Suffrage

The most information about women is found in general articles on women and woman suffrage and rights. *Merit Students, Britannica Junior,* and *The New Book of Knowledge* view women primarily through their roles in the nineteenth-century suffrage struggle. This one-dimensional view tends to limit the kinds and amount of information they provide about women. Women's involvement with other causes, especially the antislavery movement, receives brief notice. The treatment of their attempts to achieve educational and vocational opportunity is scanty. In contrast, the sections on women in *World Book* and *Compton's* are generally vehicles where fuller and more recent information is included. Both discuss or mention at least twice as many individual women of importance as the other articles. In addition to basic facts on the suffrage struggle, *World Book* reviews the whole range of activities and areas in which women have involved themselves. In addition to the more well-known suffrage leaders like Elizabeth Stanton, the article cites women like Julia Lathrop, first chief of the Children's Bureau of the Department of Labor and Florence Kelly, first factory inspector of Illinois. *Compton's* includes female rulers of foreign countries in addition to American political leaders. It is the *only* set to mention Harriet Tubman and Sojourner Truth in its major article. And it also provides substantial sections on legal status, work, politics, feminist philosophies, reform movements, and the rise of women's liberation. Discussions of various types of discrimination against women, relevant legislation, changes in the status of American women, comparisons with other countries, and collective and individual contributions of women throughout history are relatively up to date—at least to 1970. Both *Compton's* and *World Book* offer bibliographies which include *The Feminine Mystique* by Betty Friedan and the report of the President's Commission on the Status of Women.

Unfortunately, significant historical omissions are common to most of the sets. The early attitude of the established church, which supported the concept of female inferiority, is mentioned only in *Compton's*. Specific kinds of past legal discrimination against women in areas such as guardianship, property rights, legal status of married women, et al., are rarely noted. The involvement of black women leaders like Sojourner Truth is rarely mentioned in discussions of the development of the nineteenth-century Suffrage Movement. Little attention is paid to Alice Paul, Ernestine Rose, Esther Morris, and other lesser known but significant leaders. These omissions may be related to the tendency to avoid mention of the militancy and protest tactics of some factions of the American movement. But, what about the procedural conflicts between organizations and individuals in the suffrage struggle? Are not such specific sources of opposition to the women's struggle as the liquor interests, big business, political machinery, and Jim Crow supporters worthy of attention?

The variety of methods used by the nineteenth-century women to press for reforms—petitions, picket lines, referenda, etc.—is rarely presented and the magnitude of their struggle simply does not come across. Relevant publications by individual women or organizations are overlooked. Surprisingly, not one set mentions the 1876 Declaration of Rights for Women.

The description of the women's struggle ends with the passage of the Nineteenth Amendment in most of the articles. Again, only *Compton's* mentions the Equal Rights Amendment and devotes attention to the scope and variety of the women's liberation movement in the main context of the article. Most of the others fail to note the passage of post-Nineteenth Amendment legislation which has affected the status of women. Recent Presidential task forces and state Commissions on the Status of Women are ignored.

While some of the inadequacies may be attributed to a slow response by children's encyclopedias to the concerns generated by the current women's movement, it is also possible that these omissions result from the underlying attitudes and philosophies of the writers on women. A comparison of some of the statements in *Compton's* and *World Book* articles reveals diverging points of view.

> Homemaker and mother is a woman's most important role. The love and training she gives to her children are vitally important to the individual, the community, and the nation. Throughout history, women have taken care of their families and their homes. (Caption for an illustration showing a mother measuring the hem of a child's dress in *World Book*.)

While this statement may be accurate and relevant to the lives of many women, it fails to point out that some women are legitimately attributing equal or greater importance to roles outside marriage and motherhood. On the other hand, *Compton's* shows an awareness of this development in another caption, this time for an illustration showing a woman feeding a baby: "Feminists do not deny the importance of marriage but feel that women should have a wider choice of life styles."

World Book acknowledges discrimination, admitting that the "world still gives men most of the advantages and opportunities for advancement and leadership," but resolves the discussion with optimism: "Feminist leaders point out that women have usually achieved the goals they desire." This statement is supported by only one quote from Mary Beard's *Woman as a Force in History*. Surely there are many past and present women's movement leaders who would disagree. By neither airing diverging points of view, nor stating the various arguments and concerns of the current women's liberation movement, *World Book* commits an important sin of omission.

Compton's, less optimistic about quick solutions, points out that:

> Today, contraception and, in some areas, legalized abortion, have given women greater control over the number of children they will bear, but—although these developments have freed women for roles other than motherhood, the cultural pressure for women to become wives and mothers still prevents many talented women from finishing college or pursuing careers.

This article takes cognizance of the persistence of economic discrimination against women in the late 1960s, despite recent legislation, as well as the relatively small percentage of women in the various professions.

Unlike *World Book, Compton's* includes a lengthy section on the women's liberation movement, mentioning a variety of organizations from SALT (Sisters All Learning Together) to NOW (National Organization for Women). The article defines the scope of the movement's philosophies and activities and draws some comparisons between the philosophies of the nineteenth and twentieth centuries.

Objectively, neither of these sets gives equal treatment to both sides of the current women's liberation debate, though *Compton's* must, at least, be credited for explaining the argument—more than any other set does in the body of its article.

Among the other major articles on women there is one example of "girl watching." *Britannica Junior* describes Susan B. Anthony as, "Tall and plain, but with a most kindly and tolerant expression, she commanded respect by her fearless honesty and her logical arguments." *The New Book of Knowledge* exemplifies the hausfrau role stereotype when it says, "Some of these women were wives and mothers, like Mrs. Stanton who had seven children or Lucretia Mott, a quiet Quaker lady who had five." But, the most important limitation of these articles is the number of significant omissions of important historical and current facts and concepts.

Colonial Life: the Revolution

The same substantive limitation applies to articles on various phases of American history. In most cases, historical omissions are related to the description of women's roles as housewives, without mention of the other roles they actually did assume. Describing women as wives who cooked, sewed, baked, gardened, and took care of the children is not wrong in and of itself. Many women during colonial and pioneer days probably did devote much of their time to these pursuits and, in so doing, provided essential services. But, many colonial women did run businesses and did strike out for themselves in a variety of endeavors, including the professions. Some were missionaries as well as independent settlers, gold seekers, and homesteaders. Barely noticed are any kind of religious, legal, social, or educational disabilities suffered by women.

While *Merit Students, Compton's,* and *World Book* refer to Anne Hutchinson as a colonial dissenter, they neglect to mention that she challenged the position of the established church. A mention of dame schools, or the fact that girls generally dropped out of school earlier than boys, is about all there is on education for women during America's early period.

Illustrations of colonial women stress hausfrau activities—cooking, weaving, spinning, cleaning, etc. Occasionally women are shown with men at social events, on a stagecoach, or going to church. But, men are used to illustrate classes of people (blacksmiths, Indians, and Pilgrims) and are more actively involved in a greater variety of nondomestic activities, e.g., printing, trading, manufacturing, fishing, and reading.

Women are mentioned only three times in relation to the American Revolution. *The New Book of Knowledge* has a biographical insert about Molly Pitcher, *World Book's* "related articles" list mentions Molly Pitcher and Betsy Ross.

What kinds of information might an adequate treatment provide? What about such women's organizations as Daughters of Liberty and their boycott of British goods? (The Sons of Liberty are mentioned in the *Merit Students* and *New Book of Knowledge* articles, and a related article on them appears in *World Book*). A discussion of whether or not the kinds of freedom envisaged by the Declaration of Independence were applicable to women as well as men would be valuable. Statements implying that *only* men held opinions or beliefs tend to reinforce the image of women as having little or no active interest in the Revolution:

> The Stamp Act provoked almost unanimous opposition in America. Many influential men who had ignored the ministry's earlier actions or who had even favored them now gave support to the cause of the patriots. (*Merit Students*)
>
> Many of the wealthiest men in America remained loyalists. (*Compton's*)
>
> There were a few men in the colonies who wanted independence long before it came. (*Britannica Junior*)

The idea that women too were patriots came across only once, in a *Merit Students* illustration showing men and women, "American patriots pulling down the statue of King George III in New York City." This set also has the only other illustration which even includes women; it shows them watching Washington's triumphal entry into New York—from the background. Of course, there are many portraits of male leaders and pictures of men participating in great events.

Civil War

The Civil War had a significant impact on the position of women. Many women entered paid employment for the first time, a large number going into teaching and government work; women also did heavy manual labor to keep family homesteads going. They served as volunteer nurses in army hospitals and worked in the Sanitary Commission, bringing food, clothing, and other essentials to the men. They also served as spies, scouts, saboteurs, and guides. After the war, women continued in government work and taught in freedmen's schools. A number of black and white women were active and outspoken abolitionists. They held meetings, organized into the National Women's Loyal League, and petitioned the Senate to abolish slavery. Here they learned the value of organization, which was to help in the fight for suffrage. How much information about these activities is there in the relevant sections of children's encyclopedias —i.e., Civil War, Abolition, and Reconstruction?

Harriet Beecher Stowe and the impact of *Uncle Tom's Cabin* are mentioned in *Merit Students, Britannica Junior, World Book,* and *The New Book of Knowledge. Britannica Junior* cites Lucretia Mott and Harriet Tubman. Eight male abolitionists are named in *Compton's,* as compared to zero females; Harriet Beecher Stowe is the only female among seven males in *Merit Students. The New Book of Knowledge* illustrates a woman teaching in a freedman's school in the South. *World Book* is the only set to mention Dorothea Dix and Clara Barton.

In addition to Stowe and Mott, it should not be so difficult to come up with the names of such noted female abolitionists as Lucy Stone, Anna Dickenson, the Grimké sisters, Sojourner Truth, and Frances Ellen Watkins Harper. These sets ignore the variety of women's employment on the home front and closer to the battle lines. Aside from one or two female abolitionists and nurses, the image of female participation in the war effort is negative, implying lack of involvement. In the main, the illustrations depict male roles in the war—battle scenes, war prisoners, marches, recruiting posters, and portraits of male political and military leaders. When pictures of women are used at all, they are shown as slaves, in an audience, or watching a child go off to war.

Westward Ho?

Treatment of the lives of pioneer women is uneven. *World Book* and *The New Book of Knowledge* contain two of the better articles and indicate that women worked equally as hard as men, sharing the same hazards of the frontier. But, these and other sets also contain phrases which counterbalance these acknowledgments, implying that men only were the adventurers.

> Some restless and ambitious men moved west because they loved adventure. (*Britannica Junior*)

> They (the frontiersmen) had become a special type of men who were to dominate the cause of American history for the next century. (*New Book of Knowledge*)

The lives of pioneer women were characterized by drudgery and hard work and this comes across in *Merit Students, Compton's, World Book,* and *The New Book of Knowledge.* All but *World Book* give credit to women for the education of children, doctoring, and nursing, but none of the sets indicate that the need for women and their various services (including hunting, trapping, and farming) led to the greater legal and political liberty for women in the western states. *The New Book of Knowledge* discusses progressive labor legislation affecting women in the west and *Britannica Junior* cites Wyoming as the state where women first had the right to vote. Nothing more is said.

One of the most glaring omissions in all five sets is a failure to mention the activities of single and independent women who went west as missionaries, gold-seekers, and homesteaders:

> While a woman and her children waited outside in a wagon, a pioneer settler studied the survey map in the land office. At last he counted out his advance payment and signed his name. . . . He got a certificate that he could exchange for a deed of ownership when payment was completed . . . so another pioneer family found their land. (*New Book of Knowledge*)

Descriptions like the one above offer the implicit message that women went west *only* as wives. While this may represent the typical, the exclusion of the atypical is not justifiable if children's encyclopedias are to avoid indoctrinating children to assume the more traditional male–female roles.

Labor Movements

Since the early industrial period, women have worked for long hours, lower wages, and less chance for advancement than their male counterparts. Though *Merit Students, Compton's,* and *The New Book of Knowledge* briefly note these disadvantages, they make little attempt to explain the reasons for them. While most attempts to organize women workers ended in failure, there is no reason why these activities, organizations, leaders—and even an explanation for the failures—should be excluded from a discussion of U.S. labor history. Only *World Book* even mentions the first women's union.

Modern developments are equally neglected. Again, only *World Book* bothers to cite recent well-documented statistics showing, in a chart, that more women are going to work and for longer periods in their lives. *Merit Students, Compton's, The New Book of Knowledge,* and *Britannica Junior* fail to include recent legislation applicable to sex discrimination in employment, even though they discuss other kinds of labor legislation. Only *The New Book of Knowledge* covers labor legislation, but even it does not discuss the many women who feel overprotected. *Merit Students, Compton's,* and *World Book* have no illustrations of female workers or labor activists. *The New Book of Knowledge* shows women actively involved in a labor dispute.

Thirty-six pictures illustrate male workers, labor leaders, and labor activities as opposed to four illustrations of women and nine of men and women. *The New Book of Knowledge* pictures different kinds of workers in "uniform." The females are clerical workers and nurses; males represent the skilled and semiskilled worker; the doctor, professional man, the policeman, etc.

Reform and Temperance

Only *Merit Students* devotes a whole, separate article to the reform era of American history. Ida Tarbell is the sole woman cited, despite seven mentions of specific male reformers. *World Book* treats this era in the context of its U.S. history survey article. While some sets may treat separate facets of reform in more narrowly focused articles, its omission as a separate topic deprives readers of a total picture of the very important contributions made by women in the areas of social welfare and settlement work, birth control, consumer protection, and the protection of working women.

The temperance movement, in which women also participated, rates separate articles in all five sets. Basic facts about the development, purpose, and leadership of the Women's Christian Temperance Union (WCTU) are included, but only *Britannica Junior* mentions the WCTU's broader welfare activities. No set explains the motivation for women's interest in temperance. The sets also neglect the fact that male prejudice forced women to form their own temperance societies.

The World Wars

As with the other wars in American history, children's encyclopedias overwhelmingly stress male roles in World Wars I and II. *World Book's* discussion of World War II is exemplary in its inclusion of women's roles in the war effort, in the armed forces, and on the home front, but neither the impact of the war upon the status of women, nor their varied contributions to the war efforts are mentioned in the other four sets.

A brief examination of the U.S. history survey articles reveals little or no information on the lives and problems of women during the last few decades, though other recent events in the areas of foreign affairs and domestic problems are covered. This is not really surprising, as there is little recent coverage in most of the major articles on women.

The Language of History

The image of women which results from the emphasis on hausfrau roles, stereotyped illustrations, the emphasis on pictures of men, and the omission of important female contributions as compared to the numbers of male activities included, is reinforced by the language used to describe and explain history.

The linguistic category which accumulated the greatest number of examples is "subsuming terminology." Subsuming terms are masculine terms which are commonly believed to include or refer to females. Masculine pronouns are consistently used in all sets to refer to classes of people —pioneers, settlers, Puritans, Negroes, workers, farmers, students, shopkeepers, indentured servants, Virginians, et al. The use of the words "man" and "men" is prevalent. It is unlikely that the mental image a child forms when reading the following sentences will include women:

> There is little an ordinary worker can do by himself to guarantee benefits. He can improve his skills so as to increase his chances of advancing. (*Merit Students*)

> On the frontier, a man could begin life anew. (*Britannica Junior*)

> Some men worked as miners, millers, shopkeepers, shipbuilders, or merchants. (*New Book of Knowledge*)

Expressions such as red man, white man, common man, manpower, also fall into this category. Burr, Dunn, and Farquhar also object to subsuming terms on the ground of ambiguity. They say, "it often becomes a matter of making an educated guess as to whether the author means males and females both, or males only. It is also possible that such terms are employed to conceal the author's lack of information concerning the sexual composition of a group."

Metaphors occasionally found in these articles also have a male orientation. *The New Book of Knowledge* article on the Revolutionary War says, "Americans were like a young man who had grown up and was determined to manage his own affairs. The British government was like a father who wanted his grown son to obey him."

Hypothetical persons in all sets are invariably male. The *Merit Students* article on the labor movement tells the reader that "the labor effort may be organized in many ways. For example, to make bread one man might plant the wheat, mill the flour, and bake the loaves himself or many men might divide the labor among themselves."

The implication that men only have actively participated in work situations comes through again and again with the use of masculine occupational terms such as professional man, repairman, newspaperman. Women are treated as objects or more specifically as mindless luggage: "They were shipped wholesale to Louisiana in its French period and were married off as fast as they arrived" (*New Book of Knowledge*).

Women in these articles do not represent people in general, but are referred to as wives of certain classes of people, e.g., "the planter and his wife," "the farmer and his wife." Male-oriented quoted material, such as "All men are created equal," without explanation of the male orientation reinforces the effects of subsuming terminology.

These history articles in children's encyclopedias contain many more examples of linguistic conventions which serve to exclude women from the developments of history and to imply that women are of little importance.

Cultural Achievements

Another dimension of children's encyclopedias' treatment of women is evident in their articles on education, fine and performing arts, religion, black studies, and various professional areas in which women participate. The criteria for an adequate article would include a presentation of the collective and individual contributions of women and current opportunities, problems, and disabilities women face. But, while individual articles vary in their treatment, there is rarely any mention of the disabilities or discrimination women encountered. Though articles on education may mention dame schools, female academies, the opening of the first women's colleges, roles of women in the development of the kindergarten, nursery, and PTA movements, they do not describe the arduous struggle waged by women to attain equality of educational opportunity. Except for the inclusion of Emma Willard in the *Compton's* and *The New Book of Knowledge* articles (she is listed in "Related Articles" in *World Book*), there are few references to individual female educators involved in this struggle. There is no indication or explanation of the increasing educational gap between men and women. Of the five education articles, only *Compton's* includes a discussion of women in the teaching profession.

Neither the early inability of women to gain admission to medical schools recognized by the American Medical Association, nor their subsequent attempts to earn medical degrees in Europe are noticed. The free dispensaries and hospitals they founded to provide themselves with clinical experience while caring for the medical needs of the poor, and their entrance into public and school health work because of the difficulty in establishing private practices, are ignored.

The articles on the Negro or Negro history seem to mention a greater number of women than the other articles, perhaps because these articles have recently been revised. Many of these same women should, indeed, be included in articles describing the areas of expertise which they represent. Also, even these articles do not discuss the unique and specific roles and problems of black women. The treatment seems partially a result of the subject under discussion. Individual women are numerous in most articles on the dance, literature, theater, and film. Occasional mention is also made of collective contributions in these areas. But, there is no indication that women in the theater and film are anything but actresses. Most articles note that women account for a majority of the professionals working in library science, nursing, and home economics, with some indication that more men have been entering these fields. Generally, there is adequate coverage of women's participation in sports. But, articles on science, social work, religion, music, and fine arts give women scant attention. Even in library science, the names of individual women, particularly pioneers in the area of children's librarianship, are excluded, though male founders are cited.

Articles on religion never discuss the limitations on participation by women in various religious sects. No attention is paid to discrimination against women in the arts in the early days of America. Other artists and musicians often published works of women, sometimes relatives, under their own names. Nowhere is this brought out.

Children reading about religion in America will not learn of the numerous female founders of sects, rebels against religious orthodoxy, missionaries. Only *Merit Students* contains a good section on vocational opportunities for women in its Religion and Religious Vocations articles. If children read a general article on music they will not learn of the many achievements of women in vocal music, since the general articles are largely devoted to composers, most of whom have been males. In the art sections only about three or four individual women artists are mentioned. Mary Cassat appears in *Merit Students* and *World Book*, Rice Pereira and Loren MacIver are included in *Compton's*, and sculptors Anna Hyatt Hunting and Malvina Hoffman are noted in *Britannica Junior*.

The achievements of individual women in commercial art and illustrations are ignored, as is their increasing participation in contemporary art. Articles on science rarely include more than one individual mention (usually Mme. Curie) of a woman scientist.

With some exception, in the areas which have been traditionally associated with women—e.g., nursing—or in which women's achievements are widely known—e.g., acting—coverage is relatively good.

Vocations

General articles on vocations, occupations, or the world of work do not discuss past or present limited vocational opportunity for women—or the current concern of the women's movement about equality of opportunity. *World Book*'s article does contain a chart showing Annual Income in the United States by Amount of Education, Age, and Sex—which indicates a discrepancy between the incomes of men and women at the same age and educational levels. But this fact is not mentioned or explained in the text of the article.

Male and female work roles are rather sharply differentiated in examinations of types of work. Clerical work and nursing are viewed as "good fields" for girls; feminine pronouns refer to teachers and stenographers. Illustrations show women in these and other roles—ballet dancer, librarian, office worker, design student. Males are pictured as engineers, bank tellers, veterinarians, physicists, draftsmen, farmers, policemen, etc.

Girls and boys are usually assigned traditional roles, e.g., *Britannica Junior* says: "There are many kinds of part-time jobs; running a paper route is a job some boys like; girls often choose babysitting." Again, hypothetical persons are male, as in the *Merit Students'* Vocational Guidance article. An illustration shows a male guidance counselor talking to a boy: "A trained vocational guidance counselor can be of great help to a young man trying to determine the right career for himself."

Compton's article contains a chart indicating "Major Occupations for Men and Women" which lists specific kinds of jobs for each sex under different occupational groups. Women are totally excluded from the Skilled Worker Group because, "so few of them hold jobs under this classification." Among the other groups—Professional, Sales, Service, Semi-Professional, and Clerical—there are a few jobs listed in both the "men" and "women" columns—e.g., waiters, waitresses, stenographers, secondary teachers. But most are assigned to only one of the two sexes. Engineers, lawyers, physicians, policemen, real estate agents, and mail carriers are listed only in the male column; nurses, social workers, cooks, dancers, and office machine operators are listed in the female column only. My quarrel is not with the accuracy of the chart, but rather with the article's failure to say that women do participate successfully in jobs which are listed in the male column and vice versa. Neither is it explained that social attitudes and lack of vocational opportunity may at least partially account for the lack of female participation in the past. Children and young people glancing at such a chart may assume, or be reinforced in their assumptions, that certain kinds of jobs are primarily meant for males and certain others for females. The implications of the *Compton's* chart are found throughout the vocational articles of all sets, reinforced by occupational terms like advertising layout man, public relations man, hatchery man, and check-room man.

The Family

While most articles on the family say that wives may work, they assign the more typical, traditional female roles to women in the family context. Thus, *Compton's:*

> The father is usually responsible for his family and the mother for keeping the home liveable and attractive. Her day is busy. . . . Even though she is her own boss, her job is to plan and work unselfishly for the best interests of her husband and all her children. The thoughtful family shows its appreciation of the mother's efforts by praising good cooking.

The author of this article does not see any relationship between those traditional family roles of women and a situation described elsewhere in the article: "A middle aged wife may find much spare time on her hands after her children are married. This sometimes leads to unhappiness and a feeling that she is no longer useful to herself and her family."

Other articles briefly discuss families in other countries, in which equality between husband and wife varies, and the family during early human history. Here, too, the typical male–female roles are brought out. Articles in *Merit Students* and *Britannica Junior* mention a male–female division of labor within the family unit, stressing traditional roles, current and historical. For example *Britannica Junior's* article explains that: "The father usually teaches the son a man's way of doing things, while the mother is in charge of training her daughter."

Unfortunately, this emphasis upon traditional roles omits several important points. No article mentions the problems and conflicts of the child-bearing mother who must interrupt her career to bring up her children. More important are the facts that increasing numbers of modern families are headed by women and that the decisions of individual women to seek employment outside the home are usually based on economic reasons. Only *The New Book of Knowledge* mentions family arrangements such as those in Israel and Russia which are designed to free women for work. It is also the only set which shows a wife who enjoys keeping accounts and a husband who enjoys being in the kitchen. But even here, "Mr. Carlson enjoys being in the kitchen and cooking a meal when he has time; on weekends he may help his wife with some of the heavy family chores. . . ."

Compton's article on Child Development exhorts girls to act like girls and boys to act like boys. Girls who do not live according to approved social patterns for girls will receive society's disapproval by being labeled a "tomboy" and will discover that boys do not like them, girls scorn them, and adults reprove them. The possibility that the social ideal may be changing or is, at least, being questioned, has not occurred to the writer.

Biographical Component

In order to judge the adequacy of children's encyclopedias' biographical treatment of women, a list of noted women was generated and the names on the list were searched in the index of each set and checked off if present. The list was based on names found in *Index to Women of the World From Ancient to Modern Times* (F. W. Faxon, 1970), compiled by Norma Olin Ireland. Women included in Ireland's *Index*, who appeared in four or more collective biographies, were included.

While it is difficult to decide upon a numerical criterion, or the percentage of women from the list which would indicate adequate coverage, the results are as follows: *New Book of Knowledge:* 29 percent, *Merit Students:* 28 percent, *Britannica Junior:* 22 percent, *World Book:* 36 percent, *Compton's:* 40 percent.

The percentage of entries in the encyclopedia indexes is significantly higher for women who had appeared in ten or more collective biographies, indicating better coverage for women who are better known: 69 percent, 64 percent, 57 percent, 76 percent, and 77 percent, respectively.

The smaller percentage of biographies of lesser known women in children's encyclopedias may simply reflect the general lack of scholarship in the areas of women's history. But, this results in the omission of many women in certain classifications. Ireland included women who were pioneers in their fields. Some of the fields in which a significant number of women received zero or one mention among all five sets are: businesswomen, Civil and Revolutionary War soldiers, heroines, and patriots; religious leaders, women in aviation; fashion designers; social leaders; playwrights; editors, journalists, authors, pilgrims; colonial printers, publishers, merchants; nurses; scientists and engineers; instrumentalists and composers; sculptors and painters; physicians; social reformers, and politicians. It is not surprising that many of these are the same subject areas as articles in which few, if any, of the roles and contributions of women were mentioned as compared to numerous male.

Several women, quite famous in their fields, are also excluded by all or at least four of the five sets. Feminist Abigail Duniway was not included in any set. Neither were social reformer, poet, and lecturer Frances Ellen Watkins Harper, Congresswoman and nurse Frances Payne Bolton, and pioneer feminist physician Mary Jacobi. Lydia Maria Child, social reformer and editor, is included only in an index article in *Compton's;* feminist and social reformer Abigail Kelley Foster has a separate article in *World Book* but is mentioned nowhere else; fashion designer Edith Head receives one mention in *Merit Students.* Feminist and social reformer Sarah Grimké is mentioned only once by *World Book.* Educator, author, social reformer Catherine Beecher rates one separate article and an additional mention in *World Book,* and engineer Lillian Gilbreth is mentioned only once in *World Book.* In contrast, Beecher was included in 14 collective biographies in Ireland's *Index,* Gilbreth and Child in 13, Jacobi in 12, Bolton in 11, Duniway in six, Harper and Foster in five, and Head in four.

Perhaps if a little less space was devoted to the biographical treatment of the more obscure wives of presidents there would be more room left in the sets for biographical treatment of women who distinguished themselves independently.

Conclusion

In conclusion, the analysis of the treatment of women by children's encyclopedias turned up examples of each of the following content categories in greater or lesser degree:

Significant omissions from history.

Role assigning, the implication that most or many present-day work roles are necessarily distributed along sex lines; emphasis upon women collectively as housewives, to the exclusion of their other roles, past and present; pointing up the "hausfrau" dimension of important individual women who should be noted only for their unique and individual qualities; and assigning mutually exclusive roles to boys and girls within the family unit.

Exclusion of illustrations of women, preponderance of stereotyped portrayals of women as housewives, generally in the background, and an overwhelming number of illustrations in which men only are shown or in which they are dominant.

Glorification of males and the implications that men only held opinions and that they are or were the only people in the social milieu.

Girl watching, noting the physical attributes of particular women even when these are irrelevant to the discussion at hand.

Subsuming terminology, use of terms such as man, men, or mankind in the sense of human beings, he meaning both he and she and subsuming terms such as manpower and brotherhood.

The hypothetical person as male. For example, "if a man traveled from New York to Virginia in 1800 . . .".

Male-oriented quoted material which is not identified as such, for example, "These are the times which try men's souls."

Nobody knows her name, females referred to as wives, daughters, or mothers of males clearly identified by name and occupation, e.g., Archduke Ferdinand and his wife.

Differential generic terminology, in which men stand for people in general and women do not, e.g., peasants versus peasant women. This category gives women a separate and less than equal status.

Women as luggage, language implying that all women were involuntarily shipped, taken, or brought along by men during various migrations when, in fact, some independent women did set out on their own.

Male-oriented glossing of terms, the definition of words applicable to either or both sexes as though they applied exclusively to males, e.g., "A farmer is a man who farms."

Male-oriented occupational terminology, use of occupational terms ending in "man," e.g., cameraman—which suggest that certain fields of endeavor are closed to women.

Feminine suffixes, e.g., laundress—which imply that females are a special and unequal form of the correct neuter expression.

The first five categories are applicable to the substantive content of the various articles. But language, too, communicates ideas and expresses shared assumptions. It transmits implicit values and behavioral models to all those people who use it. Since children interpret language quite literally, special care should be taken to use language which honestly transmits values, ideas, and facts. Linguistic conventions used in children's encyclopedias tend to reinforce unequal treatment of men and women. Children's encyclopedias have not yet fully responded to the concerns of the women's movement, nor have they fully begun to examine the unintentional bias against women which pervades many of their articles. Even *Compton's* and *World Book*, which appear to have recently revised their major articles on women, still fail to integrate the increased amount of information about women into the variety of relevant articles throughout their sets.

To end on a hopeful note, the editors of all five sets were informed of the nature of this study and their response was, on the whole, encouraging. While they were somewhat defensive about the final judgment of their particular set, most editors were supportive of my effort and expressed interest in the final result. A few even indicated that their coverage of roles and images of women may have been less than adequate. Hopefully, they will be able to use the results of this study to overcome past weaknesses. This may mean a readjustment of priorities in decisions as to what information to include so that more information on women will be integrated into all relevant articles. A reexamination of biased presentations may result in the elimination of the preponderance of stereotyped images of women included. A greater utilization of past and current scholarship in the area of women's history would result in a more accurate and less stereotyped view of women in our past, and a closer attention to current social research and statistics will reveal the real nature of women's roles and problems in the present.

Sexism in History Or, Writing Women's History Is a Tricky Business

> If we have come to think that the nursery and the kitchen are the
> natural sphere of woman, we have done so exactly as English
> children come to think that a cage is the natural sphere of a parrot—
> because they have never seen one anywhere else.
>
> George Bernard Shaw

Sexism, like racism, is an ideology of oppression. It is a set of social attitudes based on the fundamental belief in the natural inferiority of women.

Sexism in historical writing is much like sexism in daily life. For the most part women are made invisible. When discussed at all, women are treated with the same set of narrowly defined attitudes that oppress most women throughout their lives. Usually, they appear as part of the domestic scenery behind the real actors and action of national life.

This should hardly be surprising. History, after all, is written by professional historians whose ideas and values reflect the attitudes of our dominant white male culture. The writing of history in general, and the writing of Women's History in particular, has been largely influenced by unchallenged assumptions about the "nature" of history and the "nature" of woman. It is only recently that these assumptions have been seriously questioned by a few concerned historians and many angry women.

Traditional history has been most concerned with the re-creation of the elite intellectual military, economic, and political powers that fashioned the course of events. Most general histories have ignored minority groups and women. Instead, they are records of diplomatic decisions,

Note: By Ruth Rosen. Reprinted by permission of the National Council on Family Relations and the author from *Journal of Marriage and the Family,* August 1971, 541–544.

military maneuvers, and economic exchanges. Biographies of white male authors, soldiers, industrialists, and politicians have crowded the library shelves labeled "history." History has been the record of those who controlled other people's lives.

Recently, I asked my students to scour their favorite monographic history for information on women. They discovered that women were invisible in history. Jane Addams, Susan Anthony, then a few fleeting words about the suffrage movement and the topic was closed.

The recent social pressure exerted by minority groups has created a new awareness of cultural voids in historical writing. New interest in working-class culture, black and Chicano studies, and yes, even Women's History, has led historians to question the nature of traditional history. Resurrecting the history of the oppressed, re-creating the voice of the inarticulate, and giving life to the muted discontent of the enslaved have more and more *become acceptable* activities for socially concerned historians.

Though the nature of history has been challenged, assumptions about women have remained culturally unchanged. The American woman still sees herself defined as a female who happens to be a human being, while men are viewed as human beings who happen to be male (Adams, 1967). Most forms of written and visual media still portray the American female as the happy recipient of biological destiny. In short, American men and women continue to be educated, conditioned, and bombarded with images of woman's natural inferiority.

Consequently, there is a serious problem in the writing of Women's History. While historians attempt to resurrect women's past, they are burdened with the stereotypes and prejudices of the present. For many historians, this creates a serious dilemma. Unless their own experiences challenge their conditioned responses to the role of women in society, historians have little but their prejudices with which to guide them into the unfamiliar world of female feelings, motivations, and ideas. Unfortunately, their attempts to understand Women's History have often been examples of error and misjudgment.

It is no wonder that Women's History should be the Waterloo for many a competent historian. Women's past, like their present, is filled with the unfamiliar and foreign language of the oppressed. Writers of Black History learned that the external obedience of the lackey often concealed the inner rage of the slave. Historians of women's past will also have to learn to avoid the serious and false conclusions that have so glibly been made in the past.

Coy behavior, for example, can be seen as an example of woman's generally sweet nature, or as a method of manipulating a master's power for her own needs. A woman's desire to be a man can be interpreted as evidence of Lesbianism or as the envy of men's social, economic, and political privileges. In a male supremacist society, writing Women's History is a tricky business. There is much myth to dispel.

Re-creating the past has never been an easy task. Re-creating a social group's past, whose accommodational language has been developed deliberately to avoid male comprehension, is indeed a formidable job. Despite these obvious difficulties, books on Women's History continue to roll off the presses at a fantastic rate.

In general historical studies, one is no longer shocked to find women characterized as docile, passive, fragile, inane creatures. One expects an author to dismiss a woman with the easy familiarity of a superior or to discuss a woman's appearance instead of her achievements. In serious studies on Women's History, however, one would expect more serious consideration of women's past. Unfortunately, this is not the case.

Too often historians have written about women without the slightest sympathy for or understanding of their subject. They have sometimes revealed this fact in statements of their aims and beliefs. William O'Neill (1969) for example, wrote the following passage in the Preface to his *Everyone Was Brave: The Rise and Fall of Feminism in America:*

> This book, then, is first of all an inquiry into the failure of feminism . . . To begin with, I have avoided the question of whether or not women ought to have full parity with men. Such a state of affairs obtains nowhere in the modern world and so, since we cannot know what genuine equality would mean in practice, its desirability cannot fairly be assessed.

The reader need only substitute the word black for women, and white for men, to see the obvious prejudices informing such a work:

> This book, then, is first of all an inquiry into the failure of the *Black Movement* . . . To begin with, I have avoided the question of whether or not *blacks* ought to have full parity with *whites*. Such a state of affairs obtains nowhere in the modern world and so, since we cannot know what genuine equality would mean in practice, its desirability cannot fairly be assessed.

One wonders whether this would still be considered serious history or racist propaganda.

Page Smith (1970) in his introduction to *Daughters of a Promised Land*, not only revealed his private opinion of his wife, but also admitted his inadequacy as a historian of women's past:

> The writing of this book owes nothing to my wife. She viewed the whole enterprise with undisguised skepticism, interrupted me fre-

quently to ask if the Joneses would make good dinner partners with the Browns or whether the Thompsons will go with the Johnsons, seduced me from my labors with delicious meals (so that my girth grew with my book) and, most unnerving of all, said periodically, "How you could pretend to know anything about women . . . !" Which of course I don't.

Professor Smith then goes on to prove this ignorance in the following 392 pages.

The problem is that most historians begin their journey into women's past with a sexist definition of woman's "nature." The results, like the early histories of the "American Negro," reflect the narrow categories and conditioned prejudices of the author's consciousness.

In his chapter on "The Nature of Woman," Page Smith (1970) announces that "Anyone who writes about women has to confront, sooner or later, the question of the 'nature of woman.'" The assumption that women, or any social group, would have an "identifiable nature" is a form of pseudobiological determinism. Such assumptions are always at the root of racist and sexist ideas.

Smith's definition of woman's nature leads him to conclusions that will surely return to haunt his reputation as an historian. Consider, for example, his following declarations on woman's nature: "A woman 'is'; a man is always in the process of becoming." and "A man wishes an audience of millions; a woman will create for one man she loves." Such conclusions are not analyzed as socially conditioned responses; they are stated as eternally true, biologically determined facts of the female and male condition.

Many of Smith's conclusions are outrageous because they are based on unchallenged assumptions about woman's nature. Women, he decides, are not as sexual as men, because they do not respond to traditional pornography. It never occurs to him that women are less stimulated by such performances because they are depicted as the victims and slaves of sexual abuses, rather than as equal participants in sexual pleasure. In another historical blunder, Smith states that women can rarely make great chefs. "A woman's cooking is personal," he declares. "She cooks for those she loves and wishes to nurture; thus her cooking is sacramental."

This is the same kind of historical analysis that not so long ago concluded that black slaves were the happy, contented, mindless servants of their beneficent masters. Women, in Smith's view, love their "natural" position as domestics. The economic and social obstacles which prohibit women from achieving professional status for their cooking, cleaning, and teaching as housewives and mothers are never mentioned. We are to conclude, as does he, that all women love their masters and that their cooking is an act of love.

In one final admonition, Smith authoritatively defines the natural boundaries of the female role. "Unless women respect this order," he warns, "childhood, girlhood, and grandmotherhood, they will end up frustrated and unhappy wayfarers in the Valley of the Dolls." Women are not "meant" to be lawyers, historians, or chefs. Their biological "nature" determines their social position.

Such nonsense is an example of the serious dangers present in the writing of Women's History. If women are to be viewed as only mothers, wives, daughters, and lovers, then historical writing will result in flagrant sexist distortion of their past.

William O'Neill (1969) for example, repeatedly used the term "spouse surrogate" to define the intense relationships that suffragists had with one another and with the movement in general. He could not view women outside of their relationship to and need of a "spouse."

Women's Histories are filled with such false assumptions about woman's nature. And these mistakes are not always made by male historians. Mary Massey (1967) (*Bonnet Brigades*) for example, in her study of women during the Civil War, asserted that "it is woman's nature to prefer working with a group." Mildred Adams (1966) (*The Right to Be People*) wrote how Mrs. Catt's organizing efforts were impeded by "the innate frivolity of feminine minds." The examples are numerous; the conclusions degrading.

Writing Women's History is not an impossible task. It requires serious consideration of the subject—women. Eleanor Flexner (1959) in her narrative of the women's suffrage movement, *Century of Struggle*, treats women's intellectual activities, economic position, and educational needs as serious historical problems. Her writing is noticeably free from assumptions about women's "nature" and mocking condescension. Interested in women's activities and ideas, Flexner never dwells on women's marital status, sex life, or children unless such information is historically relevant. Unlike William O'Neill, who emphasized every woman's social and sexual relationships to men, Flexner treats intellectual and activist women as she would have treated their male counterparts, that is, seriously.

In the *Emancipation of the American Woman*, Andrew Sinclair explores more topical problems in Women's History, such as the "Lady" in American culture and the effects of religion on women's lives. This serious investigation into women's social history successfully integrates women into the broader context of American social movements.

Finally, Aileen Kraditor (1968) in *Ideas of the Women's Suffrage Movement* creates a moving intellectual history of the Suffrage Movement by analyzing the racism and zenophobia of feminist progressive ideas, and the social and economic origins of their thought. The work is a splendid example of serious consideration given women's ideas and action in the past.

These three works are only examples of what can be done in the writing of Women's History. To approach women's past, the historian must recognize two things: first, the basic fact of women's social and economic oppression and secondly, that women have no readily identifiable "nature." Furthermore, the history of women must not focus solely on men's images of women, as in Kate Millet's literary history, *Sexual Politics*. Women's History is also the resurrection of women's own past thoughts and actions.

One cannot assume that every woman was either a docile servant or a rebellious feminist. Obviously, some women could and did accept the limitations of their narrowly defined social roles. Other women boldly risked condemnation in their serious efforts to broaden the boundaries of those female roles. Many women, however—terrified of losing men's economic and physical protection—concealed their rage in ways that have yet to be identified..

Women's History is the record of all these responses to the female's role in society. Sometimes it is the story of untold tragedy: the history of wasted lives. Other times it is the story of untold greatness; the history of hidden thoughts and actions. If one is serious about women, then serious history will result.

Bibliography

ADAMS, MILDRED. 1967. *The Right to Be People*. Philadelphia: Lippincott.

FLEXNER, ELEANOR. 1959. *Century of Struggle*.

KRADITOR, AILEEN. 1968. *Ideas of the Women's Suffrage Movement*.

KRADITOR, AILEEN. 1968. *Up from the Pedestal*. Chicago: Quadrangle.

MASSEY, MARY. 1967. *Bonnet Brigades*. New York: Knopf.

O'NEILL, WILLIAM. 1969. *Everyone Was Brave: The Rise and Fall of Feminism in America*. Chicago: Quadrangle.

SINCLAIR, ANDREW. 1965. *Emancipation of the American Woman*. New York: Harper and Row.

SMITH, PAGE. 1970. *Daughters of the Promised Land*. Boston: Little, Brown.

SUMMARY OF SECONDARY LEVEL LANGUAGE ARTS PRESENTATION

Our study included an analysis of two aspects of the current English curriculum in the Boulder schools. First, a comparative study of anthologies used in junior high schools and, second, an overview of some of the English courses offered at one of the high schools.

The study compares two sets of anthologies—the older published by Ginn & Co. in 1964, edited by Eller, Reeves, and Gordon. The title is *Introduction to Literature* and it is used in seventh grade; the second is *The Study of Literature* and is used in eighth grade. The latter was published by Macmillan in 1968. It was revised from a 1962 edition and comprises four separate books—*Currents in Fiction, Currents in Poetry, Currents in Nonfiction,* and *Currents in Drama.* Each book has a single editor—of the four, two are women and two are men.

Because of the growth of the women's movement in the 1960's, as well as the increasing number of women in the work force, and the more active roles women have taken in politics, one would expect the newer series of anthologies to include more female authors. But such is not the case. In the illustrations the newer series has drawings on the covers of the four books—none within the text itself. Fourteen men and boys appear on the covers; one woman seems to appear, but it is possible that the bespectacled person is a man.

The older series contains pictures within the text. In the *Introduction to Literature* 179 males and 38 females appear. In the *Study of Literature* 189 males and 21 females appear.

Next we examined the authors whose works appear in the two series. The newer *Currents* series contains 112 works by 84 male authors

Note: Reprinted with permission from the Education Task Force Report, December 1972, National Organization for Women, Boulder, Colorado chapter.

and 19 works by female authors. In the older series, works by 124 male writers and by 31 female writers appear. Percentage-wise, 20 percent of the authors in the older series are women and 15 percent in the newer series are women.

Brief biographies of the authors appear in both series. In the new series (*Currents*) a biography of one author—Angelica Gibbs—does not appear. In the older series the name of Rosemary Carr Benet is printed with a note that refers to the biography of her husband, Stephen Vincent Benet, in which she is briefly mentioned.

Another aspect that we investigated was the titles of works. In the newer series 15 titles contain the names of men, and two titles contain the names of women. In the older series 42 titles contain men's names, and nine contain women's names. Expressed as percentages, 18 percent of the older series titles and 12 percent of the newer series titles contain women's names.

The final topic considered was the appearance of men and women as main subjects of works. In the newer series, women were main characters in 10 percent, and in the older series, women were the main characters in about 30 percent of the works.

We would like to point out that these observations concern the contents of the anthologies. Not all of the selections are read and there is no way of knowing which readings are selected by the teachers for the students to study, or which aspects of the work the teacher chooses to emphasize; however the overall tone is set by these anthologies. We recommend that the teachers give consideration to this survey when they make their lesson plans and presentations.

We also conducted an overview of some English courses offered at the high school level. Sharon Christman provided us with reading lists from various high schools, and we arbitrarily chose the one from Fairview. In no way do we mean to challenge the professionalism of the teachers involved in these courses particularly since we are not personally acquainted with the teachers at Fairview. We have tried to be as objective as possible in reviewing the course offerings, but always with the point of view of a woman concerned with the representation of women in literature.

Advanced Placement English used the works of 14 authors, all male, from Sophocles to Fitzgerald and Arthur Miller plus a couple of anthologies by 12 American writers. All the main characters of the novels are men.

The course on Satire included works by seven authors, all male. All main characters in the selections are men.

Science Fiction selections were also all by male authors.

Man in Conflict used seven authors, all male. With the exception of Salinger's *Franny and Zooey* all main characters are male.

American Drama used six authors including one woman.

American Novel used 12 authors, all male, and 15 books. In two of the books, there are two female main characters—Lewis' *Main Street* and Hawthorne's *The Scarlet Letter.*

American Hero used eight authors, two of them women. There was one woman main character—Cather's *My Antonia.*

Frontier Literature used no female authors or female main characters.

British Novels used 16 works by 14 authors. One novel by a female author was included—Woolf's *To the Lighthouse.* Women main characters include Mrs. Ramsey in *To the Lighthouse* and Becky Sharp in *Vanity Fair.*

European Novels used 15 works by 14 authors, all male. All main characters in the novels are male.

Throughout this survey, we wondered why these courses omitted: works by the Bronte sisters, Hannah Green (*I Never Promised You a Rose Garden*), Sylvia Plath (*The Bell Jar*), Joyce Oates, Edith Wharton, Gertrude Stein, Bel Kaufman (*Up the Down Staircase*), Ayn Rand (*Fountainhead*), Susan Sontag, Simone deBeauvoir, Anne Frank (*Diary*), Muriel Spark (*Prime of Miss Jean Brodie*), and Lorraine Hansberry. In conclusion, we ask that the Language Arts Consultant and teachers:

1. Write to publishers of anthologies urging that more women authors be included, as well as works in which women are main characters.

2. Include in the classroom discussions of how novels or stories portray women and what the author's viewpoint of women seems to be.

3. Invite women active in writing and other professions to participate in the classes.

SEX STEREOTYPES IN MATHEMATICS AND SCIENCE TEXTBOOKS FOR ELEMENTARY AND JUNIOR HIGH SCHOOLS

I. The Sex Component of Set Theory

Is the following an innocent exercise in permutations and combinations?

> There were 4 boys and 5 girls at a party. In how many different ways can one girl be matched with one boy for a game?
>
> (Deans et al., *Developing Mathematics*, Book 3 [Gr. 3])

Problem: To diagram the proper relationship between boys and girls. Answer:

$$\begin{array}{c} G \\ G \quad \text{(serving food)} \end{array}$$

G G B		
TABLE	B	(Note boys at head of table.)
G G B		

> (Abstraction of picture found in Keedy et al., *Exploring Modern Mathematics*, Book 1 [Gr. 7])

Are the following sets joint or disjoint?

> The set of all boys who play football and the set of all boys who play baseball.

Note: By Josephine Mlinar. Reprinted with permission from *Report on Sex Bias in the Public Schools*. Copyright © 1973 by the Education Committee, National Organization for Women, New York City Chapter (28 East 56th Street, New York, New York 10022).

The set of all girls who have short hair and the set of all girls who have blue eyes.

(Gundlach et al., *Mathematics 5* [Gr. 5])

Clearly, it is implied that the set of children (boys) who are characterized by their physical activity and the set of children (girls) who are characterized by their physical appearance are disjoint.

Consider the following family activities in a camping scene from a second-grade text (Duncan, *Modern School Mathematics, 2* [Gr. 2]):

Female: Mother cooks on outdoor grill; girl watches baby.

Male: Father sets up tent; boy helps father; boy sails boat; boy romps with dogs.

The female members of the family are occupied with "homemaking" activities. The male members, by contrast, are involved in physically vigorous, "building" or "play" activities. The two boys at play are obviously engaged in *optional* activities, which permit them to develop independence and to increase their range of experience. No such choice is apparent in the female activities.

Let's examine the first-grader's view of male and female roles. Consider the pictures found in the first 100 pages of a first-grade text (Duncan, *Modern School Mathematics 1* [Gr. 1]):

Female:	*Activity shown or implied:*	*Male:*	*Activity shown or implied:*
Indian girls	none	sailors	sailing
queen	ruling (with king)	band members	marching, playing music
dolls	none		
witches	casting spells	king	ruling (with queen)
Eskimo girls	none	bakers	baking
girls	buying balloons	pirates	plundering ships
girls	skipping rope	circus performers	performing
		knights	jousting
		man	observing stars
		clowns	clowning
		man	selling balloons
		boy	raising pumpkin
		boys	swimming
Indeterminate:		Indian chiefs	ruling Indians
skiers		Indian men	war dancing
		variously dressed men	none

There are curious differences between the male and female images. In the first place, there are many more male images (15 to 7). In the second place, only one male picture is totally passive (no action shown or implied), whereas nearly half of the female pictures (three) are passive. The varied male adult roles are generally realistic (sailor, band member, baker, circus performer, astronomer, clown, balloon salesman) and include several ways of earning a living. The female adult roles are not realistic (queen, witch) and no reasonable way of earning a living is shown. The girls, however, may *spend* money (buying balloons).

The seventh grade sees the pattern repeated in problems (Keedy et al., *Exploring Modern Mathematics*, Book 1 [Gr. 7]):

Female activities: Buying chocolate creams; using flour; buying gingham; baby-sitting to earn *extra* money; walking to school; being 4 feet tall; finding mixed numerals in an easier way (than boys); writing a fractional numeral; using a skirt pattern; serving candy; using lace on a blouse; ordering a floor tile; making towels; making dresser scarves.

Male activities: Gardening; building scenery; growing $2\frac{1}{2}$ feet taller; planting grass; cutting a board; painting a room; hiking 50 miles; running 100-yard dash; being 5 feet tall; finding an average; copying a house plan; having a 7 foot board; finding mixed numerals; showing a shorter way (than a girl's) to write a fractional numeral; painting a living room; driving; trying to correct a fractional numeral; filling boxes with candy; making baskets (basketball); delivering groceries by bicycle; cutting bookshelves; cutting a board; dividing fractions; carrying the ball in a football game; selling pine trees.

Girls and women spend a great deal of time sewing and cooking. Walking to school is their most strenuous activity. Girls baby-sit to earn "extra" money. Their accomplishments are the private production of clothing and food, which wear out and are eaten respectively. Girls, unlike boys, don't spend leisure time playing or relaxing.

Boys and men spend considerable time in carpentry, painting, and gardening, which result in relatively permanent accomplishments. They engage in strenuous sports in which they achieve public recognition. They earn money (delivering groceries, selling pine trees) or practice money-making activities (copying a house plan)—and nowhere is it suggested that this money is "extra." Male examples are used 26 times; female examples only 15 times. Only in school may boys and girls participate on an equal basis.

Finally, let us consider the field of mathematics itself. What role models are presented? Surely there could be no problem here, since mathematics is intrinsically abstract and asexual.

Female mathematicians: None.

Male mathematicians: Eratosthenes; Goldbach; Euclid; John Napier; Fibonacci; Pascal.

The great algebraist Emmy Noether is not even mentioned. Even Stein's book which is very abstract, conforms to the practice of omitting female role models (Stein, *Fundamentals of Mathematics* [Gr. 8–10]). All the mathematicians above are cited with corresponding accomplishments. A girl could not help but conclude that there are no female mathematicians; and if there are, they have never done anything worthwhile.

Is there a ray of hope in the darkness? The Spitzer et al. series, *Elementary Mathematics,* appears at first to be totally unbiased as to sex. The reason for this is that nearly all of the examples of boys and girls in the text (on nearly every page) depict class participation. Thus, nearly all the examples are nonstereotyped. Nevertheless, nonclassroom activities are very much stereotyped:

Female activities: Papering cupboard shelves; using red ribbon; filling an aquarium; reading.

Male activities: Assembling a fishing rod; playing with planes; making a boardwalk across a puddle; buying paint (Spitzer et al. [Gr. 4]). Loading a truck with newspapers; loading a truck with melons; marking cans in a grocery; finding the height of a water tower; finding how far radar signals travel in 1 hour; racing a boat; practicing music; catching fish; helping in a local paper drive (Spitzer et al. [Gr. 6]).

Here we have all the usual stereotypes: female restriction to indoor, nonstrenuous, nonremunerative, and nonscientific activities which produce no permanent result. Boys may also engage in such activities, but generally their activities have some, if not all, of the opposite characteristics, and are much more varied.

The art of mathematics sex stereotyping is obviously far advanced and all-pervasive. Some recommendations to remove sex stereotyping are:

1. Inform publishers that henceforth texts will be screened for frequency and type of male and female role models and examples. Only nonstereotyped books will be acceptable.

2. All current texts should be screened similarly. Publishers should be notified of necessary corrections. Books should be dropped from the official textbook list if corrections are not made immediately.

II. Sex Education in the Science Lab

> A scientist is a human being like yourself. *He* has much the same sort of everyday problems you have. But *he* also attempts to solve problems about what is in the world around *him*. To do this, *he* is always looking for facts that will help answer *his* questions. (Emphasis added.) (Beauchamp et al., *Everyday Problems in Science* [Gr. 8–9])

Grade 1: Establishment of adult sex-role models

Aim: To establish clear differences between adult male and female sex roles. To prepare girls for later invisibility via paucity of pictures of adult women.

Means: Examples of children imitating adult sex roles and pictures illustrating appropriate sex-role differentiation.

Adult female pictures: Walking in the rain; shooing pigs into a sty; checking a thermometer and putting a coat on a boy; taking a coat from the closet; getting caught in an elephant's trunk.

Adult male pictures: Walking in the rain; holding balloons; setting out smudge pots in orange groves; holding a briefcase; walking against the wind; swimming around a capsized boat; extricating a truck from the mud; painting a gutter; introducing a circus act; clowning; selling balloons; spilling nails; riding a motorcycle; hosing down a sidewalk; putting cows in a barn.

Adult role model imitations
Boy raises chair above head, while girl holding chair waist-high looks on admiringly.

Father paints, boy piles fallen twigs in wagon, boy mows lawn, girl sweeps.

Man rides motorcycle, boy drives horsecart, boys climb tree, girl bounces on pogo stick.

Grade 2: Establishment of acceptable female sex roles outside the home

Aim: Establish appropriate female occupations. Contrast with male occupations which tend to exert control over the immediate environment. Emphasize female service to males. Accustom girls to invisibility via a lack of pictures of girls, combined with many pictures of boys encompassing a wide range of experiences.

Means: Pictures indicating acceptable behavior and subjects.

Adult female: Nurse describing a heart, showing pulse to boys, and giving them shots; packers in an assembly line packing corn.

Adult male: Driving a combine; herding cattle; spraying trees.

Girl: No activity.

Boy: Exploring woods; watching a butterfly; climbing a log; dismembering a flower; listening to a nurse describe a heart; observing a pulse as shown by nurse; eating a sandwich; holding a grapefruit; getting a shot from a nurse.

Grade 3: Establishment of feminine nurturance; establishment of male technological aptitude

Aim: To prepare girls for their future duties as homemakers via appropriate adult and child role models. To inculcate a sense of male technological monopoly in all areas except homemaking.

Means: Pictures illustrating homemaking and nurturant behavior in females. Careful exhibition of acceptable uses of technology by each sex.

Adult female: Sewing; ironing; baking.

Adult male: Reading the paper.

Girl: Feeding goldfish; placing a plant in the sun; looking at a plant; looking at teeth in a mirror; exploring woods; polishing a floor; watching TV.

Boy: Holding mirror for a girl; wearing an outgrown suit; feeding a puppy; exploring woods; demonstrating a magnetic field of electric current; watching TV; drawing with a soldering iron; experimenting with current.

Grade 4: Inculcation of male leadership role

Aim: To present leadership as an inherently male function. To drive home the connection between power and maleness. To further emphasize the invisibility of females outside the classroom. To present scientists as exclusively male.

Means: "Investigation pages" to encourage student experimentation, with males shown as leaders in experimental activities. Pictures and text which depict males almost exclusively. Description of the work of male scientists only.

A. Investigation Pages:

"Chemical and Physical Changes"

1. A male short-order cook frying pancakes.

2. Melting ice—A boy checks a thermometer and records temperature while a boy and a girl watch.
3. Physical state of butter—Two girls check a thermometer and record temperature.
4. Physical changes: a man saws wood, a boy breaks twig, a girl tears paper.
5. A boy in a baseball uniform eats lunch.

"Energy to Do Work"

Two girls make a pendulum, then—a boy measures the pendulum, swings pendulum, adds weight to pendulum, and shortens pendulum.

B. Pictures:

Adult female pictures: Removing cake from oven.

Adult male pictures: Putting anti-freeze in a car; extinguishing a candle with a jar; extinguishing a candle with a tweezer; adjusting chemical equipment; James Prescott Joule; packing boxes; driving a tractor; driving a locomotive; adjusting equipment in a plant.

C. Text:

Adult female: No activity.

Adult male: Joule's work; Einstein's work.

Girl: No activity.

Boy: Pushing a box; playing baseball.

D. Scientists Described:

James Joule, Percival Lowell, Clyde Tombaugh, other men indexed.

Grade 5: The male as paid worker

Aim: To firmly inculcate the image of the male as paid worker. To emphasize the concept of woman as child; to denigrate the value of her work. To further stress women's invisibility. To present male scientist role models.

Means: Pictures of males in various remunerative occupations. Text references to males in various activities, especially science. Omission of females in pictures. A "Scientists in Action" section acclaiming the accomplishments of male scientists.

A. Scientists in Action:

Luther Burbank (botanist)
Robert Hutchings Goddard (rocket developer)

John H. Glenn (rocket pilot)
Vilhelm Bjerknes (meteorologist)

B. Pictures

Adult female: Watching male TV image; singer ("girl").

Adult male: Using a solar cell; repairing a telephone line; shaving with an electric shaver; TV cameraman; male announcer; male TV image; satellite ground controller; disk jockey; doctor; TV engineer; driving a car; riding a rocket chair.

Girl: Talking on the telephone; schoolgirls "transmitting a picture."

Boy: Talking on the telephone; jumping off a wagon.

C. Text

1. "You have heard your *father* talk about the battery in *his* car. You know *he* cannot get the car started without it." (Emphasis added.)
2. Discussion of Isaac Newton and Newton's Laws of Motion.
3. Discussion of action and reaction when boy jumps out of wagon.
4. Action and reaction with reference to man riding a rocket chair.
5. Transportation necessary to visit one's grandmother in California.
6. "The girl here is singing into a microphone." (Picture of a mature woman)
7. Thomas Edison's inventions.
8. Policemen's use of radar.

Grade 7: The male scientist

Aim: Depiction of male participation in various scientific activities. Admission of Marie Curie to the male scientist elite.

Means: Pictures of male scientists at work. Text describing male scientific accomplishments. Multiple male scientist role models. Emphasis on male use of technology.

A. Pictures

Female: Madame Curie in lab; radioactive testing of piston wear.

Male: Pierre Curie in lab; researching of radioactive substances; radioactive testing of piston wear; inspecting an atomic reactor; assembling a satellite; Ernest O. Lawrence by his cyclotron; observing a fusion demonstration; adjusting a stellerator; Newton; Rumford; Joule; lighting a piece of wood in a solar furnace; with fuel cell; generating electricity with a teakettle; with sunlight collector; with cesium cell; with biochemical cell.

Indeterminate: Using Geiger counter.

B. Text

1. Scientists whose accomplishments are described

Female: Marie Curie.

Male: Antoine Henri Bequerel; Pierre Curie; Ernest Rutherford; Ernest O. Lawrence; Milton S. Livingston; Enrico Fermi; Otto Hahn; Glenn Seaborg; Edwin McMillan; Abelsun; Aristotle; Sir Isaac Newton; Benjamin Thomson Rumford; James Joule; Thomas Edison.

2. "Primitive *man* used only *his* muscles to produce energy, but *he* soon found out that *he* could not do very much work by *himself.* Animals were probably *man's* first outside source of energy, but they could not provide all the energy *man* wanted. *Man* then built machines to use the energy of wind and water and eventually began to use fuels such as wood, coal, and later oil to supply the energy needed to run *his* machines."

"*Man* needs a great deal of energy to operate the large machines that do *his* work. Before the invention of engines that burned fuel to release energy, the only available sources of energy, in addition to *man's* own muscles, were animals, water, and wind. Water wheels are one of the earliest known machines used by *man* to obtain energy from flowing water for *his* needs. . . . The wind has long been a source of energy used by *man.*" (Emphasis added.) (Blanc et al., *Man, Matter, and Energy* [Gr. 7–9])

Grade 8: A career in science (women need not apply)

Aim: To establish masculinity of scientific careers and behavior.

Means: Coordination of generally nonsexist text with pictures portraying males in various scientific fields. Use of male scientist role models. Depiction of males as scientific thinkers.

A. Text: How Do Scientists Think and Work?

Female: None.

Male: Aristotle; Galileo; Louis Pasteur; Thomas Edison; Jan Lippershey; Zacharias Janssen; Anton von Leeuwenhoek.

B. Pictures

Female: Observing through microscope.

Male: Repairing a generator; observing electronic equipment; checking gauges; chemist testing material; physicist using equipment; geologist studying rock samples; geologist charting rock layers; biologist simulating Martian conditions; man ("you") solving problem of extricating a model plane from a tree; using an electron microscope; using high-speed photographic equipment; using analytical balance; working in a lab.

Mathematics Textbooks

Grade	Text	Section (pp.) Reviewed
1	Duncan, *Modern School Mathematics 1*	1–100
2	Duncan, *Modern School Mathematics 2*	100–200
3	Deans et al., *Developing Mathematics,* Book 3	50–150
4	Spitzer et al., *Elementary Mathematics,* Book 4	1–25
5	Gundlach et al., *New Laidlaw Mathematics Program,* Mathematics 5	1–50
6	Spitzer et al., *Elementary Mathematics,* Book 6	25–50
7	Keedy et al., *Exploring Modern Mathematics,* Book 1	100–200 (pictures) 150–200 (problems)
8–10	Stein, *Fundamentals of Mathematics,* Second Course	1–100

Science Textbooks

Grade	Text	Section Reviewed
1	Beauchamp et al., *Science is Fun*	Weather We Move Things
2	Mallinson et al., *Science 2*	Man among the Animals of the World
3	Beauchamp et al., *Science is Exploring*	How Do Living Things Get Food? Electric Current
4	Jacobson et al., *Probing into Science*	Materials of the Earth Energy to Do Work
5	Munch-Syrocki *Book V*	Energy and Matter Scientists in Action
7–9	Blanc et al., *Man, Matter, and Energy*	Matter and Energy Forms and Sources of Energy
8–9	Beauchamp et al., *Everyday Problems in Science*	How Do Scientists Think and Work (includes quote used to introduce science section)

FEMINIST CRITICISM: AN OVERVIEW

Feminist criticism of juvenile books rests on certain assumptions: that society is sexist; that the products of society—e.g., its books—are guilty of incorporating and passing on society's sexist values; that in so doing they constitute propaganda; that this propaganda stifles potential and aspirations and therefore must be countered by sensitive, concerned, and able critics.

In the April 1971 issue of *School Library Journal,* author Phyllis Whitney remarked that unless an author is ". . . unabashedly writing propaganda (in the pejorative sense of that word), he should avoid it because it is both misleading and dull. But use of clichés, or having characters repeat common expressions, or adopt common attitudes . . . does not . . . make [a story] propaganda." [1] But what exactly is propaganda? Webster's defines it as "ideas, facts, or allegations spread deliberately to further one's cause, or to damage an opposing cause; also: *a public action having such an effect*" [2] (italics mine). Whether or not a particular viewpoint is deliberately disseminated is not always the major factor. When a certain type of information is spread to the exclusion of other types of information—e.g., the sexist thoughts and standards pervading children's books—the question of intent is irrelevant. The effect of this input on impressionable readers is the issue.

Children's books are no longer essentially didactic in nature, intentionally and obviously written to instruct, admonish, and mold character —in short, to propagandize. The pleasure principle in reading has been recognized, ostensibly at least, and at least lip service is paid to aesthetic criteria. But books reflect not only their authors' philosophy but the philosophy of the society producing them. And the use of clichés, common expressions, and characters who exhibit attitudes commonly held in society—attitudes that are not always admirable—do indeed make a story propaganda. In most cases, fictional characters repeat common expressions and adopt common attitudes only because these characters are stereotypes, not because to do so would be psychologically valid for their personalities as created by an author.

Many, many studies documenting specific examples of sexual stereotyping in children's books have been done by private groups, feminist organizations, and official task forces. These studies show that many more stories have been written about boys than about girls. The boys do many more interesting and certainly more physical and fun things in a broader range of geographical settings than do the girls (indeed, it often seems that the only females who really get around geographically are witches on broomsticks). The story lines reveal that boys often have to help out passive, helpless girls; that mothers often scold and rarely work outside the home (real-world labor statistics to the contrary); that fathers are the opposite of mothers in both respects; that, unlike girls, boys look forward to and anticipate their futures, as they see men around them absorbed in various interesting professions. Numerous authors treat admirable female fictional characters and even outstanding real women as exotic freaks. At the elementary school level, such depictions are internalized by learning children as expressions of what is, and consequently, they constitute propaganda. Researchers have pointed out that girls outperform boys academically in grade school but that their grades plummet during the socially conscious high school years. Such change is likely due at least in part to the cumulative effect of sex-role conditioning from grade school readers and other children's books.

Equal representation for girls in books doesn't mean more Jane Bond/Superwoman stories—e.g., like the Nancy Drew books. This series is so popular because it represents wish fulfillment for girl readers—who, given Nancy's unreal perfection, *have* to be homelier, less independent, and less perspicacious than she is. Even Nancy's own friends are fully conscious of how inferior to her they are—and, again, the old story, of how unique she is. Nancy is the American dream girl, the blue-eyed blonde who has it all. Girls may guess the outcomes of her mysteries, but because she's so unreal, her adventures can never be truly inspirational, merely standard escape reading. There's nothing wrong with escape reading—it's often a positive pleasure—but there is a real need for real-world girls' adventure stories too; stories which could legitimately inspire young girls to say, "I can do that, and go there, too."

Feminist criticism is by no means monolithic. The fact that feminist critics can dispute the criteria used and conclusions reached by other feminist critics shows how far we've come in a short time in this one area.

Once we acknowledge how very important feminist criticism is, we can start to express what we individually feel to be the most valid and therefore the most potentially influential forms of it.

What must feminist critics be on guard against? Like all critics, they must cope with the problem of fairly isolating quotes from their contexts to persuade readers who haven't read the books in question. They must take care not to unthinkingly praise books which build up little girls at the expense of little boys (one such book is *Messy Sally*,[3] in which a rough-and-tumble girl is presented as obviously superior to a neat boy). Boys should be shown in nonstereotyped roles too—as quiet, unathletic, studious, tidy—without being derided for it. Feminist criticism, to be enduring, must be humanistic criticism.

Feminist critics should not sacrifice aesthetic standards in judging books. If the only books featuring girls and women in nonstereotyped roles are inferior ones (ugly picture books, poorly written novels, clichéd biographies), then message has to be given precedence over medium and the inferior books made available to children. But good books are being produced now, so feminist critics must judge poor ones harshly— many of which are didactic or were written and published strictly to capitalize on lib fervor and to make a buck. The establishment and feminist presses can serve to keep each other honest, the feminist presses by so increasing and perfecting their products as to put competitive pressure on the establishment publishers; the latter by putting out the quality books they can better afford and so forcing the feminist presses to attend to quality as well as message. Presses like The Feminist Press also do extremely valuable work by sponsoring community workshops which bring home to the public the problem of sex-role stereotyping in children's books.

Feminist critics sometimes disagree on whether particular types of stories and expressions—e.g., fairy tales, or the use of male/female gender for inanimate objects—are insulting to females. Some critics maintain that fairy tales depict independent, resourceful, capable women, while others point to the stock negative characters: witchy older women, insipid young princesses, etc. Some critics resent the fact that machines, boats, tractors, etc., are given male appellations in juvenile books, while others believe they're more often female and resent what they consider to be the dehumanizing of females, the making female of objects which are, after all, strictly functional things usually used by men. Abstract theorizing and argumentation should not delay or take the place of constructive change in books, but these disagreements are healthy and desirable, and discussion should continue on the issues.

Feminist critics sometimes read too much significance into animal fantasies. It is a valid complaint that the animals considered most attractive or admirable by humans are usually male in children's books. It is often misguided, however, to confuse human issues and problems with those of animals. If a female hen is outwitted by a wily male fox, for example, that's a realistic reflection of nature. The need is for stories where female foxes outwit roosters.

It's true that many of the best juvenile books are about boys. But while it is justifiable to seek more females in all forms of children's literature, it is not right to disparage specific, individual authors for not including them. If a book, though it centers on boys, is one of those rare top-quality works (e.g., books by Sendak and Seuss), it represents the triumph of creativity, not a put-down of the female, and deserves any accolades it garners. It is valid and necessary, however, to pan so-called or otherwise good books when they feature stereotyped females. And, it is imperative that publishers no longer pressure writers to make the protagonist male, e.g., in adventure stories. Girls can and do hanker for adventure as much as boys, and boys will read about girls if only they're presented as three-dimensional characters with a little spunk, intelligence, and initiative.

Feminist critics have to tread carefully in the area of historical fiction. Objecting to historical novels because the characters in them are urged to be ladylike in behavior or spend their time wondering about whom they'll marry, is ignoring history. If that's the way it was, if those were the preoccupations of people in the era depicted, then that's what an author must present. There's a fine line to be drawn here, and each critic obviously draws it for her- or himself. There is a difference between telling it like it was and an authorial tone or statement condoning how it was. For example, a statement such as "Anne daydreamed constantly about future beaux" might well be a realistic description of a typical young girl's thoughts in a particular era. (Indeed, in any era it's natural for people to contemplate their future loves and spouses.) But if an author says, "Carla found, after all, that dressing up and being a lady was much more fun than climbing trees"—that pretty blatantly obtrudes clichéd opinion and amounts to propaganda, if there's nothing in Carla's personality to warrant the turnabout. There's no reason why she can't do both.

Feminist critics *can* remind writers of historical fiction that in every era there are men and women who quietly or dramatically defy convention. And there are men and women whose life styles and activities merely seem unconventional to later generations, e.g., many Blacks in nineteenth-century America were cowboys, but only recently has this fact been made widely known to nonreaders. Unconventional women and women whose achievements were either ignored or forgotten are certainly fit subjects for historical novels.

Feminist critics must work for the upgrading of traditional female roles in children's books as well as for the expanding of female roles. Housewives and mothers are not necessarily insipid or wasting their potential; dainty little girls are not necessarily mindless or superficial. They should not disappear from the pages of juvenile books in a binge of overreaction. (Nor should traditional men and boys.) There is no reason why they and female scientists, politicians, and athletes can't comfortably coexist.

Finally, feminist critics must avoid paranoia if they are to be taken seriously. Publishers and writers haven't huddled in corners and plotted to stereotype females in juvenile literature. There hasn't been what Elizabeth Fisher calls "an almost incredible conspiracy of conditioning." [4] Sex-role stereotyping in children's books is undeniably prevalent and harmful, but it has been done unthinkingly and unconsciously. Feminist critics should make their goal the enlightenment, not the castigation, of book producers. If they're ignored, brushed off, or handed only token changes, they can then come out swinging, in print and with boycotts against particular publishers and authors.

Some writers—e.g., Mrs. Whitney in her *School Library Journal* letter—have stated that they will not be pressured into spouting the feminist or any other party line. Certainly not. However, writers must realize that any author who presents one-sided depictions of females is—though most likely unwittingly—a party hack for the status quo. Mrs. Whitney equated the pressure exerted by feminist critics with that in dictatorships, ". . . where literature must positively support the policies and theories of those in power, or else." [5] However, it's rather amusing to compare even theoretically the relatively powerless feminists' wish for fair representation for females in literature with dictatorship-controlled literature that echoes the policies of "those in power."

Succeeding historical periods always allow a new understanding of social problems. Today's publishers, writers, critics, and book buyers can avoid producing, praising, and buying titles that are offensive in their portrayal of females. But what about the older books, particularly the well-known and popular ones, that are already entrenched in libraries? The problem has been raised before in other contexts. Do we chuck out Andersen tales for anti-Semitic allusions? Toss out *Little Black Sambo* for its negative racial stereotypes? (Several groups have opted for this—e.g., the Canadian National Black Coalition.) Get rid of the novels which portray women stereotypically; the history books which barely allude to them at all?

If one seriously wanted to remove all sexist books from libraries, most of the shelves would be depleted. Some zealous feminists might describe the removal of the worst of these books as needed and justifiable corrective social action. But it would be censorship, pure, simple, and impermissible.

Obviously, it would be ideal if librarians and teachers could talk individually to each girl or boy reading a book—e.g., a historical novel—and explain to them that the book reflects a past society, past mores that are certainly not indicative of the options open to girls—and boys—now. But this is hardly feasible. It is feasible, however, for librarians and teachers to make children familiar with books, articles, etc. that explain the reasons behind the preoccupations and occupations of people in different eras. An undertaking like this on a large scale would involve much work, yet it could be enormously beneficial, considering how susceptible children are to what they read. Similar materials could elaborate on folk and fairy tales, indicating that these are records of the values, aspirations, mythical triumphs, and fears of groups of people. This might prevent such tales from being interpreted literally by readers: e.g., a member of the Redstockings Collective who, in a piece entitled "Married and Single," said, quite understandably: "My idea of the male savior and protector was reinforced by the stories of Cinderella, Snow White, and other childhood classics. I could expect a Prince Charming to come along someday too. He would take me away and we would live happily ever after." [6]

Certainly, librarians and teachers should make available critical essays on fictional works which are stylistic triumphs but in which are manifested the peculiar neuroses of an author. Children should be able to be exposed to truly good works of fiction without taking the author's philosophy or life view as gospel; they should be made to realize that fiction is a craft, and that appreciation of a craftsman or woman doesn't necessarily entail acceptance of his or her emotional/mental outlook. Again, any book, intentionally or not, can amount to a political statement for the status quo, so materials of this sort are merely balancing agents, providing a bit of historical fact or psychological background or critical cross-section of opinion to enlarge a reader's understanding of what is being read.

In any event, we must make a distinction between the concerns of adult and juvenile book critics. Adults may change their opinions on the basis of what they read, but their minds are essentially set. For example, adults who read anti-Vietnam war books were probably already against the war; those who read pro-war literature were likely to be supporters.

Or, adults may read books as debaters and rebutters, to pit their knowledge against an author's. Adult book criticism often echoes this quality of gamesmanship; it has less of a sense of urgency about it than children's book criticism has—or should have. Critical reviews of adult books often tend to be intellectual plumage displays, seemingly undertaken at a kind of leisure. They're often humorous, very entertaining to read, and their authors could probably bite and banter back and forth persuasively for a long time.

But people concerned with books for children don't have a long time. They can't afford to complacently spar with an intellectual elite, to engage in protracted salon-type discussions. They're dealing with readers who are growing up fast; whose minds are not yet completely molded, whose opinions are not yet irremediably formed, who can be, and are, life-changingly influenced by the books they read.

Book producers must share the concerns and exhibit the awareness of feminist critics. Obviously, they can show a female character as bitchy, stupid, etc. But the motivations for the character's behavior must be clear and believable. She must be unlikable as an individual, not as a stereotype of the castrating older woman, the brainless ingenue, etc. And if an author is going to comment by statement, implication, or omission, let her or him do so equally for all the characters. This isn't influencing a writer on what to write; it's demanding the kind of ultimate psychological/dramatic verity that is needed if a book is to be any good. As John Rowe Townsend said in his May Hill Arbuthnot Honor Lecture presented in April 1971: ". . . if we are to move onward from kiddy lit and all that the use of that squirmy term implies, then children's books must be taken seriously as literature, and this means they must be considered with critical strictness."

In that same talk, Townsend alluded to a distinction he had once made between "book people"—authors, publishers, reviewers, public librarians—and "child people"—parents, teachers, and school librarians. He went on to say that "different kinds of assessment are valid for different purposes" and that "different standards can coexist within the mind of the same person at the same time."

Feminist criticism provides a strong ground of common cause for book people and child people. Those principally concerned with the quality of juvenile books can, on feminist/critical grounds, point to the fact that so many juvenile books are so poor because they flagrantly stereotype the female characters. Those principally concerned with children can, on feminist/critical grounds, point to how sexist books are stunting girls' ambition and eagerness to experience and do. Townsend remarked that ". . . we would wish every child to experience to his or her full capacity the enjoyment, and the broadening of horizons, which can be derived from literature." This, I think, is all that any feminist critic wants.

References

1. PHYLLIS A. WHITNEY, Letter, *School Library Journal*, XVII: 8 (April, 1971), p. 6.
2. *Webster's Seventh New Collegiate Dictionary* (Springfield: G. & C. Merriam Co., 1965), p. 683.
3. GLADYS Y. CRETAN, *Messy Sally* (New York: Lothrop, Lee & Shepard Co., 1972).
4. ELIZABETH FISHER, "The Second Sex, Junior Division," *The New York Times Book Review*, May 24, 1970, Section 7, Part II, p. 6.
5. *Ibid.*
6. Redstockings Collective, "How Women Are Kept Apart: Married and Single," *Women's Liberation: Blueprint for the Future,* comp. Sookie Stambler (New York: Ace Books, 1970), p. 34.

PART 4

Media Mix and the Games Children Play

WONDER WOMAN REVISITED

"One Superman is worth three Wonder Woman's," I conceded, stacking, counting, and restacking comics on the sidewalk. I was an avid comic-book reader, but I pretended not to like Wonder Woman. After all, it wasn't a real advantage in our daily comic trades. The boys on my block always bid for Superman, the Green Lantern, or Batman; even Donald Duck. But never Wonder Woman. "She's just a girl," they said. And so, being "just a girl" myself, I hid my admiration for Wonder Woman and put my stakes on Superman.

But up in my apple tree, I read Wonder Woman anyway. "Breaking the fetters of evil with her strength; parrying bullets with her steel bracelets; sweeping through dimensions of time and space in her invisible plane, Wonder Woman, the Amazonian princess from Paradise Isle, brought enemies to their knees and to her command with her golden magic lasso." Who could resist a role model like that? In America she lived as Diana Prince—secretary, nurse, army intelligence officer—but she could change into Wonder Woman costume and appear from nowhere to do battle with the forces of evil. In the mid-forties she even jumped into politics with a campaign for President—a woman to save the country from war and destruction.

I loved her comic cohorts, too.

Etta Candy: fat and frustrated—who stuffed her problems with chocolate and her comments with "Woo, Woo!"

Merboy: her underwater boyfriend—all boy above and all fish below.

Hyppolyte: her mother and queen of the Amazons (like the mythical Hyppolyta), who taught goodness and justice and kept close tabs on her daughter through a mental radio-TV.

Note: By Joanne Edgar. Reprinted with permission from *Ms.*, July 1972, 1:1, 52–55.

As a kid trading comics on the sidewalk, I wish I'd known that, even though Superman never existed outside the comic-book world, Amazonian princesses did. In sixteenth-century Brazil, for instance. Picture a civilization of jungle women living in caves deep in the rain forests of the Amazon River. These fierce female warriors and powerful victors kidnaped males from neighboring tribes, and brought them to a copulatorium for a mating ritual complete with dancing and flute music. (In memory of this fearful time of women's superiority, some modern-day tribes of Indians in Brazil will not allow their women to play flutes.) Mothers slaughtered their male infants, or maimed them so that they could be used as servants. Daughters were raised in the strong, self-sufficient, and ruling-class images of their mothers.

Many historians have rejected this Amazon society as pure myth; an expression of men's fear of women. But recent archaeological discoveries support the stories of such tribes. Caves painted with triangular female symbols, a copulatorium where a male symbol appears for the first and only time, and a slaughtering basin for male infants or animal sacrifices; all this evidence has been found deep in the jungles of Brazil by German and Brazilian scientists.

Hundreds of similar societies may have existed in other cultures over a period of several thousand years. They were probably backlash societies —a reaction to the cruel, patriarchal takeover of a previously gynocratic world.

Greek myths and legends abound with stories of Amazons. Herodotus and other ancient historians and geographers wrote of such societies in the Black Sea area, Greece, and northeast Africa.

Wonder Woman captured the Amazonian spirit of strength and self-sufficiency, but added the peacefulness and revulsion toward killing that have culturally distinguished women from men.

Wonder Woman herself first appeared in 1941, the invention of a psychologist named William Moulton Marston. Attorney, inventor of the lie-detector test, prison reformer, and businessman, Marston (who wrote comics under the thinly disguised pen name of Charles Moulton) conceived of Wonder Woman as a counter to the "bloodcurdling masculinity" of most comic books. Both plot and characters were based on Marston's self-styled vision of feminist philosophy:

> Women represent love; men represent force. Man's use of force without love brings evil and unhappiness. But Wonder Woman has force bound by love and, with her strength, represents what every woman should be and really *is*. She corrects evil and brings happiness. Wonder Woman proves that women are superior to men because they have love in addition to force.

Not all of Marston's characters were heroines. "Women have been submissive to men and taken men's psychology [force without love] as their own," explained Marston, so women villains still existed, and appeared regularly in Wonder Woman comics. Cheetah, for example, was a feline fury who represented "uncontrolled power."

So much for Marston's theories. Though Wonder Woman in battle reigned supreme, Wonder Woman in love, as if lassoed back into conventionality, became the simpering romantic maiden, willing to relinquish her Amazonian birthright to follow a man. In fact, what brought her to America in the first place was her love (illicit for an Amazon) for Capt. Steve Trevor, U.S. Army.

Wonder Woman's adventures were and are full of violence, but Marston insisted that Wonder Woman herself never sought revenge, nor hurt any villain. "Evil destroys itself, unless Wonder Woman can bind it for constructive use," Marston explained. (After six pages of fierce battle in which Wonder Woman defeats a Nazi spy, for instance, he accidentally slips off a pier and drowns.) Usually Wonder Woman saved her worst enemies and reformed their characters. Exceptions included the distorted and villainized Nazis and Japanese who invaded all good American comics during World War II.

Marston died in 1947, but Wonder Woman lived on. The new writers didn't understand her spirit, however, and she lost some of her original feminist orientation. Her superhuman strength remained, but her violence increased. Rather than proving her superiority over men, she became more and more submissive. In 1968, she relinquished her superhuman Amazon powers along with her bracelets, her golden magic lasso, and her invisible plane. She became a human being. Diana Prince, clad now in boutique pant suits and tunics, acquired conventional emotions, vulnerability to men, the wisdom of an adviser (a man, of course, named I Ching), and the skills of karate, kung fu, and jiujitsu. In other words, she became a female James Bond, but without his sexual exploits. The double standard applied even to her.

Next year, Wonder Woman will be reborn. With the help of her first woman editor, Dorothy Woolfolk, she will rise again as an Amazon, complete with superhuman powers. Ms. Woolfolk also plans to decrease violence in the plots and return our heroine to the feminism of her birth. And maybe to politics, too?

"Great Hera!" says one of the new 1973 comic-book covers. "Wonder Woman, the beautiful Amazon Princess, is alive and well and living on Paradise Isle." And why not? After all, even Wonder Woman needs a Key Biscayne.

But will she still have to trade three for one against Superman?

WHY CHILDREN'S FILMS ARE NOT RATED "R"

I have acquired a reputation for having an offbeat sense of humor, because on assignment for *WLB* I have questioned producers and distributors of children's feature films about sex in their products. It would seem that sex simply doesn't exist in this medium. There is no law which I could locate, written or otherwise, which would dictate this, but there must be a tacit agreement among producers. A terribly clever, futuristic film called *What on Earth* (Contemporary) pictures the automobile as the true inhabitant of the earth, as seen through the eyes of the first Martian scientist to visit here. In the film it is pointed out that sex on this planet has been done away with. When all the evidence has been assembled and studied, one must conclude that children's films have done this long ago.

There are one or two exceptions to the above. For instance, *Le Poulet* (Contemporary) does mention the sex of the animal of the title, and the little boy in the film is shown urinating against a tree. Although the film has done well for its American distributor, it has created some controversy. It has never been shown on American television, and may have been banned in some schools.

But Sexism—

As for *sexism*, it *is* there, and only too much in evidence. The most popular films in the 1967 EFLA (Educational Film Library Association) "Best of Best" list of children's films all have male leads. The best known among these are *Red Balloon* (Brandon), *Golden Fish* (Contemporary), and *White Mane* (Rembrandt). These are films which have remained popular.

Note: By Hannah Miller. Reprinted by permission from the October 1971 issue of the *Wilson Library Bulletin.* Copyright © 1971 by the H. W. Wilson Company.

The National Film Board of Canada has long been among the leading producers of films for children and adults. Some of their classics, which again have male heroes, are *Paddle to the Sea, Peter and the Potter,* and *The Chairmaker.*

Films shown on the CBS Children's Festival have a large audience. Again, one must point out that they are boy-oriented, and that girls today have become used to watching films about boys. *Skinny and Fatty, Boy with Glasses,* and *Blind Bird* (Contemporary), are some of the titles one tends to remember. These films were produced abroad, so we must conclude that this type of orientation is not limited to the United States and Canada.

In my opinion, the "Many American" series (LCA), is the best group of films about minority groups I have seen to date. Each film features a child, the members of his family, and the people among whom he lives. There is nothing maudlin or condescending about these films, but they do not spare the viewer any of the hardships and disadvantages these children must live with. There are six films in the series, and it has proved to be something of an exception to what my study of sexism in this media led me to believe. Four of the films feature boys, but *Felipa: North of the Border,* about a young Mexican-American girl, appeals to both boys and girls. It, like all the others, is a child-oriented film, and states a situation all children can identify with. Felipa teaches her uncle to read English in preparation for a driver's license test. The sixth film, *Siu Mei Wong: Who Shall I Be?* is about a Chinese-American child's desire to take dancing lessons after school instead of attending a Chinese school. Its appeal is decidedly to girls. It is possible though, as seen by *Felipa,* to appeal to child viewers with either boy or girl stars, which leads one to ask why so many of our best children's films feature boys?

If everything grand and exciting always happens to boys in the films we show our children, it is sexism. I recently came across this title in a film catalog: *Pets: A Boy and His Dog* (BFA). I happen to know a lot of girls who have pets, don't you? There is an entire series, "To Be A Musician" (Churchill) made up of three sensitive and beautiful films. All three, featuring a cellist, a conductor, and a composer, are about males.

Thankfully there is always *Madeline* (Rembrandt) to fall back on. Our heroine, although a girl, has not lost her appeal, and generation after generation has grown to love her.

Interestingly enough, except for *Anansi* (Texture), films about African folktales often cast females in strong roles. The women shown are storytellers, wives, and sweethearts who have a strong influence on the lives of their men. *The Magic Tree* (Texture), has both a good and bad woman as lead characters. Yet another folktale, *Why the Sun and the Moon Live in the Sky* (ACI), gives the female, pictured here as the moon, a role of equal importance with the male.

Only one film I know of actually tackles the sex-role problem head-on. *Masculine or Feminine: Your Role in Society* (Coronet) is an excellent film. One can hope it is the first of many to explore this area.

Why No Sex?

As for why sex is excluded from children's films, I'm sure we all have our own answers. Nevertheless, one might have hoped that the situation would have changed by 1971. Not so. In discussing the teaching of sex with members of one school system, I got the feeling that sexuality will become an integral part of education, a state of mind and an attitude passed on to students along with other moral values, rather than as a separate subject. This might be a strong argument for the inclusion of sex in children's entertainment films, but apparently no producer, director, or distributor has, as yet, been convinced of it.

Distributors Cited

ACI Films, 35 West 45th St., New York, N.Y. 10036.

BFA Educational Media (CBS), 2211 Michigan Ave., Santa Monica, Calif. 90404.

Brandon Films, Inc., 221 West 57th St., New York, N.Y. 10019.

Contemporary/McGraw-Hill Films, 1221 Avenue of the Americas, New York, N.Y. 10020.

Coronet Films, 65 South Water St. East, Chicago, Ill. 60601.

Learning Corporation of America, 711 5th Ave., New York, N.Y. 10022.

National Film Board of Canada, Suite 819, 680 5th Ave., New York, N.Y. 10019.

Rembrandt Films, 267 West 25th St., New York, N.Y. 10001.

Texture Films, Inc., 1600 Broadway, New York, N.Y. 10019.

FILM RESOURCES FOR SEX-ROLE STEREOTYPING

This list was compiled by the Resource Center on Sex Roles in Education. A project of The National Foundation for the Improvement of Education, the Resource Center states as its goals: (1) The development of sets of materials for use by administrators, teachers, parents, and students in dealing with the issues of sex-role stereotyping in elementary and secondary education; (2) the operation of a clearinghouse of resource persons and materials concerned with these issues; (3) the provision of technical assistance to states and other groups desiring assistance in the development or implementation of programs dealing with the equality of opportunities for males and females within the educational system.

Anything You Want to Be, by Liane Brandon. Distributed by New Day Films, P.O. Box 315, Franklin Lakes, N.J. 07417. A humorous depiction of the socialization of teen-age women—how do they learn their appropriate "feminine" roles.

Growing Up Female: As Six Become One, by Julia Reichert and James Klein. New Day Films, P.O. Box 315, Franklin Lakes, N.J. 07417. A 60-minute documentary in which six females, ages 4–35, examine the effect of social forces on their lives as women today.

Harriet Tubman and the Underground Railroad, McGraw-Hill, CBS TV, 1964. A film documenting Harriet Tubman's journeys on the Underground Railroad as she led Black slaves to freedom.

Multi-Media Kit of Materials for Teachers and Community Groups, National Education Association, including:

Note: By the Resource Center on Sex Roles in Education, The National Foundation for the Improvement of Education (1156 Fifteenth St., N.W., Suite 918, Washington, D.C. 20005). Reprinted with permission.

Filmstrips: *Cinderella Is Dead*
The Labels and Reinforcement of Sex-Role Stereotyping

Cassettes: *Blue is for Sky; Pink is for Watermelon,* poems by Eve Merriam
Sexism, Racism, Classism in the Schools, by Florence Howe
We Don't Know How to Grow People, by Richard Farson

Publications: *Sex-Role Stereotyping in the Schools*
"A Child's Right to Equal Reading"
"Consciousness Razors"
"Leaders Manual"
"Discussion Starter Guides"
other related materials

Our North American Foremothers, NOW, New York Chapter, 28 East 56th Street, New York, N.Y. 10022. A multimedia presentation about the history of women in the United States.

The Silenced Majority, Media Plus, Inc., 60 Riverside Dr., Suite 11D, New York, N.Y. 10024. A Women's Liberation multimedia kit which surveys the many dimensions of the status and lives of women—in the home, media, law, and employment.

To Be A Woman, Billy Budd Film Company, 235 West 57th St., New York, N.Y. 10022. Several young women discuss their sex-stereotyped roles, and their feelings toward womanhood and femininity.

The Women's Film, Newsreel, 322 7th Ave., New York, N.Y. A documentary in which women of many age groups, classes, and races talk about their lives and the activities they are involved in to change them.

There are of course many other resources available on the Women's Movement and Sexism. We, however, feel that those listed above are the most appropriate concerning sex-role socialization.

SESAME STREET AND SEX-ROLE STEREOTYPES

Sesame Street is an hour-long, daily television program designed to instruct preschool children, particularly urban disadvantaged children. Eight million dollars to create and produce the series was contributed by the Carnegie Corporation, the Ford Foundation, the U.S. Office of Education, and the Corporation for Public Broadcasting.

The content is designed to increase basic skills in recognizing numbers and letters, as well as to foster interest in nature studies and social relations. The first two do not depend on opinion. . . . However, we do not all agree on the roles that men and women must or should play in today's society. Even if most women were content with housework as their career (which I doubt), it would still be wrong to present this stereotype to preschool children. It used to be the sad case that almost all Blacks were servants and apparently content, but I don't think that Sesame Street would dare or wish to identify blackness with servitude. In the same way it is wrong to uniquely identify females with any characteristic other than the ability to have babies and to nurse them.

The following letter was sent to Joan Cooney, Executive Director of the Children's Television Workshop (which produces Sesame Street), 1865 Broadway, New York, New York 10023, and to women I think are or should be concerned with the problem. . . . I urge you to monitor this show and if you are disturbed by what you see, to take action, including writing to Mrs. Cooney, to the financial supporters of the program, to the local station and/or your congressmen.

In September, I attended the Symposium at the American Psychological Association Convention in which Gerald Lesser gave a "preview" of Sesame Street and was very favorably impressed

Note: By Jo-Ann Evans Gardner. Reprinted with permission from *Women: a Journal of Liberation,* Spring 1970, 1:3. Copyright © 1970 by *Women: a Journal of Liberation* (3028 Greenmount Avenue, Baltimore, Maryland 21218).

with what I saw. Over the past few days I have been ill and have had time to watch several shows in their entirety. My original judgment that children would learn from these was strengthened but my impression of what they would learn was seriously in error. I am very distressed by some of what I have seen. The sex-role stereotypy portrayed by the production in the social and nature studies section is extreme.

On one program, Big Bird (having said that he would like to be a member of a family and having been told that Gordon and Susan would be his family) is told that he will have to help with the work and that since he is a boy bird, he will have to do men's work—the heavy work, the *"important"* work and also that he should get a girl (bird) to help Susan with *her* work arranging flowers, redecorating, etc. There was more and virtually all of it emphasized that there is men's work and then there is women's work—that men's work is outside the home and women's work is in the home. (This in spite of the fact that 17 *million* children under eighteen have mothers who are employed outside the home; of these 4.5 million are under six.)

On another later program there was a caricature of the program "To Tell the Truth." On this one the contestant, Billy Monster, was supposed to figure out who was the *real* mother of a family which consisted of three puppets, a clearly distinguishable father, mother, and child. When he asked the (obviously father) No. 1, "Do you comb your children's fur," the father puppet replied, "No, I work, I drive a truck, I do not comb the children's fur." A question to No. 2 (the mother puppet) about keeping the cave "neat and clean for your family" elicited the response that she had never been in a cave but that she made the beds and did the laundry. A question to No. 3 "Do you teach your children to roar and growl?" communicated an image of fathers that could better be eliminated from everybody's repertoire. I suspect that the point that Billy was a monster and the consequent implication that (perhaps only) monsters roar at their children was entirely too quickly and superficially made to be appreciated by the preschool aged children.

In a segment about a trip through the woods, a small boy and girl acted out all the stereotypes—he found a spider, she professed fear; he used a net to catch a frog, she stood and watched; he led the way, she followed.

A consequence of promoting "femininity," motherhood and homemaking as the most desirable and only appropriate roles for females is that it virtually guarantees that every female child will grow up single mindedly determined to marry and have children. Such ambition may have been appropriate when it was necessary to motivate every young person to produce as many children as possible to offset high mortality rates. . . . Now that our biological efficiency has increased so markedly, we cannot afford to continue unthinkingly such social practices and institutions. Today, when the population explosion is regarded as our nation's single most urgent problem it would be better for women to be "procreationally underemployed." Necessary concomitants of being procreationally underemployed are:

1. Socialization practices that encourage the development of human beings, not just mothers;

2. Acceptance of achievement needs, of assertive independence in little girls as well as little boys;

3. Equal educational and employment opportunities for women;

4. Media representation of women as people first, females second. (We do not represent males first and foremost as fathers, do we?)

Awareness of the many calamitous effects of our "pronatalist" policies is presently at a disastrously low level. In addition to the national consequences, the personal consequences for every woman are far more serious and ubiquitous than is commonly recognized.

Sesame Street and Sex-Role Stereotypes (UPDATED WITH SUGGESTIONS FOR ELIMINATING OBJECTIONABLE FEATURES)

In their efforts to eliminate sex-role stereotyping in children's programming, Drs. Susan Vogel, Inge Broverman, and Jo-Ann E. Gardner met with Joan Cooney, of the Children's Television Workshop (CTW) and producer of "Sesame Street."

At the request of Mrs. Cooney, they analyzed the scope and sequence plan for the program and developed the following set of recommendations. Their detailed examination of the problem of sex-role stereotyping and possible solutions was submitted to Mrs. Cooney on August 7, 1970.

Recommendations for Eliminating Sex-Role Stereotyping on CTW Programs

Research investigation of sex-role stereotypes has indicated that children, as early as preschool age, form clear-cut expectations about the differing roles of males and females in our society. Long before they enter school, children can unhesitatingly designate as male or female not only toys (e.g., dolls versus electric trains), but also occupations (e.g., nurses vs. doctors) and even interests (e.g., clothes vs. sports). Hand in hand with this differentiation of activities into male and female goes an implicit and invariant judgment of their relative worth; the male role is superior to the female role.

Children's literature and TV programming provide a major source of information for early childhood learning about sex roles. In a *New York*

Note: By Susan Vogel, Inge Broverman, and Jo-Ann Evans Gardner. Reprinted with permission from the authors and KNOW, Inc. (P.O. Box 86031, Pittsburgh, Pa. 15221).

Times Book Review article, Elizabeth Fisher discusses sex-role stereotyping in children's books, pointing to the myriad ways in which children are "indoctrinated at an early age with stereotypes about male activity and female passivity, male involvement with things, women's with emotions, male dominance, and female subordination." Television programming for preschoolers often "outdoes" picture books, presenting even more clichéd sex-role stereotyping with the greater vividness the medium allows.

Many educators and psychologists have deplored the stultifying and inhibiting effects of early sex-role indoctrination upon children. We share the belief that exposure of young children to sex-role stereotyping will serve to restrict and redirect individual development. For girls particularly, achievement strivings are cut off, aspirations are lowered, and motivation "normalized." Implicitly, boys learn to disparage girls, and at even greater psychological cost, girls learn to disparage themselves.

Because of these consequences, we feel that it is imperative that sex-role stereotyping be eliminated in CTW programming. Admittedly, the TV commercials and cartoons, both of which children watch avidly, are much worse offenders with respect to sex-role stereotyping. But the fact that CTW is a recognized leader in exemplary educational programming for children makes it all the more important that "Sesame Street" be genuinely free from detrimental sex-role stereotyping. To this end, four concrete recommendations are made below. Basically, these recommendations derive from the single guideline, as follows:

> the program must avoid episodes and characterizations in which the sex of the individual is inextricably bound up with his or her *competence, expressiveness, dominance,* or *nurturance.* This linkage can be conveyed directly (e.g., episodes in which girls might be shown only in a subordinate role) or indirectly (e.g., only boys portrayed in positions of dominance). Both instances of stereotyping must be eliminated if CTW is to facilitate for all children, regardless of sex, fullest development of individual potential.

I. Increased frequency of female model presentation

In the projected outline for Sesame Street contained in the CTW "black book," males (both children and adults) are to appear in a 2:1 ratio over females. Counting only those incidences in which the sex of the person is indicated by (1) a descriptive word, e.g., little girl, lady, man, etc.; (2) a relationship term, e.g., uncle, mother, etc.; (3) a job title with pronoun, e.g., carpenter . . . he, and eliminating all references in which it could be either, e.g., person, child, character, there are 31 portrayals of males, 16 portrayals of females.

Correction of this lesser visibility of female models, which could be easily accomplished, ought to increase greatly the psychological relevance of the program for girls in the viewing audience, without minimizing its appeal to boys.

II. Elimination of existing stereotyping in projected Sesame Street episodes

A few highly stereotyped portrayals, described in the outline, could be rewritten to eliminate the stereotyping without altering the principle that the episode attempts to teach. These instances are noted below, under outline headings used in the CTW "black book."

> e.g., III. A. Problem Sensitivity (*What's wrong here?*)
>
>> 4. Inconsistencies based on sex.
>>   b. "A lady loaded with luggage while her husband walks beside her empty-handed."
>>   c. "A boxing match—in one corner is a man, in the other corner, a woman."

Here it would seem that the inconsistency is more appropriately one of size and strength, rather than one of sex per se. To portray it as sex (men carry, women don't) with individual capability irrelevant appears to undermine a much more important message: that individuals, both male and female, need to develop and make full use of their physical potential.

> e.g., IV. The Child and His World
>
>> B. Social Units
>> 1. Roles and functions
>>   ". . . Show Susan enjoying doing something nice for Gordon because she likes to make him happy."

As commendable as this sentiment may appear to be, it represents an example of insidious stereotyping, in that it emphasizes Susan's pleasing role. The emphasis upon pleasing others throughout the socialization of girls may well be a major reason why women seldom become critical, imaginative thinkers, capable of asserting and defending their own ideas.

We do feel that doing things to make others happy is well worth portraying, but care should be taken to avoid the implication that it is in any way sex-linked. Maintaining an exchange of favors is excellent (e.g., ". . . Show Susan and Gordon doing considerate things for each other . . . etc."); also using other males in "pleasing" roles is a possibility.

e.g., IV. The Child and His World

    C. Social Interactions
       1. Differing perspectives
         9. A person has a different perspective in each role
           ". . . a doctor is also a husband and father."
           ". . . a teacher is also a mother and wife."

Here, implicitly, sex and profession are being linked together, inadvertently reinforcing the notion that *only* boys become doctors and *only* girls become teachers. This stereotyping might be eliminated by using nonstereotyped occupations, or if these particular professions are preferred, by reversing the sex of the individual assigned to each one. Another solution might include, with these two, some that are non-stereotypic.

III. Substitution of female models for male models in planned episodes involving action, use of implements, etc.

Many of the projected episodes describe the use of male models even though males are not in any sense required to fulfill the instructional or entertainment value of the episode. Their prevalence seems in fact to be a function of the unconscious stereotypic thinking that links males with activity. As Elizabeth Fisher states, in a *New York Times Book Review* article about stereotyping as it occurs in children's literature, "What (girls) do not do is act. Boys do; girls are . . . a highly artificial and unsatisfactory dichotomy."

To replace boys with girls, and men with women, in some of the following incidents where individuals *act, do, use tools,* etc., would greatly reduce the program's inadvertent reinforcement of the stereotypic notion that these are male occupations.

The following examples are referred to under outline headings used in the CTW "black book."

e.g., III. C. Generating and Evaluating Explanations and Solutions
       1. "Man tries to climb tree . . . etc."
       2. "Man tries to walk on snow . . . etc."
       3. "Man tries to reach high apple . . . etc."
       4. "The man tries to swim . . . etc."

Any one (or all) of these examples of problem-solving could *as is* be executed by a woman instead of a man, thus communicating, in addition to the concrete skills of approaching and solving problems, the message that everyone can do it, whether male or female.

e.g., IV. C. Differing Perspectives
> "Given ————, who is happy and who is sad."
> 1. "Boy with a kite."
> 4. "Boy raking leaves."
> 5. "Boy stacking paper boxes."
>
> 3. "Man with a car snowed in."
>
> 1. "Boy with new bike."
> 2. "Farmer with dry crops."

Girls and women could be used in some of the above examples, as is (i.e., *not* changing kite to hanging doll clothes on line) to provide small girls with female models involved in activities that are assertive and physical.

IV. *Possible introduction of counter-stereotypic models as new and continued characterizations*

There are several points at which adult counter-stereotypic female models might be introduced on Sesame Street, perhaps as continuing characterizations. Their presence could offer alternatives to the role that Susan portrays and thus serve to correct the impression that Susan's role (married, public health nurse) is necessarily typical.

The fact that Susan and Gordon are portrayed as childless is excellent from our point of view, not only because they present a model that must be adopted if population growth is to be slowed, but also because motherhood is not touted as "woman's only fulfillment." However, from a sex-role point of view, it would also be desirable to portray (1) working mothers, and (2) women who are engaged in "male" professions.

Male counter-stereotypic models exist among the characters of the program as it stands, insofar as the men are concerned and professionally involved with children. Thus it is less urgent that new male characters, portraying counter-stereotypic roles, be introduced.

Opportunities for the introduction of counter-stereotypic characters:

1. Regularly appearing character who lives on Sesame Street. For example, a woman architect or city planner who is working on urban redevelopment problems in the neighborhood. She might take the children on tours of buildings-in-progress, involve them in the planning for a neighborhood playground or recreation facility of some sort, demonstrate the transition from two-dimensional plans to three-dimensional reality in the building of a community school, etc.

Other examples might be doctors, research scientists, taxi drivers . . . certainly the possibilities are endless.

2. Visitors to Sesame Street. Adult women and men whose occupations are counter-stereotypic might visit the neighborhood during a filmed segment of the program. This would lend itself to entertainers, particularly, as for example, a male ballet dancer, or a woman who plays a musical instrument professionally in a symphony orchestra.

3. Relatives, extended family members of Sesame Street regular characters.

A REPORT ON CHILDREN'S TOYS AND SOCIALIZATION TO SEX ROLES

Intensive analyses of toy catalogs, observation in toy stores, interviews with toy executives, and questionnaires probing adult and child attitudes toward certain toys reveal three major findings: (1) "Masculine" toys are more varied and expensive, and are viewed as relatively complex, active, and social. (2) "Neutral" toys are viewed as most creative and educational, with boys receiving the most intricate items. (3) "Feminine" toys are seen as most simple, passive, and solitary.

These conclusions and the following items are excerpted from a 1972 study conducted by Louis Wolf Goodman and Janet Lever, Yale University sociologists whose exploration of sex-typing of children's toys has yielded considerable evidence of a double standard in children's play.

In 30 hours of Christmastime observation in a toy department, no field worker reported a single scientific toy bought for a girl.

Adults seem to follow three rules in purchasing children's toys: (1) Up to the age of two years, children of both sexes can receive many of the same toys (for example, stuffed animals, blocks, or educational toys to learn colors and numbers). The older the child the greater the need to differentiate between male and female sex-appropriate toys. (2) Most adult toy buyers defined a set of "traditional boys' toys" and a set of "traditional girls' toys" according to social norms for each sex. (3) While some adults stuck rigidly to the above guidelines, others constructed a secondary rule to allow a child they knew well to request and receive a specific toy, regardless of the toy's "sex-appropriateness."

Note: By Nancy Lyon. Reprinted with permission from *Ms.,* December 1972, 1:6, 57.

While children are encouraged to share toys with their siblings, this encouragement is directed primarily to sex-appropriate toys. Playtime with cross-sex siblings is spent in "neutral" (not sex-specific) games like hide-and-seek and tag and kickball, or if the play is indoors, the time is spent watching television, playing cards, or with a board game.

When 42 boys and 42 girls were surveyed as part of the study, they reported an almost identical number of gift items. However, 73 percent of the boys' gifts were toys, while only 57 percent of the girls' gifts were toys. (Girls receive clothes, jewelry, money, and furniture more often than boys.) Boys receive not only more toys but a wider range of toys than do girls.

The observers found that adults spent more time choosing toys for boys than they did choosing toys for girls. This may be due to differences in attitudes about boys' and girls' toys, and also to the fact that a greater variety of boys' toys were on the shelves.

Male sales personnel sold the more expensive items such as gas-powered planes, microscopes, bicycles, and speedways, while saleswomen handled the less expensive items (thus reinforcing the relationship between the toy price and sex-type of toy reported below).

Three out of every four chemistry sets the researchers saw advertised pictured only boys on the box-top. The remaining 25 percent pictured boys and girls; none pictured girls alone.

Doll sales represented 18 percent of 1971's $3.7 billion business, making dolls the single most valuable item in the trade. And within the category "dolls," it is the fashion doll that is far and away the leader.

A study of the Christmas toy catalogs of nine major department stores yielded 102 distinct categories of items illustrated exclusively with pictures of boys, compared to 73 showing only girls.

Craft kits and art supplies are advertised with pictures of children of both sexes or with girls only, but rarely with boys alone (with the exception of a few items like metal-craft sets).

Building blocks that are simple wooden cubes and wedges and the old standard "Tinker toys" are shown with both sexes pictured on the package. On the other hand, complex Erector-set toys, which "teach a wide range of engineering principles," are exclusively marketed to boys.

When marketing costumes for children, one catalog casts boys in a number of different prestigious or exciting roles—Indian chief, astronaut, highway trooper, race-car driver, marine, and Superman. The girls' projected roles seem less authoritative in comparison—drum majorette, nurse, bride, ballerina, Indian princess, and fairy princess.

A doctor kit marketed for boys had "stethoscope with amplifying diaphragm . . . miniature microscope . . . blood pressure tester . . . prescription blanks, and more." The nurse kit, on the other hand, came equipped with "nurse apron, cap, plastic silverware, plate, sick tray with play food"—seemingly closer to the role of waitress than that of medical practitioner.

In catalog pictures illustrating the use of toys and games, the father is often seen in the role of "instructor" or "play companion," while the mother is placed in the role of "spectator," or, on two occasions, is shown "cleaning up."

In a parallel study this year on sex-type depictions of males and females on toy boxes, Sarah Wernick Lockeretz, Susan L. Kannenberg, and Karen Drew found that, of 860 toy boxes in a large toy store, 50 percent of the toys costing under $2 were aimed at girls, with only 31 percent of the toys in that price range aimed exclusively at boys, and the remaining 19 percent "neutral." However, in the "$5 and over" category, 18 percent were girl-oriented, but 34 percent were directed to boys.

TOYS FOR FREE CHILDREN

Once there were two parents who decided to liberate their children from rigid male and female sex roles. They recognized that whatever they brought into their kids' environment would carry some suggestion of "correct" behavior or sex-typed expectations. "No more domestic, passive toys for our daughter," said the mother. "That's the end of tough-guy toys for our son," added the father.

So on Christmas morning, these enlightened parents gave their little girl a shiny new truck. Under the tree was a soft, cuddly doll for their little boy. The parents beamed as their children took the new toys up to their playroom. "This will be the beginning of a new lifestyle," said the father. "Down with sexism in the nursery," said the mother.

A little while later, the parents tiptoed upstairs to observe their emancipated children at play. Through the doorway they saw the little girl cradling the truck in her arms and singing *aah, aah, Baby,* while the little boy was pushing his doll across the floor and bellowing *vroom, vroom, vroom, vrooommm.*

That is the gist of a comedy sketch written for television by Renee Taylor and Joe Bologna. It has never been produced because the writers themselves withdrew it from the script.

"We were afraid it would be misinterpreted," explains Ms. Taylor. "People don't realize that it takes more than one toy to undo society's conditioning of sex roles. The audience could have construed it to mean that boys will be boys and girls will be motherly, and we didn't want the sketch to end up boosting the biology-is-destiny crowd."

They were wise to worry about the moral that would emerge from

Note: By Letty Cottin Pogrebin. Reprinted with permission from the author and *Ms.* December 1973, 11:6, 48–53; 82–86.

407

the skit. But it should also be said that they were devastatingly accurate about that final scene in the playroom.

Whatever our good intentions, children will not be miraculously transformed by the nonsexist toys we may give them. A toy is not a magic talisman. It can't dispel the spirit of sexism in a society that is obsessed with notions of "manliness" and "femininity." Studies have shown that, by the age of three, children show a distinct preference for sex-typed activities which reflect what they have absorbed from the culture. Unless the adults in the home are committed to role flexibility, a child will ignore even the most inviting toys if they seem inappropriate. So there's not much to be gained by giving a set of toy dishes to a little boy whose father wouldn't be caught dead in the kitchen.

Understanding the effects of the larger environment upon the child's play interests can spare gift-givers a lot of grief and disillusionment. But having said that, we can still resolve to take toy buying very seriously. After all, healthy children spend over 10,000 hours at play before they enter first grade. Toys and games make a vital contribution to a growing character, personality, and temperament.

Toys are vehicles for brave experimentation. They can be the raw materials of childhood fantasy and the practice pieces for real life. Toys can help a child reason, create, express, manipulate, differentiate, count, spell, read, analyze, construct, categorize, and dismantle. They can teach children to compete or to cooperate. The right sort of toy can be a ready recipient for the child's love or an available outlet for frustration and rage. Toys have even been known to inspire occupational choice, unleash artistic talent, or leave an emotional imprint for life. Devotees of the film *Citizen Kane* will remember that the haunting and mysterious Rosebud turned out to be a child's sled.

Despite all this impressive potential, toys are most prized and best loved if they have one simple quality: fun. My children regularly ask their friends: "What is your funnest toy?" And their friends have no trouble answering. Kids know what they like, whether we like it or not. Which is where the problems come up.

Should we buy our daughter the "Suzy Homemaker Oven" because all her friends are getting it for Christmas, and she's dying to make a 2½-inch angel food cake? Or should we explain that we are generally opposed to toys that require use of electrical outlets, toys that trade on the happy–little–housewife ideal, toys that are overpriced, breakable, and poor substitutes for the real thing?

Should we buy an "Action Jackson" or "G.I. Joe" doll with his authentic wardrobe of uniforms and instruments of destruction, simply because the television commercials have convinced our son that no boy's life is complete without them? Or should we carry on about the masculine mystique and the phony glamorization of the military and the "Barbie Doll syndrome" that exploits pint-size consumers?

I'll have to admit that there's a "Suzy Homemaker Oven" and an "Action Jackson" somewhere in the toy closets in this very house. But that's because I used to be weak-willed, misguided, and indulgent. "Aw, Mom, it's the funnest thing" once could reduce me to compliant mush. But no more. Now I've got standards the way other people get religion. Whether buying a toy for my own children or for friends', I run it through a rigorous checklist: is it safe, made to last, respectful of the child's intellect and creativity, nonracist, moral in terms of the values it engenders, and nonsexist in the way it is packaged, conceived, and planned for play?

By now, most of us have an automatic litmus test for toys. We're alert to illustrations on game covers and toy packages. (See "More Than Child's Play," *Ms.*, December 1972.) Not just the obvious—chemistry sets showing only boys at the test tubes, or craft kits picturing all-girl weaving teams—but the subtle and more pernicious uses of stereotypes.

Remco's "Walkie Talkie" set, for instance, does show a boy and girl using the toy. But the girl is seen chattering on one end (just like a woman), and the boy is listening at the other end of the receiver with a bored and tolerant expression.

Kohner's plastic board game "Cross Over the Bridge" shows a clumsy, unhappy girl playing with a nimble, cheerful boy. While countless games and toys are illustrated with both sexes, it seems that the boy is nearly always using the set, building the structure, performing the experiment, while the girl is watching and smiling. "Activity Dashboard" (Remco) shows a boy operating the moving parts as the girl looks on. The package says: "A busy working dashboard just like *Dad's.*"

Job bias is illegal in adult society, but it proliferates among so-called educational toys. Playskool's "When I Grow Up," a matching game, contains pictures of 21 males in widely varied jobs, from mason to milkman and from sailor to scientist. The three females match up with teacher, violinist, and dancer. "Occupations," a preschooler's puzzle by Fisher-Price, gives boys five role choices; girls can pick "mother," "ballerina," or "nurse." "People and Jobs" (Questor) has four women out of 24 small puzzles. The women match up with only four jobs: librarian, teacher, waitress, and skier.

Emblematic of the trivia-is-your-life games is the "Emily Post Popularity Game" (Selchow & Righter), a game of etiquette for girls—

which is just as bone-chilling as it sounds. One sample card reads: "You handled your first date with a new boy very well. You made an excellent impression and got another invitation."

Women are no longer interested in good impressions. We want toys that don't insult, offend, or exclude one sex by inference or omission. We're refusing to buy toys "for girls" that teach hypocrisy, narcissism, and limited aspirations. We're avoiding toys "for boys" that promote militaristic values and a must-win attitude. The question now is, what's left? If we have a budget for new toys, what can we buy with confidence and enthusiasm?

In general, the best toys are the least structured ones. They're open-ended. Their playability is determined by what the individual child brings to them. And while a high price doesn't guarantee durability or child-interest, certain larger toy investments of this kind keep paying off with years of pleasure.

Blocks, for example. When our daughters were two, they were given a set of full-size unpainted hardwood blocks in all geometric shapes—arches, squares, columns, half circles, and so on. Now, six years later, the set belongs to the girls and their younger brother, and the same blocks are still the most frequently used playthings in their collection.

The children have transformed them into bridges, castles, space stations, zoos, parking lots, highways, farms, and split-level homes. The block structures have been accessorized with little rubber animals, wooden people figures, cars, trains, street signs, dandelions, and home-made taped-on curtains. Constructions have been used to hide in, jump off, climb up, and balance on. Though each block is a solid, heavy weapon, the children have been too involved in block play ever to think of hurling one around the room. We're still grateful to the grandmother who gave the set to us.

There are other worthwhile once-a-year extravagances that can be justified in terms of developing children's creativity, physical agility, and dexterity.

Consider a bicycle that's appropriate to the child's size and co-ordination (and so-called boys' bikes with the crossbar are sturdier and safer for both sexes), outdoor climbing bars, a sandbox, painting easel, bulletin board, wagon, record player, walk-in playhouse or tent, a pedal car or fire engine (boys *and* girls love the feeling of motion, power, and control), a telescope, microscope, a pair of field glasses, a secondhand portable typewriter (typewriters made especially for kids are disorganized and have all sorts of unnecessary keyboard gingerbread), a rope ladder for climbing indoors or out, a child-size desk or worktable, an illuminated globe.

When choosing these items and all toys and games, the buyer should be skeptical about *any* specification cited by the manufacturer. The terms "educational," "child-tested," "developed with psychological advisers," "for ages 3 to 6" are often just as arbitrary as the label "for boys" or "for girls." Where there is potential danger, however (use of heat or sharp objects required in the game), observe age specifications at the very least.

The stores still advertise electric train sets for "every boy and his dad," though there is nothing sex-linked about the sets themselves. A model railroad layout is an elaborate commitment that should be purchased for use by all members of the household. With carefully chosen accessories and free-ranging imaginations, trains can be instructive in the areas of transportation, city planning, engineering, ecology, geography, history, and sociology. If you can afford a set, don't knock it just because electric trains have become a cliché of feminist consciousness-raising. (It seems that "every girl and her mom" felt cheated because she couldn't have a set as a child.)

Expression of budding musical talent is what usually triggers the purchase of an instrument. However, without the child's commitment to music lessons (if they're economically feasible), this can be a wasteful and frustrating gift. Feminists have noticed that packaging tends to feature boys on the instruments you play, and girls on the instruments you turn on. Needless to say, drums for girls and flutes for boys are just fine. One can now find a performer somewhere in the classical, folk, or rock fields who provides a role model of each sex for just about every instrument—even for your son, the harpist.

Sexist packaging becomes a real stumbling block to the purchase of sports equipment. Fishing equipment, golf, archery, bowling, and even croquet sets are frequently boxed or blister-packed (under plastic) with pictures of a boy getting the big catch, the hole in one, the bull's-eye, the strike, and so on. If a girl is shown at all, she's jumping for joy—on his behalf.

As I see it, most items packaged in this fashion should be boycotted. Since it is possible to find equally good sports equipment wrapped in a neuter container, why not use consumer power to reform the Neanderthals? Baseballs, basketballs, mitts, bats, and the like can usually be bought loose from a counter display. (There's not much we can do about endorsements or autographs of male players, but we can search for equipment signed by females whenever possible: an Althea Gibson tennis racket, for example.)

A scaled-down set of lightweight tools is a great gift for anyone from the nursery school years up. But here again, it's hard to find a box that shows the tools themselves or a picture of both boys and girls using them. Tool kits also tend to be named "Handy Andy" or "Mr. Fix-It," which further inhibits our purchase.

That doesn't mean a "Handy Andy" is alienating to a girl but okay for a boy. Both sexes are better prepared for life when utilitarian objects are disassociated from any kind of sex-specific usage.

It may be impossible to find a tool kit in a neuter or nonsexist package. In that case, I would buy the offending set, unwrap it, and repack it in a plain metal toolbox bought in a local hardware store.

Similarly, if we waited for a small broom and dustpan to be packaged with a picture of girls *and* boys cleaning, we'd have quite a heap of dust in the kids' rooms. So it might be sensible to buy the "Golden Girl" (Miner) cleaning set, throw away the box with the picture of a housewife wearing a crown, and present it to the child in a plain brown wrapper. Spared the visual brainwashing, a four-year-old can sweep his or her room without embarrassment.

Most toys are sexually anonymous. It's only the way we present them to the child that reflects stereotypes and causes them to be perpetuated. Those of us who are choosing gifts might want to turn our attention from the hopeless, negative attitudes of manufacturers and turn instead to what we can do for kids with the best of what's available. And that's where "package-altering" is a stopgap answer.

Tear off the "Boys, 8–12" sticker; toss out the box the tea set came in; and put the pieces in colored tissue paper in a silver dime-store box, or cut off the protruding card showing boy astronauts and just give the child the blister-pack section that contains the toy rocket. This tactic may not reform toymakers, but it will give our kids a lot more play options.

Where a child lives might determine your choice of gift. In warm climates, rubber rafts, snorkel masks, flipper feet, and light surfboards will keep kids busy in the water until their skin puckers. Snowbound youngsters will love snowshoes, mini-toboggans, sleds, and ice skates. (Double runners are a rip-off. And don't let anyone tell you that speed skates are only for boys and figure skates only for girls.)

For the urban child, roller skates are a sure bet—and the misplaceable skate key of our youth has been replaced by adjustable clamps. You can't go wrong with kites, umbrellas, bubble bath, lunchboxes, or Thermos bottles, either. City kids who rarely see grass and nature life might enjoy a planting kit (or just seeds and a flowerpot, or a small plant of their own), a nature collector's kit (butterfly-insect net, bug house), or a flower press and a bunch of assorted live flowers, or a watering can.

Gardening shops are an untapped source of terrific "toys." In fact, some of the best buys are found not in toy departments but in specialty outlets. Art shops might offer a better selection of clay—a material that's as malleable as the child's dreams. Everyone can always use new poster paints, brushes, pastels, and colored felt-tipped pens. Team them with a fat pad of paper and add a couple of variety-store picture frames so the child can display her or his masterpieces "formally."

The stationery or office-supply store is loaded with items that become toys in the hands of a child. A pencil compass and flexible pipe cleaners are versatile tools. Hole punchers make Swiss cheese pictures; loose-leaf binders are wonderful for a diary or activity journal; scrapbooks collect favorite snapshots, test papers, report cards, drawings, or secret codes; labelmakers turn out plastic name tapes to stick on books, bikes, or whatever (and making identifying labels for things around the house helps the child's spelling); calendars keep track of club meetings and visits to the orthodontist; a stapler, glue, and cellophane tape can be used to make art out of cut-up magazine pictures; a steno book takes dictation as young children tell adults their made-up stories, or school-age kids can write spiral-bound novels in them.

At the notions store, pick up colored yarn, beads, sequins, buttons, appliqués, trim, and braiding. Put them in separate plastic bags, pop them in a Christmas box, and give the child a first-rate collage kit that beats the ready-made craft sets by far.

Childhood is a period of experimentation and let's pretend. While gender identity is essential for the healthy child, sex-role identity should be entirely flexible and subject to personal choice. In its simplest form, a role can be tried on with just a change of clothes. To encourage this, adults who aren't uptight might buy a grab-bag selection of secondhand clothes for dress-up play for both sexes. Top hats, riding boots, old lace shawls, and ropes of pearls bring out the performer in most children.

And while makeup may be a political issue for grown women, pots of color and eyebrow pencils are very helpful to a small clown or a tiny actor or actress.

Forget about finding decent occupational costumes or child-size uniforms in the toy departments—unless the little girl in your life is cut out to be a stewardess or a cowgirl. We'll know that costumemakers are liberated when they make a boy's bridegroom outfit and a girl's pilot uniform.

If one could coin a new word for dolls, perhaps people wouldn't have so much trouble giving them to little boys. Dolls have a heavy aura of all the negative-feminine associations: dainty, weak, helpless. "Doll-like" is the adjective used for diminutive, vacuous women. What would happen if we borrowed from the play *Guys and Dolls,* and called a boy doll a "guy?" Would little boys saunter off to the playground announcing, "I have to take my guy for a walk"?

Who knows. In any case, even with the label "doll," two new developments are taking place. Boys are being "allowed" (and even encouraged) to play with dolls; and male dolls (other than the "Action Jackson" type) are becoming available in most places.

Perhaps this has become acceptable because Dr. Benjamin Spock, the child-care guru, recently proclaimed that dolls are good for boys. "Dolls can be used to dramatize all the human relationships a child is sensitive to and has a compulsion to work through," Dr. Spock wrote in 1971. "A boy or girl playing with a doll has it break things or wet its pants or be rude in order to express his own rebelliousness and hostility. But then he scolds or spanks the doll as a way of placating his conscience for the naughty impulses and as a way of practicing his future role as a parent."

Small baby dolls (some are black-skinned, but not always true to negroid features) also give all children a chance to play the big shot, and to lavish love and attention on something smaller and more helpless than they. At the same time, however, because most dolls are totally flat between the legs, children receive the suggestion that there is something shameful or different about their own real-life sex organs. New baby dolls with realistic genitalia are a welcome addition. Unfortunately, because they're imported from Europe, some models are prohibitively priced. (See Shopping List.)

Many parents who have bought the realistic dolls have expressed relief that their sons can now find an approximation of their own anatomy, while daughters without male siblings can satisfy their natural curiosity about the opposite sex.

If you are not the parent of the little boy for whom you plan to buy a doll, discuss your purchase ahead of time. Someone close to the child should agree to be supportive when peers and neighbors observe him playing with his new doll.

Nanette Rainone, feminist program director for WBAI radio, recalls one of her typical journeys through her neighborhood. "My son was wheeling his doll carriage and I was walking alongside. First a fireman standing on the street said, 'Tell your mommy boys should have guns, not dolls!' Next, a storekeeper told my son, 'Your mother should give you a little sister if she wants a girl that badly.' Those guys were really disturbed. But they chose to speak man-to-man to a three-year-old rather than directly to me."

Obviously a doll carriage is not in itself an "effeminate" symbol.

Proud adult fathers wheel babies around all the time. Why should a boy's rehearsal for parenthood be so alarming? By the same token, why is there concern about a girl's disinterest in the maternal role?

Perhaps the 20th century preoccupation with "normality" has led us to discriminate so vigorously between the two sexes and to label everything each must do and become. Yet it could be otherwise. Without rigid guideposts for "normal feminine" and "normal masculine" behavior, we would learn to cope with all the surprising shadings of diverse human behavior. Our economy would have to adjust to the pragmatic consumer who needs half as much of practically everything because most things would be shared or handed down between the sexes. And toy manufacturers would have to use blank boxes and make everything suitable for both sexes because one could never be sure which children—when they're free to make the choice—would respond to which toys.

Sounds good. But until a feminist conscience takes over toyland, here are some specific suggestions for gifts that should bring cheer to *whoever* gets them.

Shopping List

Dolls (and guys)

Because of the immense selection available, no one needs help finding lovable girl dolls. For most people it's only a question of preference or price. Baby dolls inspire nurturant play while larger or life-size dolls are stand-ins for friends.

Texture is important—and dolls seem to be getting softer all the time. Pinchable plastic, rag dolls, cloth-covered foam or yarn dolls are far superior to the hard, hollow kind. Doll clothes vary from diaper-and-bunting sets to elegant outfits of foreign cultures. Fashion dolls, however, should be avoided. They encourage acquisitive values and feed the image of woman as ornament. Ditto for hairstyle dolls with "growing" hair, curlers, setting lotions, and so on. Black dolls with Afro hair are easy to find, although their faces often reflect white society's idea of beauty.

Given this extraordinary variety in girl dolls, this list concentrates on male dolls, with a few exemplary exceptions. Anatomically correct boy dolls (with genitals) are noted with an asterisk (*). And age range is suggested after each description.

JIMMY JEANS BEAN BAG DOLLS (Commonwealth, $4). Gingham-covered body wearing denim overalls; 13 inches tall. His female counterpart is Dolly Dimples. 2+.

Bob 'n betty (Dandy, $4). Gingerbread doll you make from materials supplied. Bob on one side, Betty on the other. 3–9.

Raggedy andy (Knickerbocker, $4). Ann's beloved brother. A timeless favorite. 1+.

* Sasha boy (Creative Playthings, $4). Black or white skin. Wistful face but genitals are a cop-out outline. 3+.

Laurie (Madame Alexander, $14). The boy from Louisa May Alcott's novels. 4+.

Tyrolean dutch boys (Madame Alexander, $9). Both dressed authentically. 4+.

Chico (F. A. O. Schwarz branch stores, or order by mail from Schwarz, Fifth Avenue at 58th Street, New York, N.Y. 10022, $30). Vaguely Latin face, soft body, 23 inches high, 4 pounds. 4+.

Pedro (Schwarz, $30). Same as Chico, with black skin (but a pink cloth belly). 4+.

Jamie boy (Schwarz, $9). Washable blue (natch!) yarn doll with braided legs. 1+.

Angelino (Schwarz, $20). Nifty red turtleneck sweater, blue-knit cap and pants, blond hair, 24 inches tall. White only. 4+.

* Thomasino (Schwarz, $25). Luxurious 24-inch baby with realistic sex organs. Can wet his diaper. Blond, white only. 4+. *This item is not in the catalog and Schwarz toy buyer Eileen Austin admits that stores don't display Thomasino without his clothes. But she believes in the doll and reports that it sells briskly even without exposing itself.*

Pippi longstocking (Schwarz, $13). Inspired by Astrid Lindgren's novels about Pippi, the powerhouse, pigtailed, freckled little girl who lives alone and likes it. 6+.

Wilky (Shindana, a division of Operation Boot Strap, $2.50). Black rag doll wearing mod sweatshirt and sneakers. 3+.

Dapper dan (Playskool, $9). Kids practice motor coordination and self-sufficiency with Dan's buttons, zipper, and laces. Dressy Bessy is his match. 3–6.

* Boy baby (Hans Gotz. $10). Best buy. German import with infant genitals. Wets. Blond hair, white only. Dressed in baby blue. Girl baby with suggestion of labia comes dressed in pink. 4+. (May be ordered from Bloomingdale's, Lexington Avenue at 59th Street, New York, N.Y. 10022.)

Tom (Amsco, $5). Rag doll with denims, gingham shirt, yarn hair, 14 inches. 3+.

CAMPBELL KIDS (Knickerbocker, $2.50 each). The famous soup lovers. Boy and girl rag dolls in chef's hats and aprons. 3+.

DOROTHY/THE LION (Blue Ridge Hearthside, $14). Handcrafted cloth doll has the bold visitor to Oz on one end, the engaging Cowardly Lion on the other. Two dolls in one, printed cotton clothes; charming. 3+.

NURSING MOTHER (Possum Trot, $25). Soft cotton 18-inch woman with red hair, a pink face, and a green calico dress. Unsnap her bodice and there are snaps on her breasts instead of nipples. A 9-inch baby doll (redheaded and diapered) has a snap on its mouth. Put together and you have a breast-feeding baby. Also from Possum Trot (which is an Appalachian co-op): MOTHER PIG ($15), five piglets suckle when snapped in place on the large orange-flannel mother—or they play alone; MOTHER MOO ($25), brown plush fur cow with green felt for the grass in her mouth and an udder with four snaps. The calf snaps on for feeding. *All three enchanting Possum Trot creations available at Bear Threads, 2519 Wilshire, Santa Monica, California 90403; or Children's Concepts, 2295 Broadway, New York, N.Y. 10024; or toy boutiques. Nursing human mothers and involved fathers will appreciate these "dolls" to help explain matters to younger siblings who are envious of the new baby at the breast.*

PREGNANT MOTHER (Brio, $10). No American toy distributor will handle this yet. Watch for further details in future issues of *Ms.*

JACK AND THE BEANSTALK (Playskool, $6). New this year, a "Hug-a-Book Doll" that's machine washable and dryable, and complete with cloth book on his tummy. 1–6.

RAGGEDY ANN AND ANDY EMBRACEABLES (Knickerbocker, under $4). This new item has the two tykes in a permanent hug. Excellent co-ed package picture. 1–6.

Toys for baby humans

THE ACTIVATOR (Creative Playthings, $8). Crib activity bar. Baby pulls cords to make different sounds. 6 months +.

IRMI MOBILES (Nursery Originals, $6.50). Hand-painted wooden animals dangle prettily over the crib. 0–9 months.

BEATRIX POTTER STUFFED ANIMALS (Eden, $10–$15). Jemima Puddle Duck, Peter Rabbit, and Hunca Munca are cuddlesome good company. 6 months +.

PLAY MIRROR (F. A. O. Schwarz, $4). Flexible and unbreakable with finger grips. Or MUSICAL MIRROR (Child Guidance, $3). Nothing is more fascinating than that face in the looking glass. 3 months +.

CLOTH CUBES (Creative Playthings, $9). Nine brightly decorated foam blocks are great for sore gums, clutching, and, later, for safe constructions. 6 months +.

SPACE RINGS (Creative Playthings, $2.75). Chewable teething rings in primary colors. 3 months +.

THE BUSY BOX (Kohner, $7.25). Crib activity panel includes crank, mill, drawer, door, mirror. 6 months +.

THE BABY SITTERS (Vanguard Records, SRV 3002). Alan Arkin and friends sing folk songs for babies, parents, and sitters.

HAPPY APPLE (Fisher-Price, $3). Roly-poly red plastic chiming apple with green stem for teething. 3 months +.

WALK A BYE (Child Guidance, $4.50). A push toy. 9–14 months.

BABY PANDA (Dakin, $6.50). The rare bear, a play pal of perfection. 6 months +.

SNAP-LOCK BEADS (Fisher-Price, $1.50). Giant beads interlock to make jumbo necklace, hat, colorful snake. 3 months–2 years.

ROCK-A-STACK (Fisher-Price, $1.29). A pyramid of plastic doughnuts. 6 months +.

Toys for little kids

HARDWOOD BLOCKS (Playskool, $13.75). A total of 63 pieces, 12 shapes plus animals. (Also BLOCKS from F. A. O. Schwarz, $26 for 82 pieces—15 shapes in a wooden storage wagon.)

MINIATURE FURNITURE (Lundby, $7.75). Not just dollhouse decor, but detailed cabinets, chairs, bathroom fixtures to outfit any block structure. And a boy and girl on the box. Swedish import. 4+.

THE BUSY BATH (Kohner, $8). Suctions hold to tub. Pull handle to make water pressure activate carousel, spouting fish, waterwheel, and "sea-saw." 2+.

SLINKY (James, $1.20). Metal coil waddles downstairs by itself. Not creative, but fun to watch. 3+.

PEOPLE/PLACES APARTMENT GARAGE (Samsonite, $17). Four floors of apartments, elevators, people, cars, a patio, and a pool. Pure luxury but good play value. 2–7. Also

PEOPLE/PLACES ARK ($18). Mr. and Mrs. Noah come with 18 matched sets of animals, furniture, and a spacious boat with first-class compartments. Not for anti-nuclear family types. 2–7.

PEG DESK (Playskool, $15.75). Chair is connected to desk that has writing surface, magnetic spelling board, slate. Bright green and sturdy. 3–8.

TINKER TOY (Questor, $7). The perennial; 315 parts, a million possibilities. 3+.

CREATIVE COASTER (Fisher-Price, $11). A ride-on cart with a seat, steering wheel, horn, and a payload of blocks. For solitary or group play. 2–6.

PLAY-DOH FACTORY (Kenner, $3.50). Extruder toy. Feed in Play-Doh (4 cans, 4 colors for $1) and out come cones to shape and paint. 3–7.

LOCK-UP ZOO (Playskool, $18.75). Six animals to put in cages; man, boy, woman, and girl to visit them. (Sorry about the skirts on all the females.) 2–6.

SPIROGRAPH (Kenner, $5). Kindergartners and up can make Op-Art masterpieces.

THINK AND LEARN SERIES (Ideal). Plastic take-apart, put-together firehouse ($10), truck or train ($2). Imagine! Vehicles with both sexes pictured on the package. 2–5.

BUSY STORES (Kohner, $8). Open and lock familiar neighborhood shops and arrange items that fit in each store. 2–5.

SHAPEES (Kohner, $2.70). Plastic construction set in 3-D; 55 notched pieces. 2–7.

PUNCHING CLOWN (Romper Room, $3). An inflatable to hug or aggress upon. 2–6.

FUZZY FELT (Allen, $2.50). Felt figures adhere to board to create jungle, sports, or fantasyland scenes. Skip the farm set—everyone is male. 3–6.

CASH REGISTER (Samsonite, $5). Colorful numerals, buttons, and "cash drawer." 2–5.

SEWING BLOCK (Gemla, $4.50). Spoolshape block with holes to thread with a giant wooden "needle." 2–4.

WOODEN PUZZLES (Playskool, $2 each). Good choices are "I Set The Table," "When It Rains," "Colors I See." Number of jigsaw pieces depends on age of child. 2–6.

MAILBOX (Samsonite, $5). Push different-size disks in the slots and make musical tones. (Not for the toddler who tends to swallow toys.) 2–4.

PLAY FAMILY ACTION GARAGE (Fisher-Price, $13). A car nut's paradise. 2–10.

UNIWORLD HOUSES (Aurora UNICEF Toys, $6). With tiny beanbag or wood people and accoutrements. Spanish hacienda, igloo, Oriental and African houses are delightful. Ignore the story pamphlet inside and leave play ideas to the child. (This UNICEF line is impressive, coming from the company that used to make torture toys.)

RHOMBONES (Synestructics, $3). Ten bone-shaped blocks make odd structures. 2+.

ANIMAL SETS (Britains Ltd.). The model farm contains hand-painted animals, pigsty, gate, stile, stone walls, scarecrow, and milk churns, each about 1½ inches ($12.50). The zoo includes animals, palm trees, cages ($7.50). Filler kits, $3.75. Uncommonly realistic, marvelous as block accessories. The ideal substitute for toy soldiers. 3–9.

LEGO ($4 up). Notched plastic construction cubes in sets that build one skyscraper or a full city. Almost ageless.

TYKE BIKE (Playskool, $7). Indoor-outdoor tricycle without pedals. Runs on child power with even the shortest legs. 1–4.

SHAPE-SORTING BOX (Brio, $5.50; or Creative Playthings, $6). Kids find out you can't fit a square peg into a round hole. 2+.

PASTRY SET (Brio, $5.25). Wooden rolling pins, pastry board, tin cookie cutter, and fluted pan. Boy and girl rolling dough on the package make baking fun for all. 3+.

BASKETBALL (Fisher-Price, $7.95). Tot-size hoops and ball develop a sure eye. Sex-integrated picture on backboard but not on outside package. 2–8.

YOUNG CAREERS (Playtime-Fun, 79 cents–$1.29). Noticeably non-sexist. "Flyer" not pilot or stewardess; "Medic" not doctor or nurse; both sexes get a chance to "Be a Superstar" in sports, too. 3+.

ETCH-A-SKETCH (Ohio Art, $5). Draw with two knobs. Design appears under plastic screen. (Formerly glass, now completely safe.) 4+.

SUM FUM (Educational Ideas, $3.75). A bingo game that calls for adding and subtracting skills. 4+.

HOPPITY DUCK (Sun, $12). Huge, hard-rubber ball with a duck's head. Sit on it, hang on tight and bounce. 4+.

SOAK AND SHAPE (Loeher, $1.75). Mix with water to make a pliable modeling compound that dries to indestructible finish. 3+.

RHYTHM BAND (Creative Playthings, $11). Six instruments (tambourine, triangle, cymbals, and so on) for a glorious symphony or a solo performance. 3+.

HOUSE OF CARDS (Creative Playthings, $4). A total of 54 oversize, slotted cards with photos of uncommonplace things. 4+.

SPIN ART (Rapco, $7). A carnival activity for the home. Squeeze paints and spin a different picture every time. 3+.

SEE-THROUGH MUSIC BOX (Creative Playthings, $4). Crank out "Swan Lake" while peeking at the mechanism inside. 2+.

BLOCKHEAD (Saalfield, $5). Pile up tricky-shaped blocks without a mishap. 3+ and great at adult parties, too.

PUPPETS (Creative Playthings). Five finger puppets with wooden heads, $2.75 for either people or animal set. Pliable, heavy plastic hand puppets (duck, frog, whale, dragon, or wolf), $2.25 each. 3+.

STETHOSCOPE (Creative Playthings, $4.25). There are lots of these on the market but this one is professional quality and has a consciousness-raising package illustration: a girl doctor listening to a boy's heart. 4+.

BUILD A PICTURE (Creative Playthings, $7.50). Any 40 of these 126 interchangeable parts make a zany picture. 3–6.

UNIWORLD COLOR 'N DRESS DOLLS (Aurora UNICEF, $3.75). Outfits and accessories to dress three wooden dolls in clothes of other lands. No male figures, but dolls are black, oriental, and caucasian.

MINIATURE SILVERWARE AND UTENSILS (Creative Playthings, $1.75 up). Slightly overpriced, but worth it to get a neuter package for these functional items. 3+.

JUDY PUZZLE (General Learning Corp., about $3). Appears to be a policewoman guiding two kids across the street. 3–5.

CARRY-ALL KIT (Montessori Play & Learn, $6). Features life-size Billy and Judy puzzles that teach parts of body. 2–8.

NESTING CARS (Montessori, $2). Cut off the boy picture sticking up from package. This is fun and manipulative for 2–5.

GONE FISHING PUZZLE (Galt, about $2.50). Put together a boy and girl with fishing nets. Take puzzle apart and see very natural, naked kids underneath. Matter-of-fact acceptance of nudity. 3+.

MINI-TRUCKS (Henschel, $2) and TINY-TONKAS ($1.25). Come with no propaganda on the box, when you buy individually, not in boxed sets.

FREE TO BE . . . YOU AND ME (Bell Records, $5.95). The one and only nonsexist kids record, featuring Marlo Thomas & Friends. A Ms. Foundation Project. 4–ageless.

Toys for bigger kids

ACTION LABS (Edcom, $2 each). Age-graded experiments such as visible hydraulic pump (8+), solar heater (10+), and waterspout (6+).

WEAVING LOOM (Spears, $5.50). The package shows the loom only —and it's fine. 6+.

MULTIWAY ROLLWAY (Creative Playthings, $9). Make tracks and chutes. Balls will career on your runways. 6+.

MAGIC (Merit, $6.50). 25 tricks of prestidigitation with instructions. 10+.

BAG-A-BEAST ($1.95 from Children's Concepts, 2295 Broadway, New York, N.Y. 10024). Clever paperbag sculpture kit. 6+.

TURN-A-WORD (Creative Playthings, $3.50). Blocks turn on a hinged bar to form 72 possible three-letter words. 5+.

DELUXE CAMPING KIT (F. A. O. Schwarz, $16). Everything for an overnight in the woods—or backyard or rooftop. Only for 8+ because of the ax.

AFRO-AMERICAN HISTORY-MYSTERY GAME (Theme, $5). Four women (including dancer Katherine Dunham and abolitionist Sojourner Truth) are among 24 men featured in this interesting puzzle-board game. Volume II, on sale in March, has more "Lost Women" from black history. 6+.

NEEDLEWORK KITS (Whistlework, $4, or Spinerin, $8). Make an owl, elephant, or graphic design—plush. 7+.

LIVE BUTTERFLY GARDEN (Insect Lore Products, $6). Watch caterpillars feed, grow, shed furry coats, and emerge as butterflies. Guaranteed to live two weeks. 8+.

SCATTER RUGS (various brands, $3 up). Soft rugs are fun to sprawl on whether they're decorated with flowers, alphabets, or Scrabble or Monopoly board designs.

JOHNNY HORIZON (Parker, $13). Get past the name and you'll find 10 pollution experiments for water and air—to be performed by Johnny and Janie Horizon and a supervising adult. 9+.

THE BUG HOUSE (Tierney, $1.50). A sensible wire-screen container for your special catch. 5–9.

ELECTRIC MOTOR, ELECTRIC BELL, or HYDRAULIC PUMP KIT (Educational Resources, $2.29 each). Put them together and learn how they work. 9+.

MIX AND SPELL (Uncle Milton Industries, $6). A human anagram game for eight players. Each wears a letter bib and spells with themselves. 8+.

BIRDHOUSE KIT (Hyde Bird Feeder, $2.50). Easy to build and capable of luring woodpeckers and bluebirds. 7+.

OPTILE (Schaper, about $8). Invented by two women amateurs. Objective: cover your board with the tiles that count most. Glamorous couple on box are a turnoff, but game is fun. 8+.

CANDLE SCULPTURE (Rapco, $9). Create elaborate candles, but only if you're at least 9 and *very* careful.

MARBLE PAN (Creative Playthings, $1.75). Dexterity exercises of increasing difficulty. 8+.

APPETEASER PUZZLES (Springbok, $1.50 each). Round jigsaws of a tempting apple, olives, popcorn, or salami. 6+.

TEXTURE PLAYNTS (Kenner, $4). Squeeze thick paint from tube for a design, and it hardens to make a striking plaque. 5–10.

PORTABLE ACTION LABS (Gilbert Chemcraft, $34). A major investment for a future scientist. Both sexes on wrapper. 10+.

WFF 'N PROOF (Learning Games Associates, $8). A brain-twister game of modern logic. 10+.

LINCOLN LOGS (Playskool, $8.75). Building logs in the pioneer motif. 5–10.

FISCHER TECHNIK (starter set, $15; deluxe set with motor, $23). The most sophisticated engineering toy on the market. 8+.

SCIENCE FUN EXPERIMENTS (Logix-Kosmos). All races and both sexes illustrate Electrics Set ($16) and Electronics ($10).

WIRE ART (Synergistics, $7.50). Make designs with wire stretched on nails. 10+.

THE BLACK EXPERIENCE GAME (Theme, $4). Poet Gwendolyn Brooks, Rosa Parks (the woman who started the Montgomery, Alabama, bus sit-in), Patricia Harris (lawyer), Harriet Tubman (abolitionist), and Congresswoman Shirley Chisholm are among the many black people honored in this American History Game. 8+.

CORGI CARS AND TRUCKS. Made in England with precise detail: doors, trunks, and hoods open and close. A wide assortment from $1.50 to $20. To use or collect. 5–12.

TINY TABLE TENNIS (Atech, $10). Miniature Ping-Pong table (2 feet by 3 feet) with the ball on a rubber band suspended on a wire arc. 8+.

ECOLOGY KITS (Urban Systems, $6 each). "Predatory Prey," "How Fish Breathe," and "What Moves Life?" teach about the environment. 10+.

LIFE (Milton Bradley, $8). A board game that offers a nonsexist trip through your future. Anyone might "start own business" or "add baby daughter," etc. 9+.

CONSTRUCT-O-STRAWS (Parker, $2.50). Bendable straws as creative material. 5+.

HEAD TO HEAD (E. S. Lowe, $3.50). Two players race to build high-scoring words before the timer runs out. 8+.

CAREERS (Parker, $5). Anyone-can-be-anything board game. 8+.

QUICK MASTER CHESS (Learning Games, $15). Instruction disks teach the way chess pieces move. Approved by U.S. Chess Federation—shows girl player on cover. 6+.

SILK FACTORY (Natural Sciences, $6). Start culture to produce silk moths that produce silk as you watch. 8+.

MAKE AND SHOW SLIDES (Ideal, $11.95). Battery-operated projector shows slides that kids create from magazine pictures. 8+.

THUNDERBOLT BREAK TIME (General Fix, $18). Play darts without dangerous points. Velcro material sticks to board. 7+.

MAGIC HOCUS-POCUS SHOW (Jumbo, $6). Thirty-five baffling tricks. 9+.

FOR THEIR ROOM FROM DETERMINED PRODUCTIONS: RAGGEDY ANN & ANDY clock, $10.50; bookends, $8; or sleeping bags, $19. Peanuts' characters banks ($4 each)—Lucy with bat, Linus with security blanket, are most irresistible. Snoopy wristwatch, $17, or bulletin board, $6.

POTTERYCRAFT (Gilbert, $15). Make ceramics with motorized potter's wheel, paints, and glaze. 10+.

VISIBLE MAN AND VISIBLE WOMAN (Renwal, $6). Not the highest-quality plastic reproduction, but a unique inside look at human-like systems, including the often neglected reproductive and urinary organs. Visible Woman includes "Miracle of Birth" adapter kit for pregnant female. Unfortunately, the faces are rather grotesque and notably white. Suggested for 12+ or with younger children, adult guidance is essential.

ROCK TUMBLER (Skil-Craft, $32). Make sleek gemstones from beach pebbles and common rocks. Basically passive activity until the child makes something of the polished stones. Fantastic results. 8+.

THE RUG MAKER (Skil-Craft, $10). Choice of patterns for a 12-inch-square rug. 9+.

LEATHERMAKING (Rapco, $10). Buy with care. One of their kits says "strictly for girls," the other doesn't. 10+.

COOTIE (Schaper, $3.50). Plastic bug comes apart, and kids roll dice to see who can reassemble it first. 5–10 and time-tested.

CIRCUIT PUZZLE GAME (Creative Playthings, $5). Can be used as puzzle or board game for two. Challenging. 8+.

JUMP SHOES (Rapco, $6). Zany spring coils provide a bouncy walk. 6+, but only for kids with strong ankles.

PIVOT POOL (Milton Bradley, $19). A family game endorsed by Lucille Ball, who is shown playing it competently on TV—the only "sportsy" game promoted by a woman. Also P. D. Cue Bumper Pool, ($23).

PERFECTION (Reed, $8). A 60-second timer ticks as you rush to fit pieces into the right-shaped slots.

In the foregoing list, all retail prices are approximate. One can usually do better at discount stores.

Special thanks are due to Mr. Joe Tischler, toy buyer for Bloomingdale's, whose cooperation, sensitivity, and raised consciousness were of immense help to me in researching this toy list. Many of the toys cited in this article are available at Bloomingdale's branches.

The classics

Monopoly, Parcheesi, Checkers, Chess, Chinese Checkers, Scrabble, Backgammon, Playing Cards, Bingo, Dominoes, Silly Putty, Frisbee, Jacks, and Pick-Up Sticks. *Note:* These and virtually all games come with instructions that denote the player as "he." Whether or not the manufacturers use this generically, sensitive adults will alter the pronoun when reading the rules to female players.

Recommended by Allenna Leonard †

Years 0–3: By far the easiest group to find good and nonsexist toys for, such as: STUFFED BEAR FAMILY (Sutton, $7), SESAME STREET WALKING LETTERS (Educational Toys, $1).

† Acting Toy Coordinator for National NOW.

Years 3–6: Of special interest are: "HAVE YOU EVER HEARD OF A SKY FLOWER?" and "FARMER GREEN TAKES US THROUGH HIS GREEN FACTORY," sturdy booklets with plants included (Growing Concern, Inc., $15); MAGNET TRAIN (Brio, $4.50); KENNEL TRUCK (Buddy L, $4.69); CREAT-A-KIT (Torro, $4); PARADE DRUM (Chein, $4.44); RING TOSS (Hasbro, $1.20); HOUSE BOAT (Fisher-Price, $7).

Years 6–8: Here the great majority of toys are presented for one sex or the other. There is also tendency for the toys to become more elaborate and to demand less from the child. Some exceptions: BALLANDRO NAVIGABLE SAILING CRAFT ($2–$6); CHEMISTRY I (Thomas Salter, $6.50)—with adult supervision only; AIRPORT (Fisher-Price, $13); SOCCER-KICKBALL (Wilson, $4); SPILL AND SPELL (Parker, $3.50); PLASTIC CUBE WITH REVOLVING GARDEN or AQUARIUM WITH MUSIC BOX INSIDE (Mattel, $13); CRYSTAL CLIMBERS (Pressman, $3.50); DESIGN STAMPS (Creative Playthings, $5).

Years 9–11: Selection for this age is much easier if the child is interested in science. QUBIC (Parker, $3); CHEMISTRY III & V (Salter, $11.50 and $17)—with adult supervision; ZOO PLAYSET (Airfix, $4); ORIGAMI (Child Guidance, $2).

Years 12+: PENDUL ART (Multimarketing, $10), BOTTLE CUTTING KIT (Avalon, $6).

Recommended by Pat Powers ‡

If a toy cannot be dropped to the floor from over your head without breaking, it will not hold up to rigorous use by a child, and it is probably dangerous.

CHILD GUIDANCE TRAIN ($3.66), PLAYSKOOL TRAIN ($14.88), MARY MANY-FACES (Aurora UNICEF, $4.79. The dolls from Israel and Thailand are good, but the American doll's face remains white even though her outfit changes when her skirt lifts up. These are the only dolls made of flame-retardant material.) CENTER RING CIRCUS (Aurora UNICEF, $6.49, men and women from various countries in a trapeze act). PLAY FAMILY CAMPER (Fisher-Price, $7) and PLAY FAMILY NURSERY (No authority figures; wooden females and males can fill all roles), FUN WITH STICKS (Whiting, $1.60), SUPER STRUCTURES (Synestructics, $5), ERECTOR SET (Gilbert, $20, two girls on package).

Recommended by Steven Caney §

RUBBER PARQUETRY (Lauri, $4.75). Foam rubber in 168 pieces, four shapes, four different colors to make designs. 4+.

‡ PACT spokesperson.
§ Toy consultant, author of "The Toy Book" (Workman, $3.95).

U2 PLASTIC TABLE AND CHAIR (Rodadyne, $32.50). The most versatile kids equipment imaginable: a desk, bridge, igloo, tunnel, rocker, bed, cave. Great colors. 2–10.

POSTER CARDS (Milton Bradley, $3.95 each). Three sets: homonyms, synonyms, and antonyms. 6–11.

INDOOR GYM HOUSE (Creative Playthings, $36). Solid wood construction with ladder, slide, and hiding place. Long-lasting child interest. 1+.

CARDBOARD BLOCKS (Creative Playthings, $10). Brick-blocks are durable and lightweight. There is no frustration for the child because there is no right or wrong way to use them. 2+.

TAN GRAMS (Berea College Student Industries, $1). Ancient Chinese puzzle with 7 pieces and endless possibilities. 8+.

The following mail-order companies will send catalogs and their toys are uniformly excellent. (*Author's Note:* The catalog illustrations are horrendously sexist.)

Child Life Play Specialties, 1640 Washington St., Holliston, Mass. 01746. Unconditionally guaranteed, highest quality outdoor play equipment. 2–teens.

Community Playthings, Rifton, N.Y. 12471. Not the most aesthetic but functional and indestructible cars, climbers, shelves, chairs, and tables. All ages.

Bill Muller Wooden Toys, Rockhill Industrial Park, 87 Commerce Drive, Telford, Pa. 18969. Uncomplicated, classical toys made by a man who loves kids—obviously.

Galt Toys, P.O. Box 2, Cheadle, Cheshire, England. A full selection of Britain's best toys. Items under $10 market value can enter the United States without duty.

Mr. Caney emphasizes that raw materials are still the best playthings. Staple toys such as those listed above run a close second.

The Toy People vs. the Toy Barons

To promote toy standards on a nationwide basis, Public Action Coalition on Toys (PACT, Suite 503, 2000 P Street N.W., Washington, D.C. 20036) was formed last February by several women's and consumer groups, among them the National Organization for Women, Ralph Nader's Citizen Action Group, Parents for Responsibility in the Toy Industry, and several state consumer assemblies.

PACT is attempting to pressure toy manufacturers to take a more socially responsible position in designing and marketing toys. This year, they presented to Toy Manufacturers of America, the industry's trade association, a list of demands covering dangerous and sadistic toys, the sex-stereotyped sell, deceptive advertising and packaging, and the lack of minority and female representation in ads and on illustrations.

Several NOW chapters have active toy committees whose members research toys on the market, address complaints to retailers, toy buyers, manufacturers, and TV shows that run sexist commercials.

Among these, the studies done by Mary Bailey and the late Ann Pollard White for Montgomery County NOW (Maryland), and by Allenna Leonard of the Howard County chapter are among the most extensive. A Boston study of more than 800 toys is available from one of its authors, Susan Kannenberg, 279 Winter Street, Weston, Massachusetts 02193. Ask for "Sex-Typed Depictions on Toy Boxes" and send $2 to cover costs. Nicki Montaperto has written "Report on Sexism in Toys," which is available from the Union County (New Jersey) NOW chapter, via Ms. Montaperto at 483 West Third Avenue, Roselle, New Jersey 07203. (25 cents each)

Movement behavior

Investigators such as Sheflen, Birdwhistle, Fast, and others have in recent years begun developing a science of "Kinesics" which seeks to examine and classify the ways in which persons communicate with the body. "Body Language" includes any nonreflexive or reflexive movement of a part or all of the body used by a person to communicate an emotional message to the outside world. Nonverbal forms of communication include action signals, systematized action language, reflexive motions, expressive movement, gestures, and postures.

Movement is a preverbal language, much of which is learned by children before they learn the abstract symbolism of speech. The movement patterns of a culture serve both as a system of information about that culture and as a means of communication within and between cultures. Movement behavior within a culture delineates age, social and economic status and, most especially, sex. Birdwhistle (1970) and others found in their investigations of a number of societies that what is male and what is female differed in specifics from society to society but that interpreters could always identify stereotypical male and female movement either by rough description or by acting out.

Movement is valued in our society, but the degree of approval granted movement participation varies according to sex. Movement-centered activities are a chief means of ascribing gender roles to little girls and boys, the dimensions of whose movements are clearly defined as to space, time, and force.

The *space* that girls use for movement is limited by the nature of so-called "girls'" toys and "girls'" games. A sample list of these will show that girls play in a small, limited space: Ring Around the Rosy, London Bridge, Drop the Handkerchief, Hopscotch, Jump Rope, Jacks, "May I,"

Note: Copyright © 1974 by Elizabeth C. Umstead.

429

Redlight, School, Store, Freeze Tag, and Statues. For boys, an analogous list would include: Cowboys, Cops and Robbers, Spacemen, Bows and Arrows, Football, Climbing, Baseball, King of the Mountain, and Capture the Flag.

So convinced are we that girls should not exhibit speed that we use the term "fast girl" or "fast woman" to express our negative judgment of females with questionable moral standards. Parents and friends will chuck a little girl under the chin or hold her gently, while they playfully punch a little boy, ride him on a knee, or wrestle with him.

Space, time, and force dimensions of masculine-feminine activities were analyzed by Rosenberg and Sutton-Smith (Cratty, 1967) who studied 67 games. They found that the boys' games involved forceful physical contact, the dramatization of conflict between males, propulsion of objects in space, and complex team organization. The girls tended to play games involving men and women in static activity, ritualistic, noncompetitive actions, and rhythmic activities. In the eighth year, there was a marked sex-role differentiation, with the difference more marked in males than in females. In the third grade, games and sports become positively associated with sex-role identification (pp. 67–68).

Many children's movement activities not only prescribe space, time, and force according to gender, but have built-in selective rewards and punishments which echo those of the social system. One example is the simple game called "Here We Go Gathering Nuts in May" (Newell, 1963). This game had its origin in the custom of marriage by capture. The "Nuts in May" were originally "Knots in May," the knots signifying flower garlands worn by the girls. The pull over the line in our present game reenacts the physical capture of a wife in another time (Newell, p. 236).

Even exercise programs are guilty of sex-role stereotyping. The media would still have us think that males and females should exercise for different reasons. Women exercise to become more appealing in looks, presumably to become more attractive to men. Men exercise to feel "more like a man," to improve health, to live longer, and to increase efficiency.

Effect on Girls of Movement Restriction

What is the effect upon girls and women of these imposed norms for movement activities? Eleanor Metheny (1965) says:

> Our acceptance of averages as norms that indicate what a "real man" or a "real woman" should be like, has condemned many men and women to an unhappy choice between two grim alternatives. Either they feel they must try to be something they are not, or

they must live with a feeling of failure and rejection born of being
or doing what a man or woman should not be or do. (p. 153)

In a society where all skill and efficiency in movement are assigned to
boys, a skilled girl may feel something is wrong with her. If she is good
at ball games, she is told, "You throw just like a boy." She may succumb
to subtle pressures and give up her athletic activities, at the cost of real
human joy. Or, she may continue, but on the defensive, feeling herself
to be an outcast, glaringly different from other girls. In an even worse
position, perhaps, is the poor young boy who is told "You throw like a
girl" (Smith, 1968, p. 43).

At the present time, an athletic girl finds a great deal of discussion
going on about her role. One extreme position was expressed by a
psychiatrist addressing a National Football Coaches Association meeting.
Dr. Leo Madlem said:

> The experiential value of athletics and especially football is
> that it is an encounter with another and one's self that is real, con-
> crete, naked, and out in the open for all to witness. Athletics is one
> of the few endeavors left where a young man can have an experi-
> ence in masculinity. As a matter of fact, the word is getting around
> these days that "the men are getting more feminine and the women
> more masculine, and that probably this is a good thing." I, per-
> sonally, feel this is a bad state of affairs. . . . As a matter of fact,
> I'd like to go on record as being against the building up of women's
> athletic teams to compete with the Russian gals, as my own per-
> sonal response to the development of athletic females is "who the
> hell wants a bunch of fast running women?" (Vanderzwaag, 1972,
> p. 45)

At the other extreme are advocates and supporters of women's boxing
and professional football teams.

Clothing and Movement

Clothing customs and fashions must share a good deal of the blame
for restricting the movement of girls and women. Tight skirts, tight
girdles, and high, wobbly heels hardly permit, either physically or
psychologically, the free expression of a girl's movement needs. Some
of the stereotypical movement behaviors described by Birdwhistle are
undoubtedly the result of patterns dictated by clothing.

Today, however, there is clear evidence that both Seventh Avenue
and American women have seen the light. Clothing conventions for
women are changing at a marvelously rapid pace. Prudish mothers,
demanding males, and self-imposed personal preferences may still seek

conformity to traditional norms, but the influence of Chanel, Levi Strauss, Chinese women, and Rosie the Riveter can't be denied.

The Meaning in Movement

It is a contemporary phenomenon to seek the "meaning" in our activities. Meaning-centered education, fostered by the writings of Maslow, Rogers, Phenix, May, and others, has prompted us to look at the meaning of movement, especially in its forms of sport, dance, games, and exercise.

We move to learn—to learn about ourselves, our capabilities, our environment. Some people have found in movement, as nowhere else, a feeling of wholeness, a symbolic all-outness, or as Smith (1968; p. 64) called it—"an inner *aistheticos,* a feeling of 'just-rightness.'" The freeing capacity of play frees one from predictable demands. The capacity to move describes one's power to shape one's self, and the freedom to manipulate space, time, and force makes this possible.

One area of meaning in physical activity little explored thus far but exciting in its prospects may be found in "eustress-seeking." In a 1970 article, Harris described eustress as being:

> . . . associated with adventure, excitement, and thrilling experi-
> ence . . . a pleasant type of stress as opposed to painful, un-
> pleasant type of stress or dystress . . . The role that stress-seeking
> plays in the motivation of persons to participate in physical activities
> has yet to be determined. . . . The male has traditionally been
> the stress-seeker; adventure, excitement, and the thrill of battle
> have been the male prerogative. The American culture provides
> and approves stress-seeking activities for the male, but few for the
> female. There is no reason to suspect that women are any less stress-
> seeking than men. Boys have grown up testing their physical
> strength, their bodily skill, and their courage while girls tradition-
> ally have needed no such assurance. (pp. 33–40)

Eustress needs have been identified as human needs. Sports and participation in physical activity seem to serve as one of the few socially accepted avenues left for eustress-seeking. If, indeed, the evidence extant on why men move is valid evidence for movement's meaning, then its meaning-making potential would be denied those whose movement opportunities are limited.

A study done in 1958 at the Fels Research Institute was cited by Maccoby (1963). In a study done on the IQ of young girls, an *increase* in IQ was shown by those girls who were described as "competitive, self-assertive, independent, and dominating in interaction with other children." These obviously are not the characteristics we associate with femininity. A *decline* in IQ was noted in those girls described as passive, shy, and dependent.

A Fels researcher, when asked what kind of developmental history was necessary to make a girl into an intellectual person, replied: "The simplest way to put it is that she must be a Tomboy at some point in her childhood" (Maccoby, p. 33).

Perhaps some researcher will soon answer a similar question this way: "The developmental history necessary to make a girl into a fully functioning person must include full opportunities to *move* as she needs and wants to."

Bibliography

BIRDWHISTLE, R. L. (1970). *Kinesics and Context.* Philadelphia: University of Pennsylvania Press.

CRATTY, B. (1967). *Social Dimensions of Physical Activity.* Englewood Cliffs, New Jersey: Prentice-Hall, Inc.

FAST, J. (1970). *Body Language.* New York: M. Evans and Company.

HALL, E. T. (1959). *The Silent Language.* New York: Doubleday.

HARRIS, D. (1970). In *Quest.* XIII, Winter 1970. National Assn. for Physical Education of College Women and National College Physical Education Assn. for Men.

MACCOBY, E. (1963). *The Potential of Women.* New York: McGraw-Hill.

METHENY, E. (1965). *Connotations of Movement in Sport and Dance.* Dubuque, Iowa: William C. Brown.

NEWELL, W. W. (1963). *Games and Songs of American Children.* New York: Dover Publications, Inc.

SMITH, H. (1968). *Introduction to Human Movement.* Reading, Pennsylvania: Addison-Wesley.

VANDERZWAAG, H. (1972). *Toward a Philosophy of Sport.* Reading, Pennsylvania: Addison-Wesley.

Notes on Contributors

Carol Ahlum works at The Feminist Press and The Clearinghouse on Women's Studies in New York where she teaches inservice courses on sexism in the schools to teachers. Ms. Ahlum is coauthor of *Feminist Resources for Schools and Colleges: a Guide to Curriculum Materials* and *High School Feminist Studies.*

Drs. Sandra and Daryl Bem are psychologists and the first husband and wife to hold full faculty appointments in the same department at Stanford University, California. Sandra Bem studies sex differences and sex roles; masculinity, femininity and androgyny; and personality. Daryl Bem's research focuses on expressive behavior, personality theory, self-perception, and attitude change. Both have written and lectured on sexism.

Dr. Inge K. Broverman is Principal Psychologist at Worcester State Hospital, Massachusetts. She does research in the field of sex-role perception and behavior, and she has published extensively in professional journals.

Elizabeth Burr is Assistant to the Chief Psychiatrist and codirector of the Suicide Prevention Center and Institute for Studies of Self-Destructive Behaviors in Los Angeles. She is also Editorial Consultant for *Vita,* the newsletter of the International Association for Suicide Prevention; cofounder and coordinator of the Westside Women's Committee of Los Angeles; and a founding member of the Southern California Section of the National Women's Political Caucus.

The Commissioner's Task Force on the Impact of Office of Education Programs on Women was established in May 1972 by then Commissioner of Education Sidney P. Marland, Jr. The task force examined the problems women face in American education, considered the relationship of HEW education programs to these problems, and outlined an agenda for action.

The Committee to Eliminate Sexual Discrimination in the Public Schools is a loose-knit group of women in Ann Arbor, Michigan, whose studies of sexism in industrial arts, home economics, building, and athletic programs, reading texts, etc. were gathered together and written up by Marcia Federbush as the report, *Let Them Aspire.*

Dr. Dan Donlan is Assistant Professor of Education at the University of California at Riverside. He is coauthor of the books *Voices I* and *Voices II,* and has published articles in *Clearing House, English Journal,* the *Peabody Journal of Education* and other publications.

Susan Dunn designed and currently teaches the introductory course in women's studies at the University of California at Los Angeles. She has worked to end sexism in the educational system and in the English language, and is coordinator of the Women's Resource Center at UCLA.

Joanne Edgar is an editor at *Ms.* Magazine with a special interest in politics and economics. She was formerly a writer for *Facts on File,* a weekly news digest, and is a member of the New York Women's Political Caucus and the National Organization for Women.

Deborah Eifler is a graduate student in the sociology department at Yale University, Connecticut.

The Emma Willard Task Force on Education is an independent group based in Minnesota. Its members teach courses and hold workshops on sexism, work as consultants, sponsor TV programs, and hope to establish a resource center on sexism in elementary and secondary education to be called "Education for Personhood."

Norma Farquhar free-lances editorial services, has coauthored several articles on sexism in education, and will be associate editor of a new scholarly journal, *Contemporary China.* She lobbies against and occasionally lectures on sexism in textbooks, language, and the public schools.

Marcia Federbush is spending a year as a consultant with the New Jersey State Department of Education where she is trying to get the Y's and the Public Recreation Department to offer courses on a nonarbitrary basis to both sexes. She normally resides in Ann Arbor, Michigan, where she lectures, writes, and works for solutions to sexism and other social problems.

Feminists on Children's Media is a collective of teachers, librarians, mothers, etc. who lecture on sexism in children's literature using slides, tapes and readings. They have produced a bibliography of recommended nonsexist books about girls, *Little Miss Muffet Fights Back,* and *A List of Literature on Sexism in Children's Books.*

Jackie Fralley has worked at the Valley Women's Center in Northampton, Mass. with the University of Massachusetts Women's Studies Program, and at The Feminist Press. She has taught at "Our Bodies Ourselves" workshops and is coauthor, with Carol Ahlum, of *Feminist Resources for Schools and Colleges: a Guide to Curriculum Materials* and *High School Feminist Studies.*

Monroe H. Freedman is Dean of the School of Law at Hofstra University in New York, and a member of the American Civil Liberties Union Board of Directors.

Dr. Jo Freeman is Assistant Professor of American Studies at the State University of New York, College at Old Westbury, where she teaches American politics and women's studies. She has written extensively on women and women's liberation, and has edited a feminist anthology.

Dr. Jo-Ann Evans Gardner is a psychologist, Eastern Regional Co-Director of the National Organization for Women, and Articles Editor of KNOW, Inc. She has published extensively in the professional journals, particularly on sexism.

Diane Gersoni-Stavn, formerly Associate Editor of *School Library Journal Book Review,* has lectured and written extensively on children's literature. She is presently a free-lance writer and reviewer whose critiques of adult and juvenile books have appeared in the *New York Times,* the *Greensboro Daily News,* and *Library Journal,* among other publications.

Elizabeth Hokada is finishing her last year as an undergraduate at Yale University, Connecticut.

Florence Howe is President of the Feminist Press, a former chairwoman of the Modern Language Association's Commission on the Status of Women, and coauthor with Paul Lauter of *Conspiracy of the Young.* She frequently writes and lectures on sexism in the schools, literature and society.

Suzy Kitman is 14 years old and presently attending an alternative high school in Leonia, New Jersey. Her particular interests are journalism, drama, women's history, and dance.

Linda Kraft was formerly Children's Librarian at the Kensington Park Public Library, Montgomery County, Maryland and has been a Social Studies and English teacher in New York City.

Julius Lester is a writer of both adult and juvenile books, including *Search for the New Land, The Seventh Son: the Life and Writings of*

W.E.B. Du Bois, Long Journey Home, Two Love Stories, To Be a Slave, and *The Knee-High Man and Other Tales.*

Betty Levy is a doctoral candidate at Teachers' College, Columbia University, New York. Her dissertation will deal with teachers' judgments of children's achievement-related and pupil role behaviors. Ms. Levy has taught a Women's Revolution course at City College of the City University of New York, and she is an organizer and member of the New York-based Feminist Psychology Research Group.

Dr. Marcia Lieberman is Assistant Professor of English at the University of Connecticut at Storrs, where she initiated and teaches a Women in Literature course. She has been an officer of the Connecticut chapter of the Women's Equity Action League, and her article, "Sexism and the Double Standard in Literature" was anthologized in Susan Koppelman Cornillon's *Images of Women in Fiction: Feminist Perspectives.*

Nancy Lyon was formerly on the editorial staff of *New York* Magazine. She is now a free-lance writer who has done travel pieces for the *New York Times* and specializes in behavioral subjects.

Hannah Miller, a former teacher, is now a free-lance writer and reviewer of children's films. She has published in *Film News, Film Library Quarterly, School Library Journal,* and other journals, and she frequently prepares film guides for commercial distributors of children's films.

Dr. Patricia P. Minuchin is Professor of Psychoeducational Processes at the College of Education, Temple University, Pennsylvania. For many years she was Senior Research Associate at Bank Street College, where she wrote with colleagues *The Psychological Impact of School Experience.* She is currently at work on a book concerning the middle years of childhood, and is studying children with different styles of functioning within the "open classroom."

Josephine Mlinar has been active in the National Organization for Women since 1968 and heads the Brooklyn Chapter's Employment Task Force. She is now a legal assistant and has been an affirmative action specialist.

The National Organization for Women is the largest feminist organization in America. On national and local levels, its members participate in task forces on education, rape, older women, child care, sports, etc., and lobby for and against different laws and customs.

Dr. Alleen Pace Nilsen is on the faculty of the Elementary Education Department at Arizona State University. She edits a monthly column, "Books for Young Adults," in *The English Journal,* and has contributed articles and reviews to *The Reading Teacher, Jack and Jill, Elementary English,* and other publications.

Letty Cottin Pogrebin is an editor at *Ms.* Magazine with a special interest in children's features. The author of the book, *How to Make It in a Man's World,* Ms. Pogrebin writes "The Working Woman" column in the *Ladies' Home Journal* and is presently writing a book on non-sexist child-rearing, tentatively to be entitled *Down With Sexist Upbringing.*

Dolores Prida is Acting Editor of *Tiempo,* the largest Spanish-language newspaper in New York. She has edited a literary magazine, *La Nueva Sangre,* which features the work of Puerto Rican and Latin American poets; her own books of poetry include *Women of the Hour* and *Thirty-One Poems.* She frequently speaks on feminism from a Spanish-American point of view.

The Resource Center for Sex Roles in Education, a project of the National Foundation for the Improvement of Education, synthesizes materials in specific subject areas and provides content summaries and resource identification lists within these areas; develops materials for use in conferences, seminars and training programs; and responds to individual requests for information.

Ruth Rosen is a doctoral candidate in history at the University of California at Berkeley; her dissertation will deal with prostitution in the American past. Ms. Rosen has taught courses in the history of sex roles at the University of California and Sonoma State College, and has lectured and written on the history of women and the family.

Catherine Ross is a graduate student in the sociology department at Yale University, Connecticut.

Anne McEvoy Schmid is a St. Paul, Minnesota, elementary school teacher who has been active in the women's rights movement for several years. She is on the executive board of Local 28 of the American Federation of Teachers Union, and a member of the AFT's national women's rights committee.

Dr. Dorin Schumacher is Director of the Upward Bound program at the University of Maine at Orono. She has taught and written on women's studies in secondary school, masculinity and femininity, women in literature, and feminist criticism.

The late Dr. Buford Stefflre was Professor of Counseling, Personnel Services and Educational Psychology at Michigan State University, East Lansing, until his death in 1969.

Dr. Iris M. Tiedt is Assistant Professor and Director of the M.A. in Reading Program at the University of Santa Clara, California, and the current editor of *Elementary English.* She has published numerous articles on sex stereotyping and the status of contemporary women, and is the author of *Linguistics, Grammar and the Classroom.*

Janice Law Trecker is a full-time free-lance writer whose articles have appeared in the *Saturday Review,* the *West Hartford News, The American Scholar,* and other publications. She is the author of *Connecticut History, 1818–1865,* designed for high school use, and researched and wrote the first drafts of a series of film strips on women in American history.

Dr. Elizabeth C. Umstead is Associate Professor of Health, Physical Education and Recreation at the University of North Carolina at Greensboro.

Dr. Susan Vogel is Clinical Psychologist at Brandeis University, Massachusetts. She has published extensively in the professional journals, concentrating on sex role differences, parent-child interaction, and the acquisition of defense mechanisms.

Dr. Lenore J. Weitzman is Assistant Professor of Sociology at the University of California at Davis. Her major research interests are the sociology of law, sex role socialization, and symbolic interaction. She is currently working on a study of the impact of the California no-fault divorce law.

Constance Williams is a sophomore at Beloit College in Wisconsin, where she is training to be an obstetric paramedic. She is active in the statewide organization, Wisconsin Youth for Democratic Education.

Women on Words and Images is a group of Princeton, New Jersey, women seeking to eliminate sexism in elementary textbooks. They present lecture/slide shows, work as paid consultants to publishers, and plead their cause with committees responsible for approving textbooks.

(The editor was unable to locate Jamie Kelem Frisof, Karen Lindsey, and Susan Ribner for biographical information.)

INDEX